Honey
So Sweet

8

Story and Art by
Amu Meguro

Contents

Story Thus Far

Soon after starting high school, the fearsome-looking
Onise asks Nao to be his girlfriend. At first Nao is afraid,
but once she discovers that Onise is actually a gentle soul,
Nao asks him out and their blissful relationship begins.

The shy and awkward new student Miyabi Nishigaki
asks Onise for help on how to be better understood. Nao
feels the pangs of jealousy when she sees how Miyabi acts
towards Onise.

The gang decides to go to a summer festival. Nao tells
Miyabi which yukata she plans on wearing, and Miyabi
shows up wearing the exact same one! Miyabi then mimics
Nao to get closer to Onise! At first, Nao tries to squash
her feelings of resentment, but she finally announces once
and for all that she's not going to lose Onise to Miyabi.
Onise also swiftly rejects Miyabi's advances.

Although heartbroken, Miyabi summons up the courage to
apologize to Nao and Onise before finding her own path.

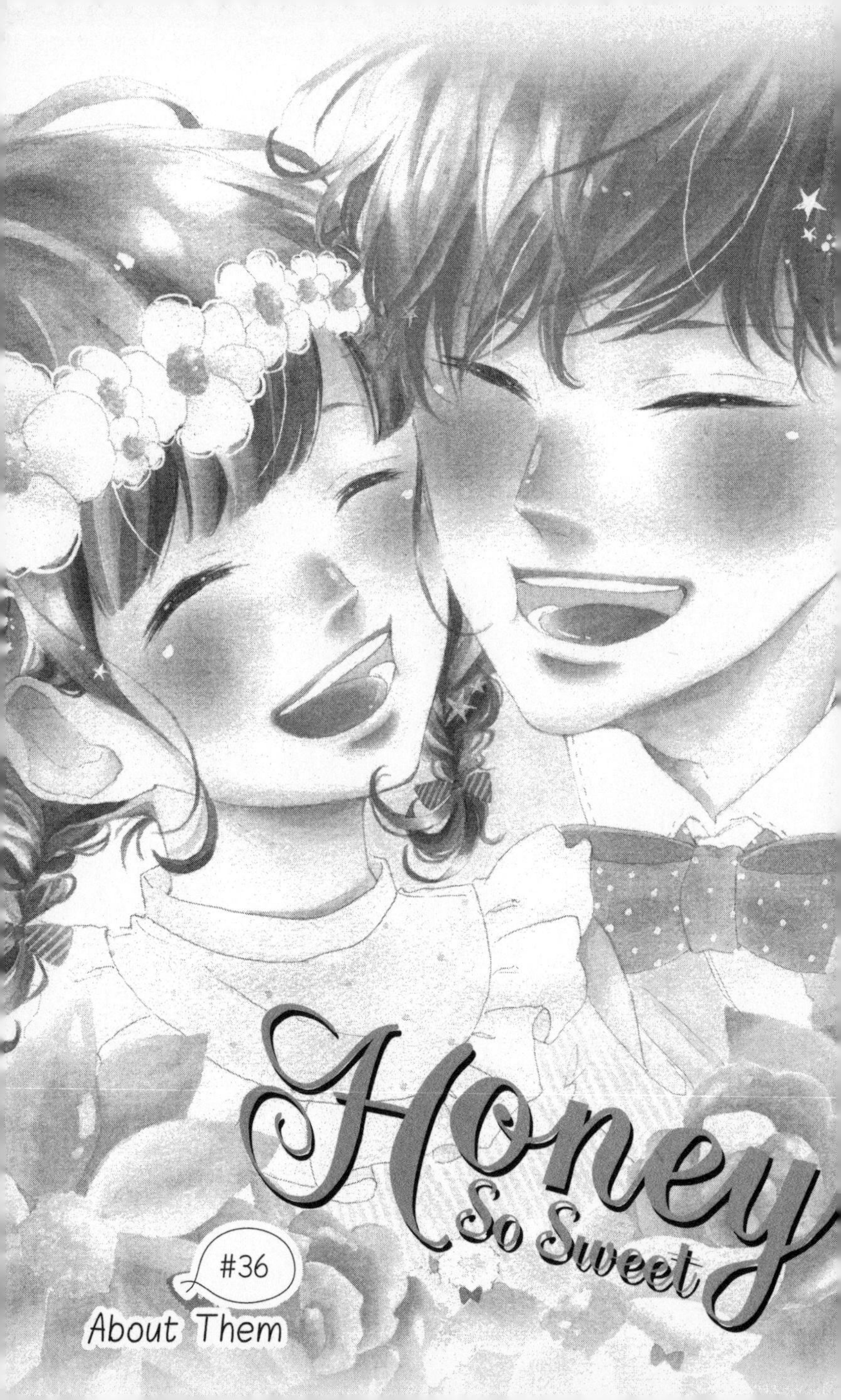
Honey So Sweet
#36
About Them

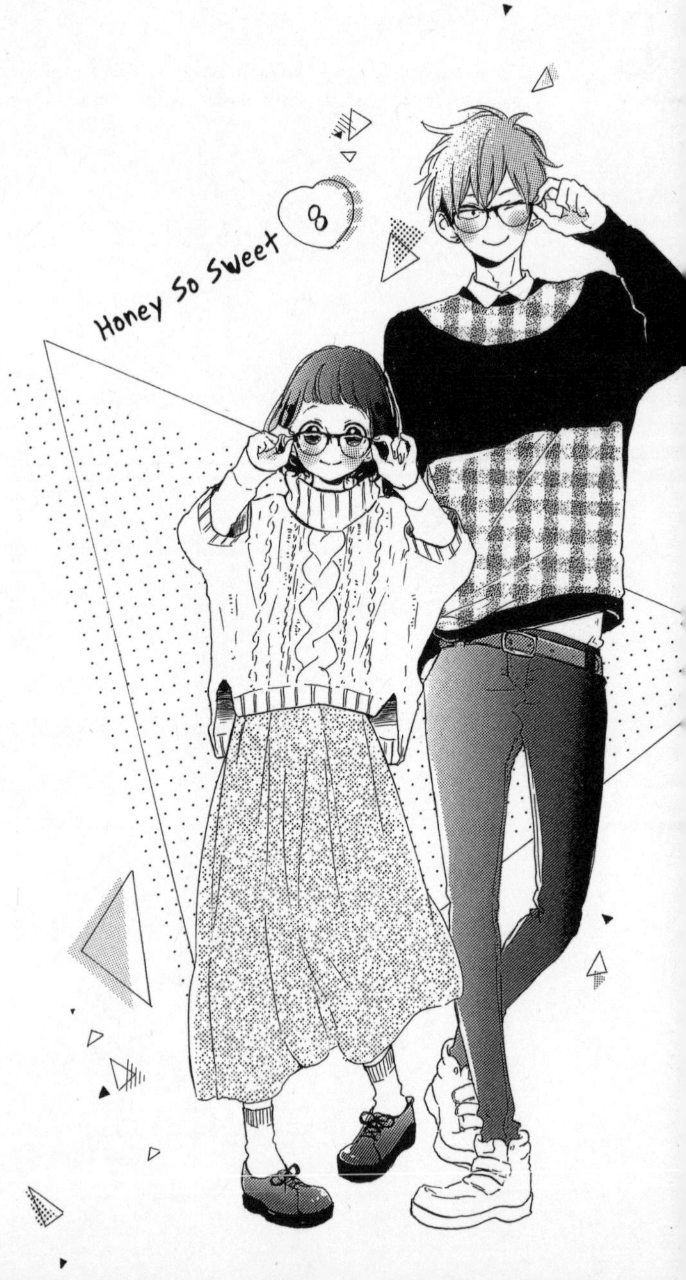
Honey So Sweet
8

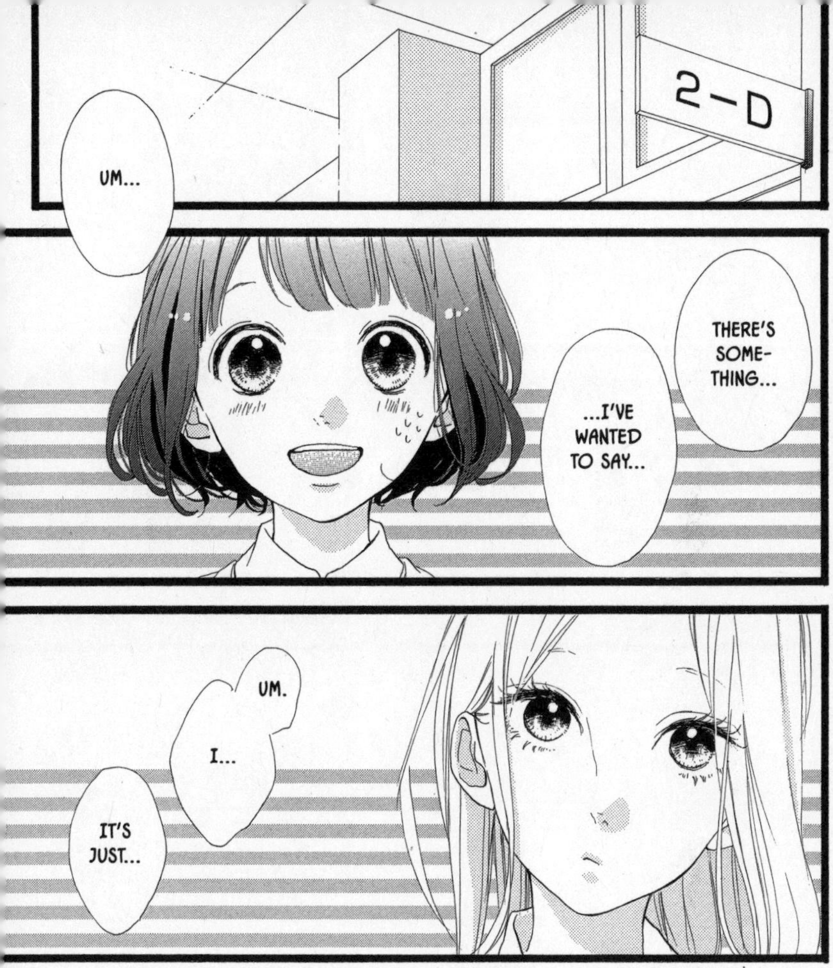
2-D
UM...
THERE'S SOME-THING...
...I'VE WANTED TO SAY...
UM.
I...
IT'S JUST...

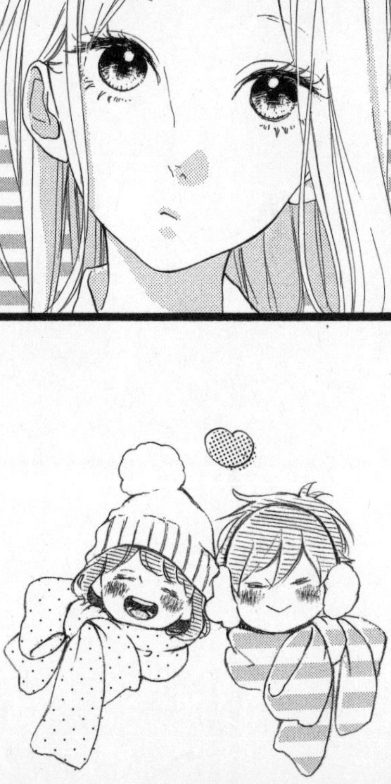

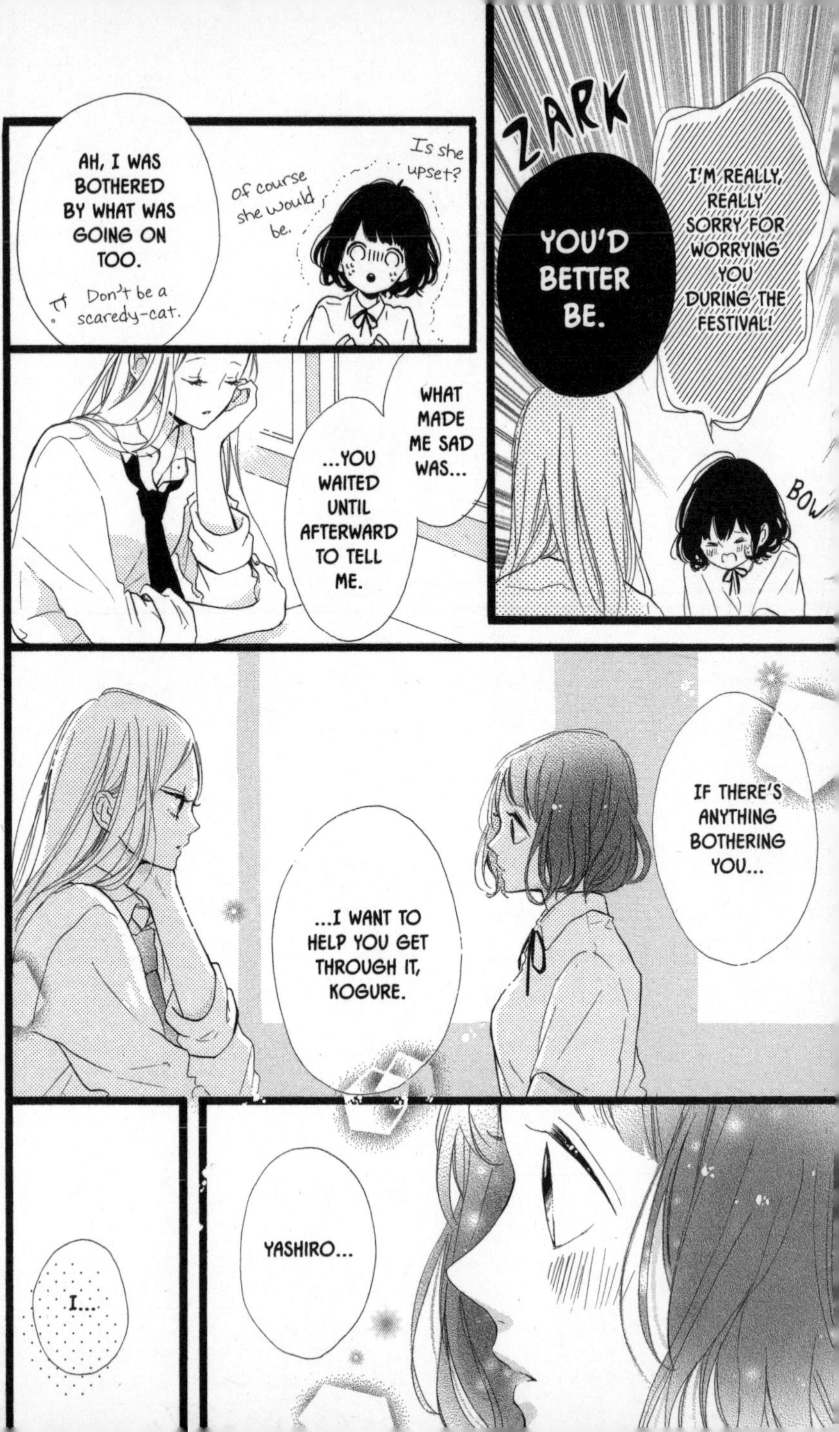
I'M REALLY, REALLY SORRY FOR WORRYING YOU DURING THE FESTIVAL!
ZARK
YOU'D BETTER BE.
BOW
Is she upset?
Of course she would be.
AH, I WAS BOTHERED BY WHAT WAS GOING ON TOO.
Don't be a scaredy-cat.
WHAT MADE ME SAD WAS...
...YOU WAITED UNTIL AFTERWARD TO TELL ME.
IF THERE'S ANYTHING BOTHERING YOU...
...I WANT TO HELP YOU GET THROUGH IT, KOGURE.
YASHIRO...
I...

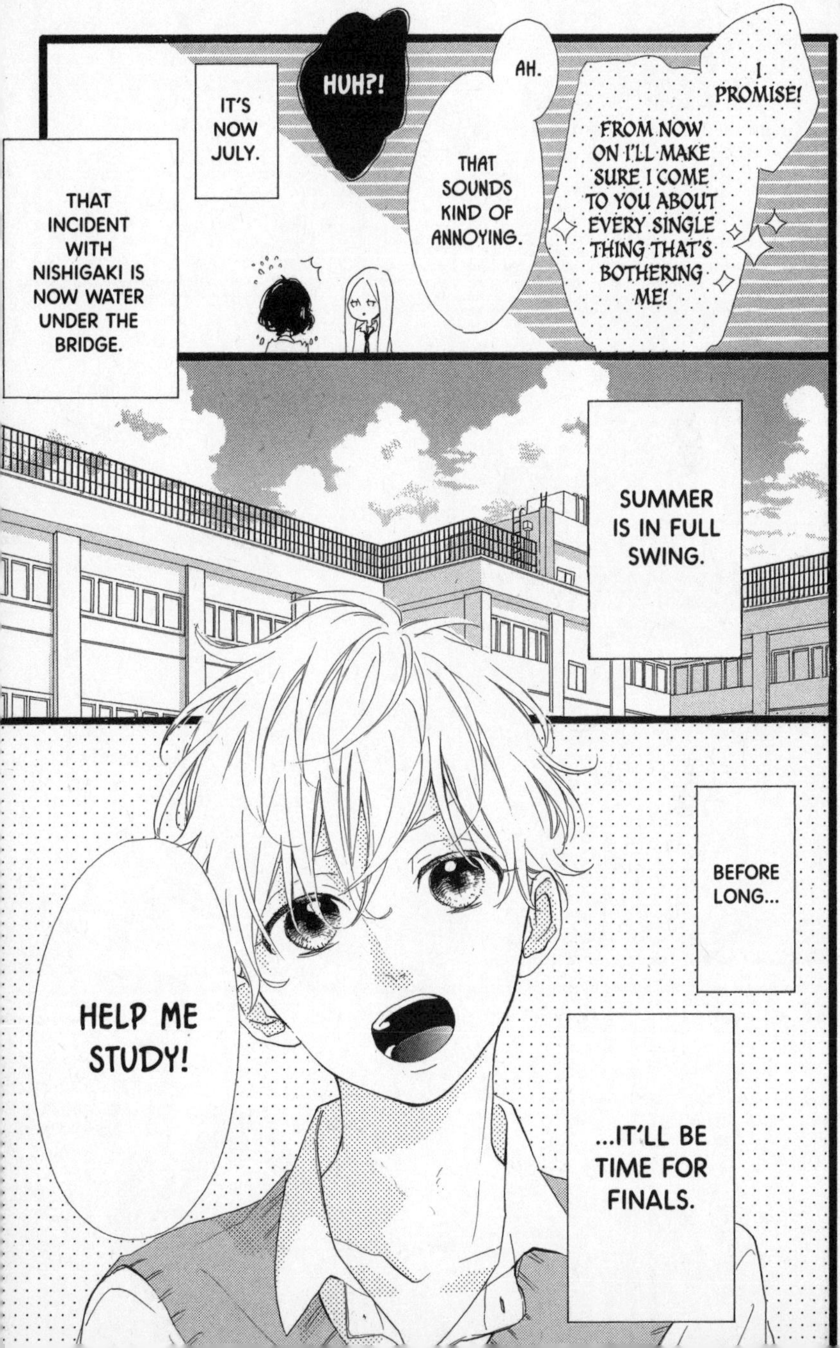

I PROMISE!
FROM NOW ON I'LL MAKE SURE I COME TO YOU ABOUT EVERY SINGLE THING THAT'S BOTHERING ME!
AH.
THAT SOUNDS KIND OF ANNOYING.
HUH?!
IT'S NOW JULY.
THAT INCIDENT WITH NISHIGAKI IS NOW WATER UNDER THE BRIDGE.
SUMMER IS IN FULL SWING.
BEFORE LONG...
...IT'LL BE TIME FOR FINALS.
HELP ME STUDY!

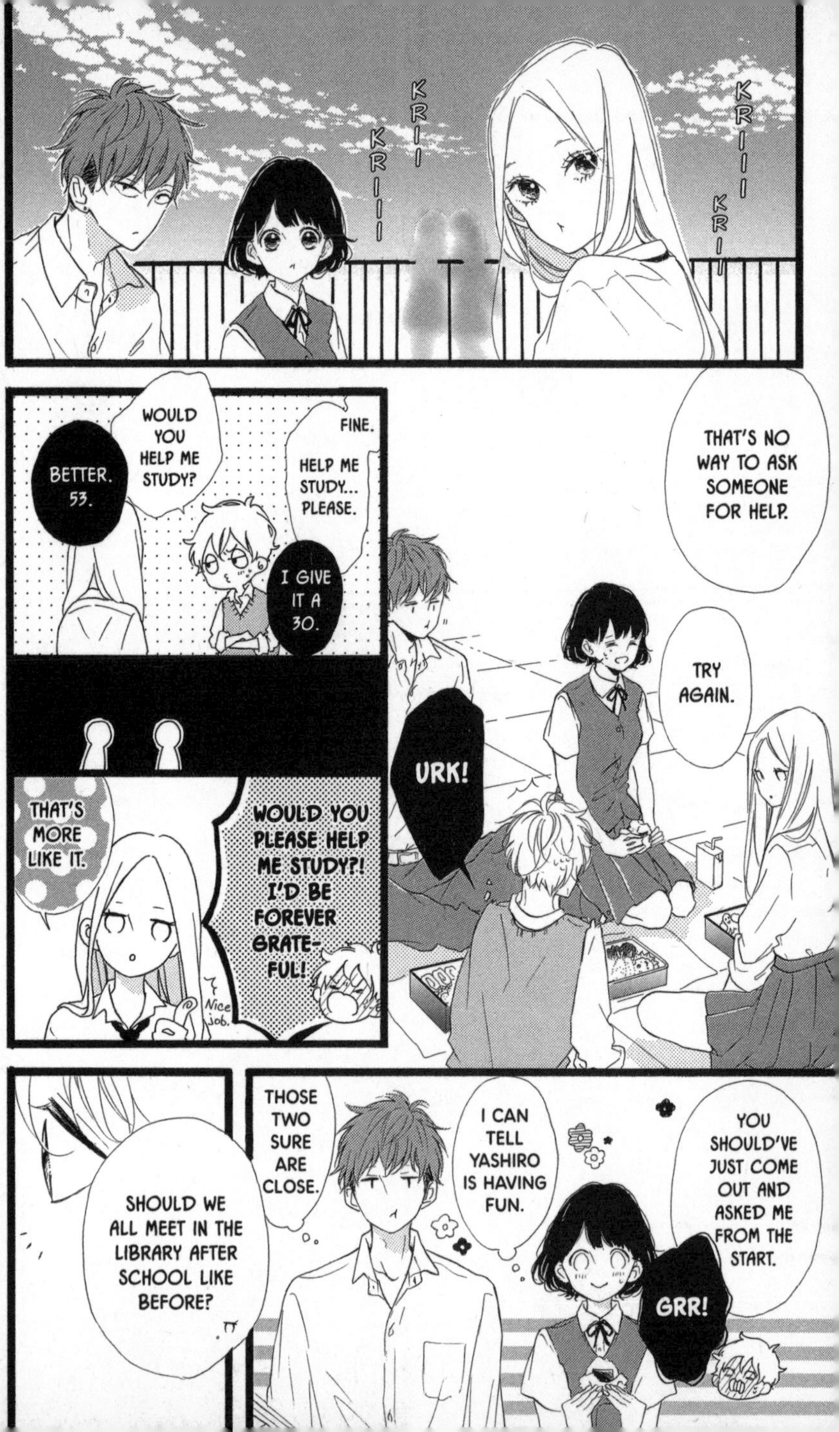
KRIII
KRII
KRII
KRIII
THAT'S NO WAY TO ASK SOMEONE FOR HELP.
TRY AGAIN.
URK!
FINE.
HELP ME STUDY... PLEASE.
I GIVE IT A 30.
WOULD YOU HELP ME STUDY?
BETTER. 53.
WOULD YOU PLEASE HELP ME STUDY?! I'D BE FOREVER GRATE-FUL!
Nice job.
THAT'S MORE LIKE IT.
YOU SHOULD'VE JUST COME OUT AND ASKED ME FROM THE START.
GRR!
I CAN TELL YASHIRO IS HAVING FUN.
THOSE TWO SURE ARE CLOSE.
SHOULD WE ALL MEET IN THE LIBRARY AFTER SCHOOL LIKE BEFORE?

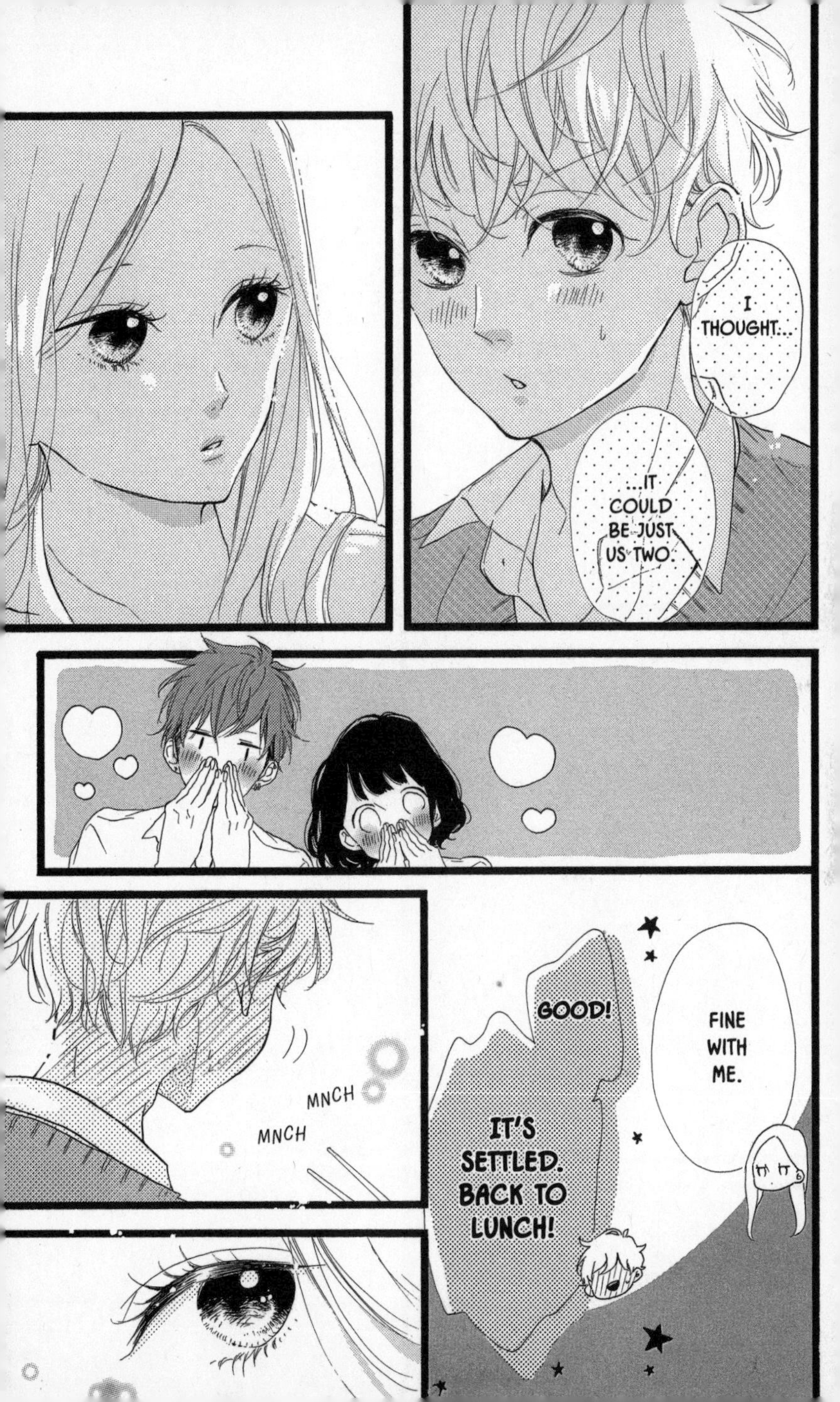
I THOUGHT...
...IT COULD BE JUST US TWO.
FINE WITH ME.
GOOD!
IT'S SETTLED. BACK TO LUNCH!
MNCH
MNCH

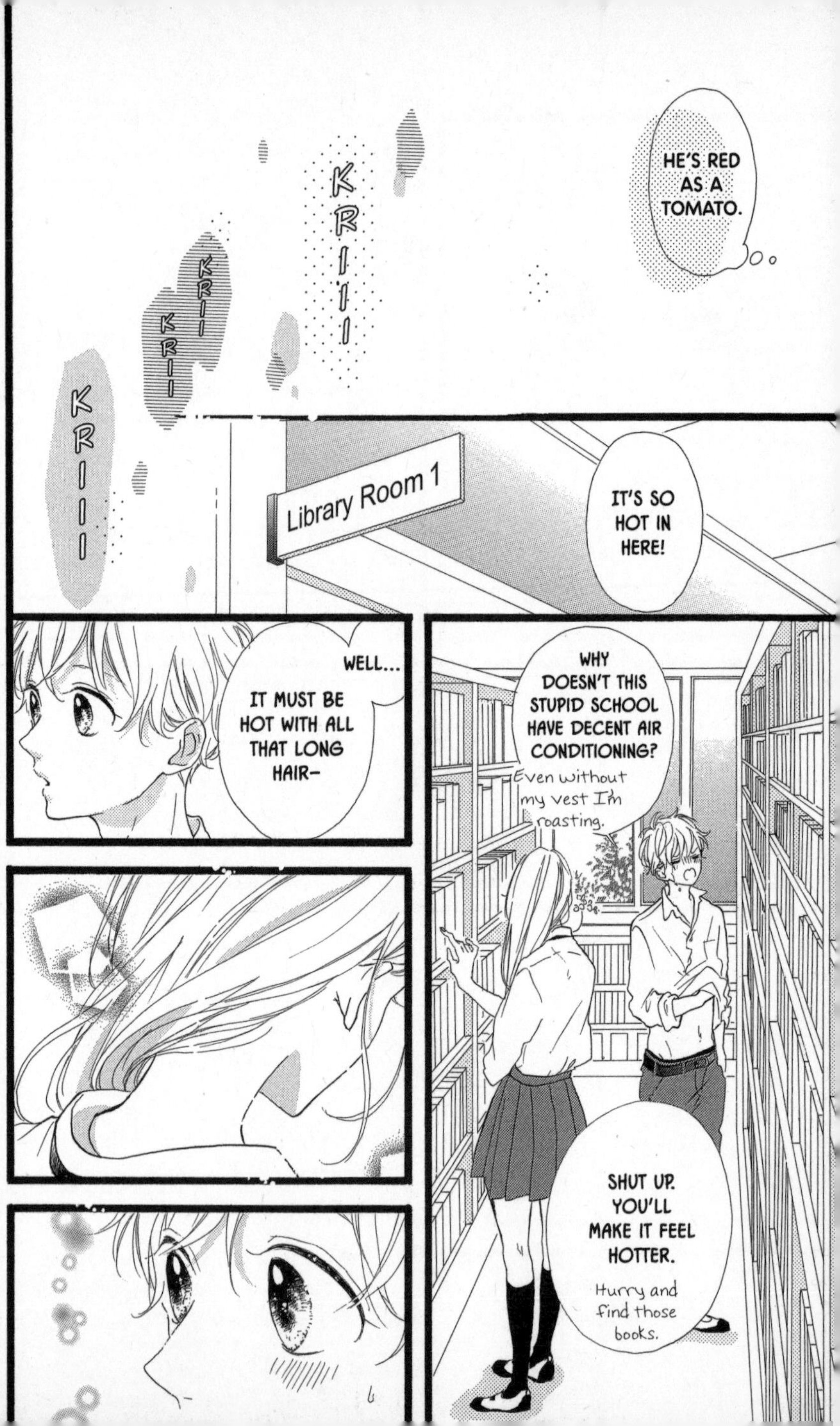
HE'S RED AS A TOMATO.
KRIII
KRII
KRII
KRIII
Library Room 1
IT'S SO HOT IN HERE!
WHY DOESN'T THIS STUPID SCHOOL HAVE DECENT AIR CONDITIONING?
Even without my vest I'm roasting.
SHUT UP. YOU'LL MAKE IT FEEL HOTTER.
Hurry and find those books.
WELL...
IT MUST BE HOT WITH ALL THAT LONG HAIR–

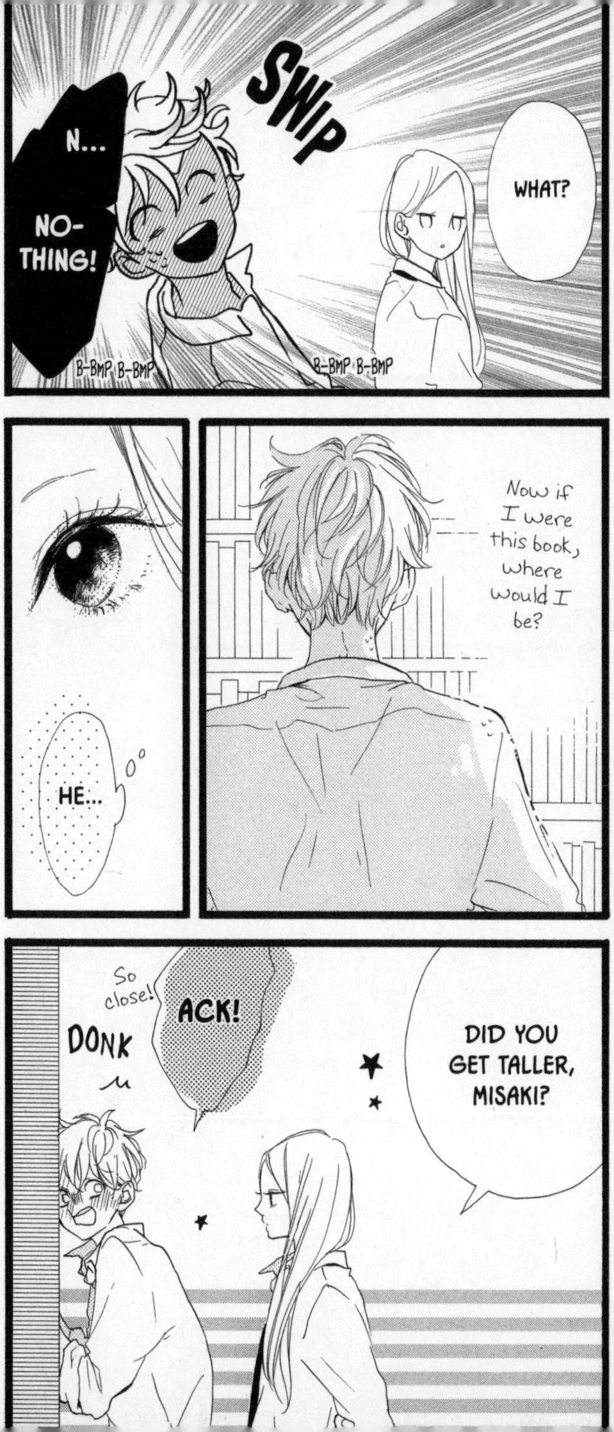
WHAT?
SWIP
N...
NO-THING!
B-BMP B-BMP
B-BMP B-BMP
Now if I were this book, where would I be?
HE...
DID YOU GET TALLER, MISAKI?
ACK!
So close!
DONK
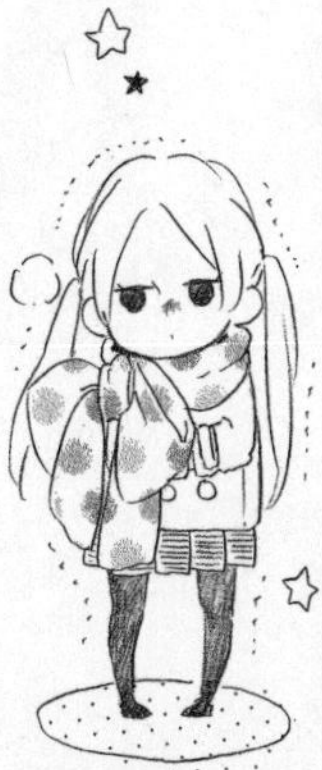

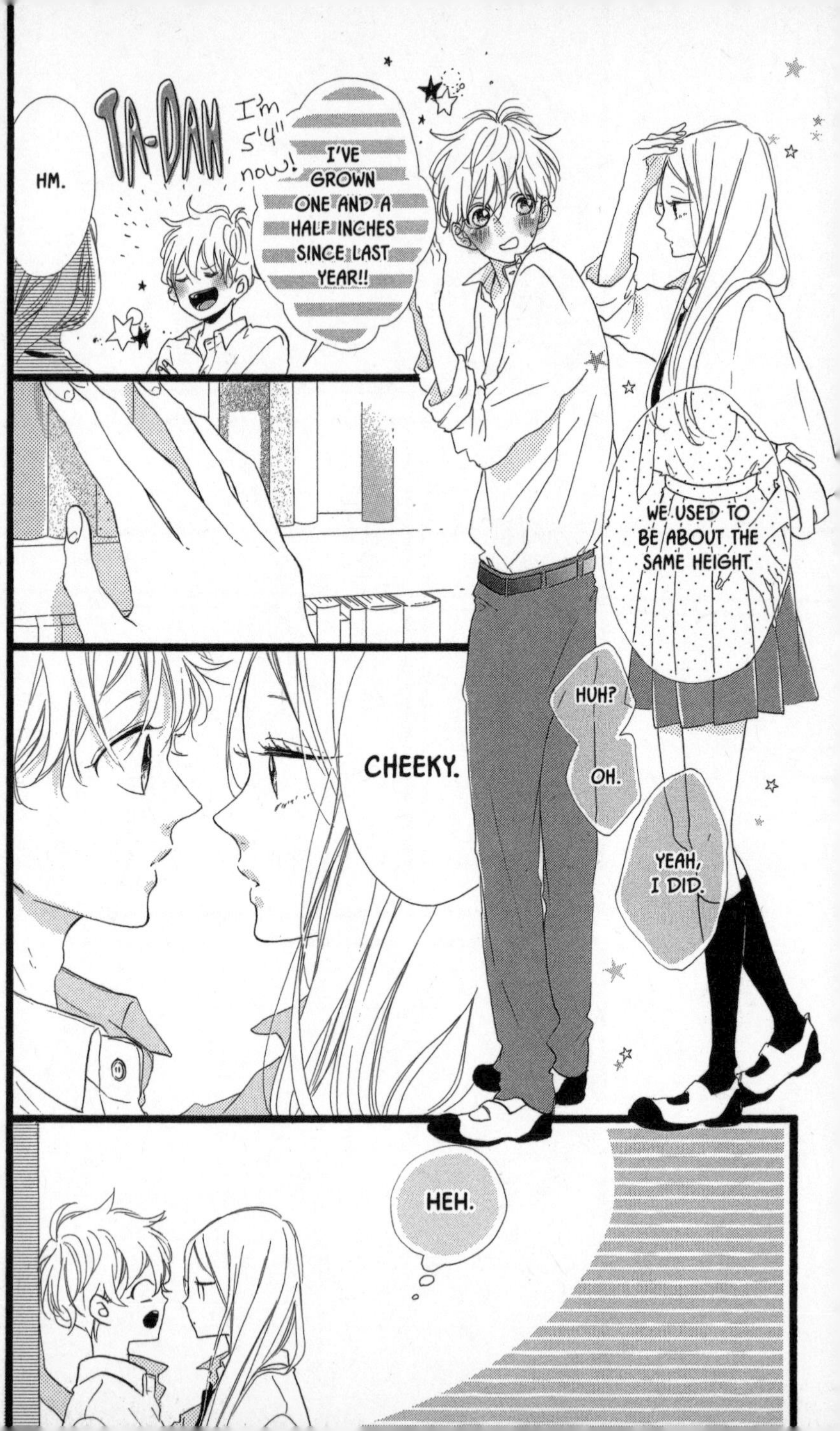

I'VE GROWN ONE AND A HALF INCHES SINCE LAST YEAR!!
I'm 5'4" now!
TA-DAH
HM.
WE USED TO BE ABOUT THE SAME HEIGHT.
HUH?
OH.
YEAH, I DID.
CHEEKY.
HEH.

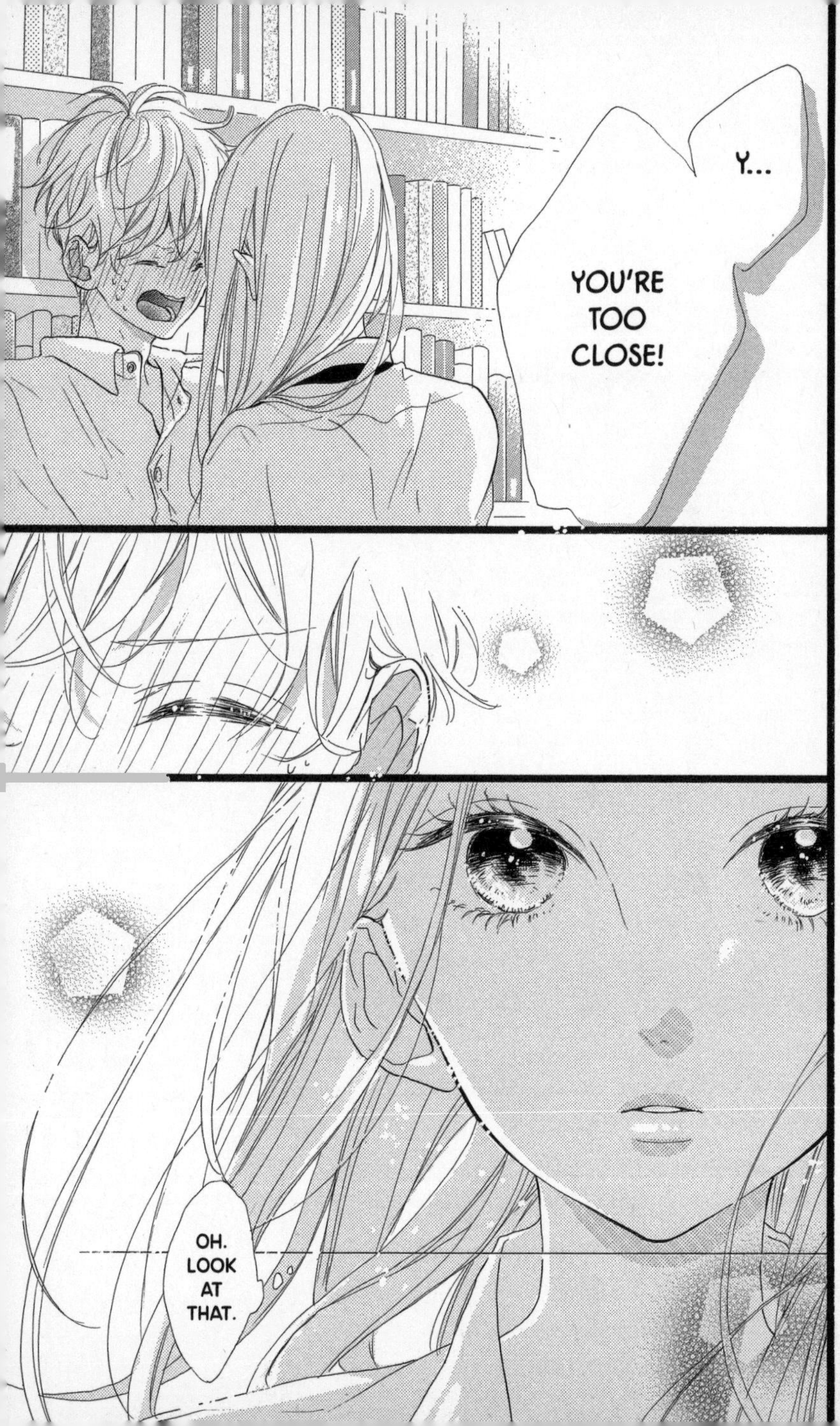
Y...
YOU'RE TOO CLOSE!
OH. LOOK AT THAT.

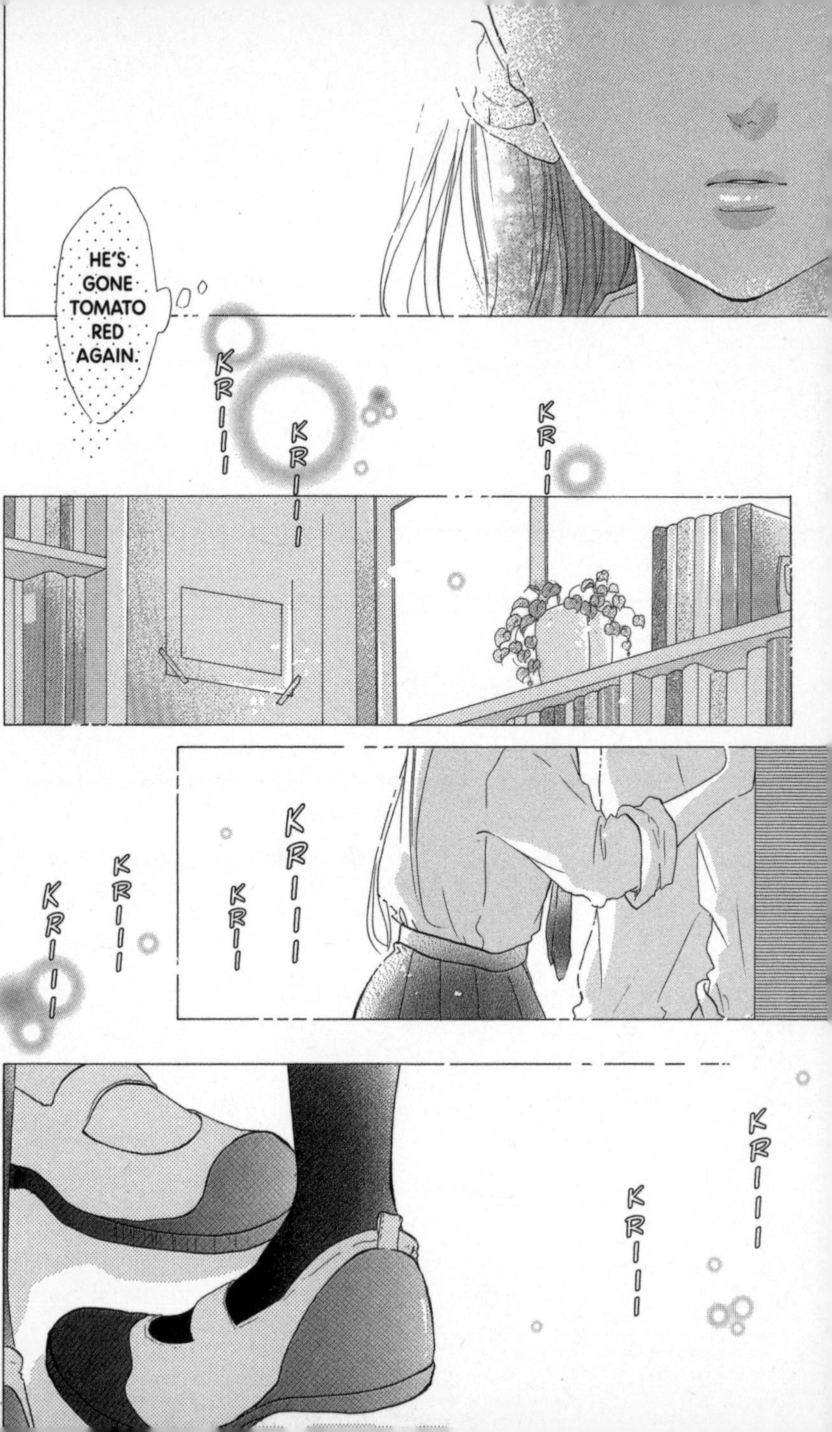
HE'S GONE TOMATO RED AGAIN.
KRIII
KRIII
KRII
KRIII
KRII
KRIII
KRIII
KRIII
KRIII

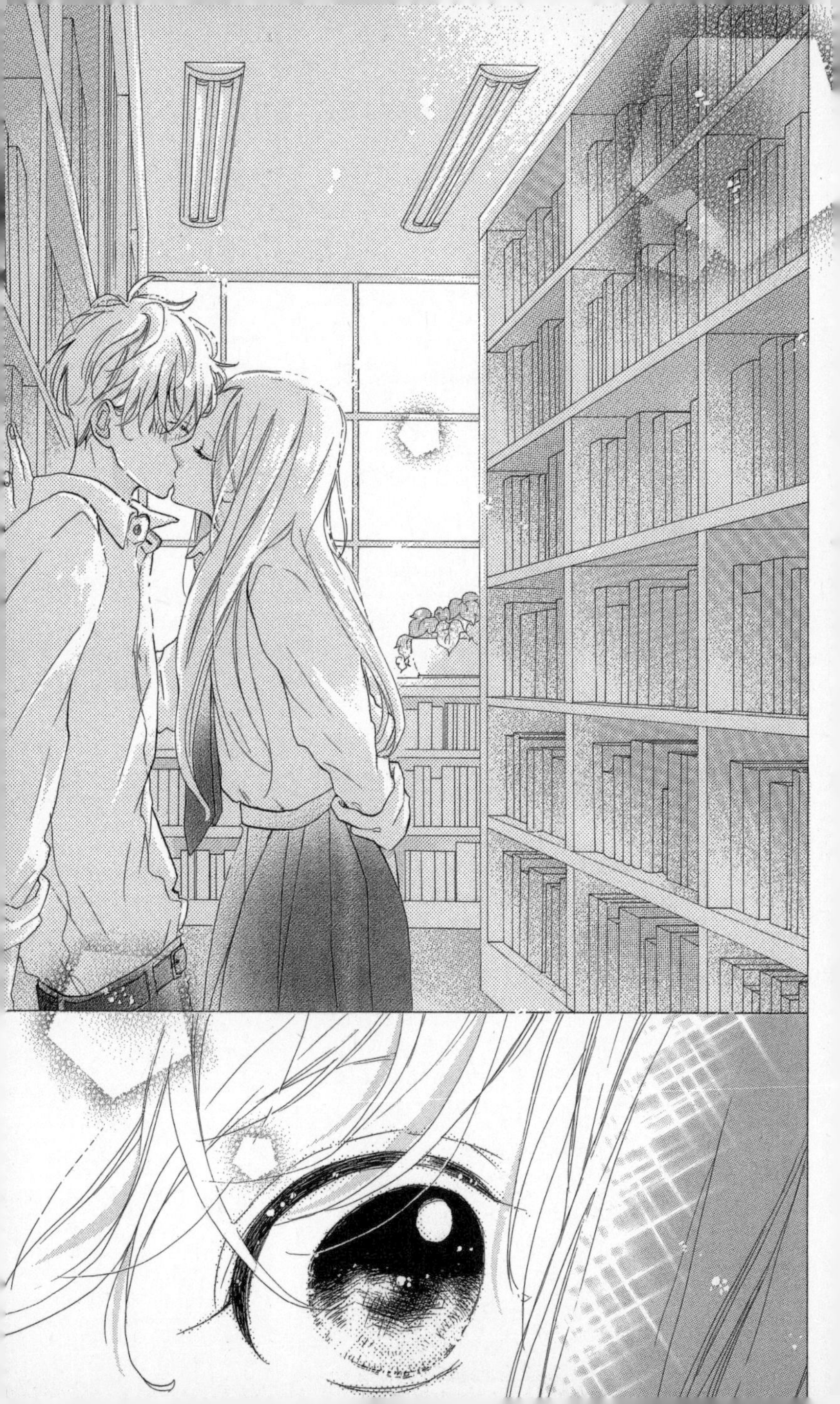

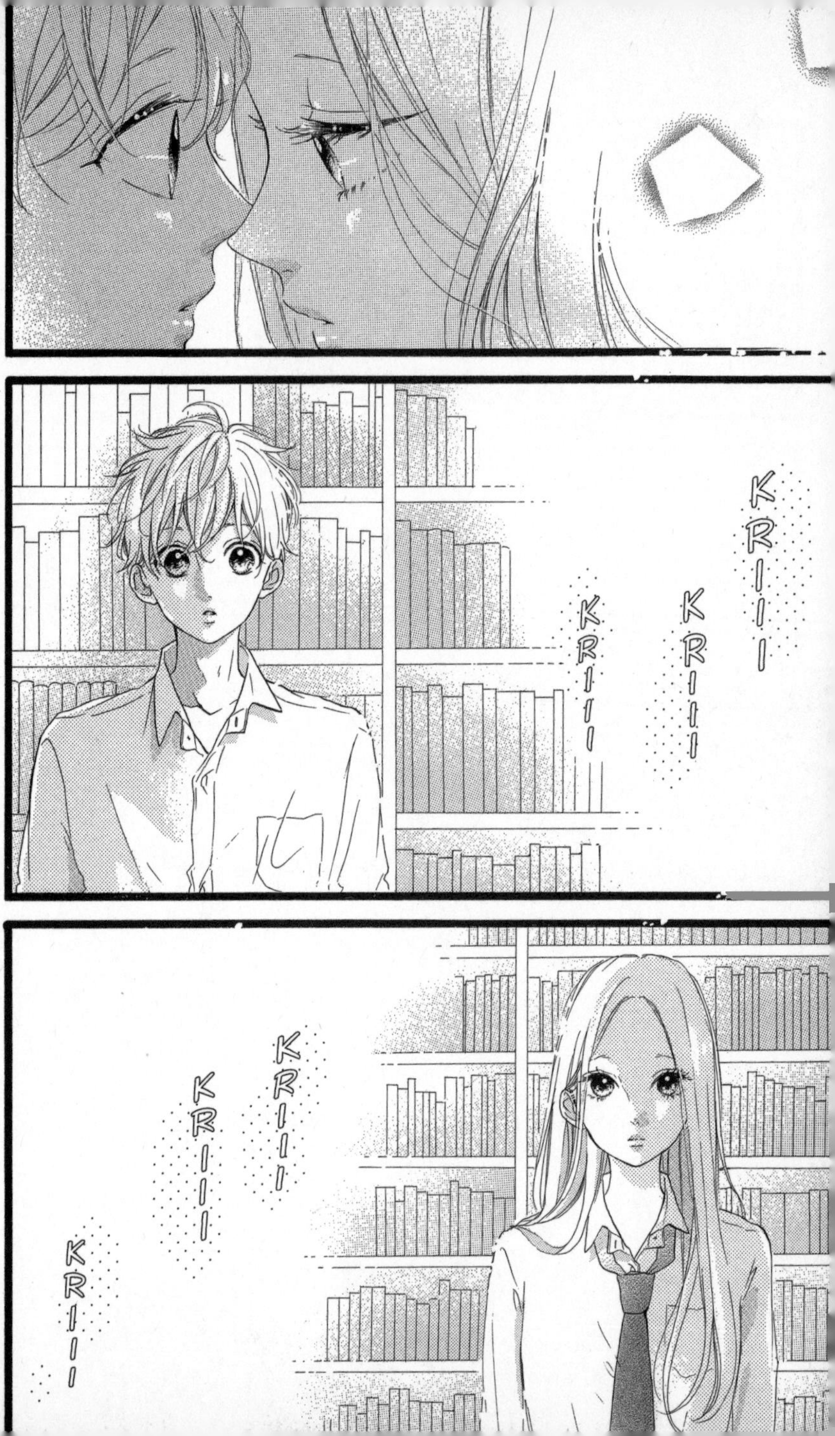
KRIIII
KRIIII
KRIIII
KRIIII
KRIIII
KRIIII

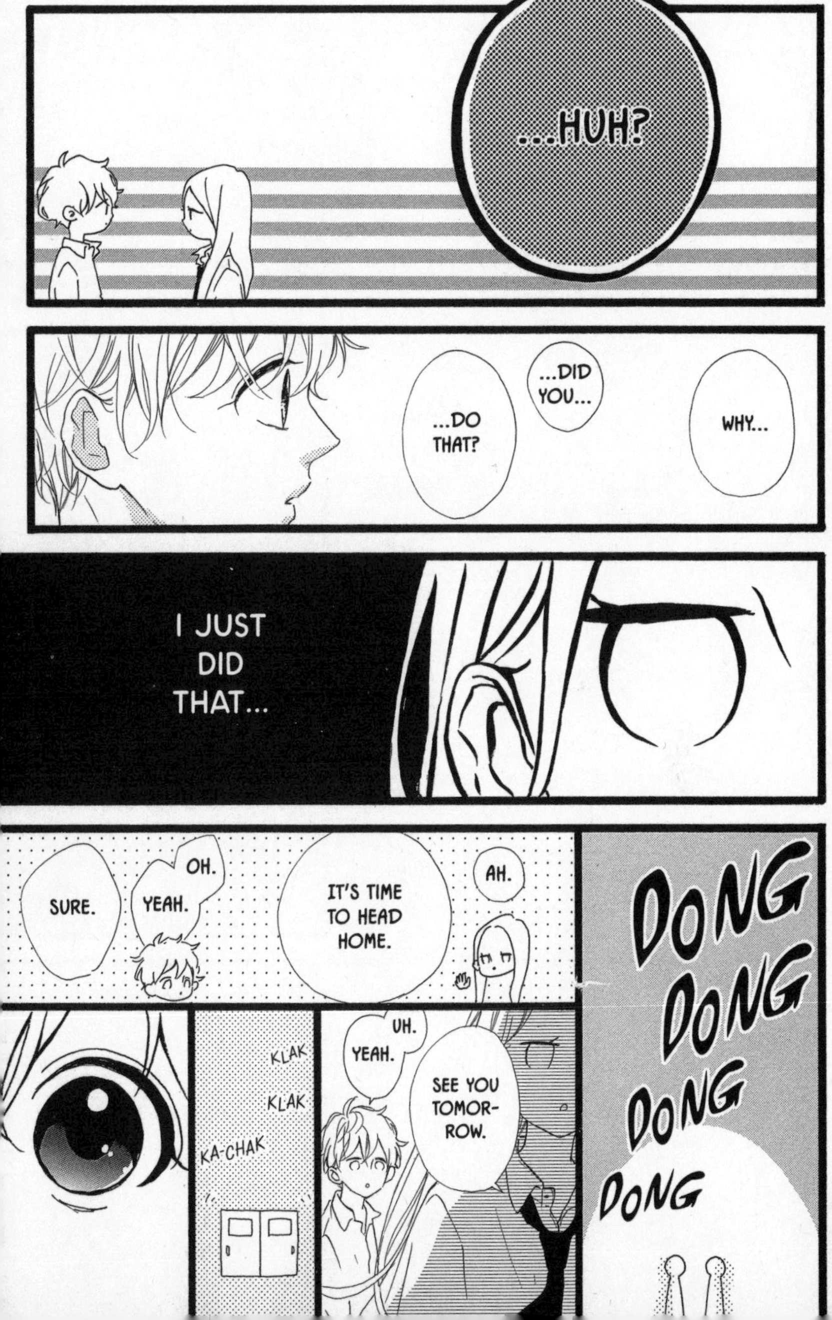
...HUH?
WHY...
...DID YOU...
...DO THAT?
I JUST DID THAT...
DONG DONG DONG DONG
AH.
IT'S TIME TO HEAD HOME.
OH. YEAH.
SURE.
SEE YOU TOMOR-ROW.
UH. YEAH.
KLAK
KLAK
KA-CHAK

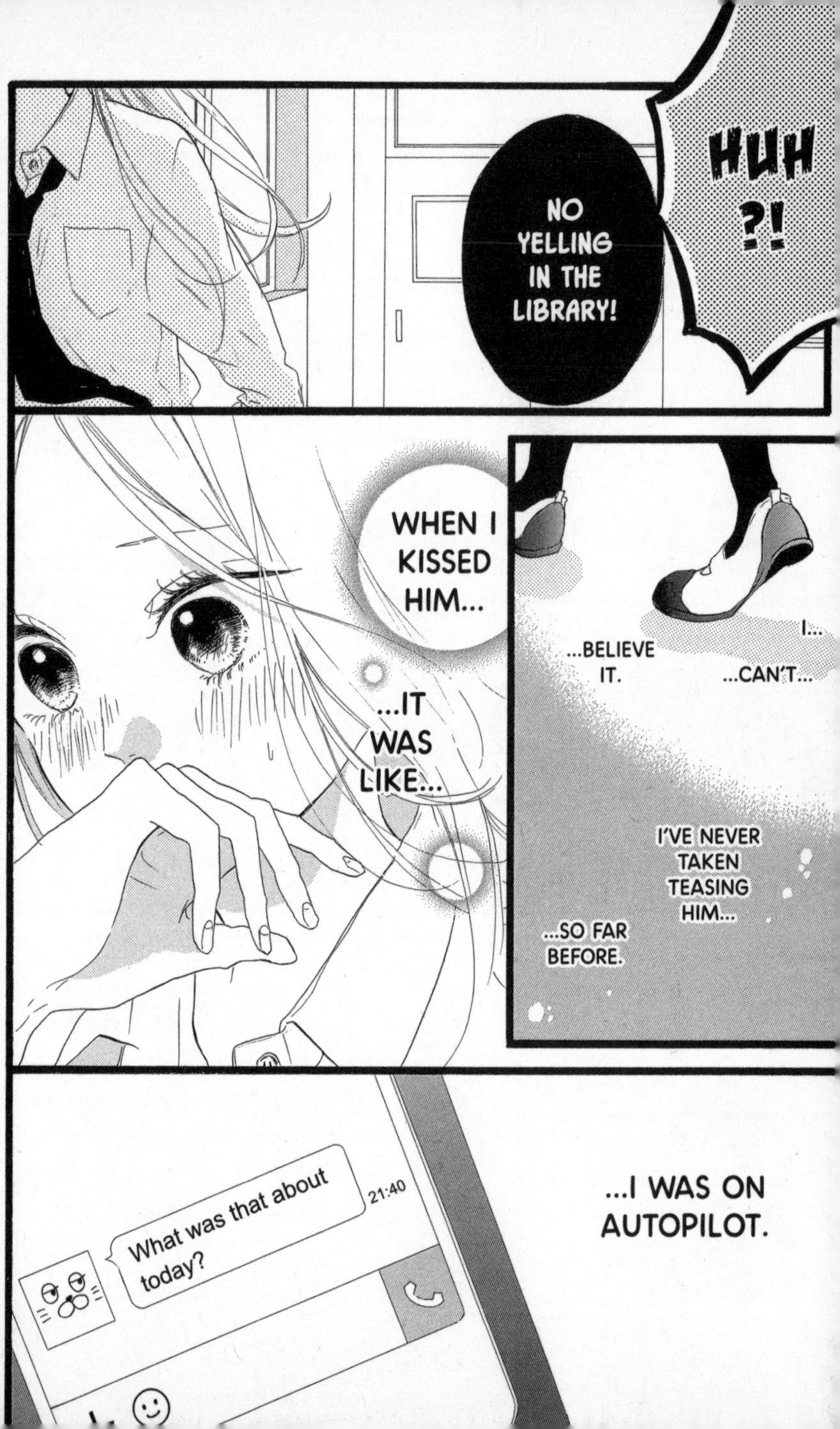
HUH ?!
NO YELLING IN THE LIBRARY!
I...
...CAN'T...
...BELIEVE IT.
I'VE NEVER TAKEN TEASING HIM...
...SO FAR BEFORE.
WHEN I KISSED HIM...
...IT WAS LIKE...
...I WAS ON AUTOPILOT.
21:40
What was that about today?

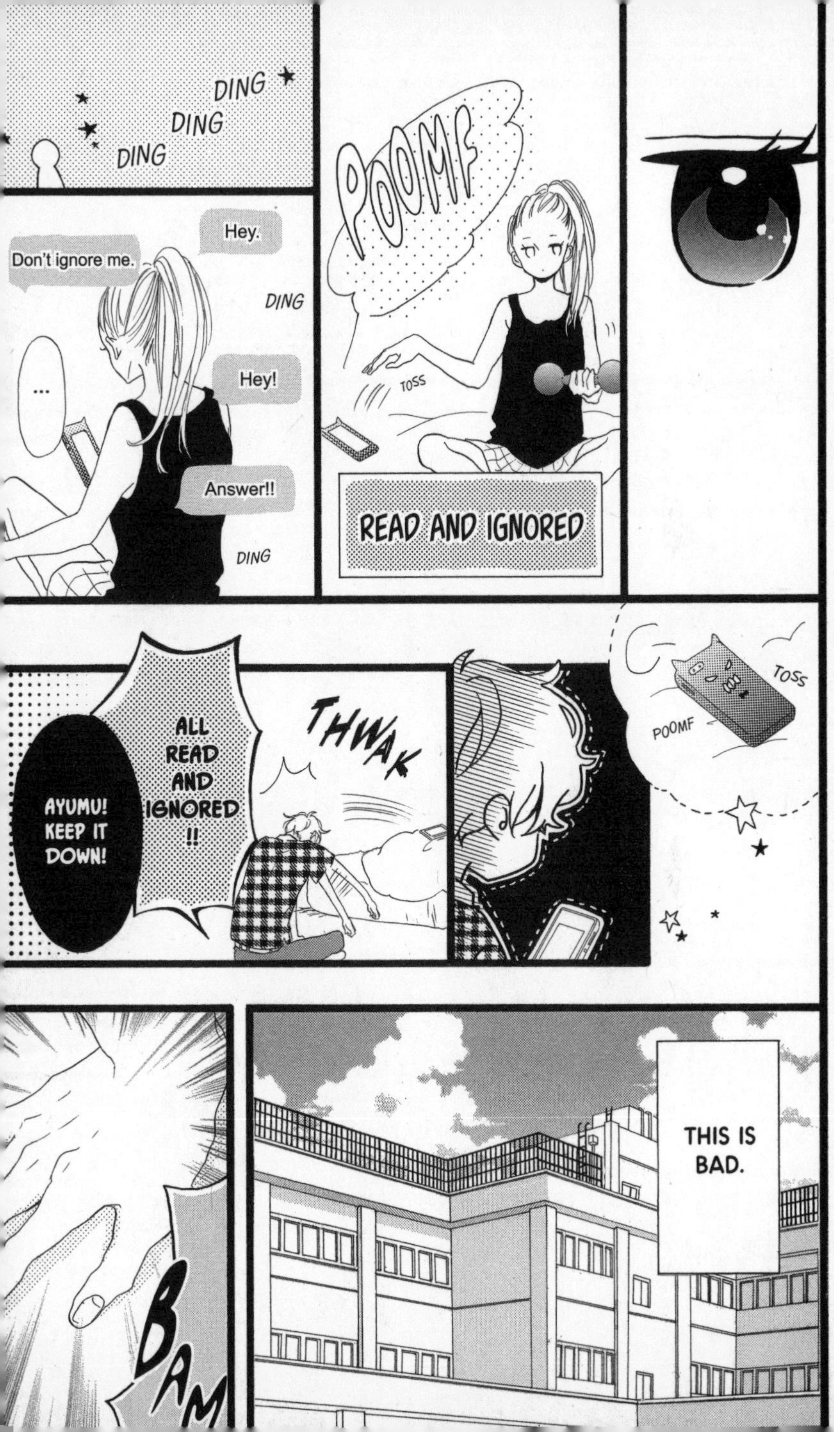
POOMF
TOSS
READ AND IGNORED
DING DING DING
Hey.
Don't ignore me.
DING
Hey!
...
Answer!!
DING
TOSS
POOMF
THWAK
ALL READ AND IGNORED!!
AYUMU! KEEP IT DOWN!
THIS IS BAD.
BAM

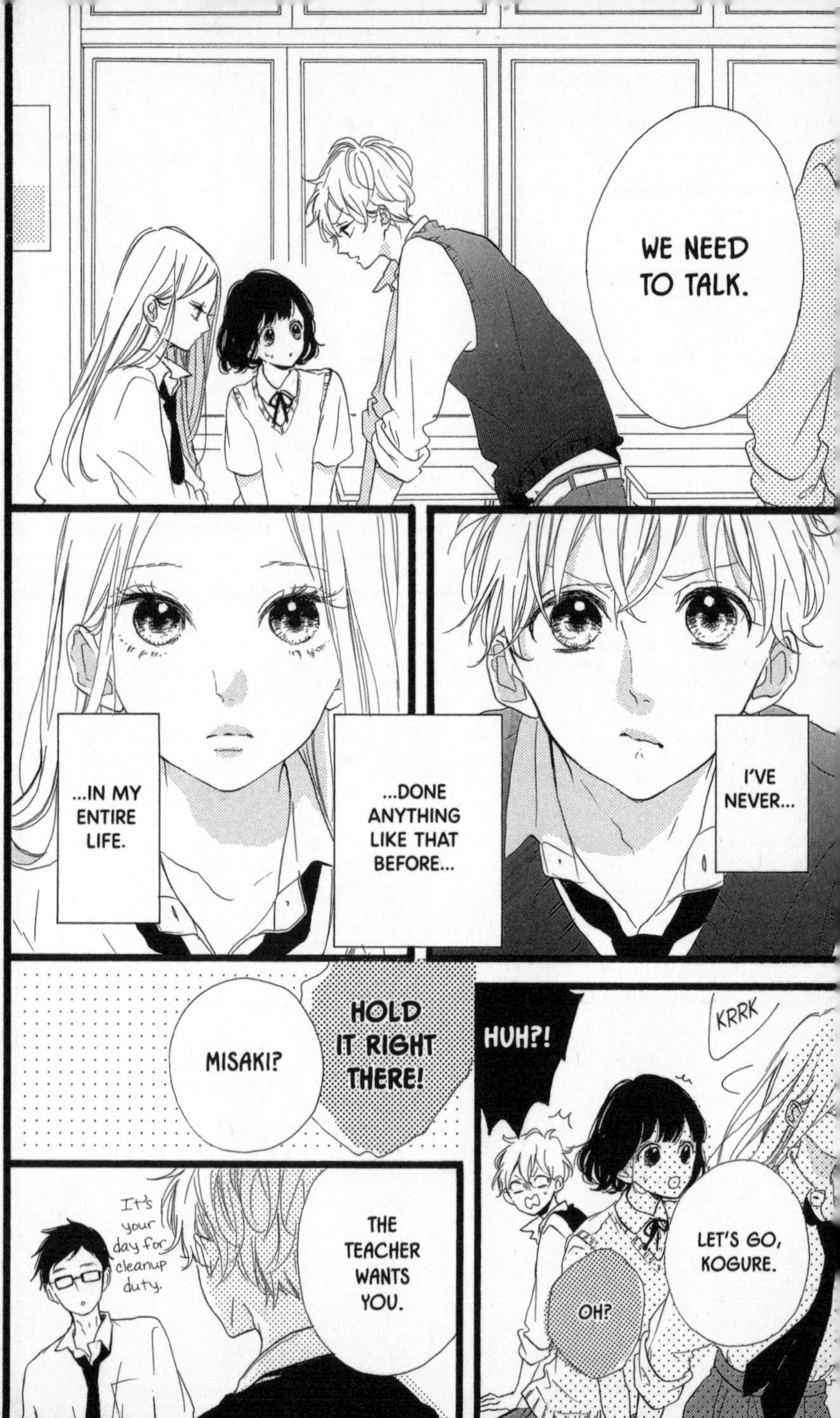
WE NEED TO TALK.
I'VE NEVER...
...DONE ANYTHING LIKE THAT BEFORE...
...IN MY ENTIRE LIFE.
KRRK
HUH?!
LET'S GO, KOGURE.
OH?
HOLD IT RIGHT THERE!
MISAKI?
THE TEACHER WANTS YOU.
It's your day for cleanup duty.

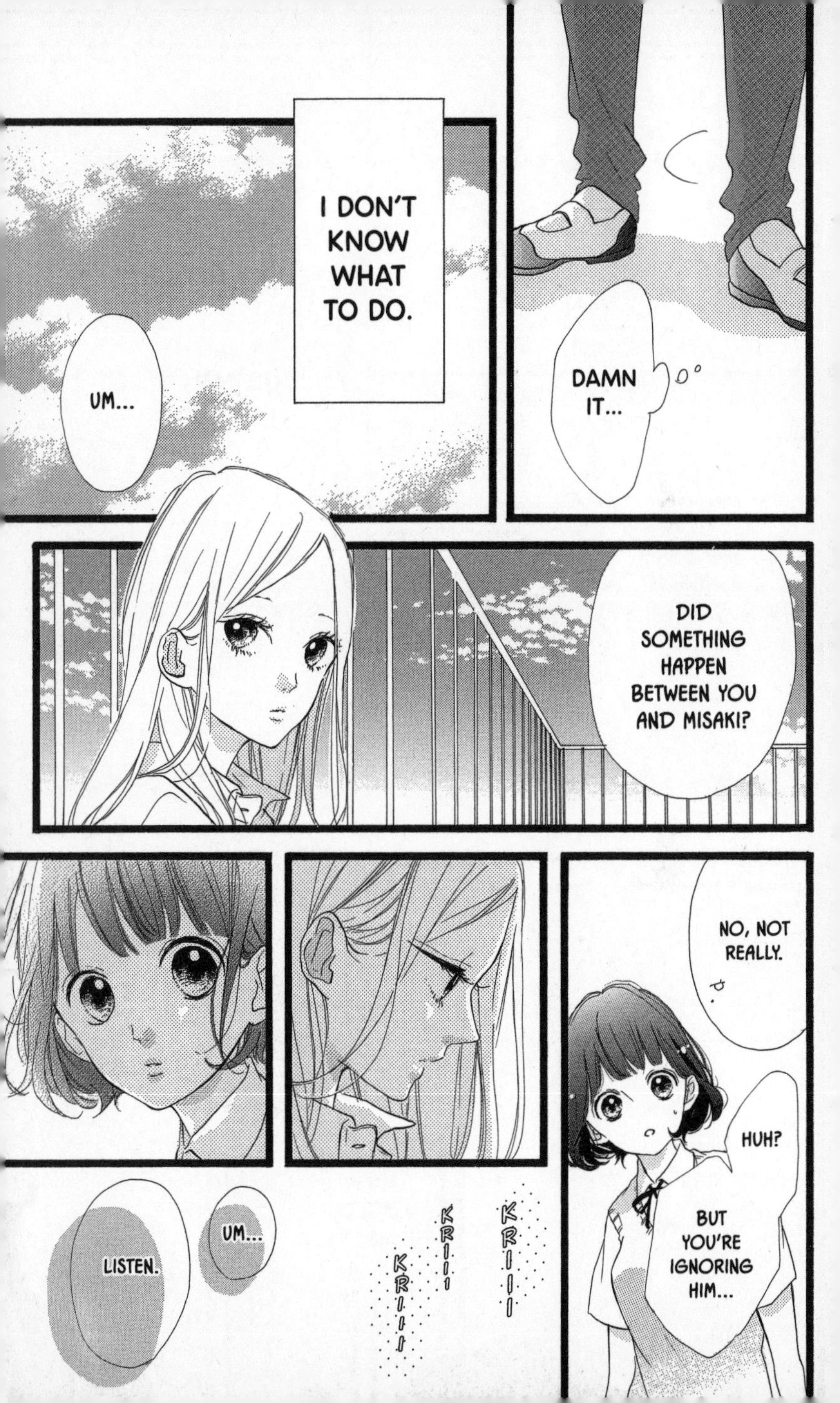
DAMN IT...
I DON'T KNOW WHAT TO DO.
UM...
DID SOMETHING HAPPEN BETWEEN YOU AND MISAKI?
NO, NOT REALLY.
HUH?
BUT YOU'RE IGNORING HIM...
KRIII
KRIII
KRIII
UM...
LISTEN.

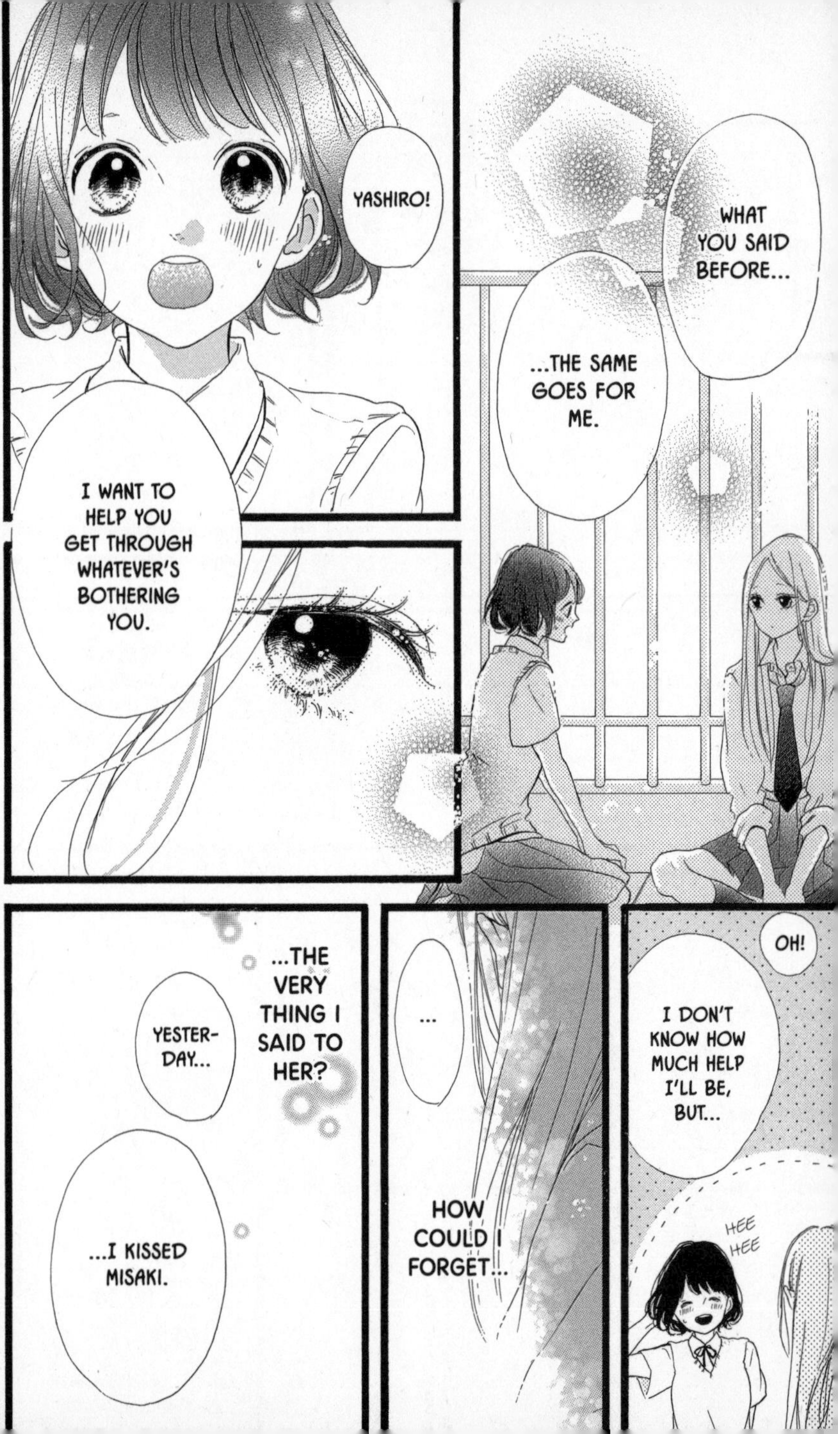
WHAT YOU SAID BEFORE...
...THE SAME GOES FOR ME.
YASHIRO!
I WANT TO HELP YOU GET THROUGH WHATEVER'S BOTHERING YOU.
OH!
I DON'T KNOW HOW MUCH HELP I'LL BE, BUT...
HEE HEE
...
HOW COULD I FORGET...
...THE VERY THING I SAID TO HER?
YESTER-DAY...
...I KISSED MISAKI.

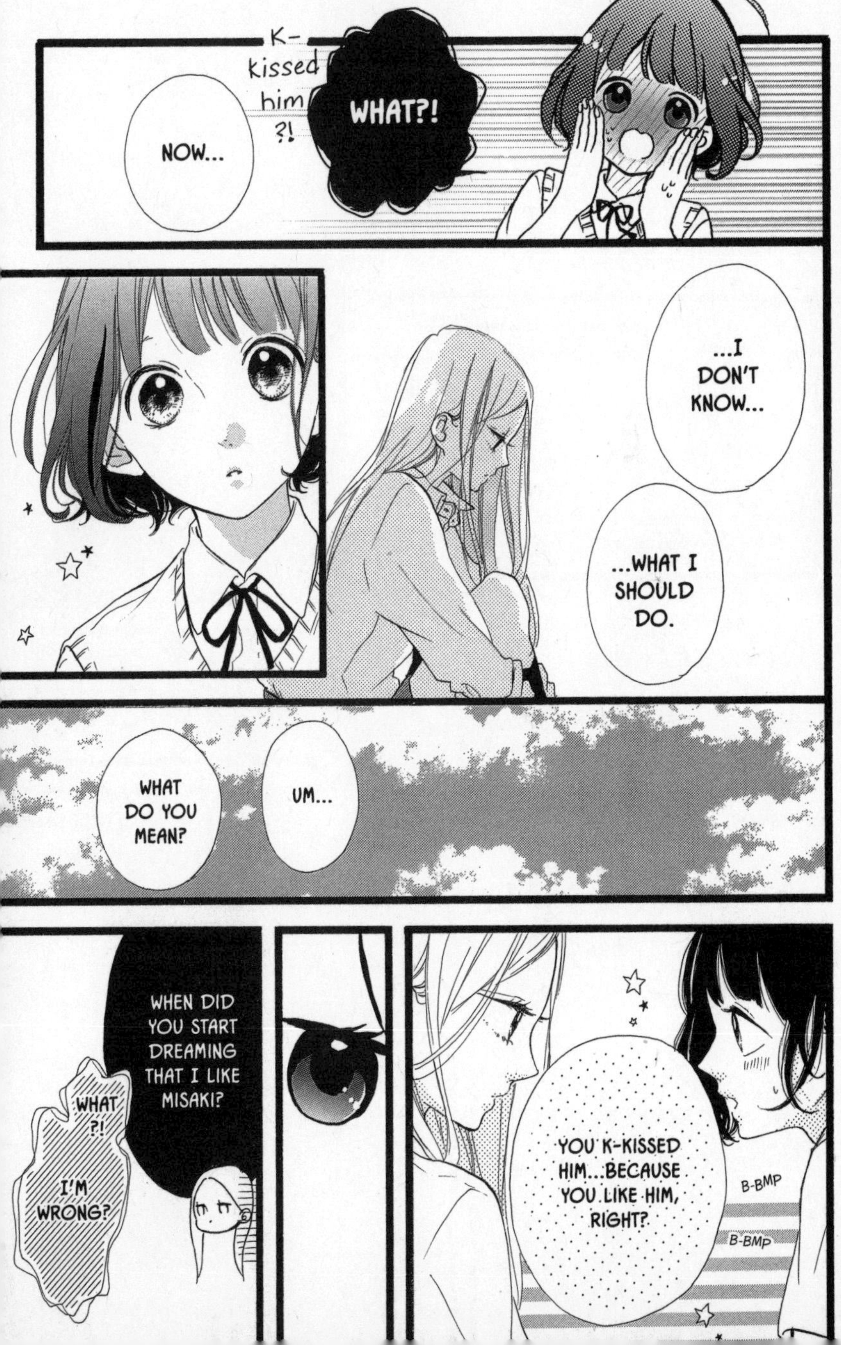
WHAT?!
K-kissed him?!
NOW...
...I DON'T KNOW...
...WHAT I SHOULD DO.
UM...
WHAT DO YOU MEAN?
YOU K-KISSED HIM...BECAUSE YOU LIKE HIM, RIGHT?
B-BMP
B-BMP
WHEN DID YOU START DREAMING THAT I LIKE MISAKI?
WHAT?!
I'M WRONG?

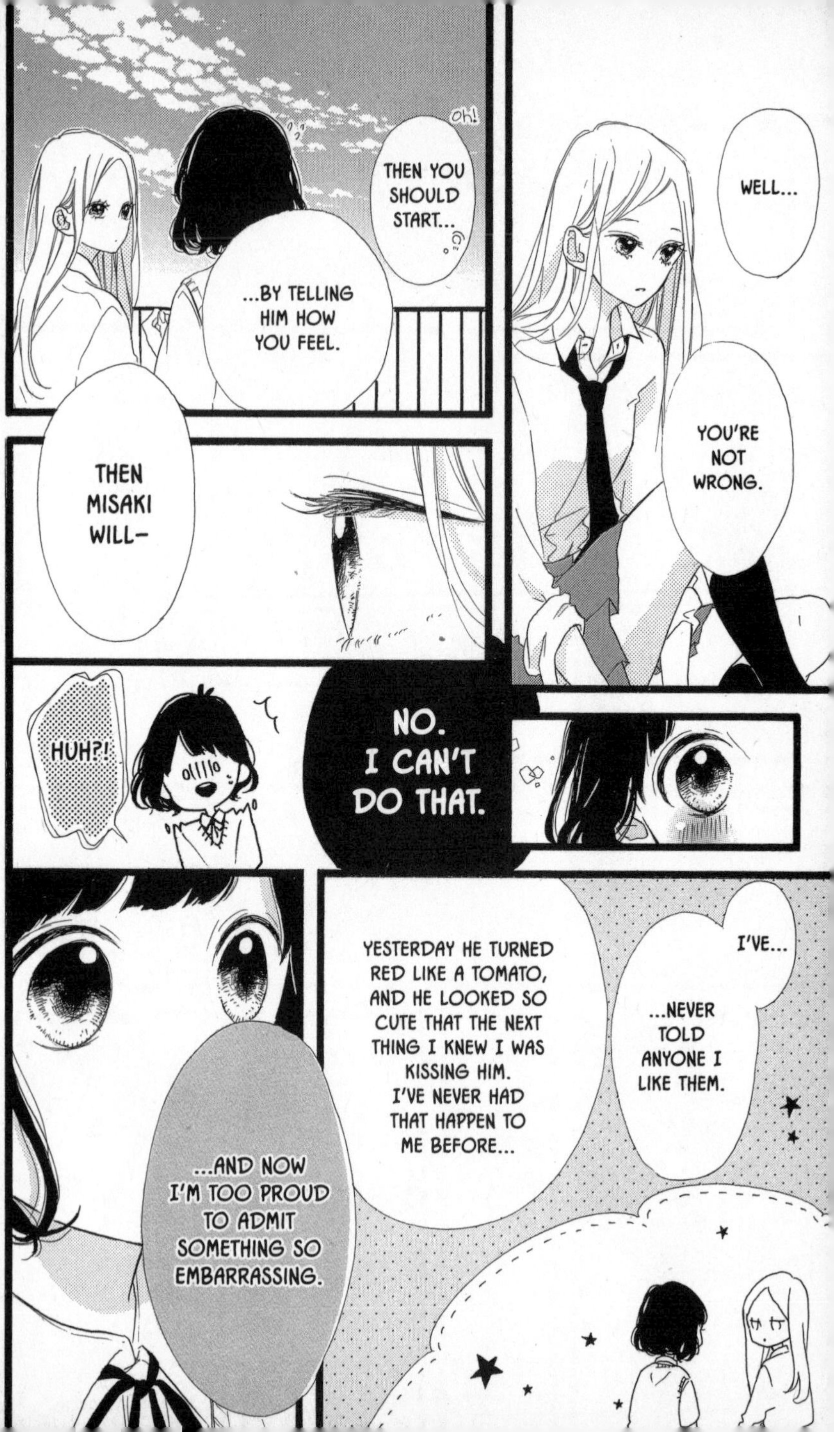
WELL...
YOU'RE NOT WRONG.
Oh!
THEN YOU SHOULD START...
...BY TELLING HIM HOW YOU FEEL.
THEN MISAKI WILL-
NO. I CAN'T DO THAT.
HUH?!
I'VE...
...NEVER TOLD ANYONE I LIKE THEM.
YESTERDAY HE TURNED RED LIKE A TOMATO, AND HE LOOKED SO CUTE THAT THE NEXT THING I KNEW I WAS KISSING HIM. I'VE NEVER HAD THAT HAPPEN TO ME BEFORE...
...AND NOW I'M TOO PROUD TO ADMIT SOMETHING SO EMBARRASSING.

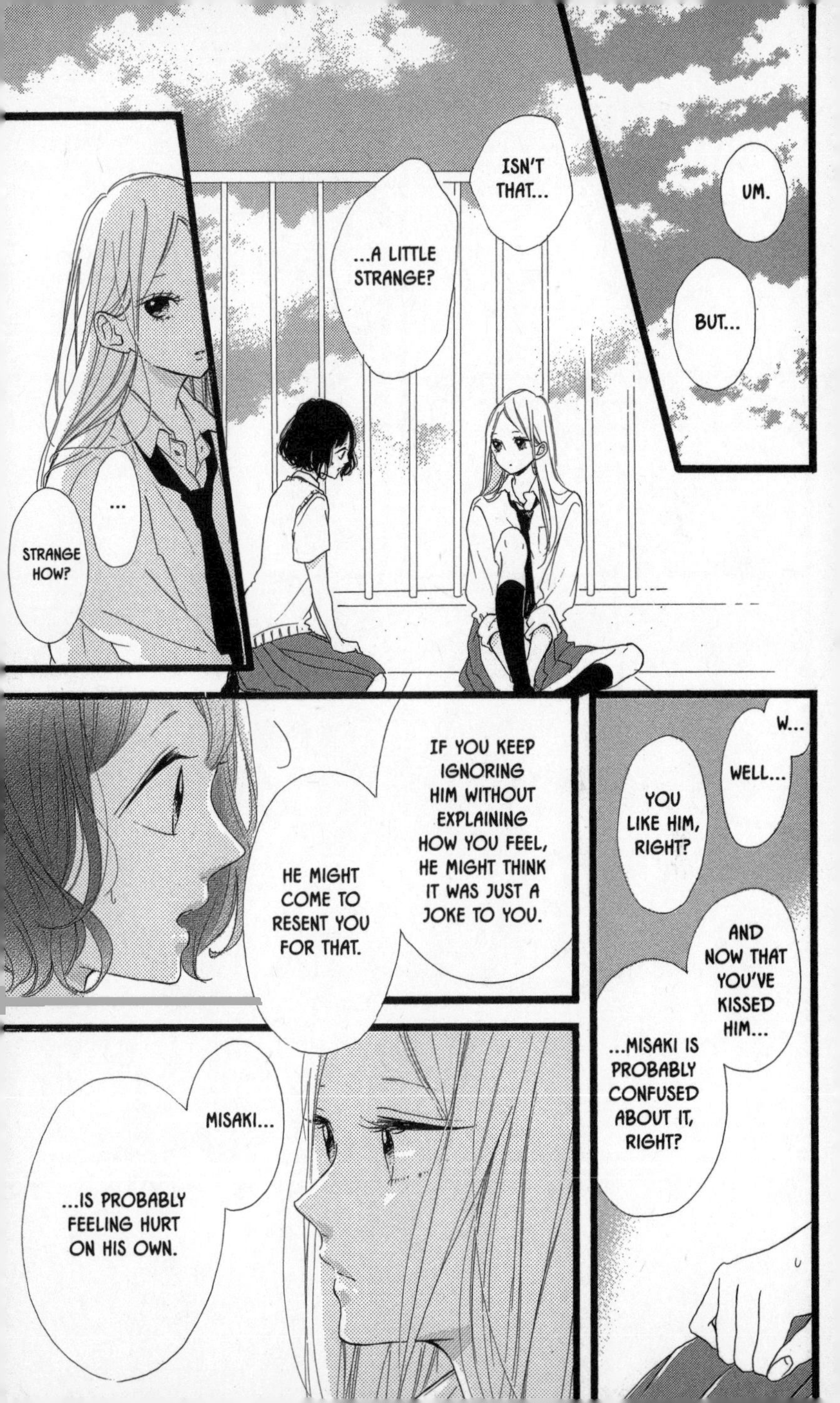
UM.
BUT...
ISN'T THAT...
...A LITTLE STRANGE?
...
STRANGE HOW?
W...
WELL...
YOU LIKE HIM, RIGHT?
AND NOW THAT YOU'VE KISSED HIM...
...MISAKI IS PROBABLY CONFUSED ABOUT IT, RIGHT?
IF YOU KEEP IGNORING HIM WITHOUT EXPLAINING HOW YOU FEEL, HE MIGHT THINK IT WAS JUST A JOKE TO YOU.
HE MIGHT COME TO RESENT YOU FOR THAT.
MISAKI...
...IS PROBABLY FEELING HURT ON HIS OWN.

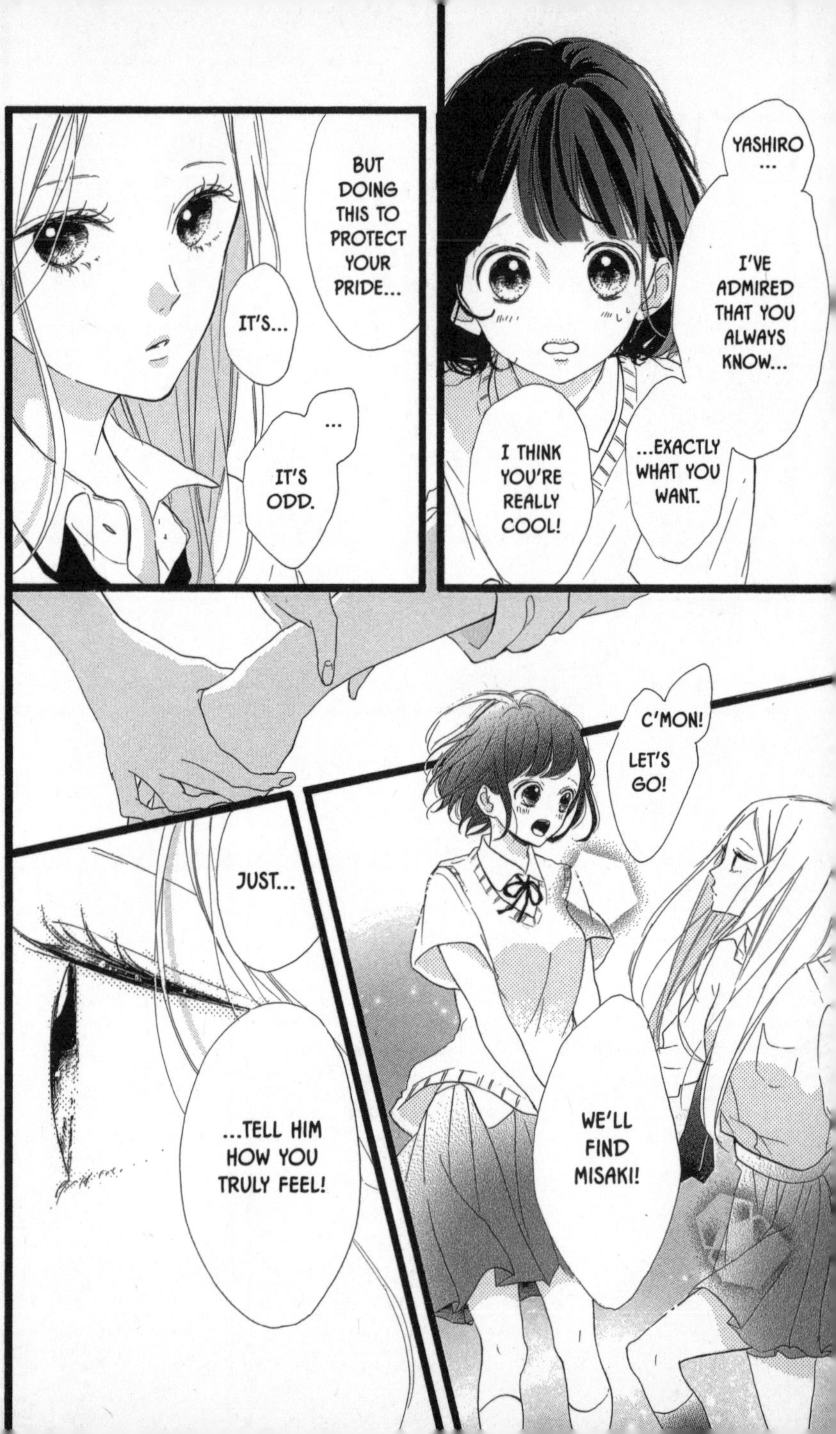
YASHIRO ...
I'VE ADMIRED THAT YOU ALWAYS KNOW...
...EXACTLY WHAT YOU WANT.
I THINK YOU'RE REALLY COOL!
BUT DOING THIS TO PROTECT YOUR PRIDE...
IT'S...
...
IT'S ODD.
C'MON!
LET'S GO!
WE'LL FIND MISAKI!
JUST...
...TELL HIM HOW YOU TRULY FEEL!

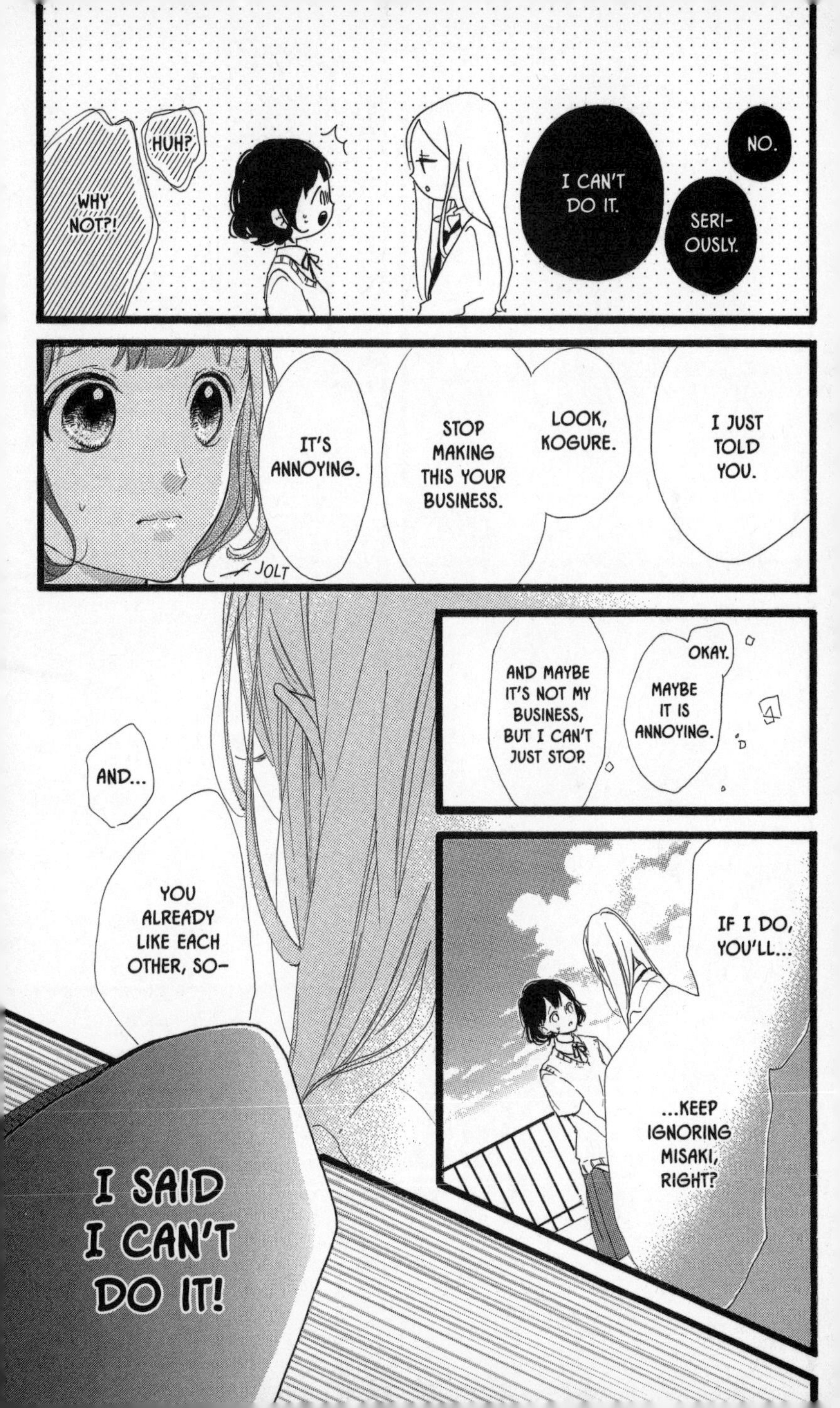
NO.
SERI-OUSLY.
I CAN'T DO IT.
HUH?
WHY NOT?!
I JUST TOLD YOU.
LOOK, KOGURE.
STOP MAKING THIS YOUR BUSINESS.
IT'S ANNOYING.
JOLT
OKAY.
MAYBE IT IS ANNOYING.
AND MAYBE IT'S NOT MY BUSINESS, BUT I CAN'T JUST STOP.
IF I DO, YOU'LL...
...KEEP IGNORING MISAKI, RIGHT?
AND...
YOU ALREADY LIKE EACH OTHER, SO-
I SAID I CAN'T DO IT!

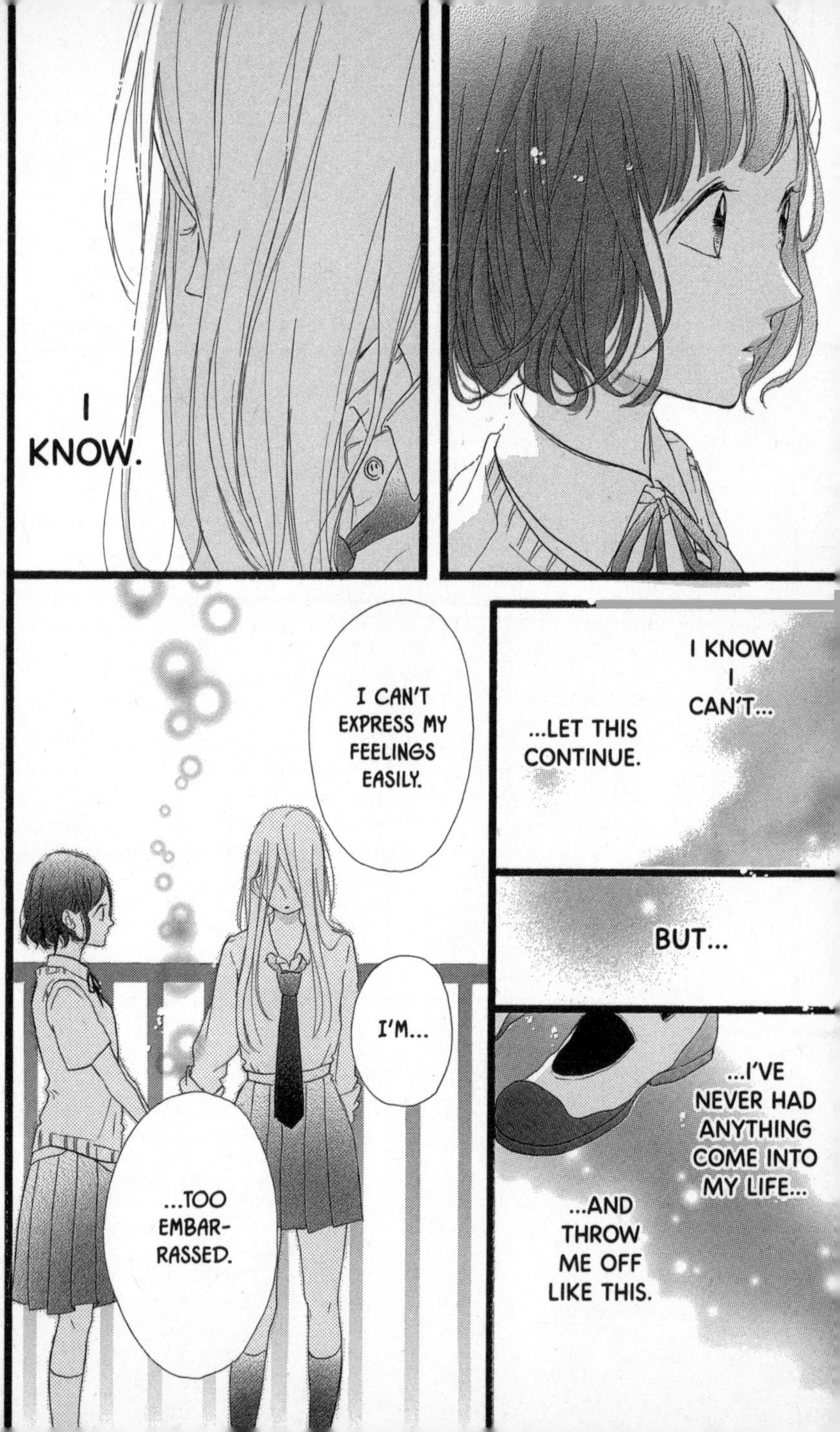
I KNOW.
I KNOW I CAN'T...
...LET THIS CONTINUE.
BUT...
...I'VE NEVER HAD ANYTHING COME INTO MY LIFE...
...AND THROW ME OFF LIKE THIS.
I CAN'T EXPRESS MY FEELINGS EASILY.
I'M...
...TOO EMBARRASSED.

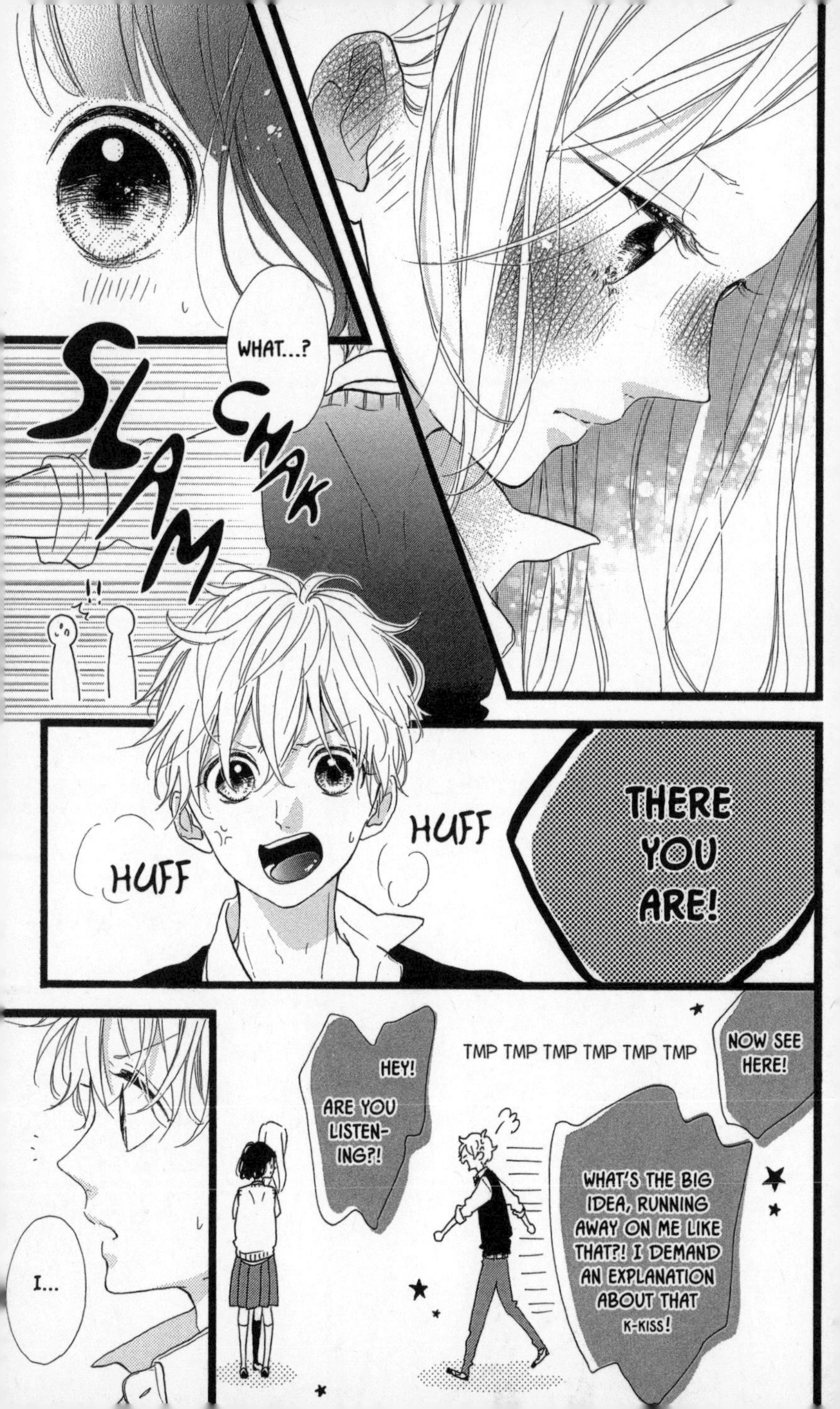
WHAT...?
SLAM
CHAK
!!
THERE YOU ARE!
HUFF
HUFF
NOW SEE HERE!
TMP TMP TMP TMP TMP TMP
WHAT'S THE BIG IDEA, RUNNING AWAY ON ME LIKE THAT?! I DEMAND AN EXPLANATION ABOUT THAT K-KISS!
HEY!
ARE YOU LISTEN-ING?!
I...

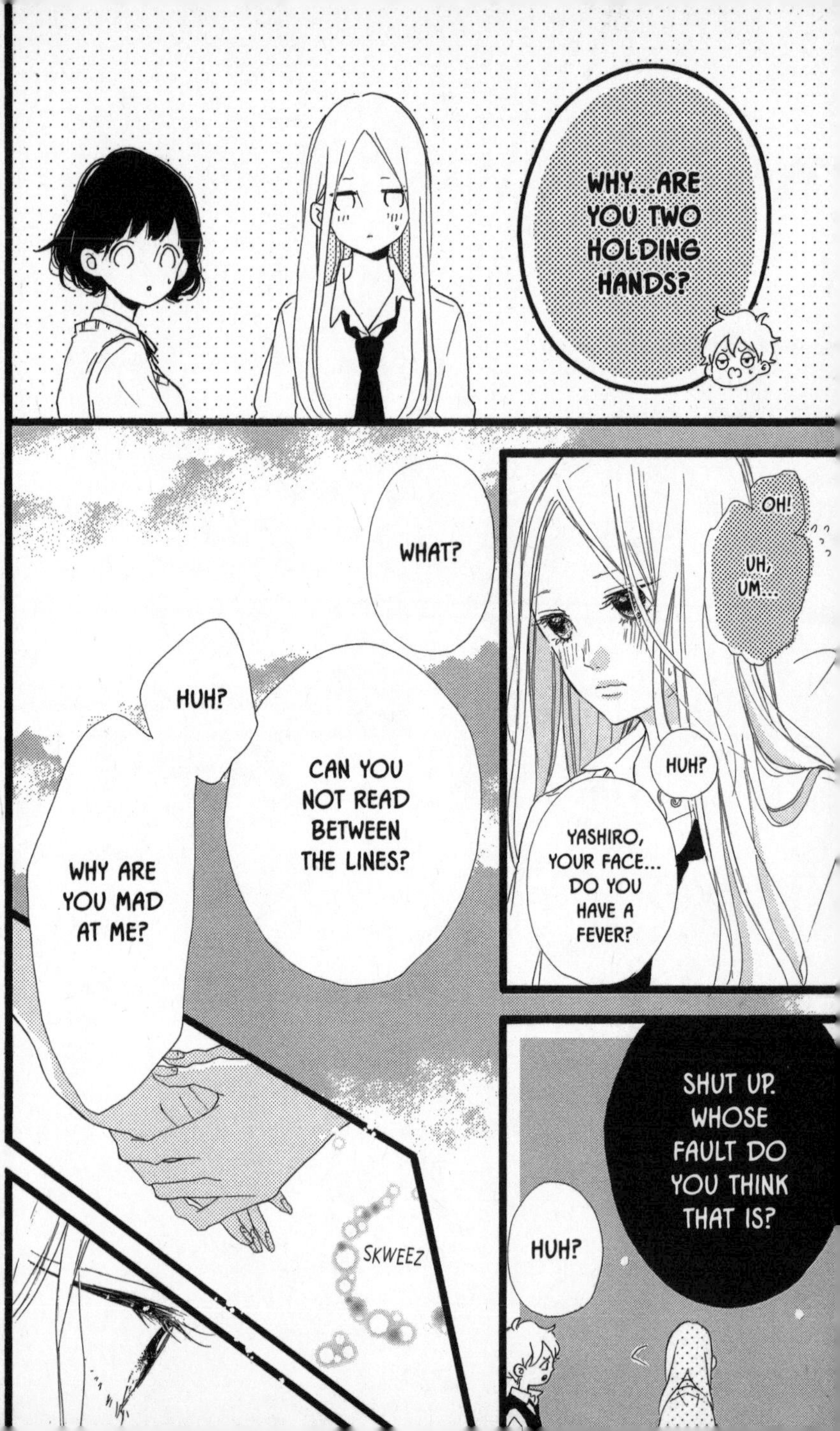
WHY...ARE YOU TWO HOLDING HANDS?
OH!
UH, UM...
HUH?
YASHIRO, YOUR FACE... DO YOU HAVE A FEVER?
SHUT UP. WHOSE FAULT DO YOU THINK THAT IS?
HUH?
WHAT?
CAN YOU NOT READ BETWEEN THE LINES?
HUH?
WHY ARE YOU MAD AT ME?
SKWEEZ

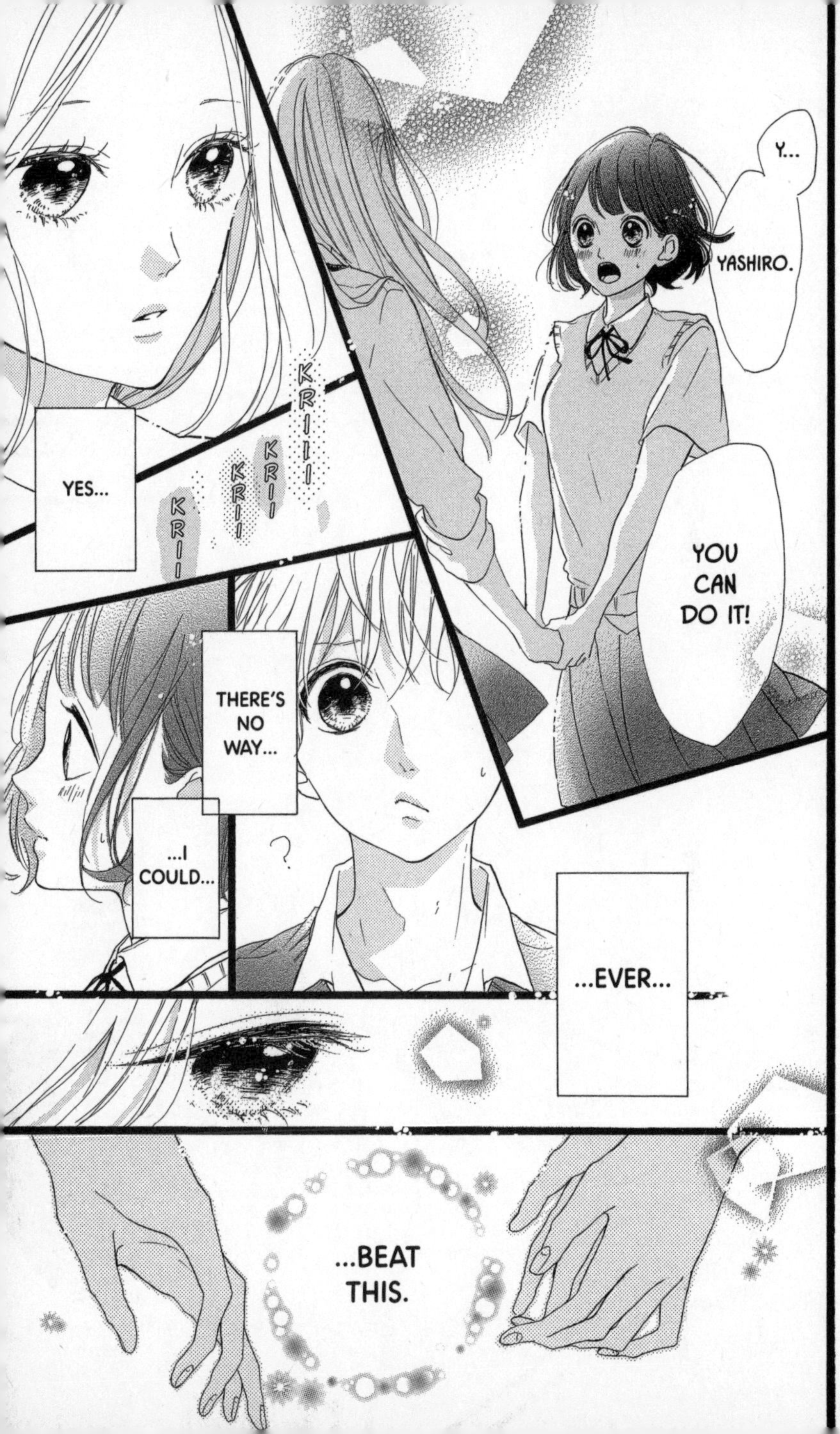
Y...
YASHIRO.
YOU CAN DO IT!
YES...
KRIII
KRII
KRII
KRII
THERE'S NO WAY...
...I COULD...
...EVER...
...BEAT THIS.

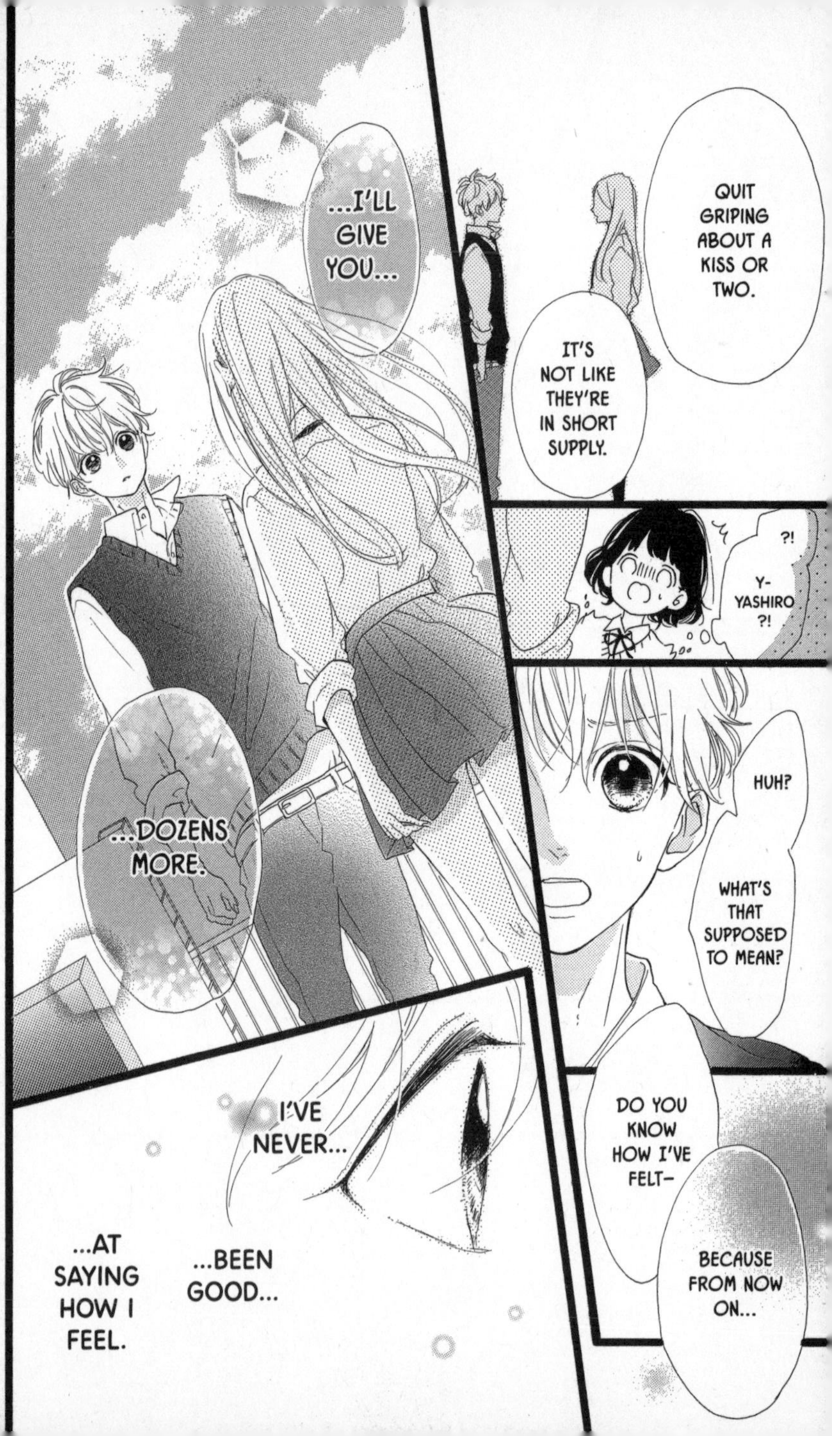
QUIT GRIPING ABOUT A KISS OR TWO.
IT'S NOT LIKE THEY'RE IN SHORT SUPPLY.
?!
Y-YASHIRO ?!
HUH?
WHAT'S THAT SUPPOSED TO MEAN?
DO YOU KNOW HOW I'VE FELT—
BECAUSE FROM NOW ON...
...I'LL GIVE YOU...
...DOZENS MORE.
I'VE NEVER...
...BEEN GOOD...
...AT SAYING HOW I FEEL.

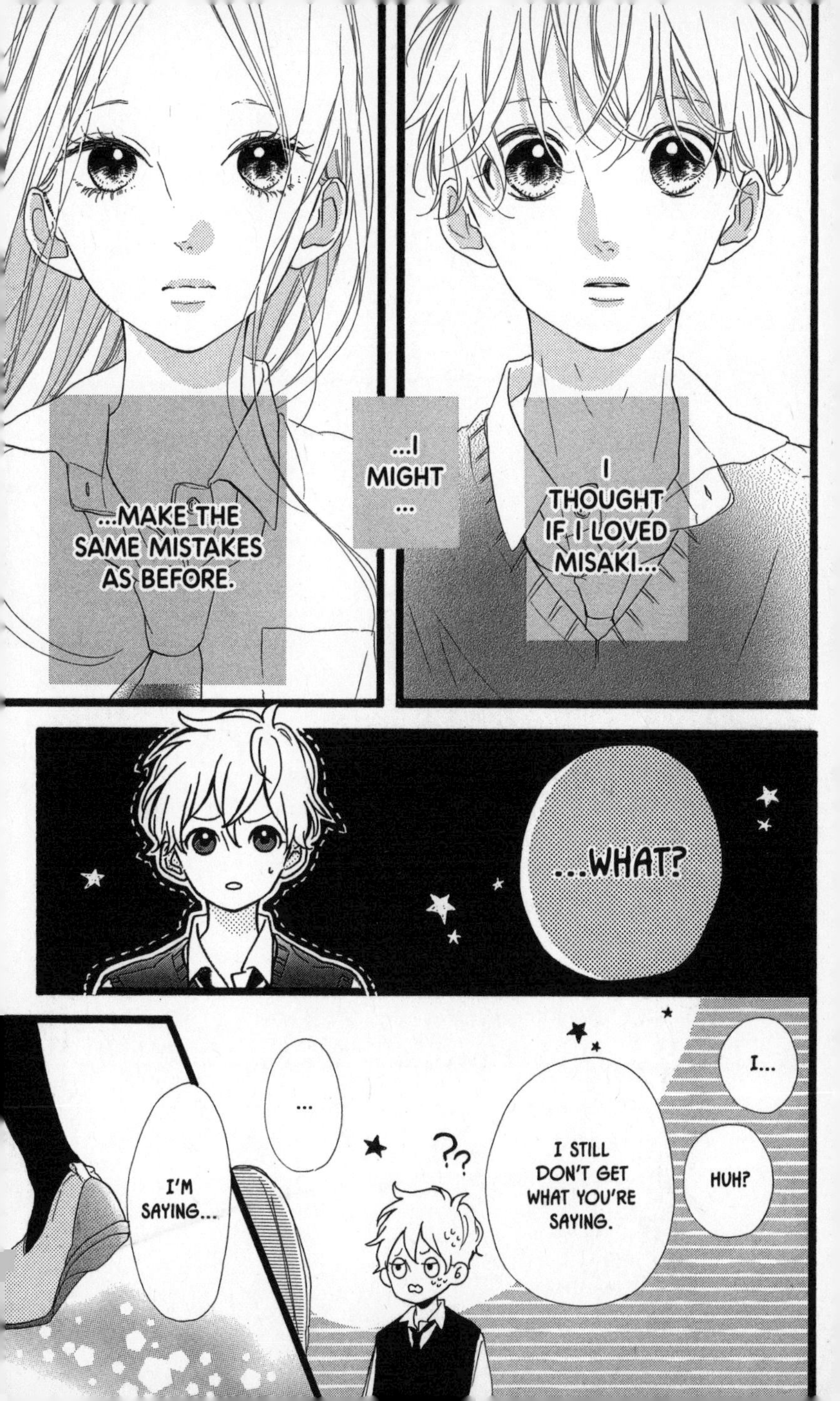

I THOUGHT IF I LOVED MISAKI...
...I MIGHT ...
...MAKE THE SAME MISTAKES AS BEFORE.
...WHAT?
I...
HUH?
I STILL DON'T GET WHAT YOU'RE SAYING.
...
I'M SAYING...

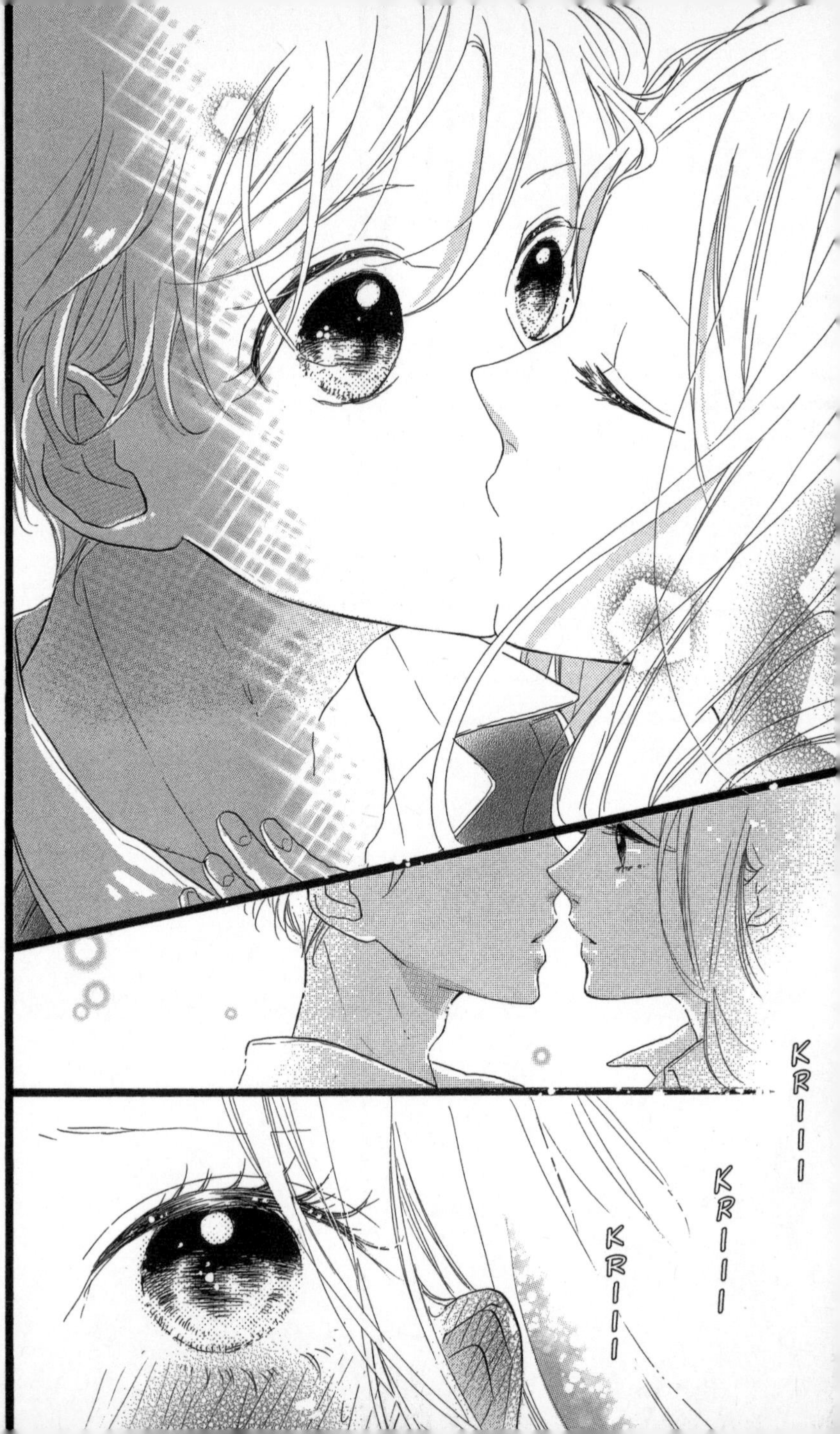
KRIII
KRIII
KRIII

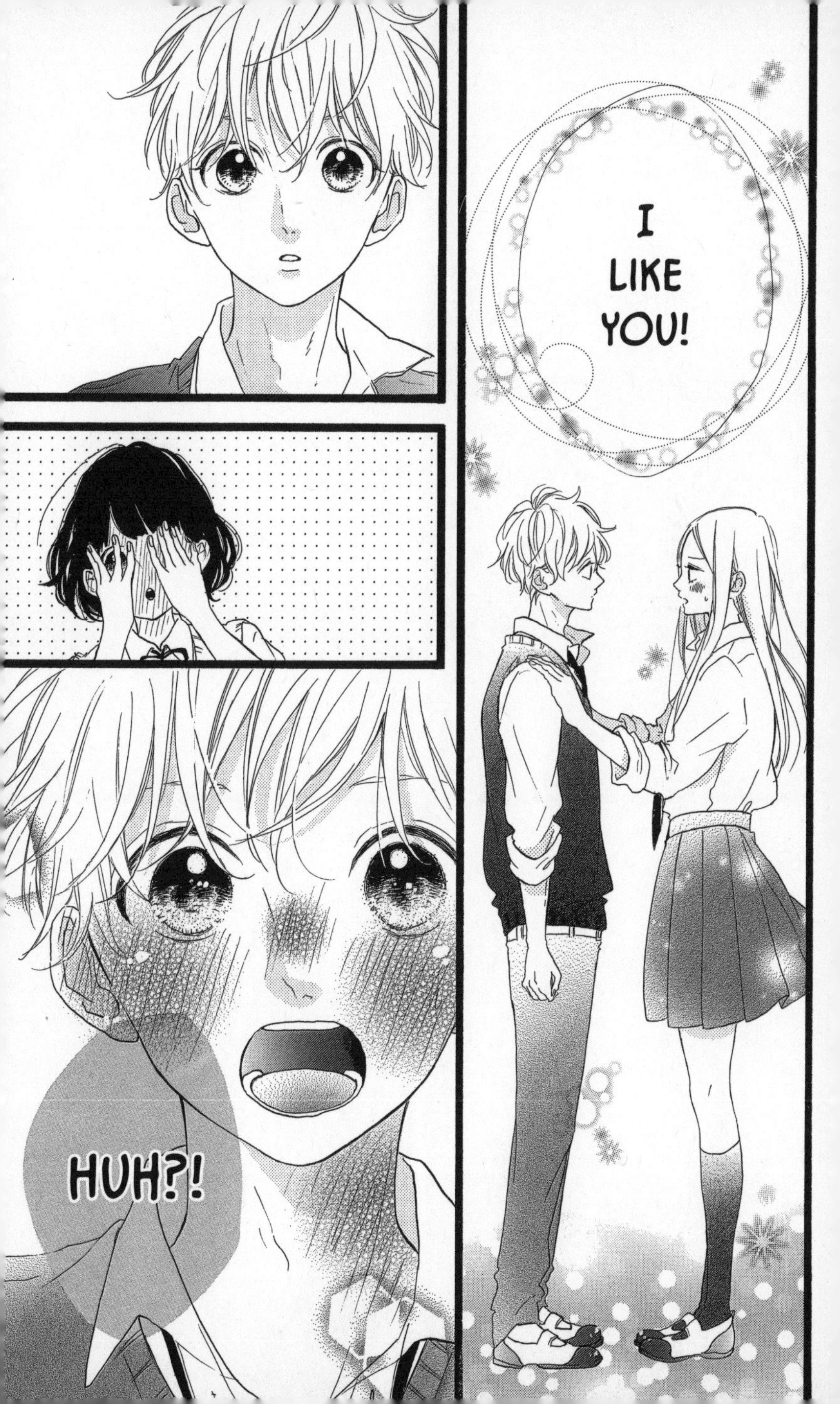
I LIKE YOU!
HUH?!

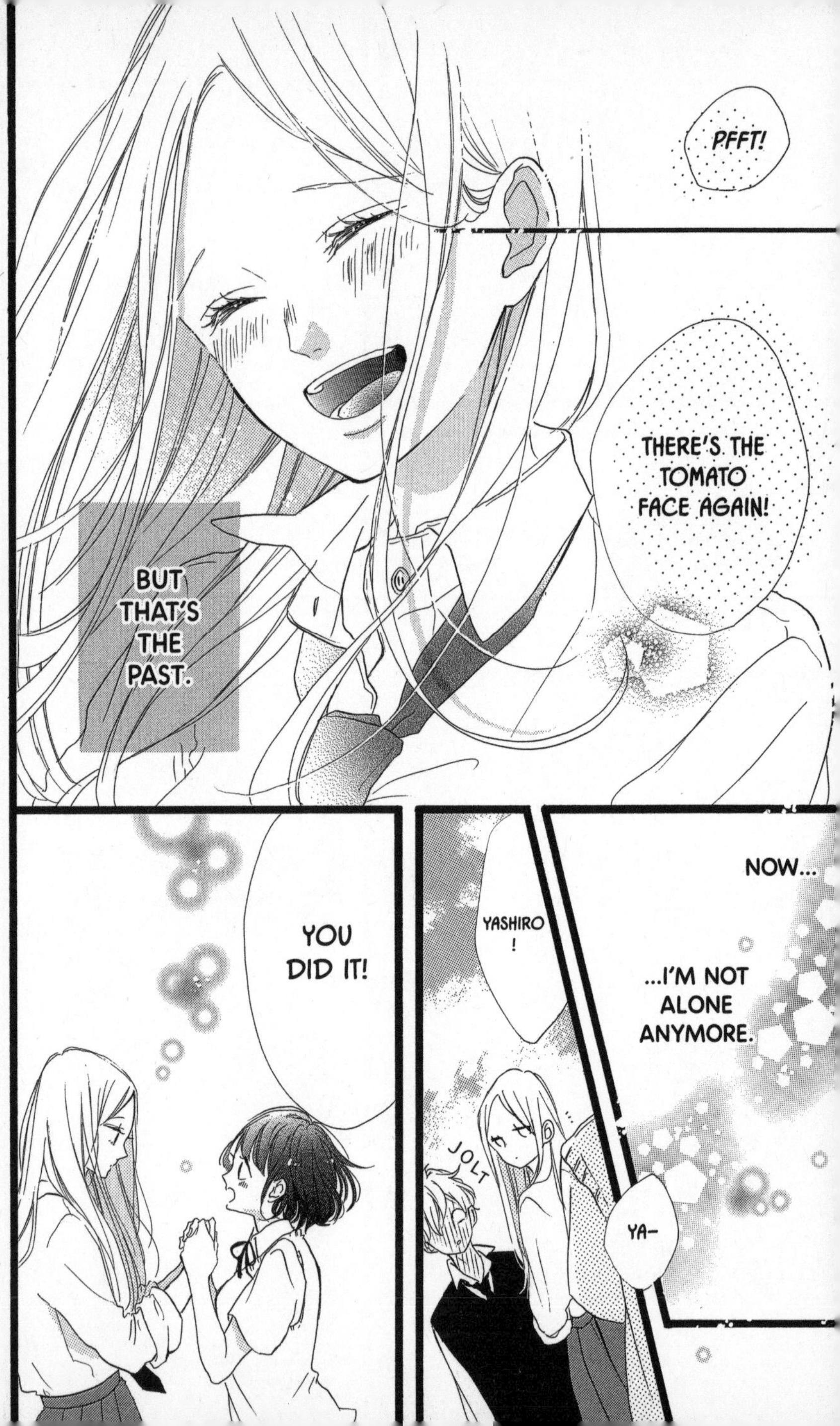
PFFT!
THERE'S THE TOMATO FACE AGAIN!
BUT THAT'S THE PAST.
NOW...
...I'M NOT ALONE ANYMORE.
YASHIRO!
JOLT
YA-
YOU DID IT!

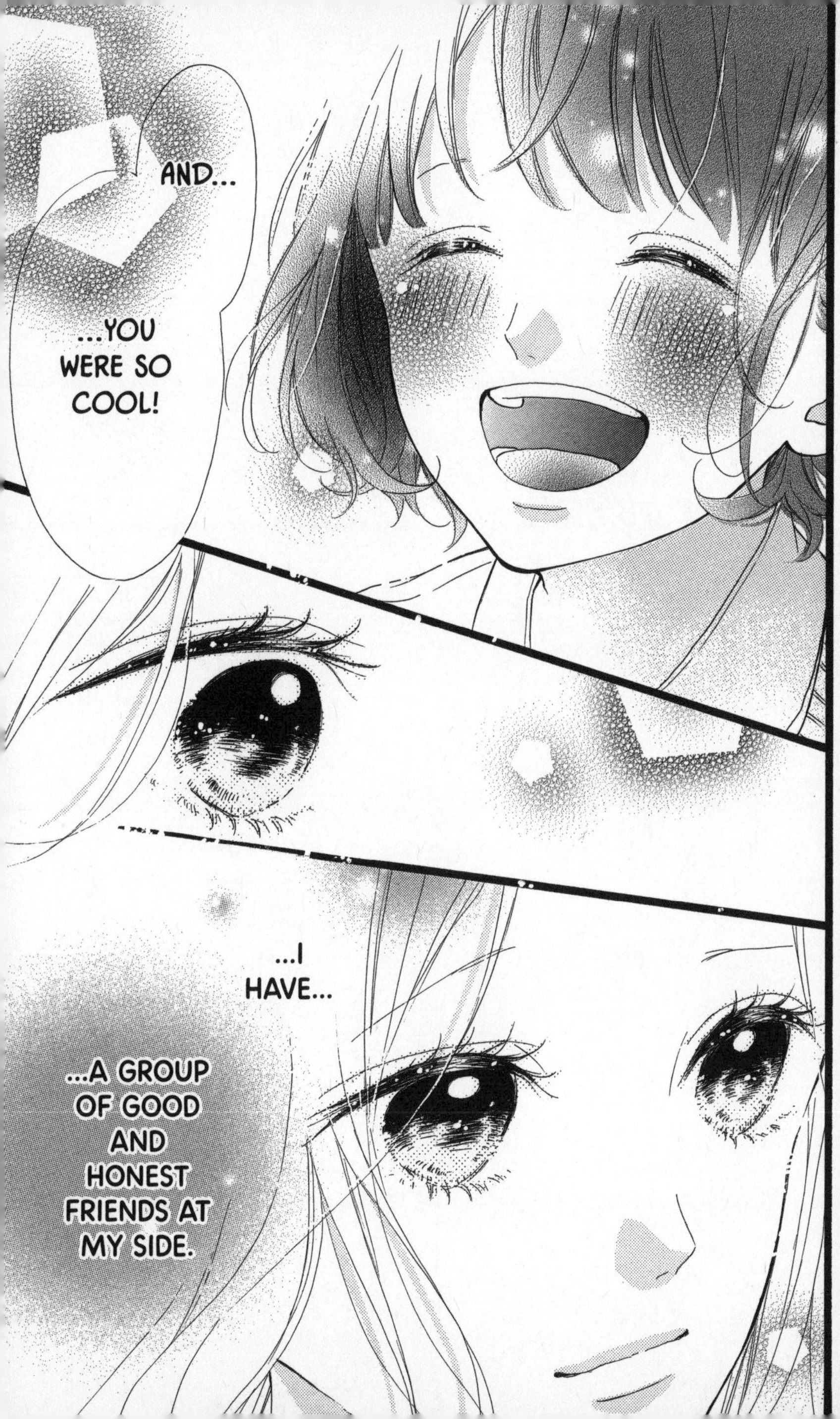
AND...
...YOU WERE SO COOL!
...I HAVE...
...A GROUP OF GOOD AND HONEST FRIENDS AT MY SIDE.

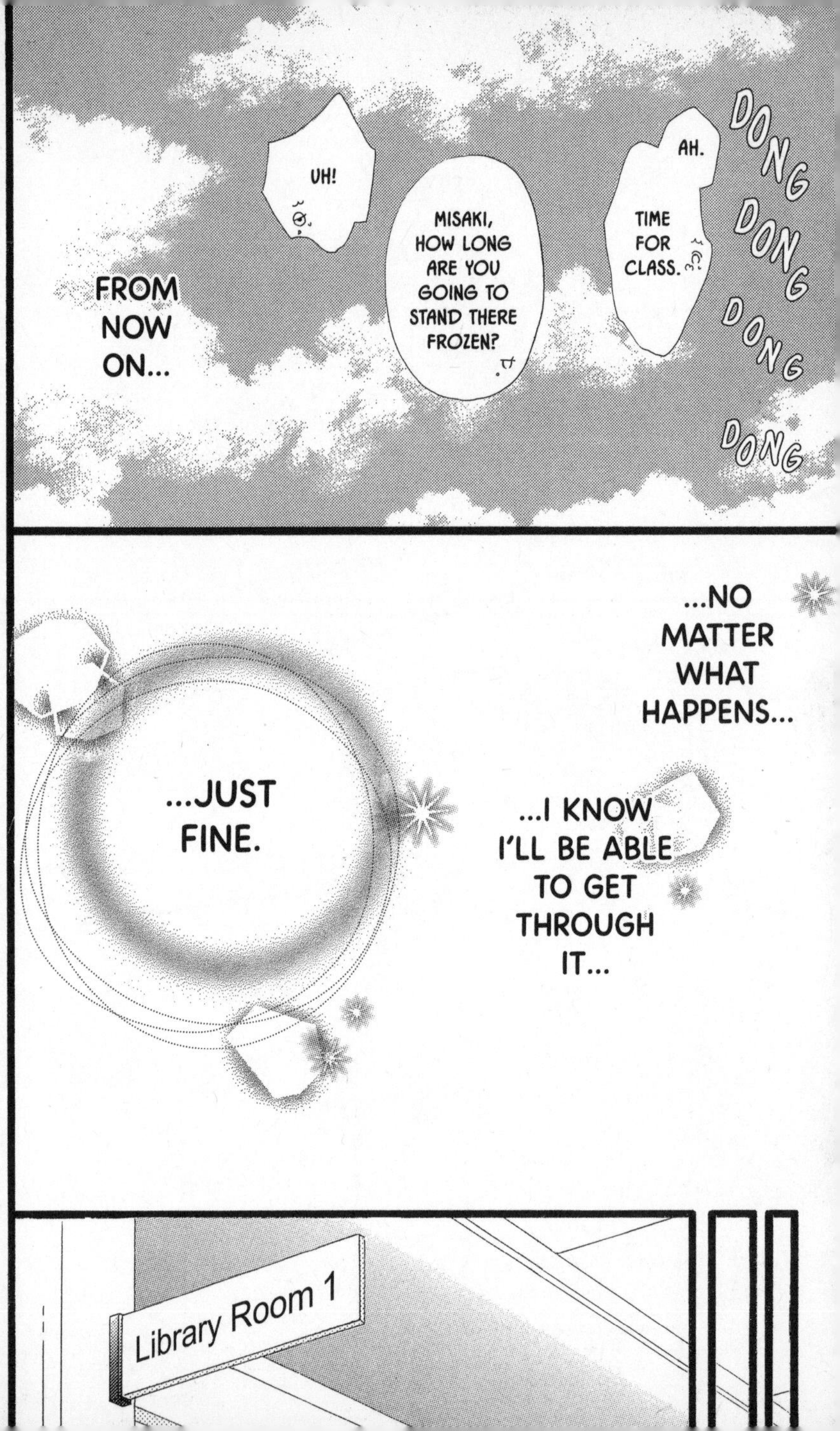
DONG DONG DONG DONG
AH.
TIME FOR CLASS.
MISAKI, HOW LONG ARE YOU GOING TO STAND THERE FROZEN?
UH!
FROM NOW ON...
...NO MATTER WHAT HAPPENS...
...I KNOW I'LL BE ABLE TO GET THROUGH IT...
...JUST FINE.
Library Room 1

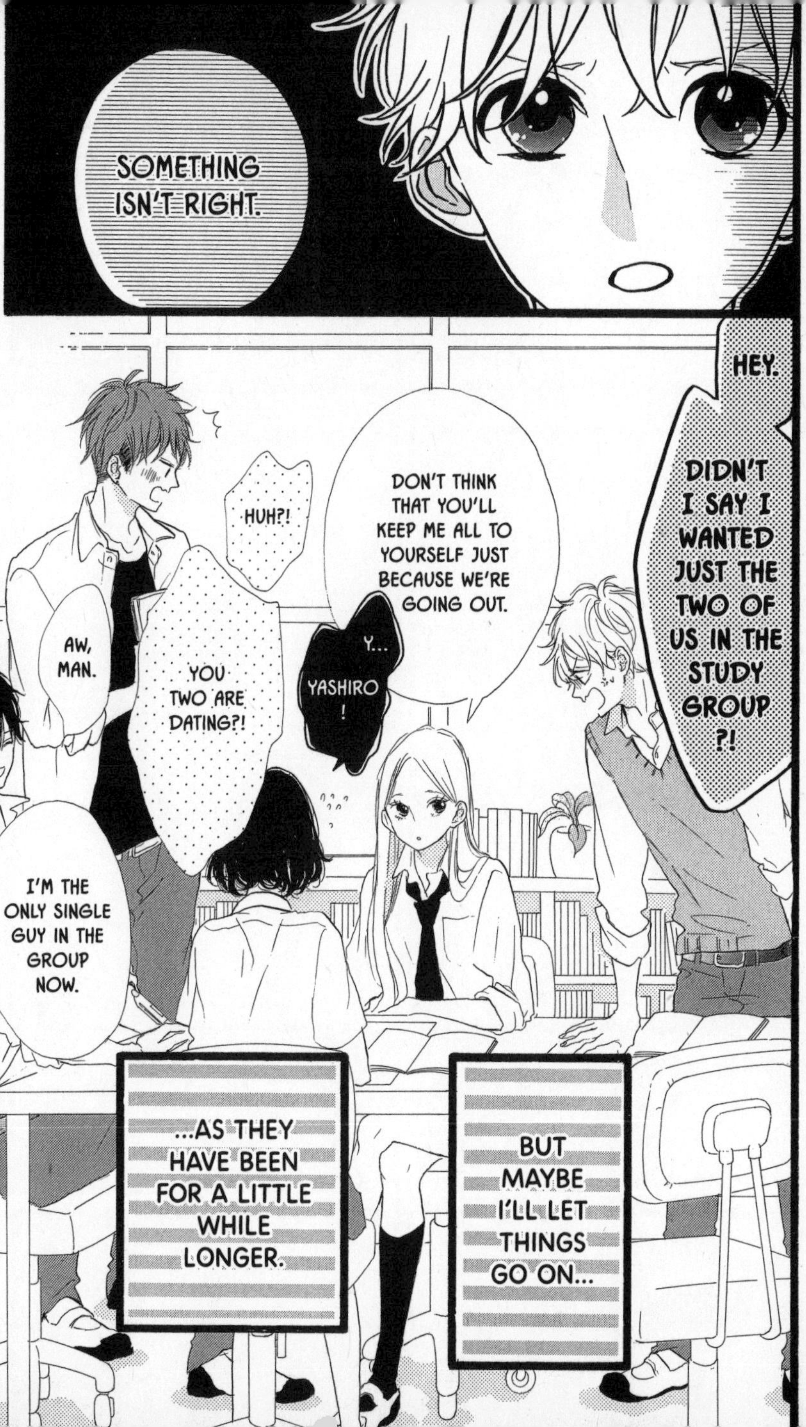

SOMETHING ISN'T RIGHT.
HEY.
DIDN'T I SAY I WANTED JUST THE TWO OF US IN THE STUDY GROUP?!
DON'T THINK THAT YOU'LL KEEP ME ALL TO YOURSELF JUST BECAUSE WE'RE GOING OUT.
Y... YASHIRO!
HUH?!
YOU TWO ARE DATING?!
AW, MAN.
I'M THE ONLY SINGLE GUY IN THE GROUP NOW.
BUT MAYBE I'LL LET THINGS GO ON...
...AS THEY HAVE BEEN FOR A LITTLE WHILE LONGER.

A Man's Pride

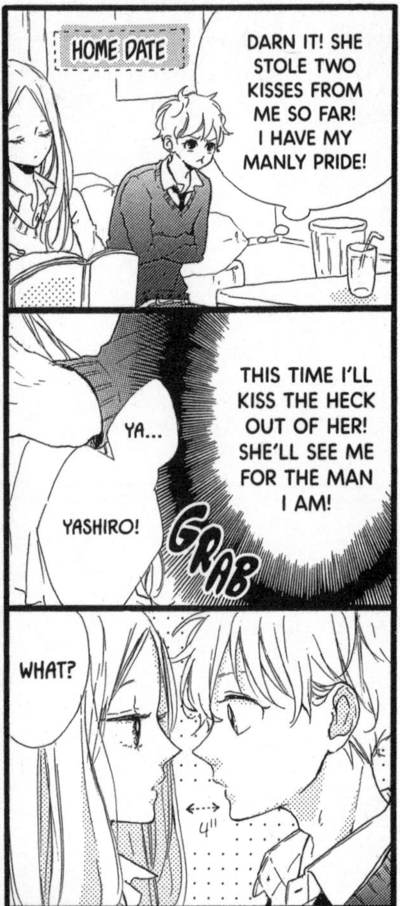
DARN IT! SHE STOLE TWO KISSES FROM ME SO FAR! I HAVE MY MANLY PRIDE!
HOME DATE
THIS TIME I'LL KISS THE HECK OUT OF HER! SHE'LL SEE ME FOR THE MAN I AM!
YA...
YASHIRO!
GRAB
WHAT?
4"
I-I'LL LET YOU GET AWAY WITH IT...THIS TIME!
HUH?
It's not that I'm too shy or anything.

Close but No Cigar

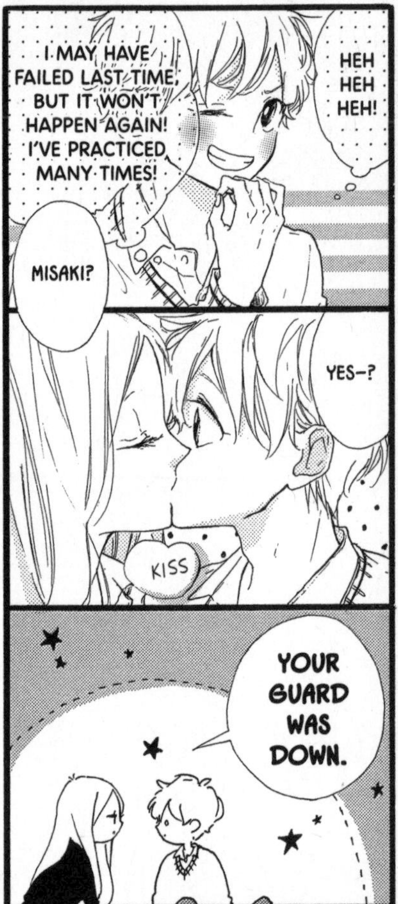
HEH HEH HEH!
I MAY HAVE FAILED LAST TIME, BUT IT WON'T HAPPEN AGAIN! I'VE PRACTICED MANY TIMES!
MISAKI?
YES-?
KISS
YOUR GUARD WAS DOWN.
AHHH! NO MORE! LET ME KISS YOU FOR ONCE!! YOU GIRL PERVERT!!!
HE'S ADOR-ABLE.
BLANKET ROLL

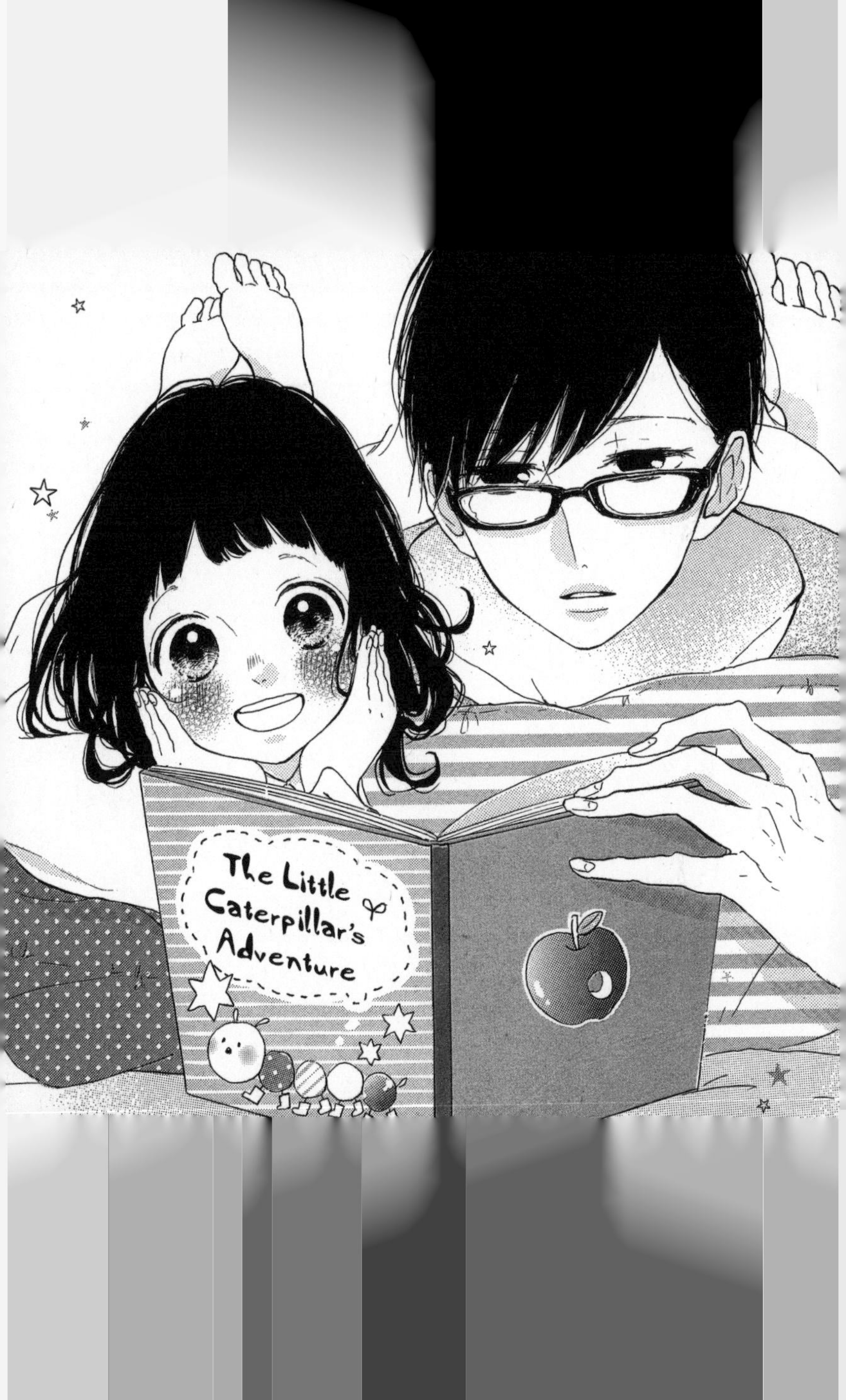
The Little Caterpillar's Adventure

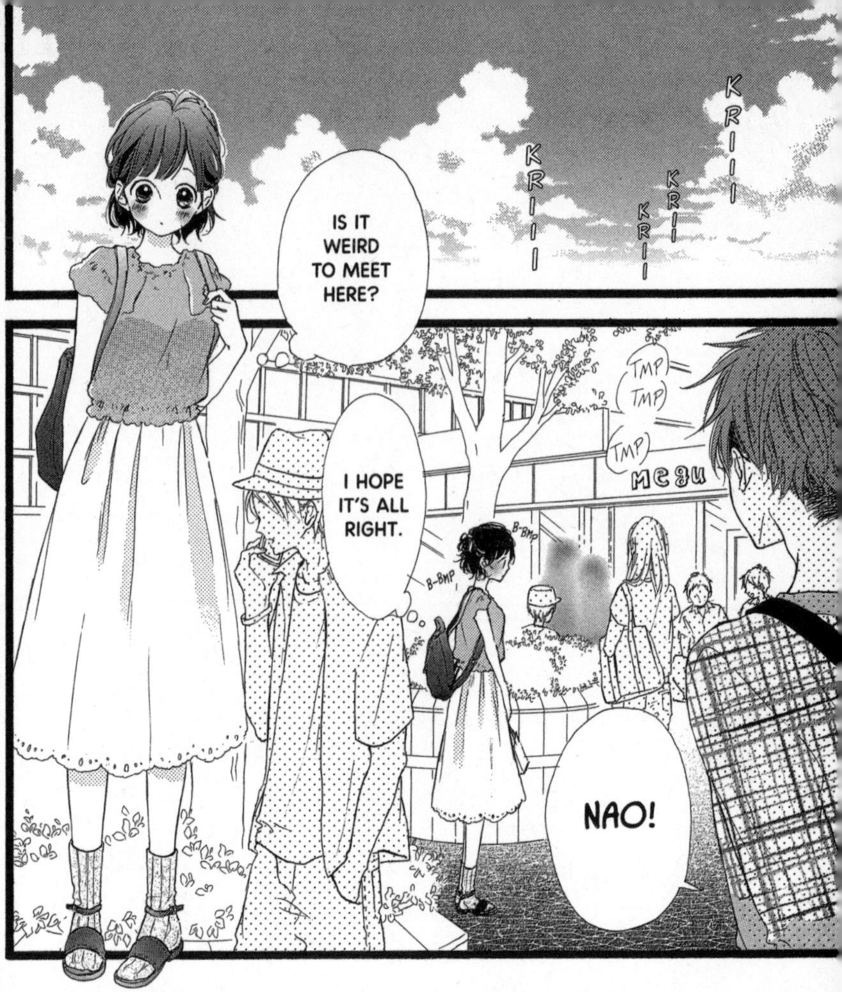
KRIII
KRIII
KRII
KRII
IS IT WEIRD TO MEET HERE?
TMP
TMP
TMP
megu
I HOPE IT'S ALL RIGHT.
B-BMP
B-BMP
NAO!

Honey So Sweet

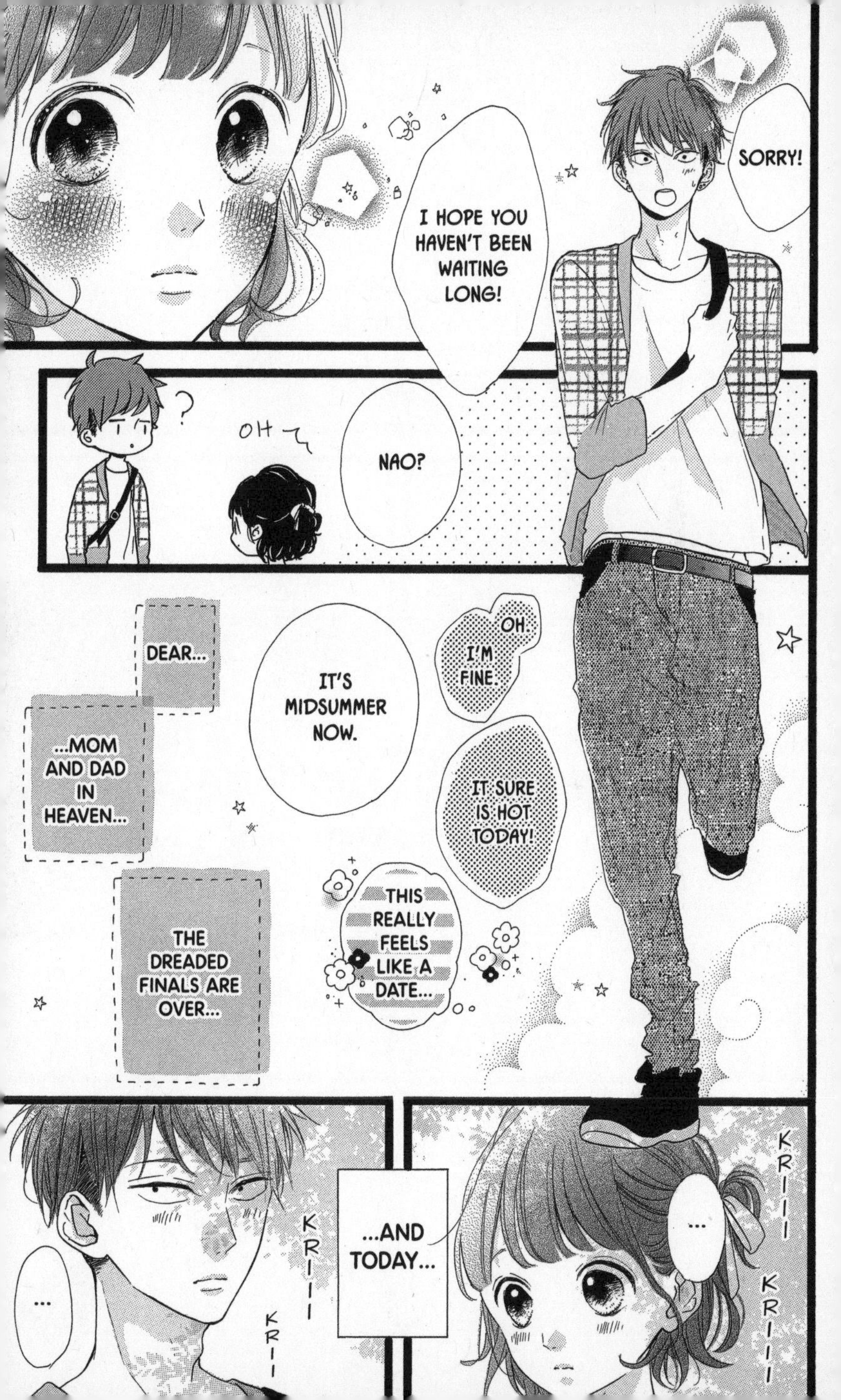
SORRY!
I HOPE YOU HAVEN'T BEEN WAITING LONG!
NAO?
OH~
OH. I'M FINE.
IT SURE IS HOT TODAY!
IT'S MIDSUMMER NOW.
DEAR...
...MOM AND DAD IN HEAVEN...
THIS REALLY FEELS LIKE A DATE...
THE DREADED FINALS ARE OVER...
KRI-I-I
KRI-I-I
...
...AND TODAY...
KRI-I-I
KRI-I
...

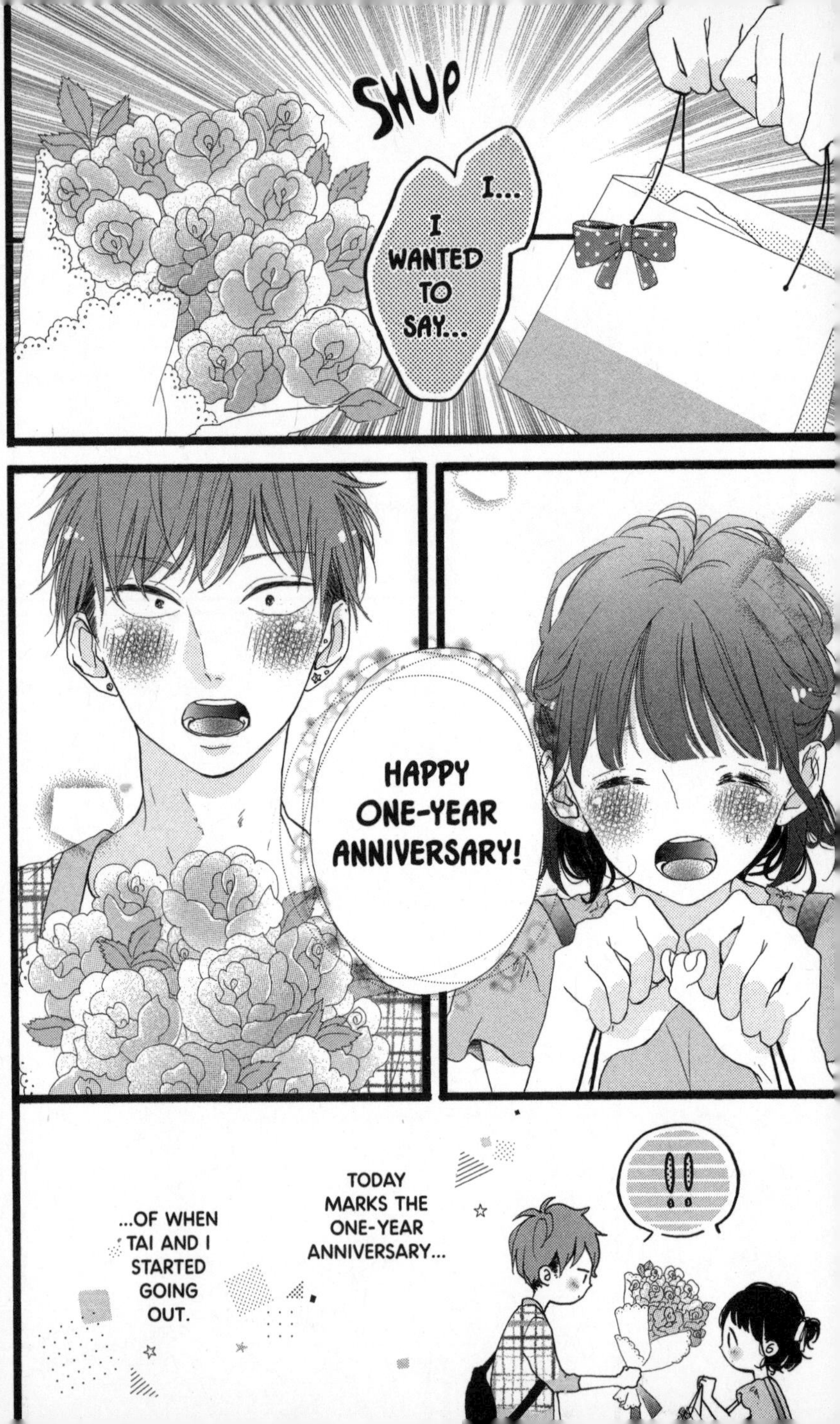
SHUP
I... I WANTED TO SAY...
HAPPY ONE-YEAR ANNIVERSARY!
!!
TODAY MARKS THE ONE-YEAR ANNIVERSARY...
...OF WHEN TAI AND I STARTED GOING OUT.

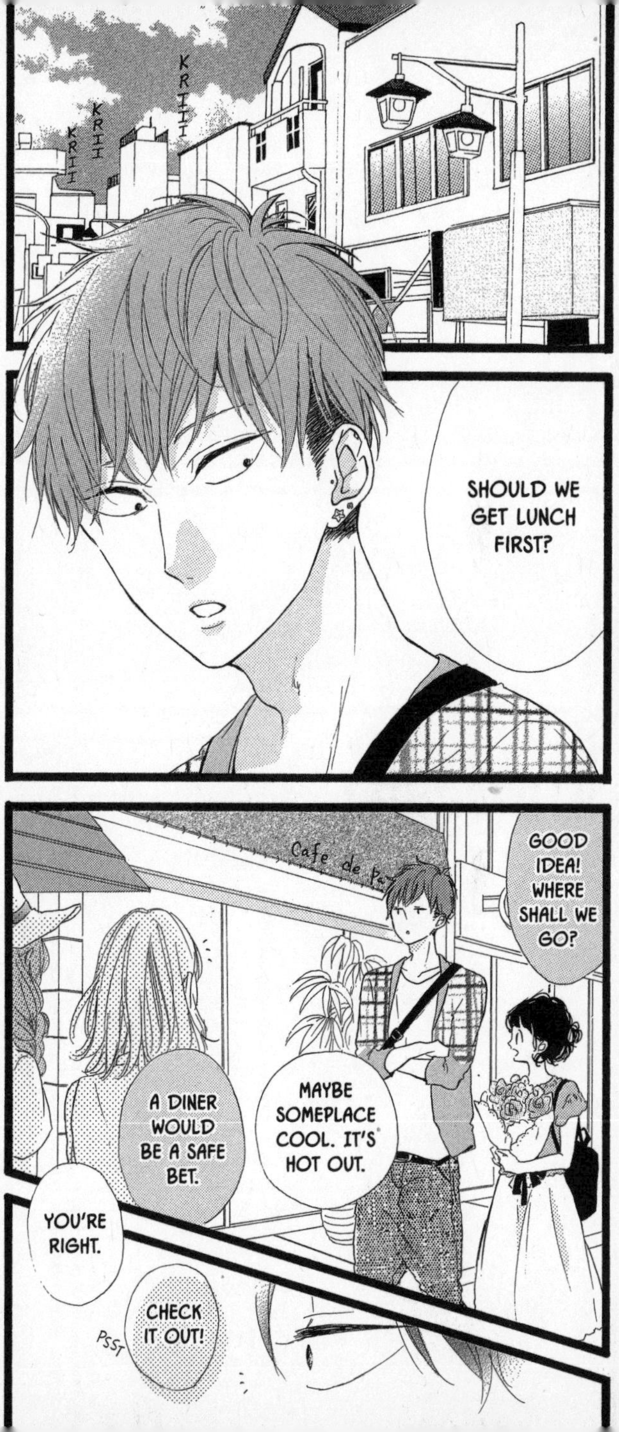
KRIII
KRIII
KRIII
SHOULD WE GET LUNCH FIRST?
GOOD IDEA! WHERE SHALL WE GO?
MAYBE SOMEPLACE COOL. IT'S HOT OUT.
A DINER WOULD BE A SAFE BET.
YOU'RE RIGHT.
PSST
CHECK IT OUT!
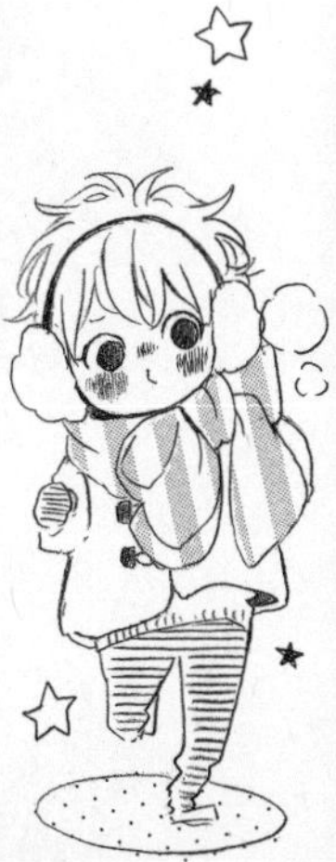

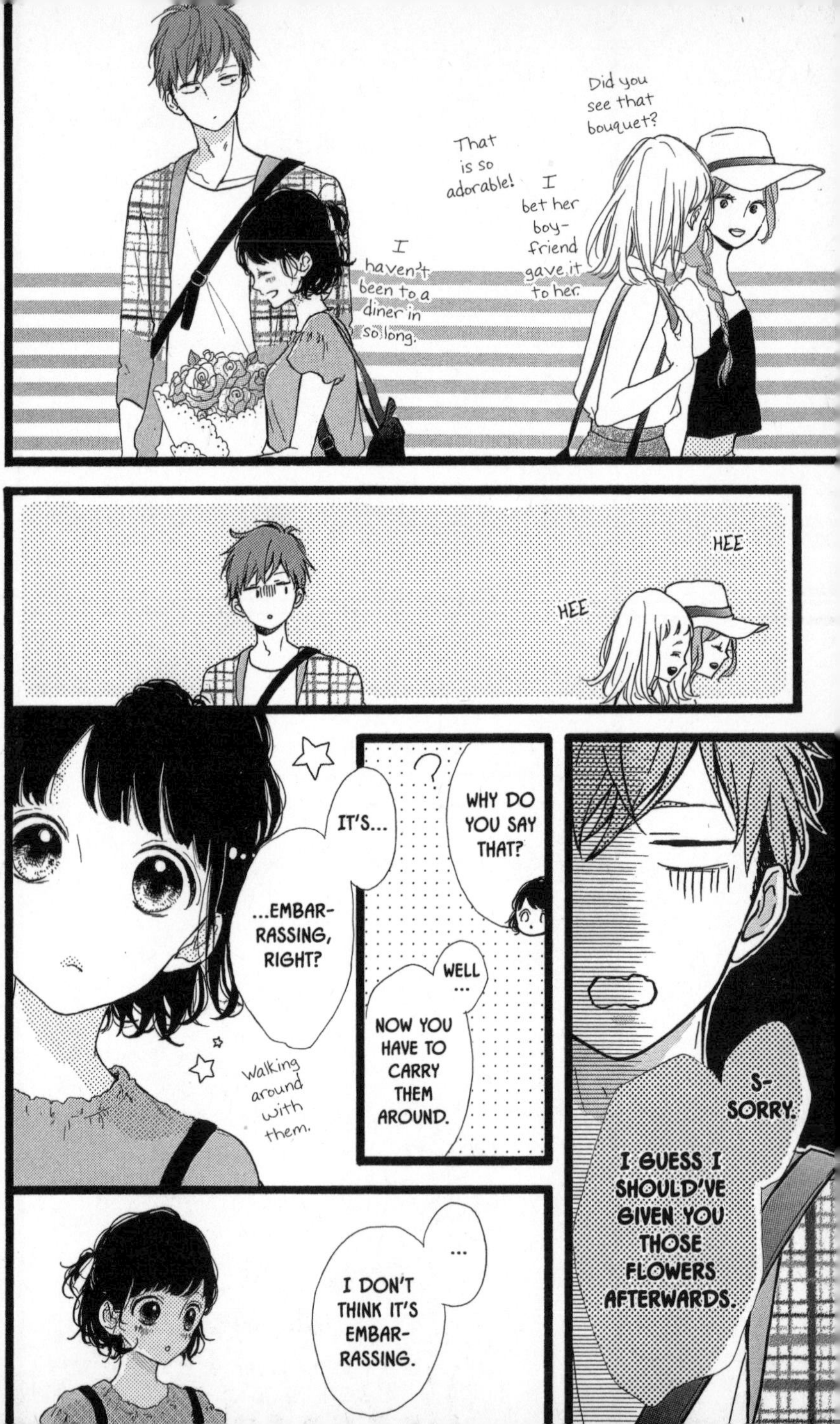
Did you see that bouquet?
That is so adorable!
I bet her boyfriend gave it to her.
I haven't been to a diner in so long.
HEE
HEE
S-SORRY.
I GUESS I SHOULD'VE GIVEN YOU THOSE FLOWERS AFTERWARDS.
WHY DO YOU SAY THAT?
WELL...
NOW YOU HAVE TO CARRY THEM AROUND.
IT'S...
...EMBARRASSING, RIGHT?
Walking around with them.
...
I DON'T THINK IT'S EMBARRASSING.

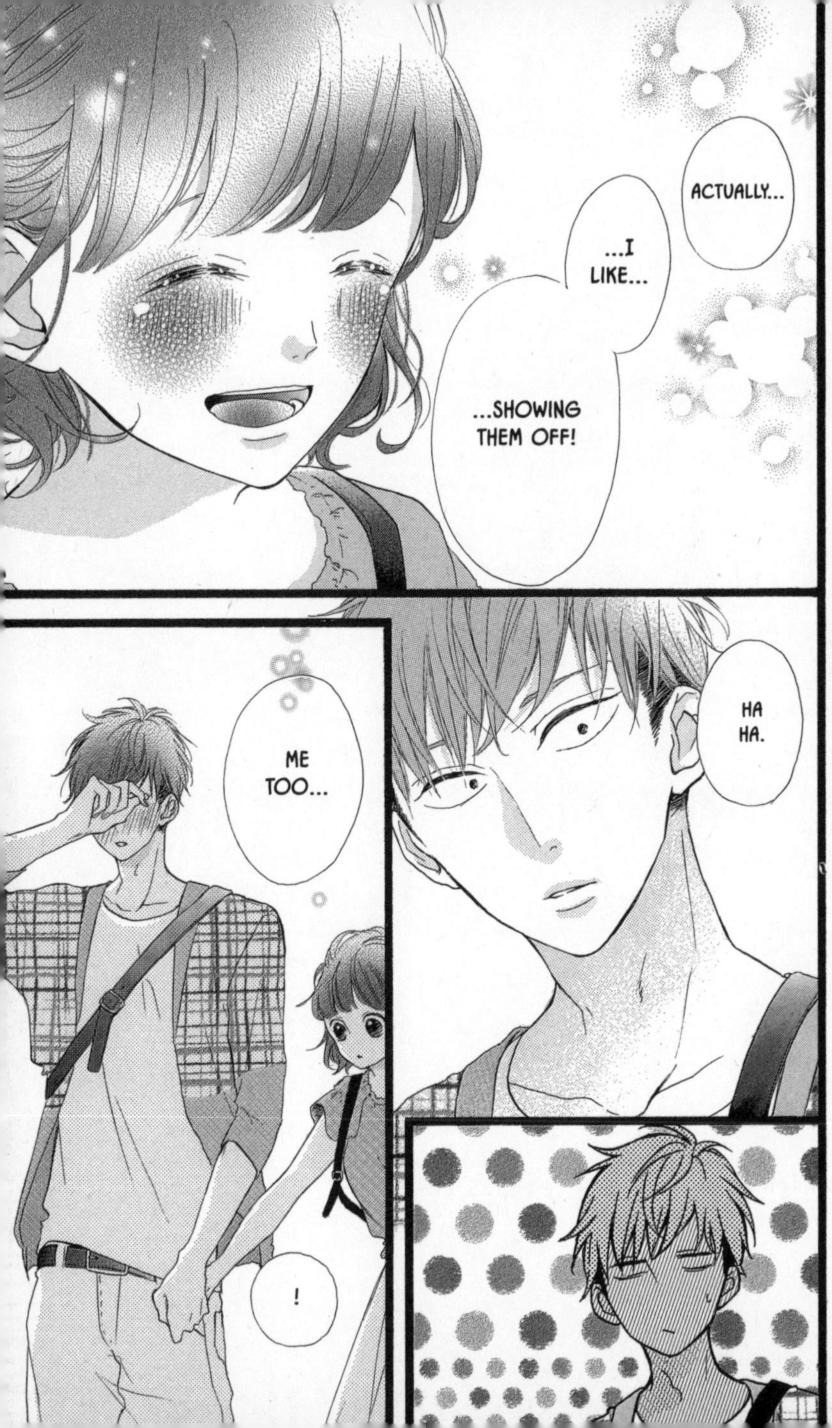
ACTUALLY...
...I LIKE...
...SHOWING THEM OFF!
HA HA.
ME TOO...
!

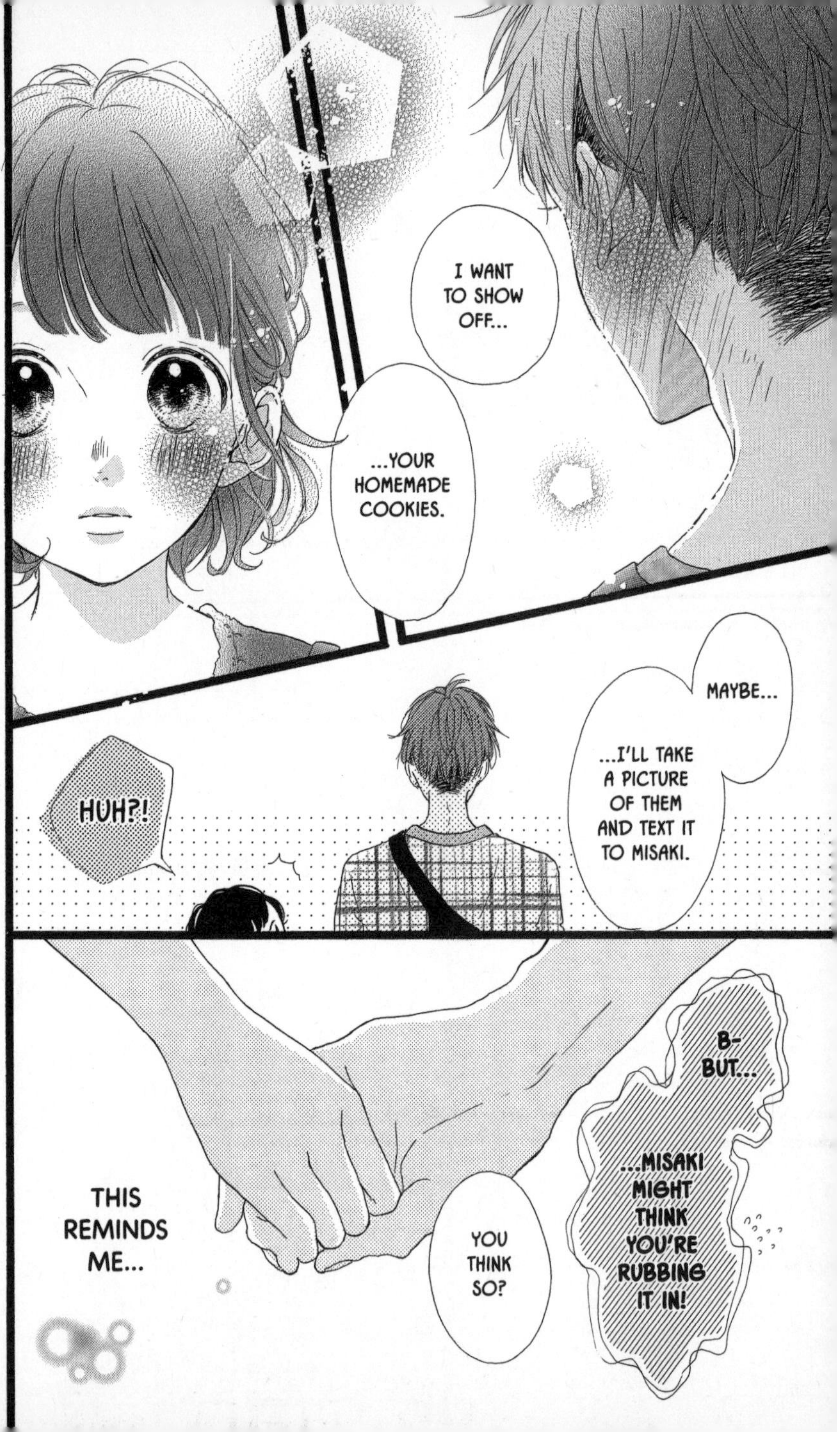
I WANT TO SHOW OFF...
...YOUR HOMEMADE COOKIES.
MAYBE...
...I'LL TAKE A PICTURE OF THEM AND TEXT IT TO MISAKI.
HUH?!
B-BUT...
...MISAKI MIGHT THINK YOU'RE RUBBING IT IN!
YOU THINK SO?
THIS REMINDS ME...

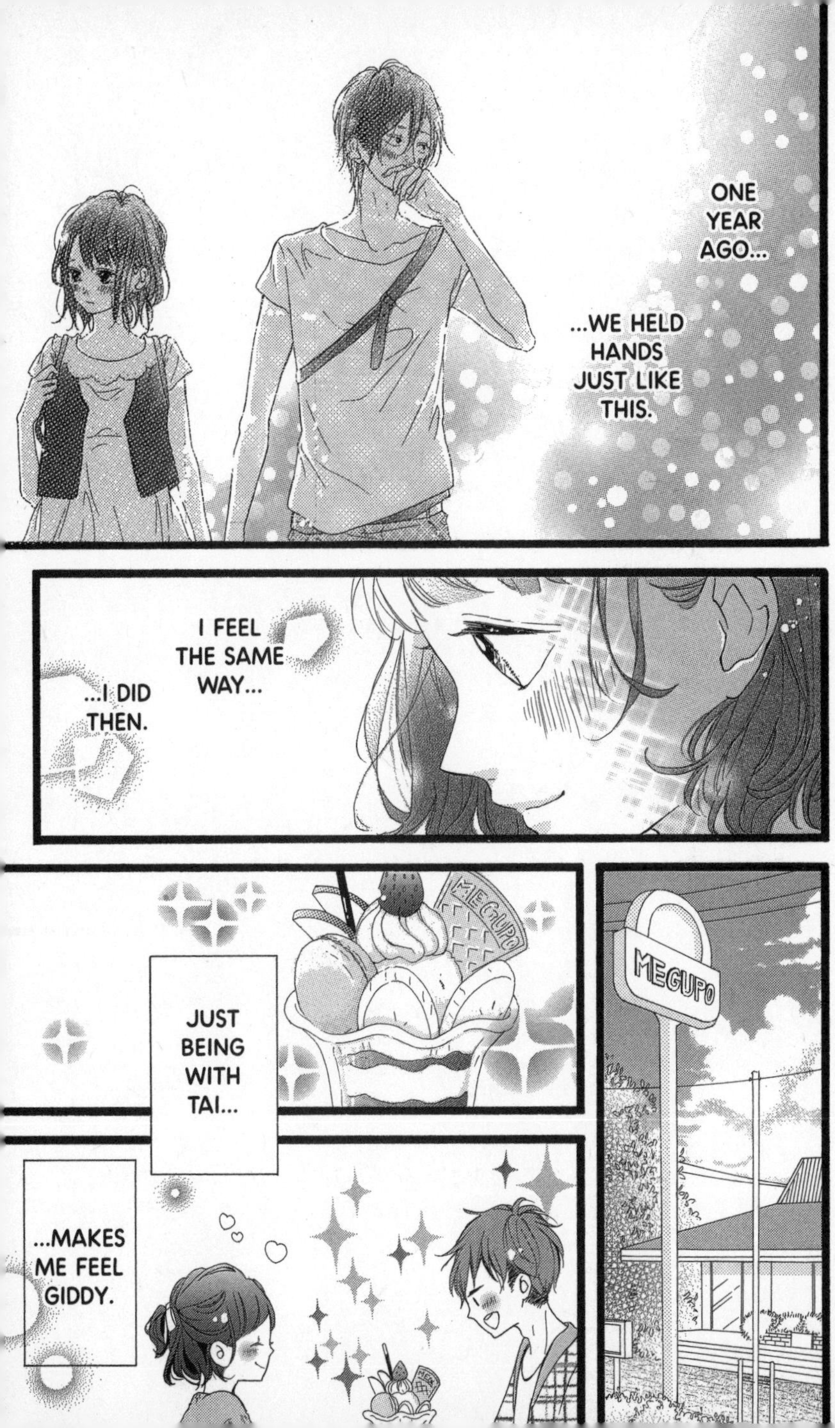
ONE YEAR AGO...
...WE HELD HANDS JUST LIKE THIS.
I FEEL THE SAME WAY...
...I DID THEN.
MEGUPO
MEGUPO
JUST BEING WITH TAI...
...MAKES ME FEEL GIDDY.

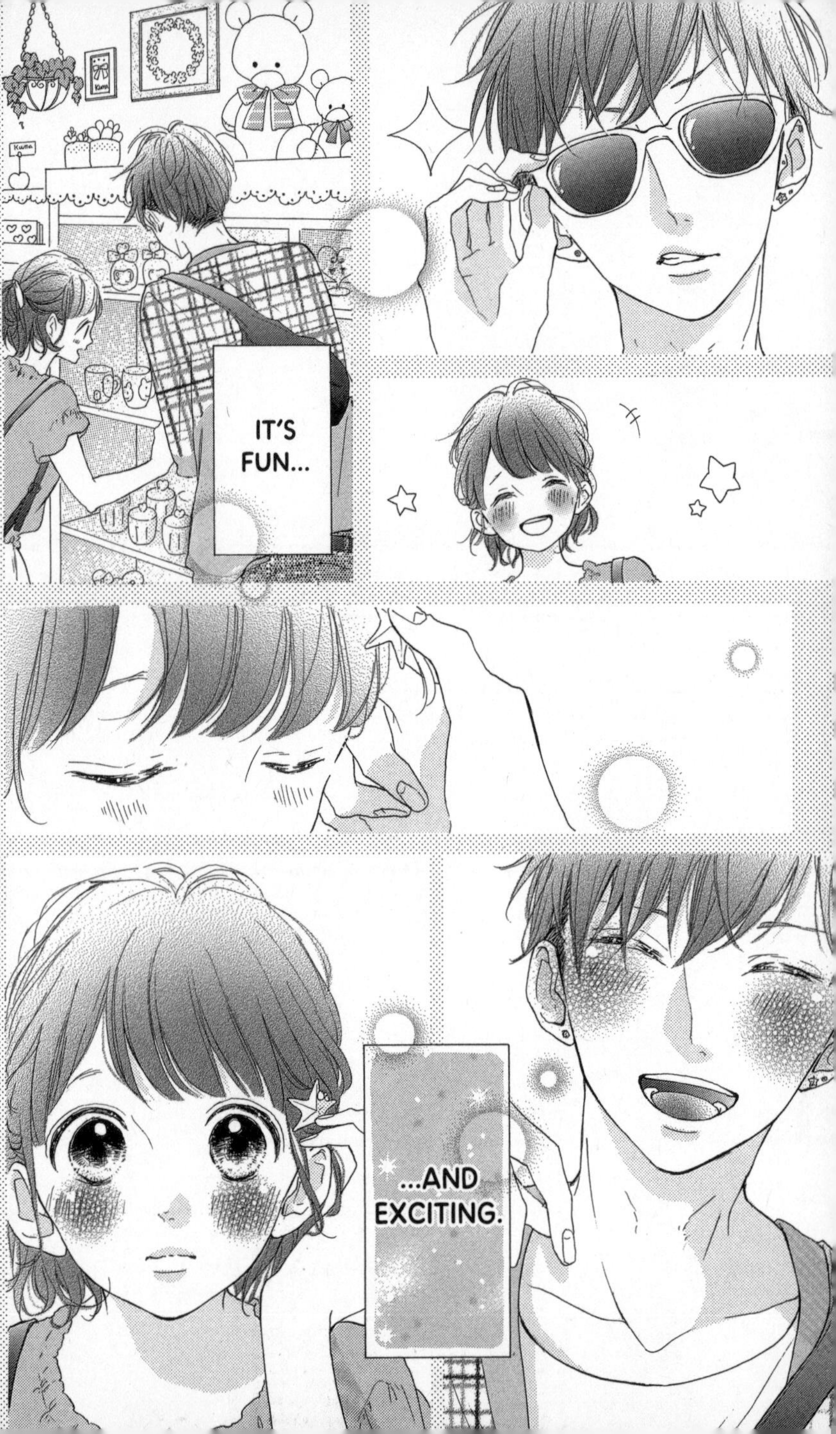
IT'S FUN...
...AND EXCITING.

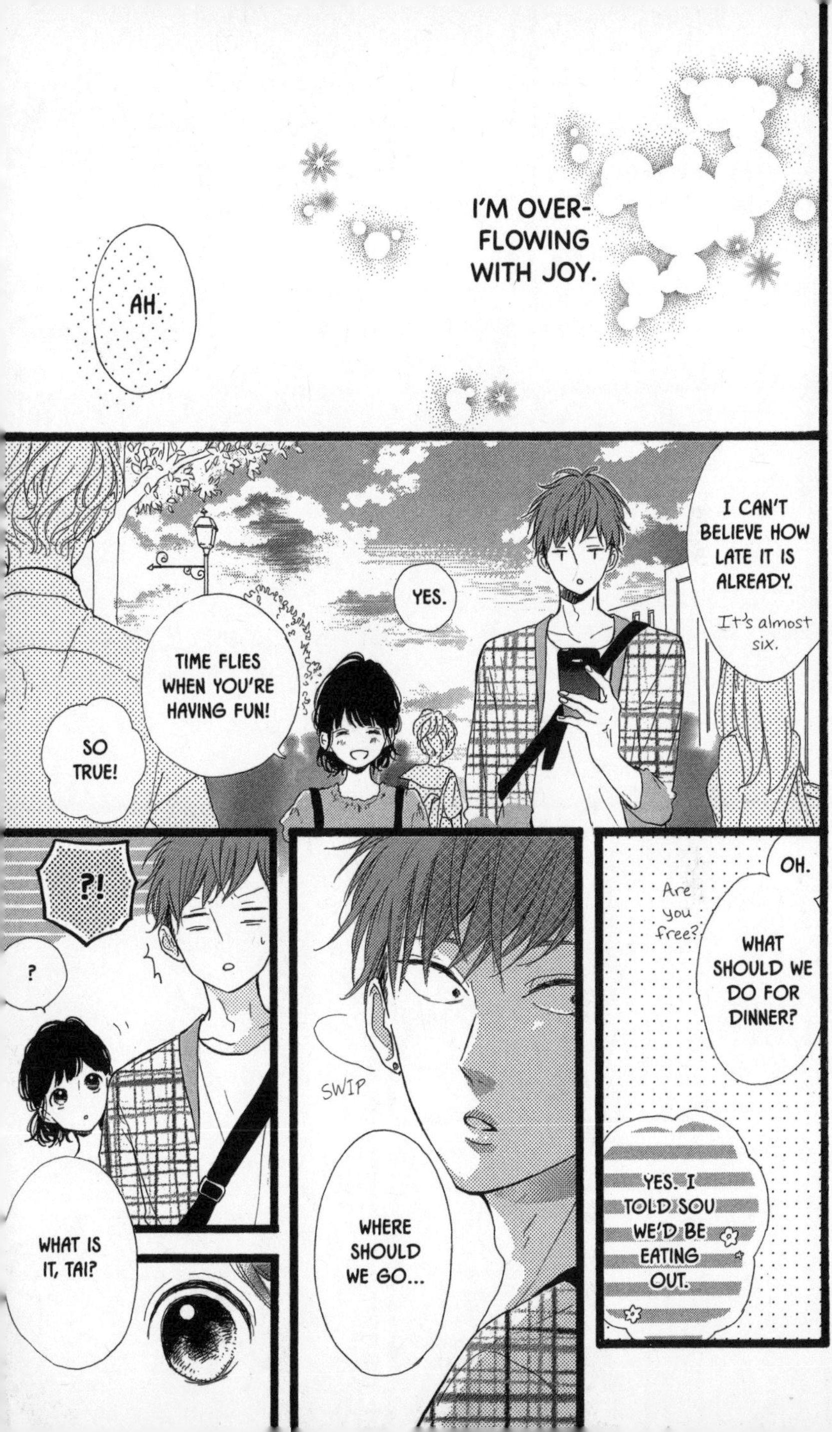
I'M OVER-FLOWING WITH JOY.
AH.
I CAN'T BELIEVE HOW LATE IT IS ALREADY.
It's almost six.
YES.
TIME FLIES WHEN YOU'RE HAVING FUN!
SO TRUE!
OH.
Are you free?
WHAT SHOULD WE DO FOR DINNER?
YES. I TOLD SOU WE'D BE EATING OUT.
SWIP
WHERE SHOULD WE GO...
?!
?
WHAT IS IT, TAI?

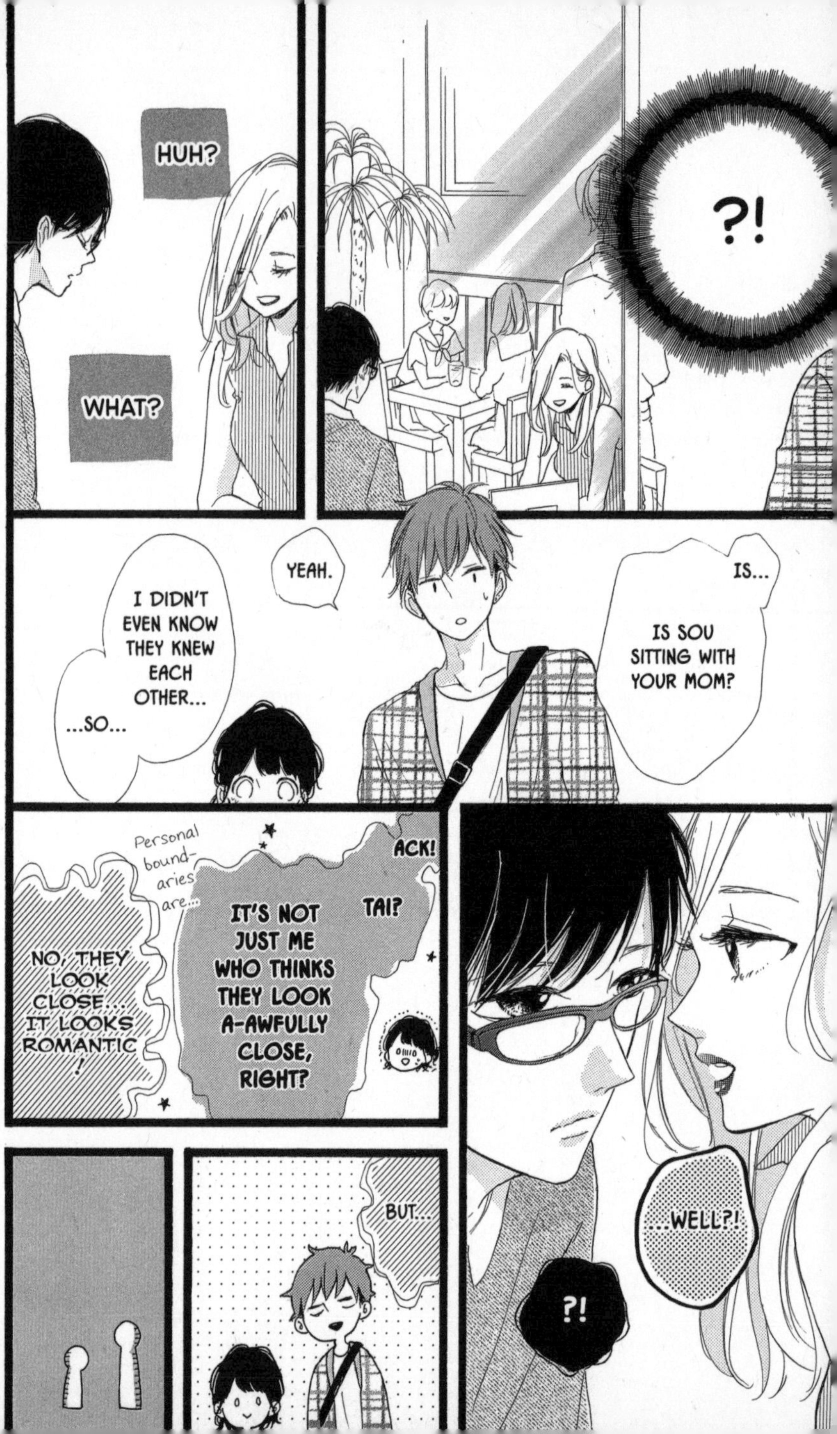
?!
HUH?
WHAT?
IS...
IS SOU SITTING WITH YOUR MOM?
YEAH.
I DIDN'T EVEN KNOW THEY KNEW EACH OTHER...
...SO...
...WELL?!
?!
ACK!
TAI?
IT'S NOT JUST ME WHO THINKS THEY LOOK A-AWFULLY CLOSE, RIGHT?
Personal boundaries are...
NO, THEY LOOK CLOSE... IT LOOKS ROMANTIC!
BUT...

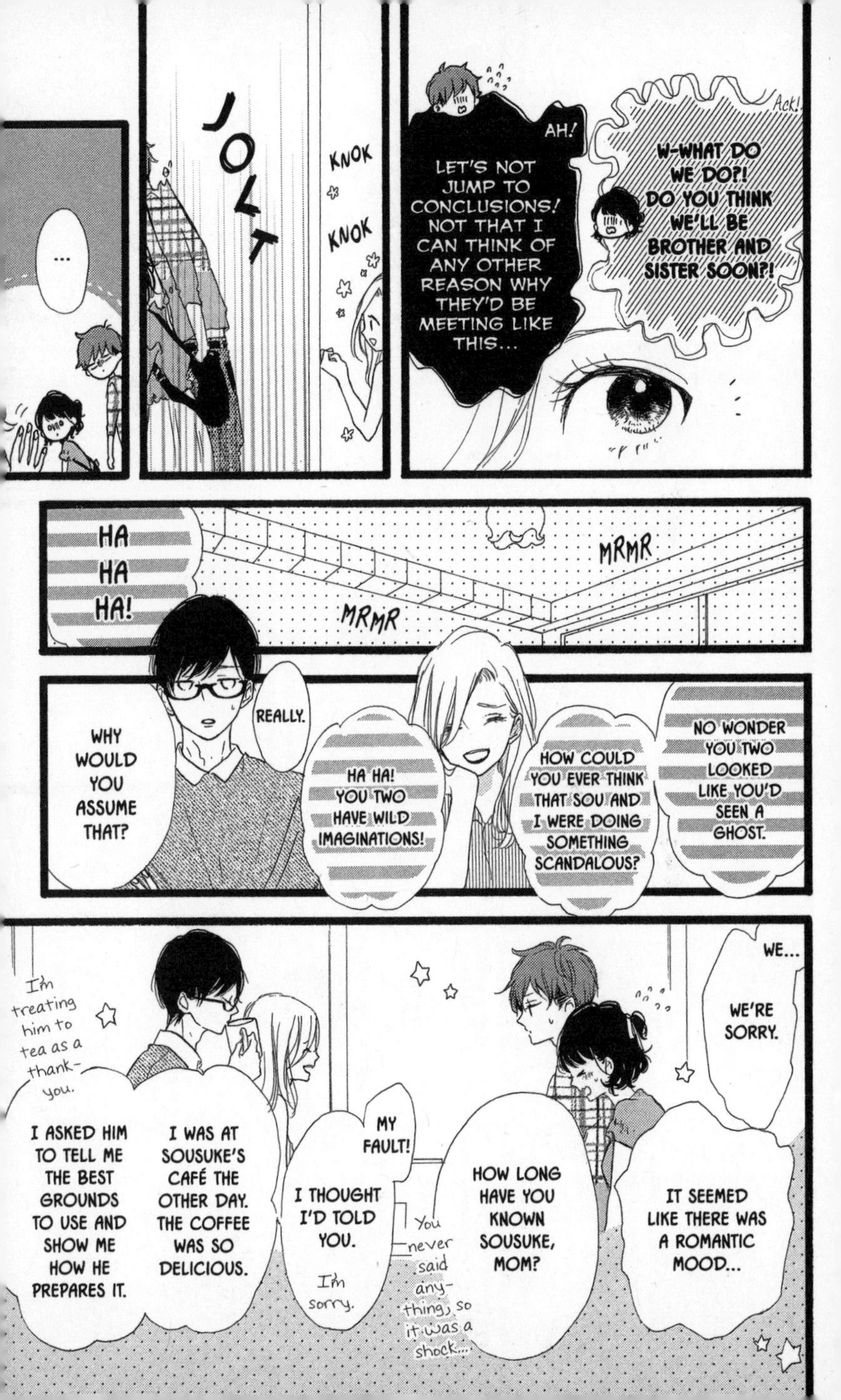
Ack!
W-WHAT DO WE DO?! DO YOU THINK WE'LL BE BROTHER AND SISTER SOON?!
AH!
LET'S NOT JUMP TO CONCLUSIONS! NOT THAT I CAN THINK OF ANY OTHER REASON WHY THEY'D BE MEETING LIKE THIS...
KNOK
KNOK
JOLT
...
HA HA HA!
MRMR
MRMR
NO WONDER YOU TWO LOOKED LIKE YOU'D SEEN A GHOST.
HOW COULD YOU EVER THINK THAT SOU AND I WERE DOING SOMETHING SCANDALOUS?
HA HA! YOU TWO HAVE WILD IMAGINATIONS!
REALLY.
WHY WOULD YOU ASSUME THAT?
WE...
WE'RE SORRY.
IT SEEMED LIKE THERE WAS A ROMANTIC MOOD...
HOW LONG HAVE YOU KNOWN SOUSUKE, MOM?
You never said anything, so it was a shock...
MY FAULT!
I THOUGHT I'D TOLD YOU.
I'm sorry.
I WAS AT SOUSUKE'S CAFÉ THE OTHER DAY. THE COFFEE WAS SO DELICIOUS.
I ASKED HIM TO TELL ME THE BEST GROUNDS TO USE AND SHOW ME HOW HE PREPARES IT.
I'm treating him to tea as a thank-you.

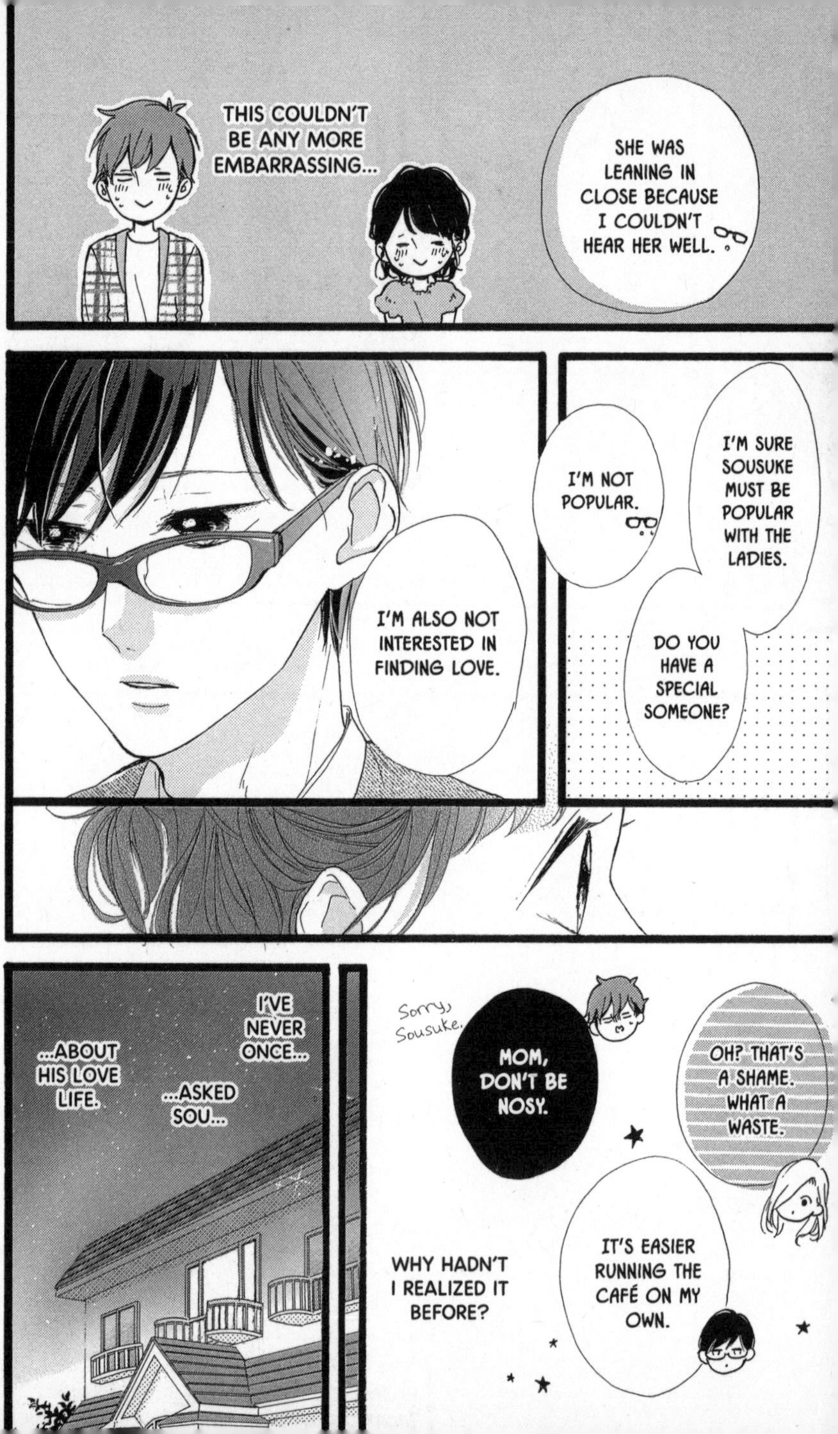
SHE WAS LEANING IN CLOSE BECAUSE I COULDN'T HEAR HER WELL.
THIS COULDN'T BE ANY MORE EMBARRASSING...
I'M SURE SOUSUKE MUST BE POPULAR WITH THE LADIES.
I'M NOT POPULAR.
DO YOU HAVE A SPECIAL SOMEONE?
I'M ALSO NOT INTERESTED IN FINDING LOVE.
OH? THAT'S A SHAME. WHAT A WASTE.
MOM, DON'T BE NOSY.
Sorry, Sousuke.
IT'S EASIER RUNNING THE CAFÉ ON MY OWN.
WHY HADN'T I REALIZED IT BEFORE?
I'VE NEVER ONCE...
...ASKED SOU...
...ABOUT HIS LOVE LIFE.

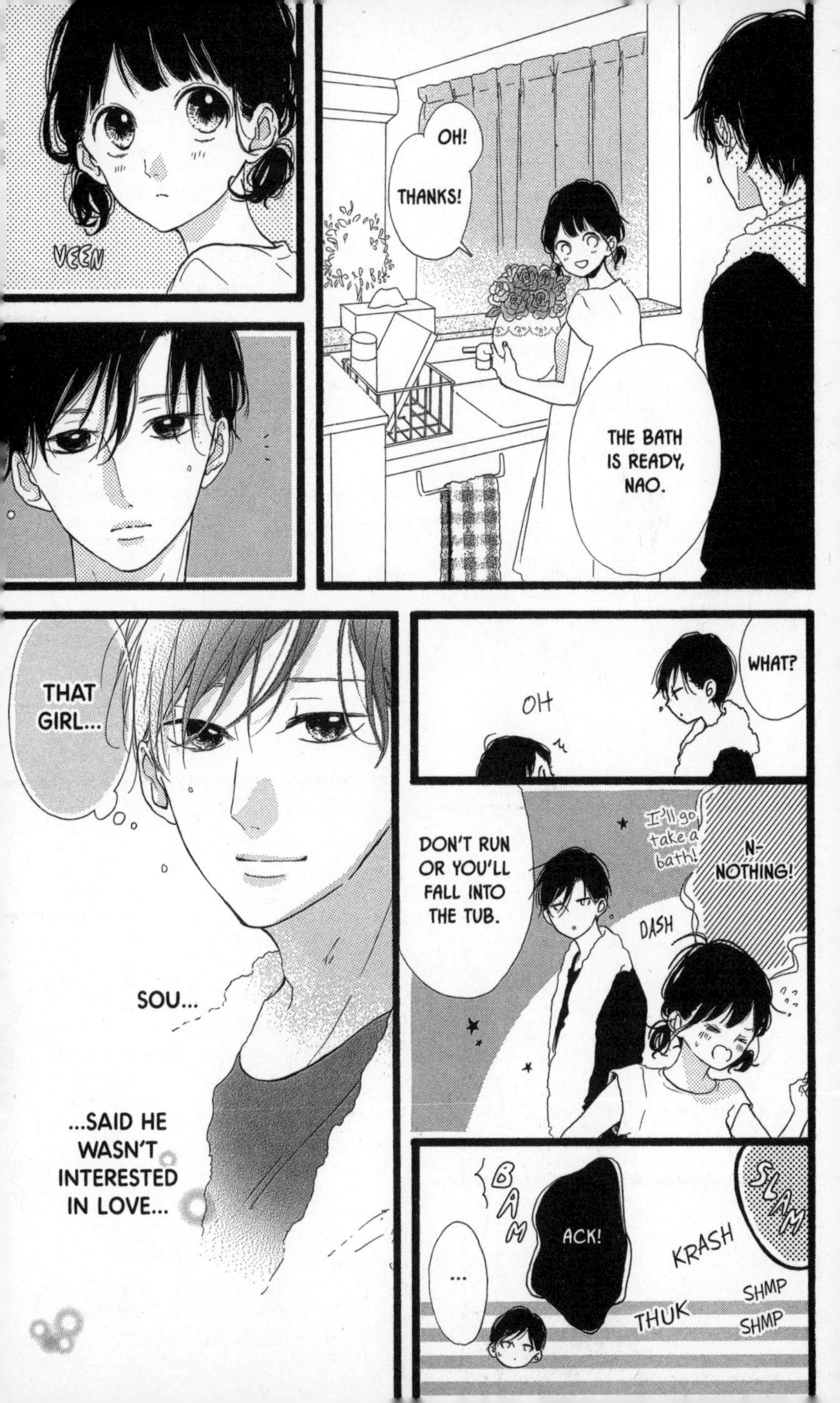
THE BATH IS READY, NAO.
OH!
THANKS!
VEEN
WHAT?
OH
N-NOTHING!
I'll go take a bath!
DON'T RUN OR YOU'LL FALL INTO THE TUB.
DASH
SLAM
KRASH
SHMP SHMP
THUK
ACK!
BAM
...
THAT GIRL...
SOU...
...SAID HE WASN'T INTERESTED IN LOVE...

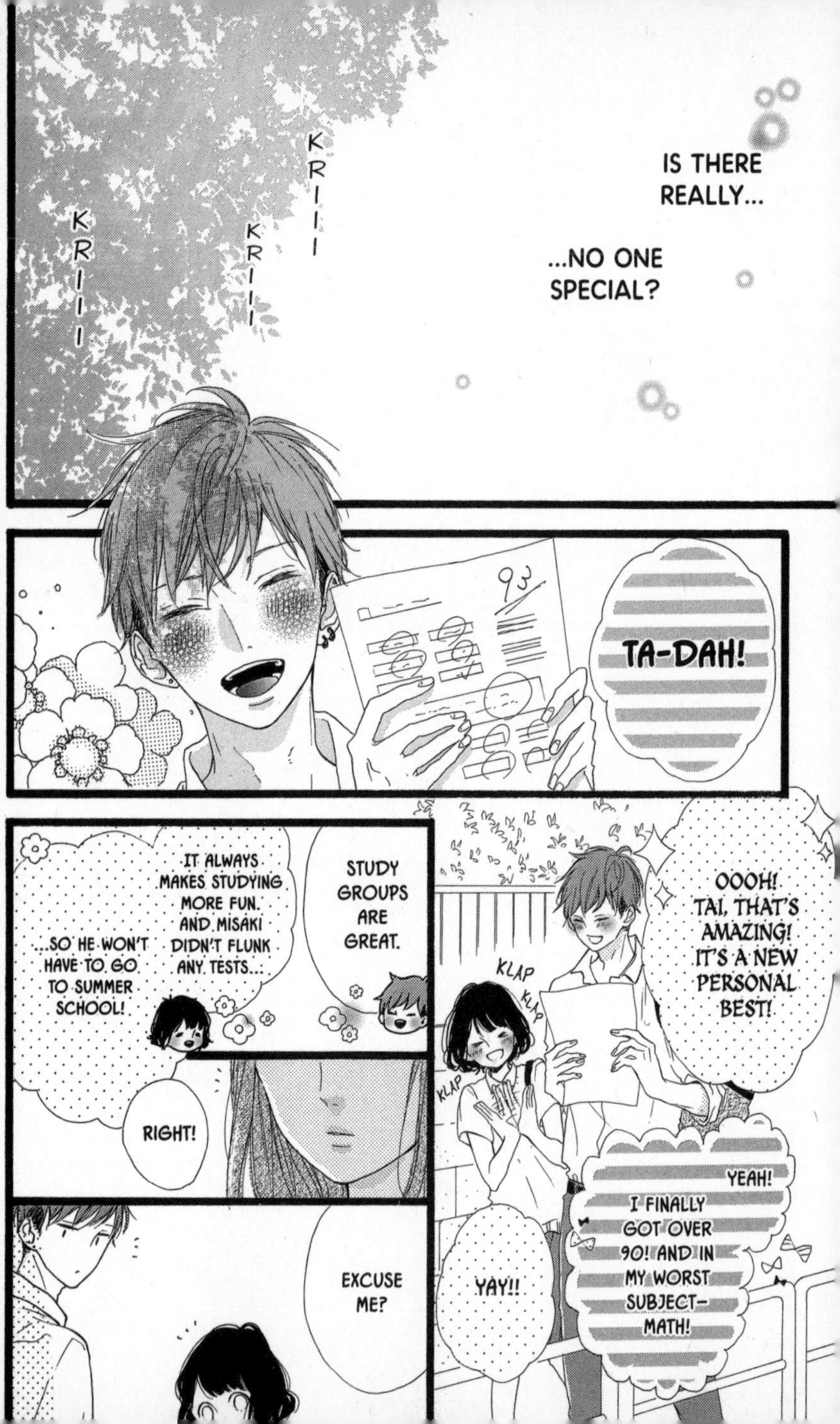
IS THERE REALLY...
...NO ONE SPECIAL?
KRIII
KRIII
KRIII
TA-DAH!
OOOH! TAI, THAT'S AMAZING! IT'S A NEW PERSONAL BEST!
YEAH!
I FINALLY GOT OVER 90! AND IN MY WORST SUBJECT—MATH!
YAY!!
KLAP
KLAP
KLAP
STUDY GROUPS ARE GREAT.
IT ALWAYS MAKES STUDYING MORE FUN. AND MISAKI DIDN'T FLUNK ANY TESTS...
...SO HE WON'T HAVE TO GO TO SUMMER SCHOOL!
RIGHT!
EXCUSE ME?

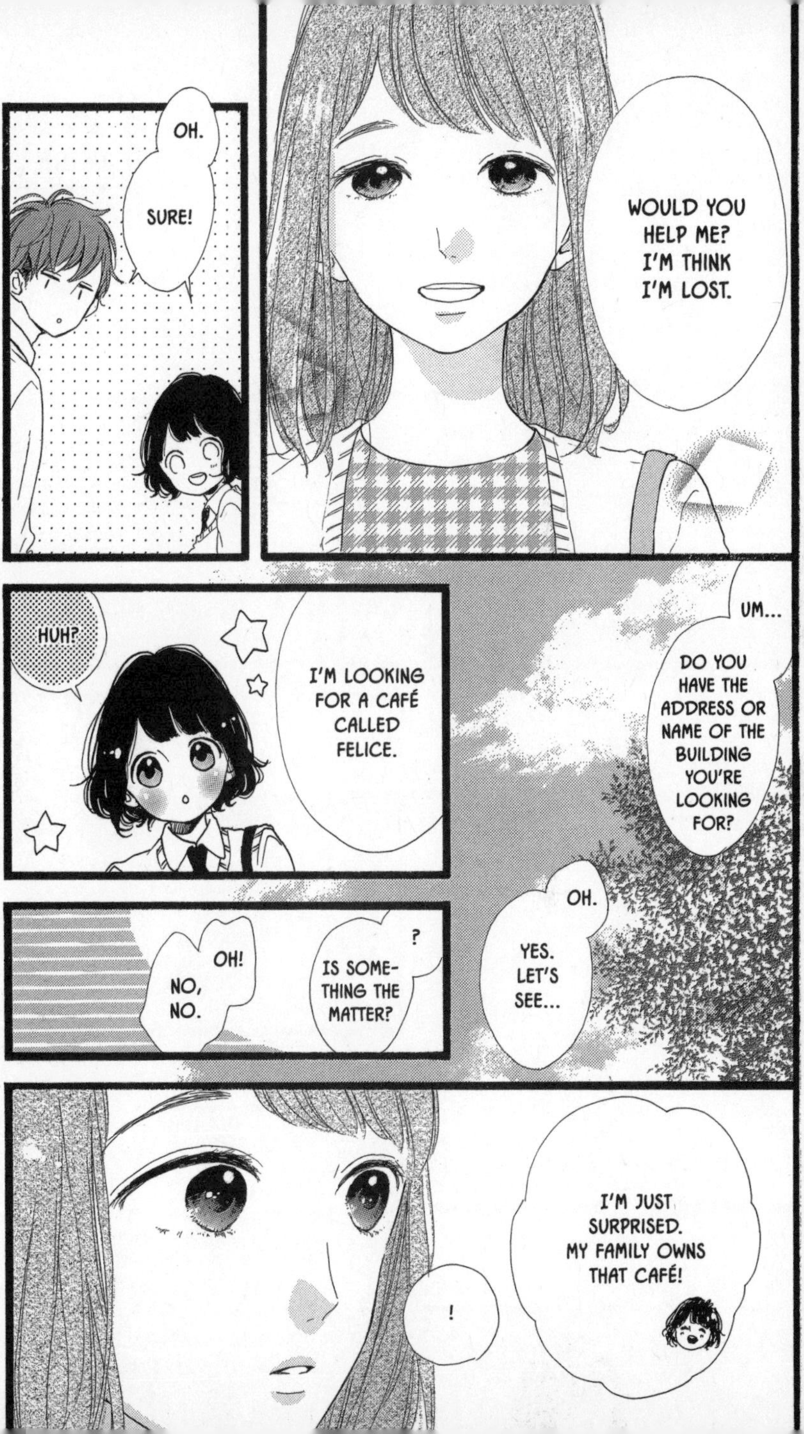
WOULD YOU HELP ME? I'M THINK I'M LOST.
OH.
SURE!
UM...
DO YOU HAVE THE ADDRESS OR NAME OF THE BUILDING YOU'RE LOOKING FOR?
OH.
YES. LET'S SEE...
I'M LOOKING FOR A CAFÉ CALLED FELICE.
HUH?
?
IS SOME-THING THE MATTER?
OH!
NO, NO.
I'M JUST SURPRISED. MY FAMILY OWNS THAT CAFÉ!
!

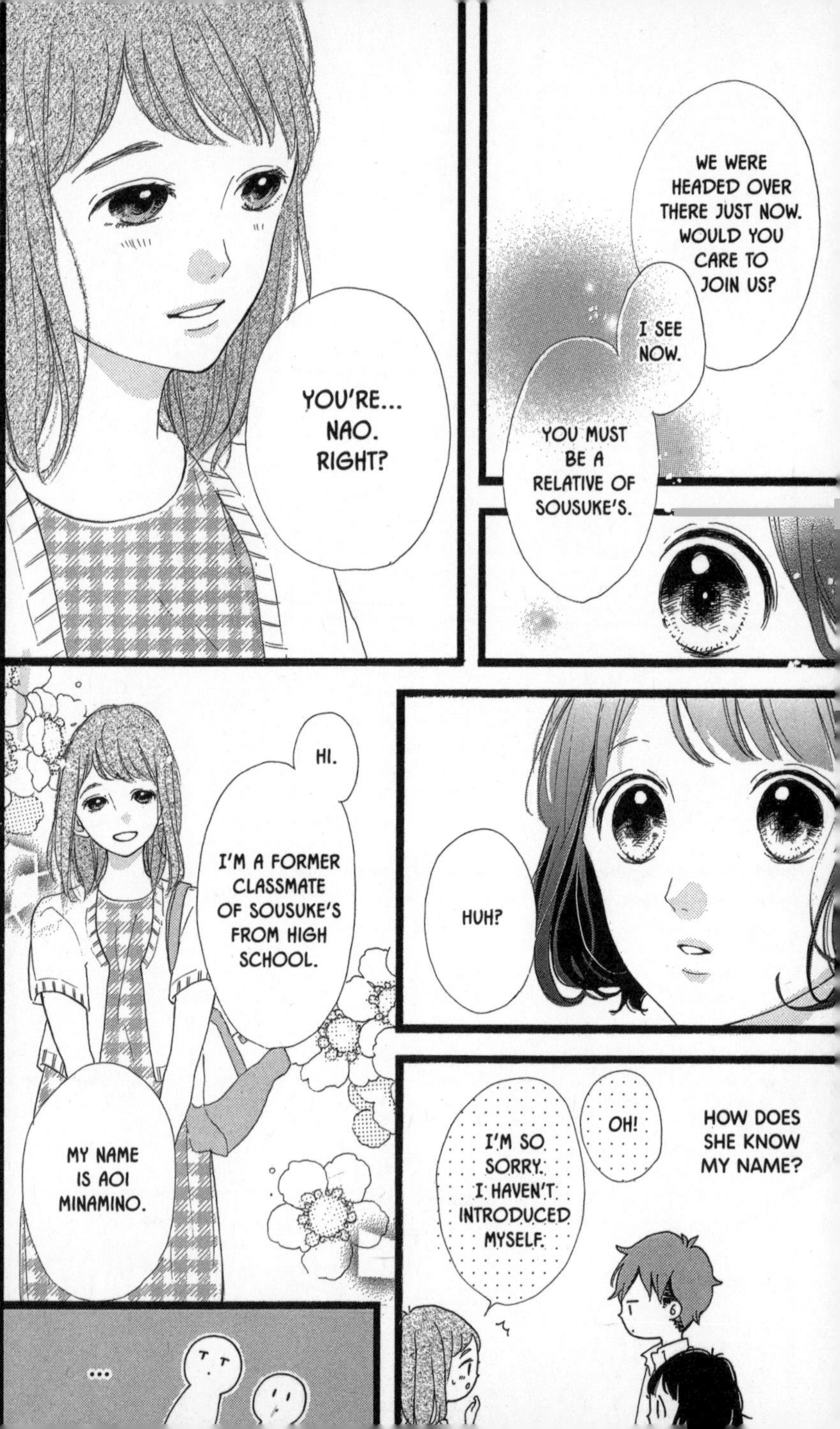
WE WERE HEADED OVER THERE JUST NOW. WOULD YOU CARE TO JOIN US?
I SEE NOW.
YOU MUST BE A RELATIVE OF SOUSUKE'S.
YOU'RE... NAO. RIGHT?
HUH?
HOW DOES SHE KNOW MY NAME?
OH!
I'M SO SORRY. I HAVEN'T INTRODUCED MYSELF.
HI.
I'M A FORMER CLASSMATE OF SOUSUKE'S FROM HIGH SCHOOL.
MY NAME IS AOI MINAMINO.
...

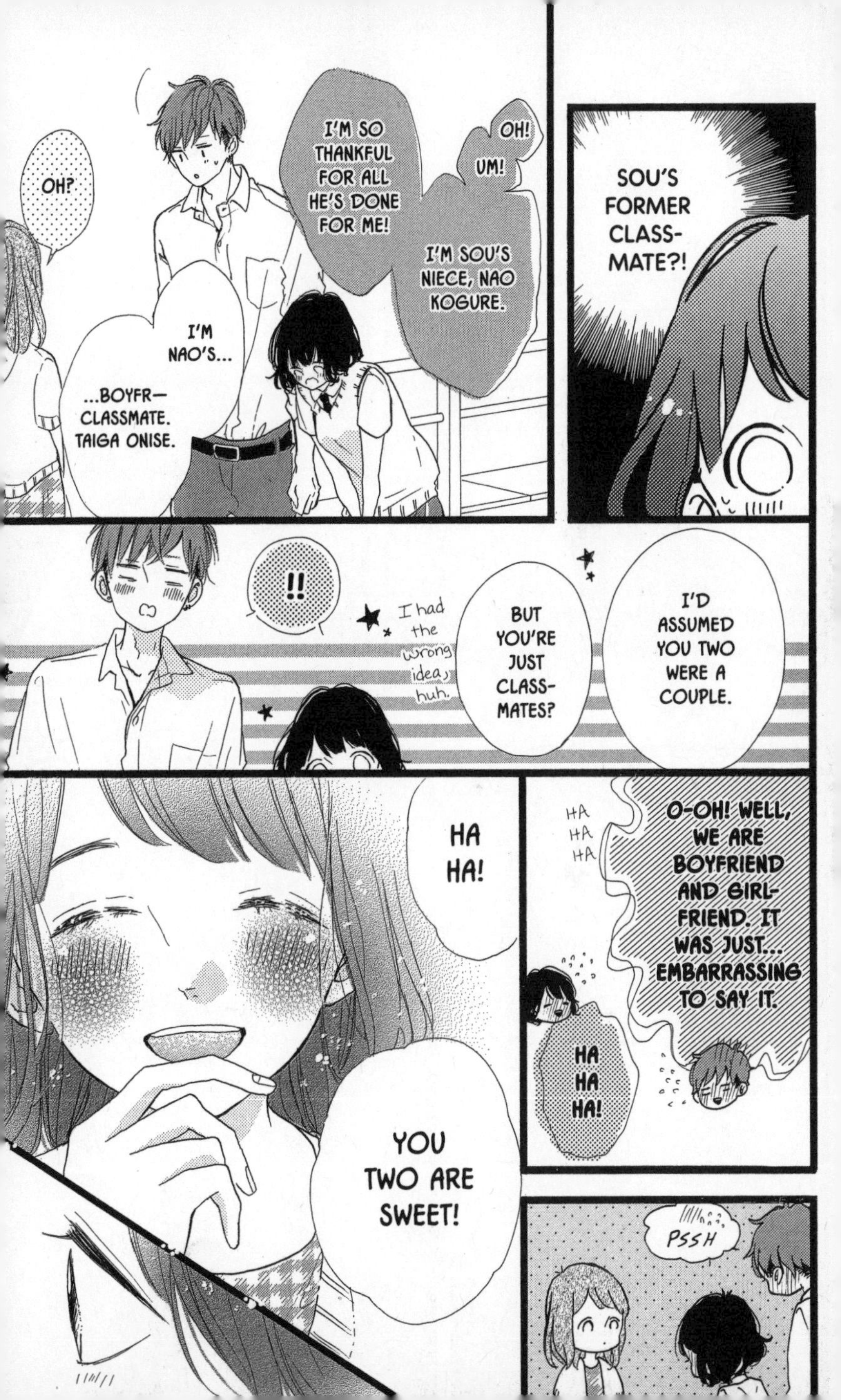
SOU'S FORMER CLASS-MATE?!
OH!
UM!
I'M SOU'S NIECE, NAO KOGURE.
I'M SO THANKFUL FOR ALL HE'S DONE FOR ME!
OH?
I'M NAO'S...
...BOYFR— CLASSMATE. TAIGA ONISE.
I'D ASSUMED YOU TWO WERE A COUPLE.
BUT YOU'RE JUST CLASS-MATES?
I had the wrong idea, huh.
!!
HA HA HA
O-OH! WELL, WE ARE BOYFRIEND AND GIRL-FRIEND. IT WAS JUST... EMBARRASSING TO SAY IT.
HA HA HA!
PSSH
HA HA!
YOU TWO ARE SWEET!

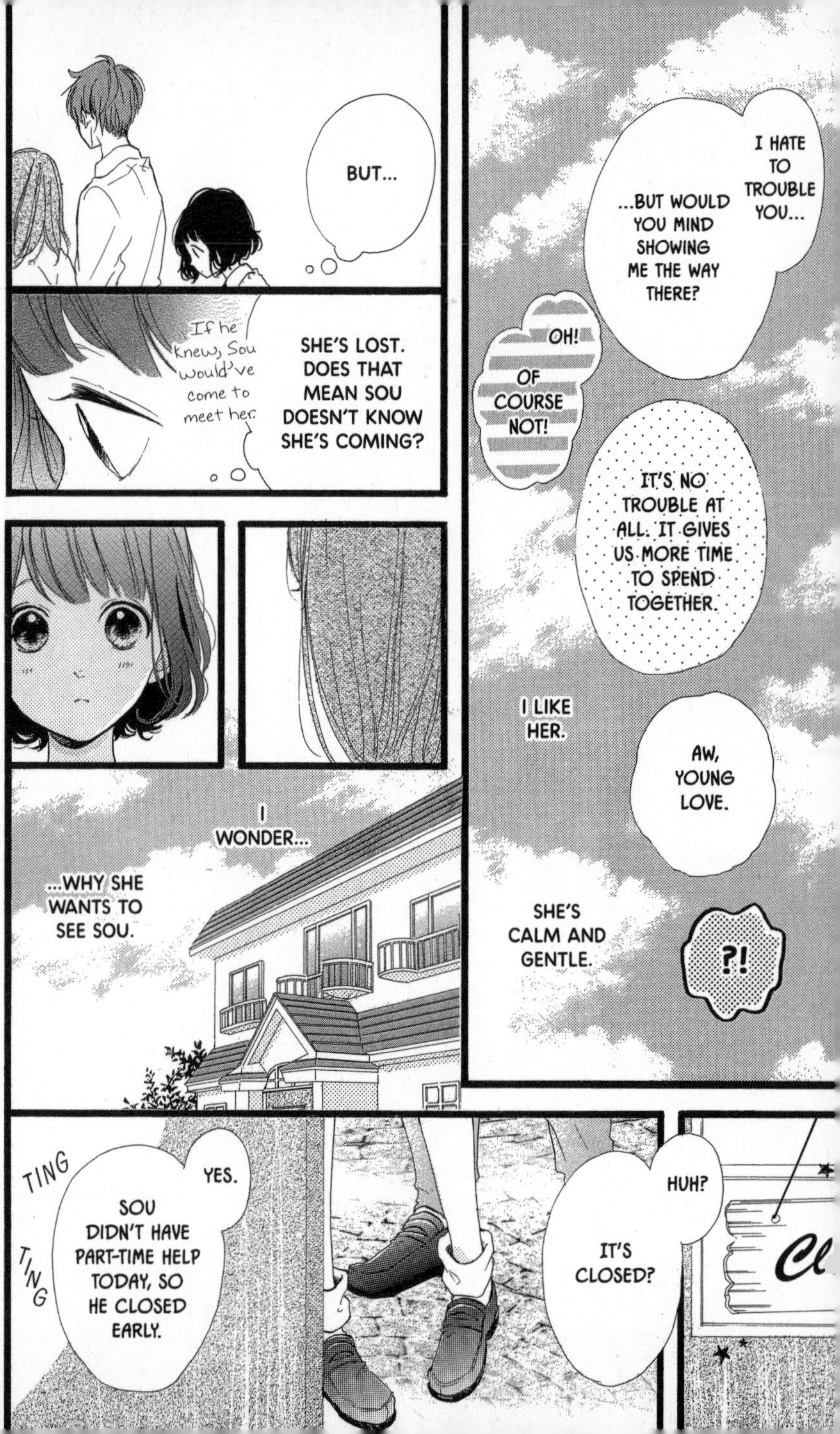
I HATE TO TROUBLE YOU...
...BUT WOULD YOU MIND SHOWING ME THE WAY THERE?
OH! OF COURSE NOT!
IT'S NO TROUBLE AT ALL. IT GIVES US MORE TIME TO SPEND TOGETHER.
AW, YOUNG LOVE.
I LIKE HER.
?!
SHE'S CALM AND GENTLE.
BUT...
SHE'S LOST. DOES THAT MEAN SOU DOESN'T KNOW SHE'S COMING?
If he knew, Sou would've come to meet her.
I WONDER...
...WHY SHE WANTS TO SEE SOU.
HUH?
IT'S CLOSED?
YES.
SOU DIDN'T HAVE PART-TIME HELP TODAY, SO HE CLOSED EARLY.
TING
TING

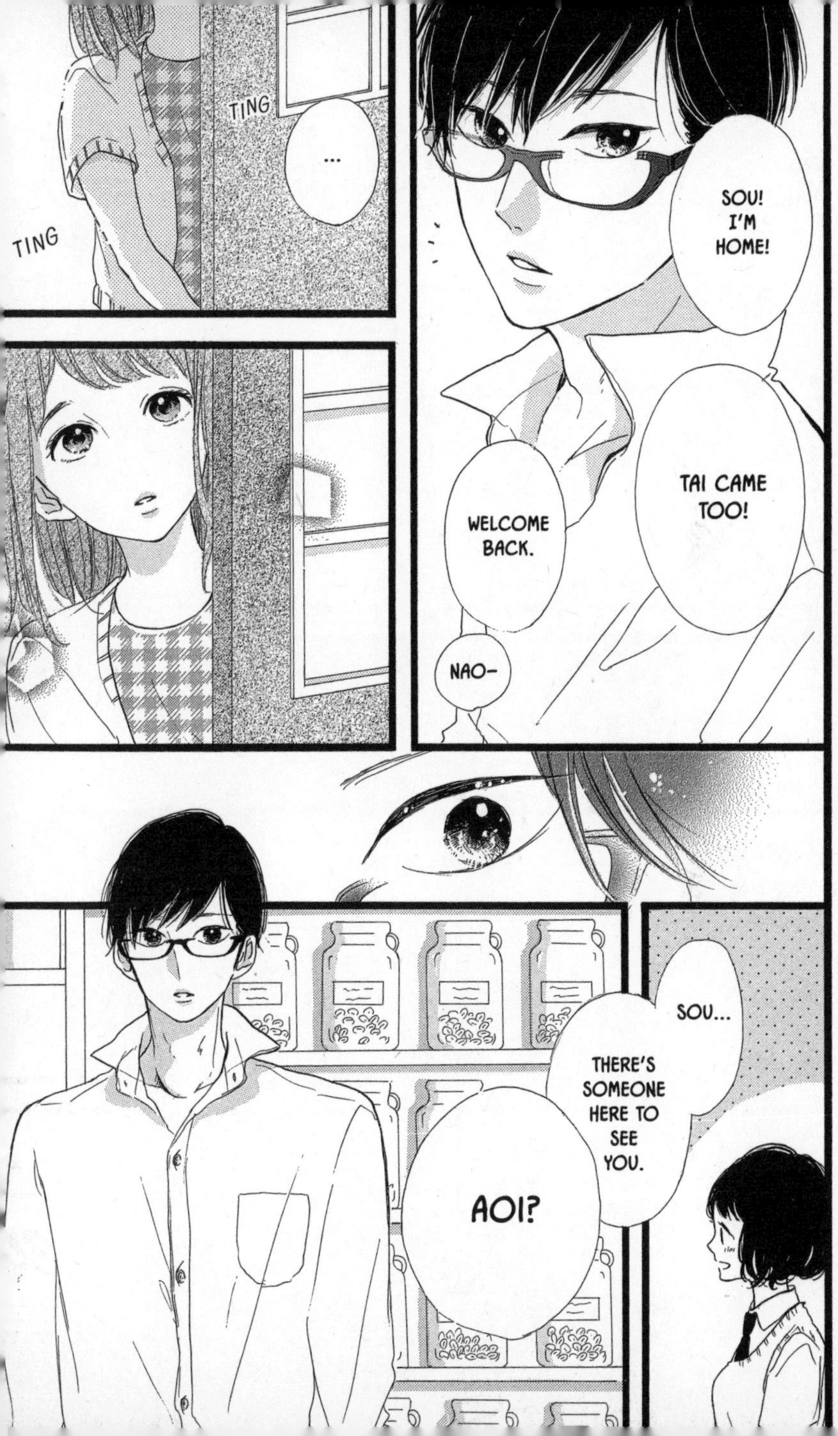
SOU! I'M HOME!
TAI CAME TOO!
WELCOME BACK.
NAO-
TING
...
TING
SOU...
THERE'S SOMEONE HERE TO SEE YOU.
AOI?

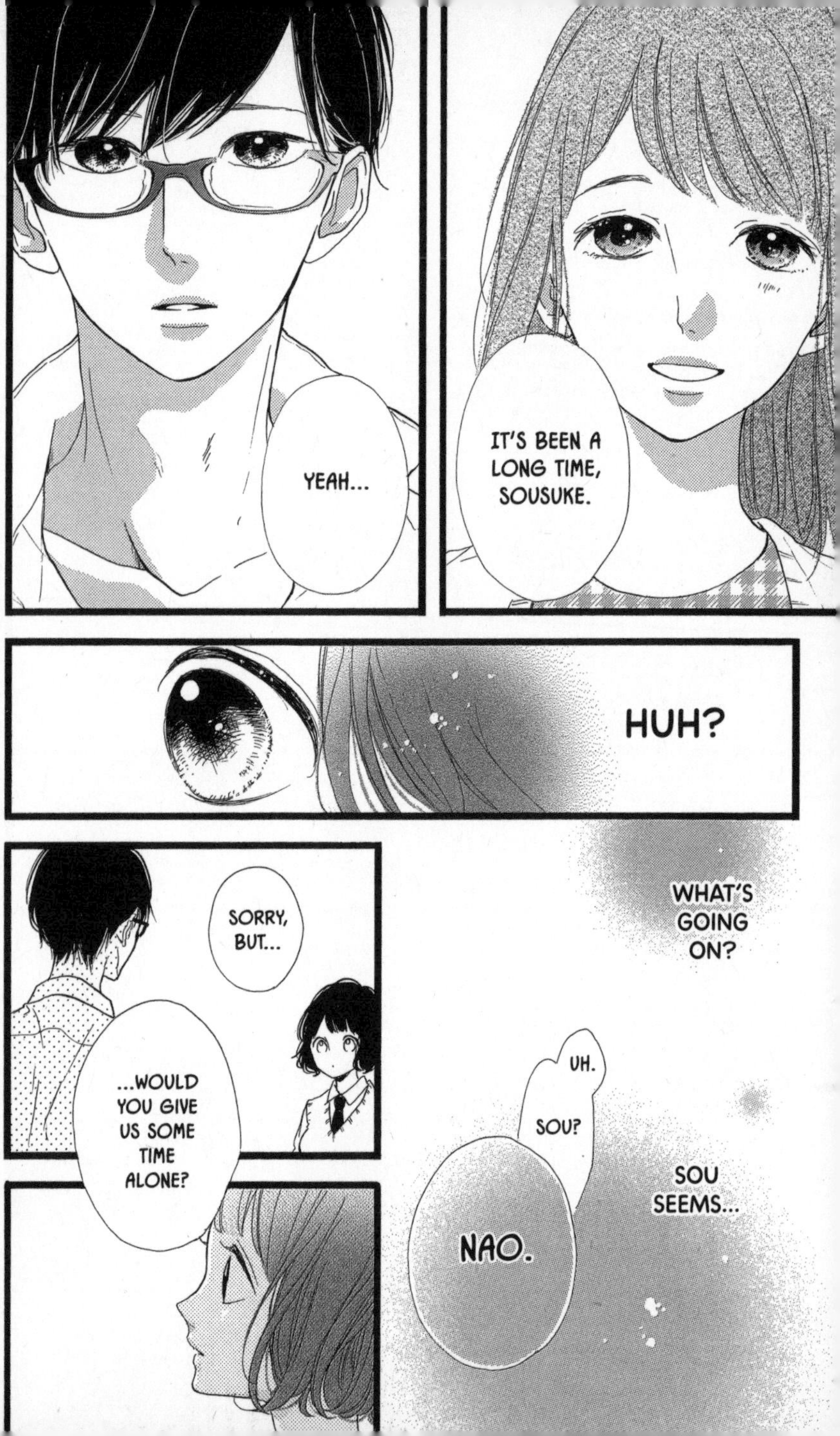
IT'S BEEN A LONG TIME, SOUSUKE.
YEAH...
HUH?
WHAT'S GOING ON?
UH.
SOU?
SOU SEEMS...
NAO.
SORRY, BUT...
...WOULD YOU GIVE US SOME TIME ALONE?

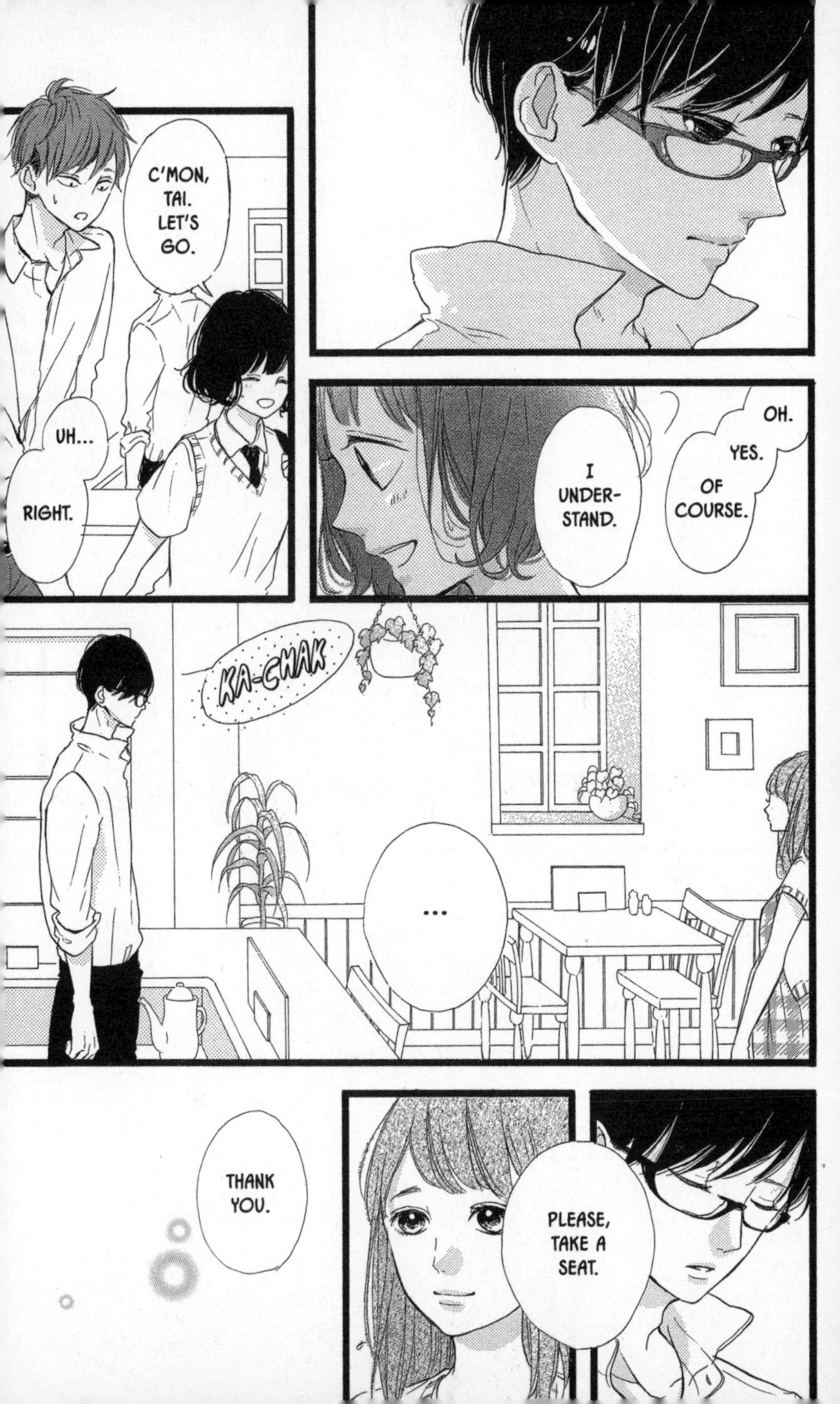
OH. YES. OF COURSE.
I UNDER-STAND.
C'MON, TAI. LET'S GO.
UH... RIGHT.
KA-CHAK
...
PLEASE, TAKE A SEAT.
THANK YOU.

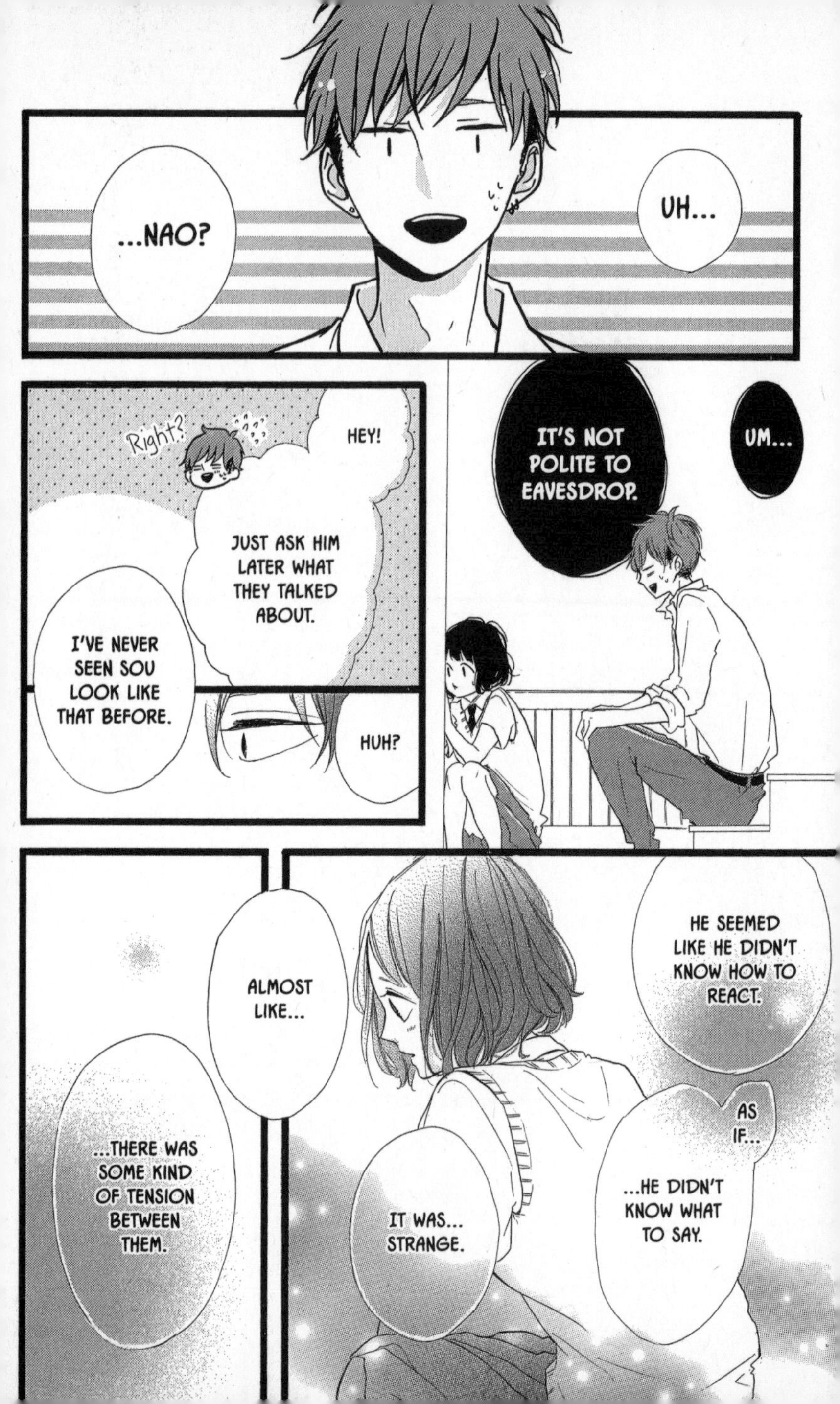
UH...
...NAO?
UM...
IT'S NOT POLITE TO EAVESDROP.
HEY!
JUST ASK HIM LATER WHAT THEY TALKED ABOUT.
Right?
HUH?
I'VE NEVER SEEN SOU LOOK LIKE THAT BEFORE.
HE SEEMED LIKE HE DIDN'T KNOW HOW TO REACT.
AS IF...
...HE DIDN'T KNOW WHAT TO SAY.
IT WAS... STRANGE.
ALMOST LIKE...
...THERE WAS SOME KIND OF TENSION BETWEEN THEM.

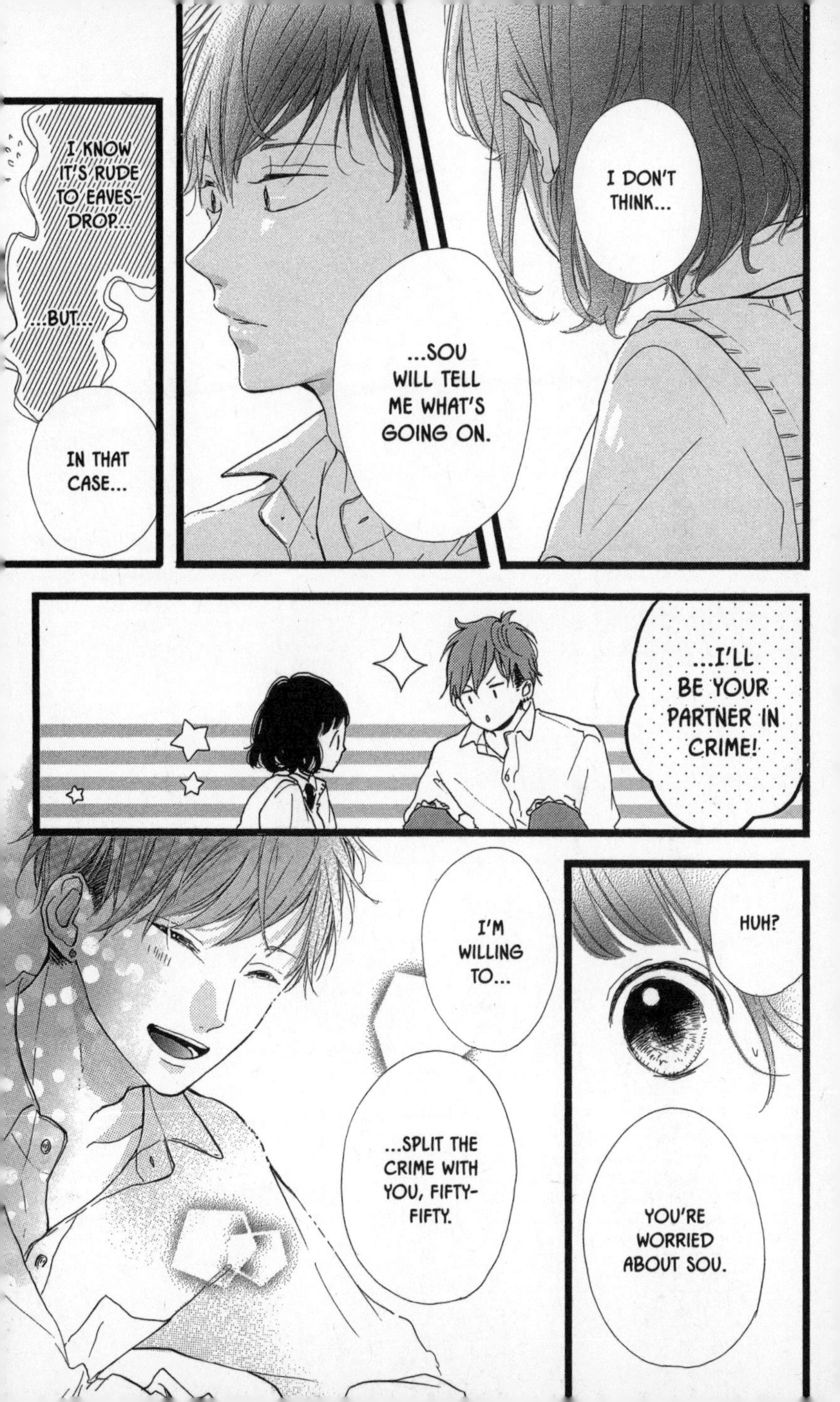
I DON'T THINK...
...SOU WILL TELL ME WHAT'S GOING ON.
I KNOW IT'S RUDE TO EAVES-DROP...
...BUT...
IN THAT CASE...
...I'LL BE YOUR PARTNER IN CRIME!
HUH?
YOU'RE WORRIED ABOUT SOU.
I'M WILLING TO...
...SPLIT THE CRIME WITH YOU, FIFTY-FIFTY.

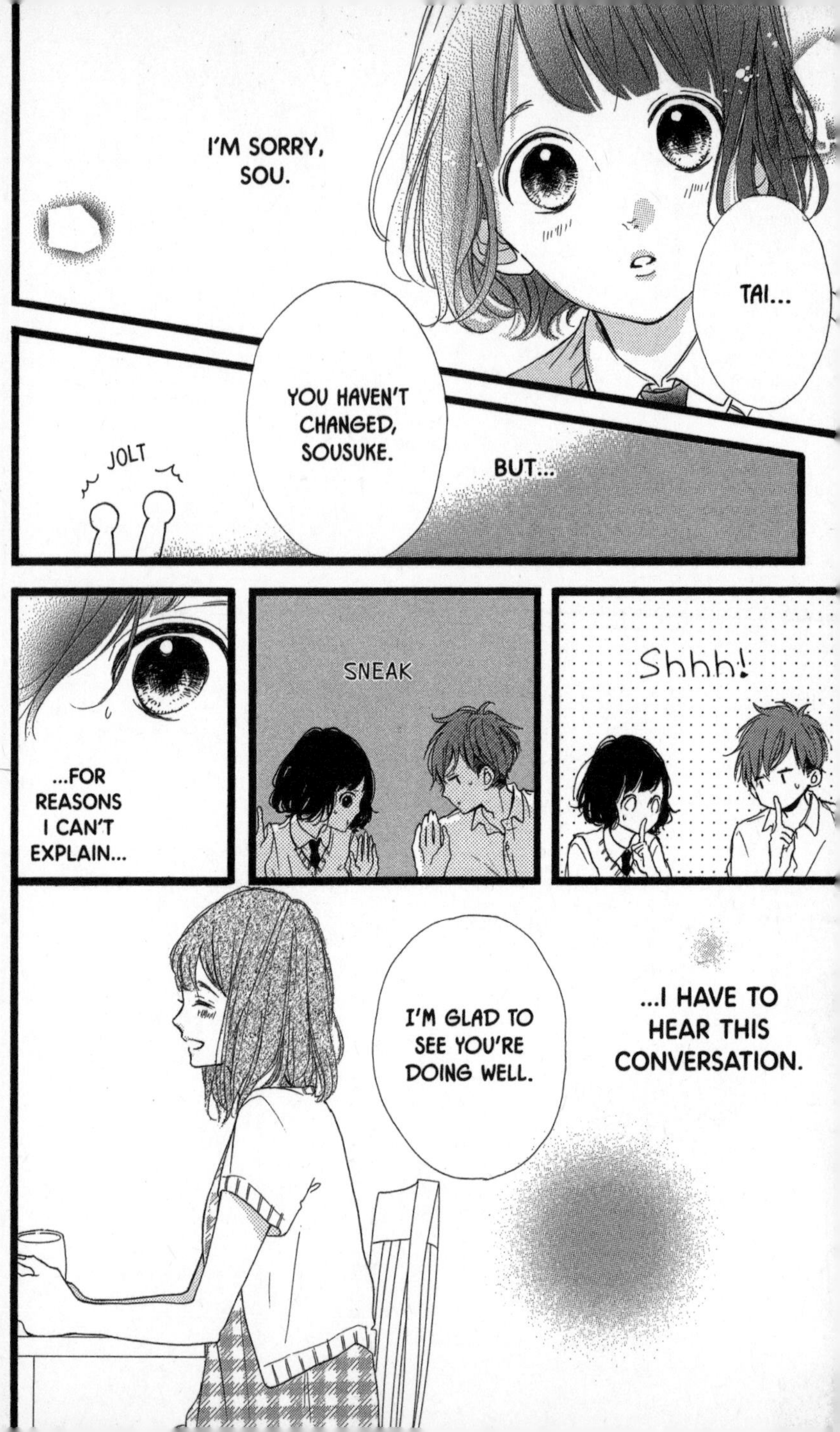
TAI...
I'M SORRY, SOU.
BUT...
YOU HAVEN'T CHANGED, SOUSUKE.
JOLT
Shhh!
SNEAK
...FOR REASONS I CAN'T EXPLAIN...
...I HAVE TO HEAR THIS CONVERSATION.
I'M GLAD TO SEE YOU'RE DOING WELL.

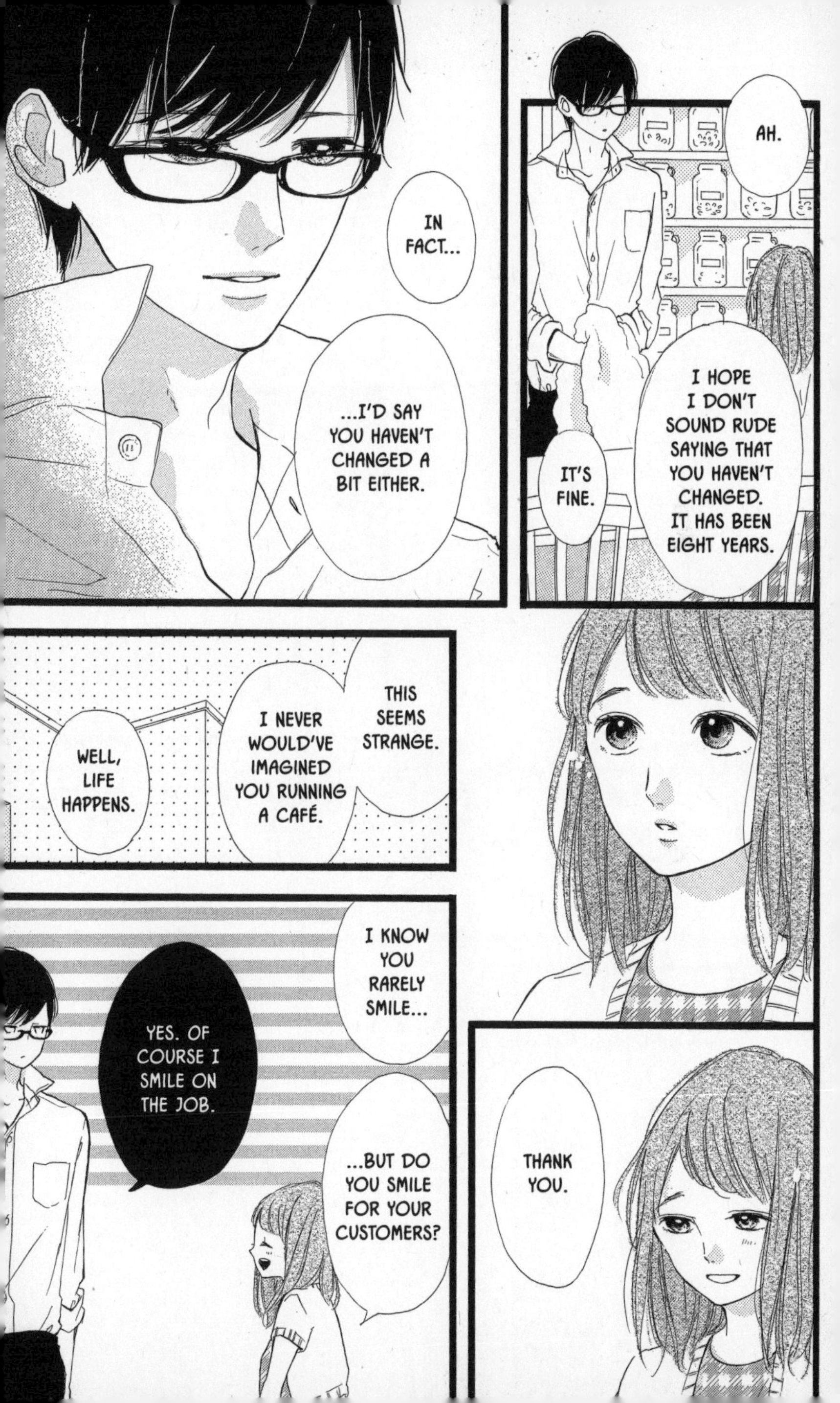
AH.
I HOPE I DON'T SOUND RUDE SAYING THAT YOU HAVEN'T CHANGED. IT HAS BEEN EIGHT YEARS.
IT'S FINE.
IN FACT...
...I'D SAY YOU HAVEN'T CHANGED A BIT EITHER.
THIS SEEMS STRANGE.
I NEVER WOULD'VE IMAGINED YOU RUNNING A CAFÉ.
WELL, LIFE HAPPENS.
I KNOW YOU RARELY SMILE...
YES. OF COURSE I SMILE ON THE JOB.
...BUT DO YOU SMILE FOR YOUR CUSTOMERS?
THANK YOU.

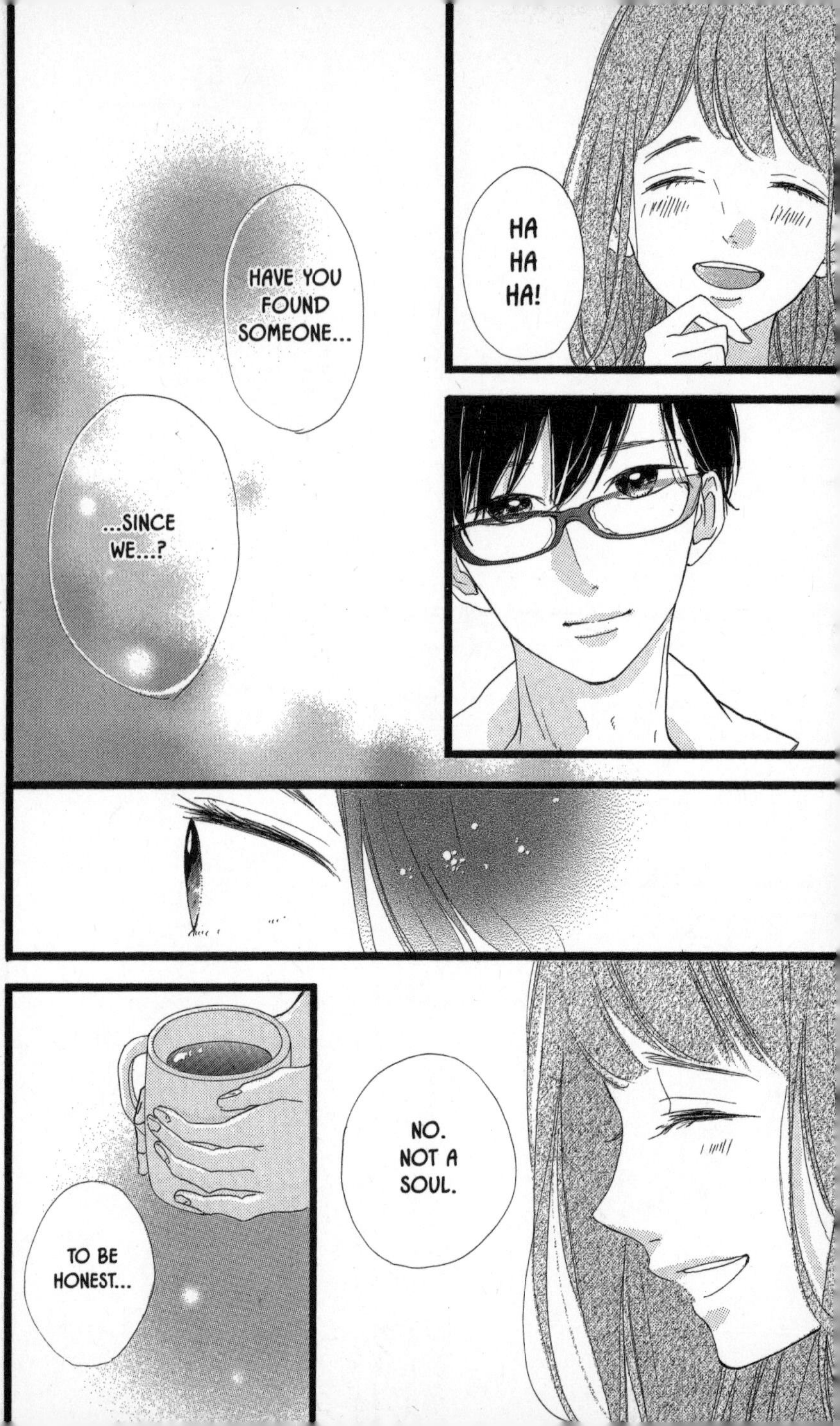
HA HA HA!
HAVE YOU FOUND SOMEONE...
...SINCE WE...?
NO. NOT A SOUL.
TO BE HONEST...

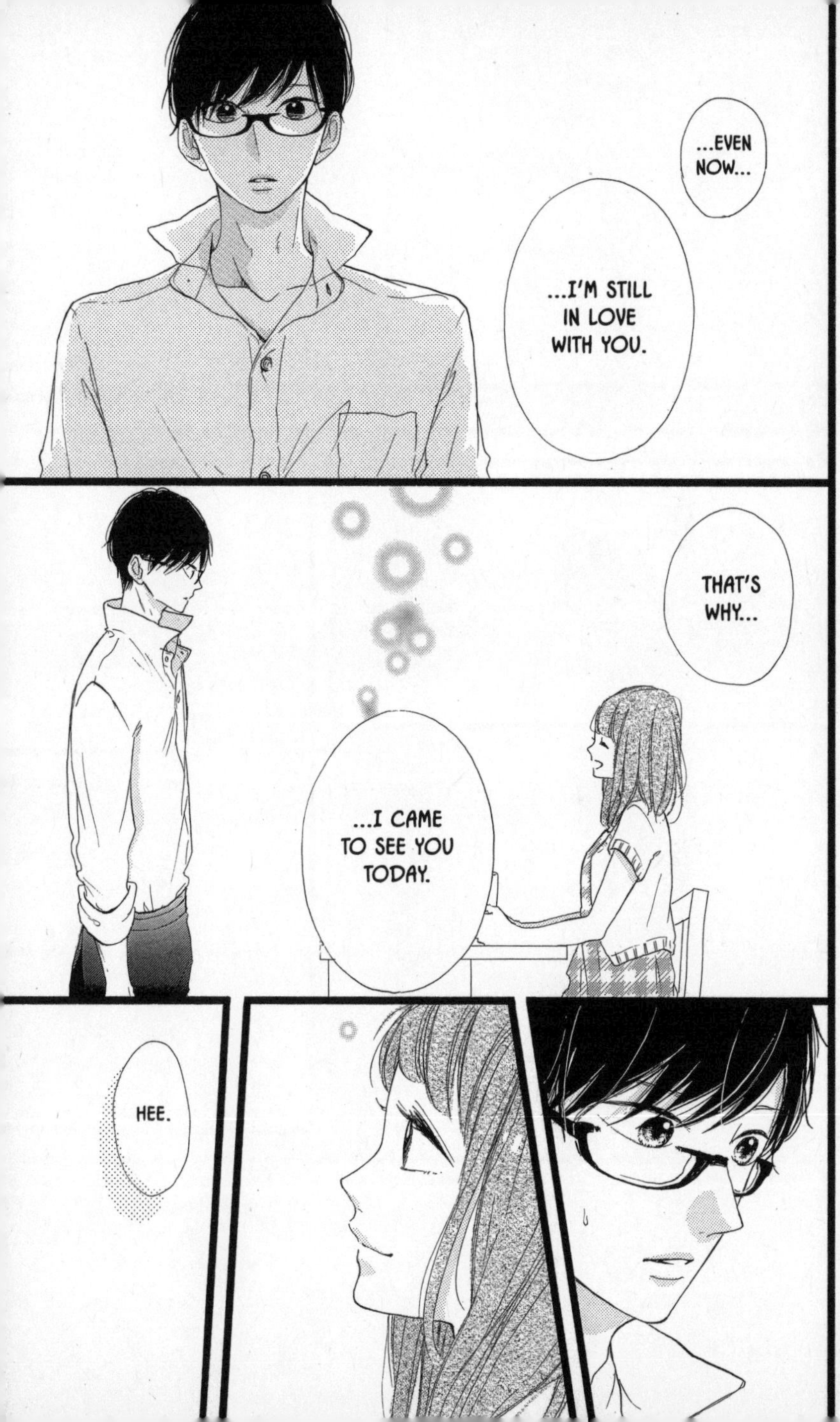
...EVEN NOW...
...I'M STILL IN LOVE WITH YOU.
THAT'S WHY...
...I CAME TO SEE YOU TODAY.
HEE.

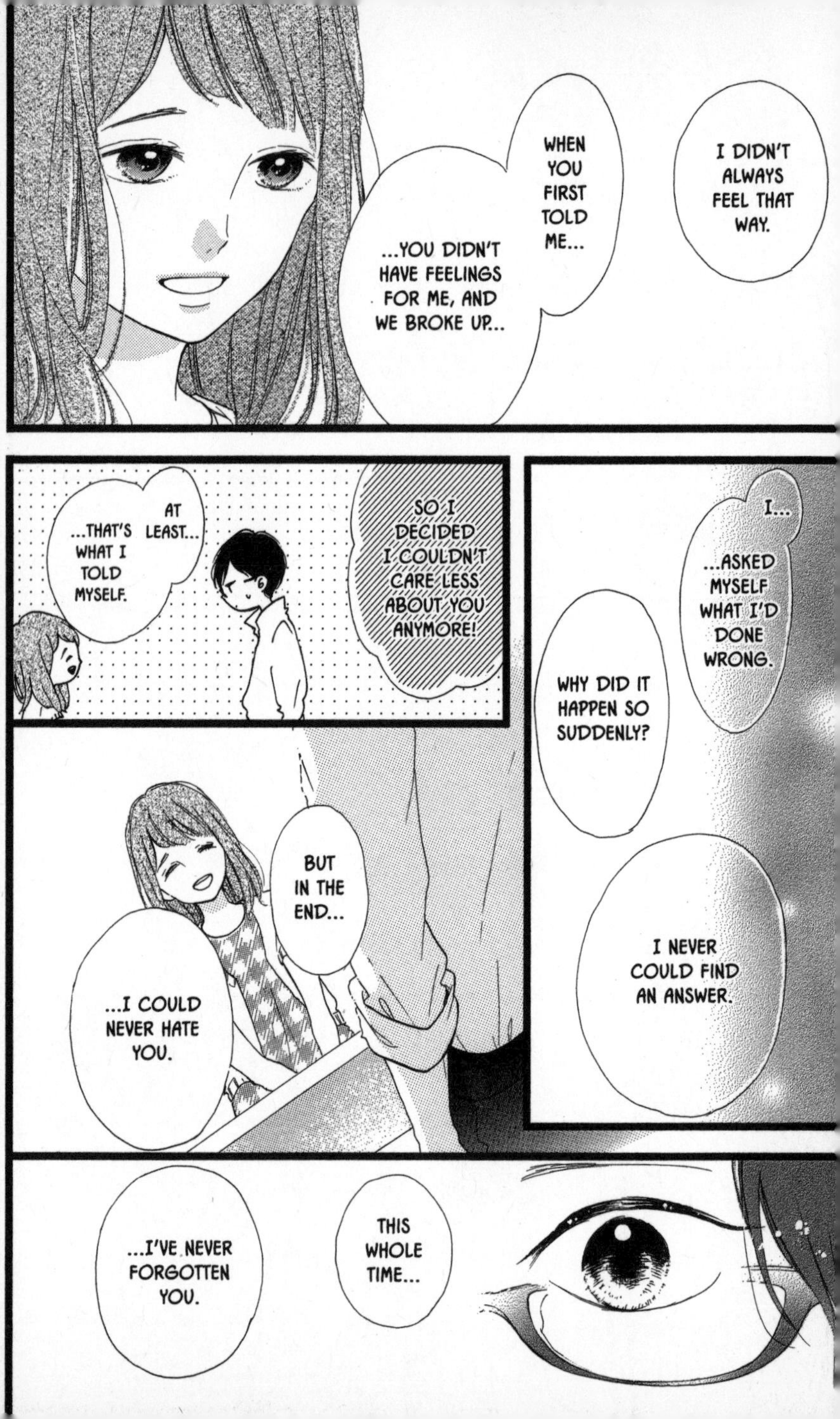
I DIDN'T ALWAYS FEEL THAT WAY.
WHEN YOU FIRST TOLD ME...
...YOU DIDN'T HAVE FEELINGS FOR ME, AND WE BROKE UP...
I...
...ASKED MYSELF WHAT I'D DONE WRONG.
WHY DID IT HAPPEN SO SUDDENLY?
I NEVER COULD FIND AN ANSWER.
SO I DECIDED I COULDN'T CARE LESS ABOUT YOU ANYMORE!
AT LEAST...
...THAT'S WHAT I TOLD MYSELF.
BUT IN THE END...
...I COULD NEVER HATE YOU.
THIS WHOLE TIME...
...I'VE NEVER FORGOTTEN YOU.

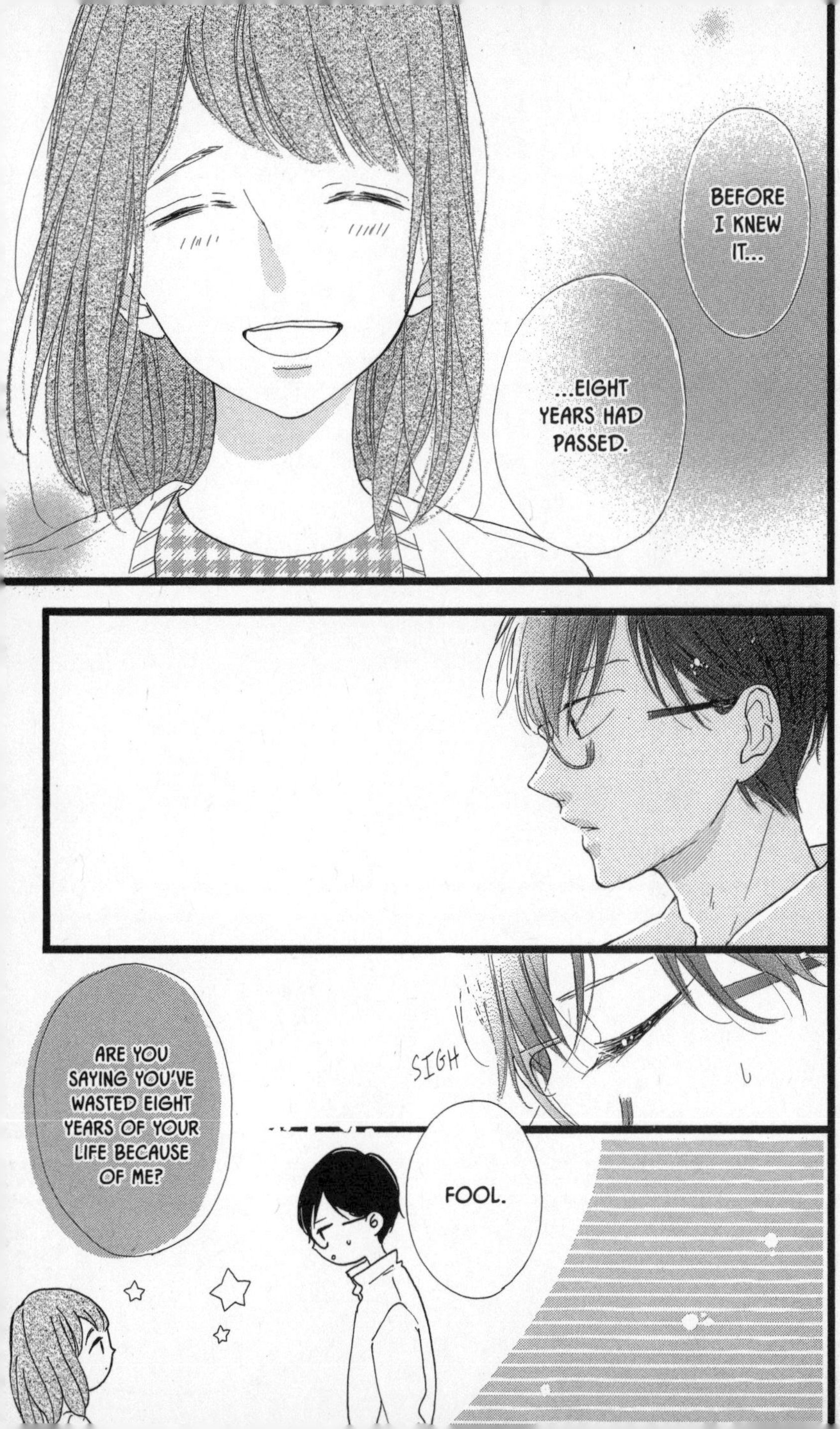
BEFORE I KNEW IT...
...EIGHT YEARS HAD PASSED.
SIGH
ARE YOU SAYING YOU'VE WASTED EIGHT YEARS OF YOUR LIFE BECAUSE OF ME?
FOOL.

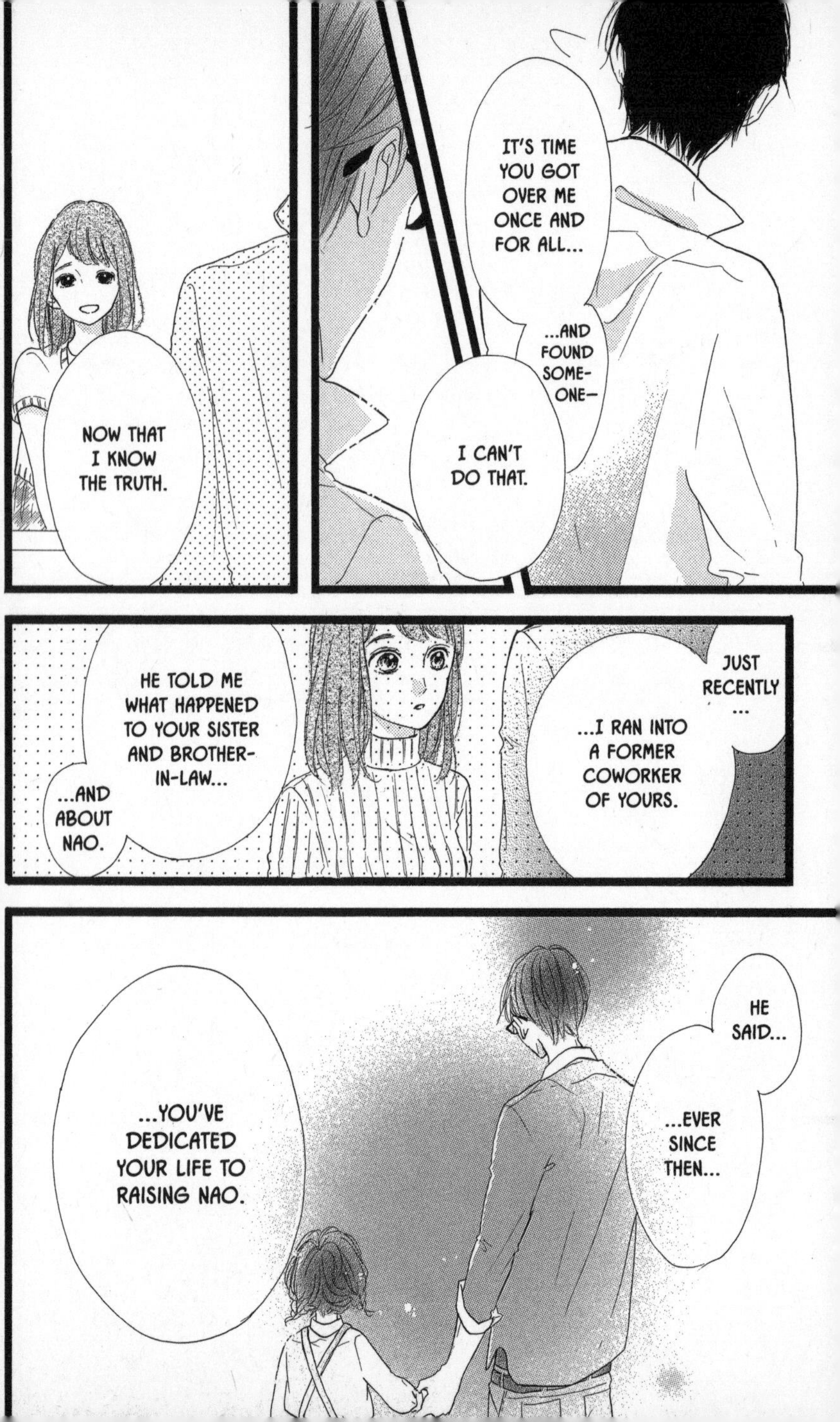
IT'S TIME YOU GOT OVER ME ONCE AND FOR ALL...
...AND FOUND SOME-ONE—
I CAN'T DO THAT.
NOW THAT I KNOW THE TRUTH.
JUST RECENTLY...
...I RAN INTO A FORMER COWORKER OF YOURS.
HE TOLD ME WHAT HAPPENED TO YOUR SISTER AND BROTHER-IN-LAW...
...AND ABOUT NAO.
HE SAID...
...EVER SINCE THEN...
...YOU'VE DEDICATED YOUR LIFE TO RAISING NAO.

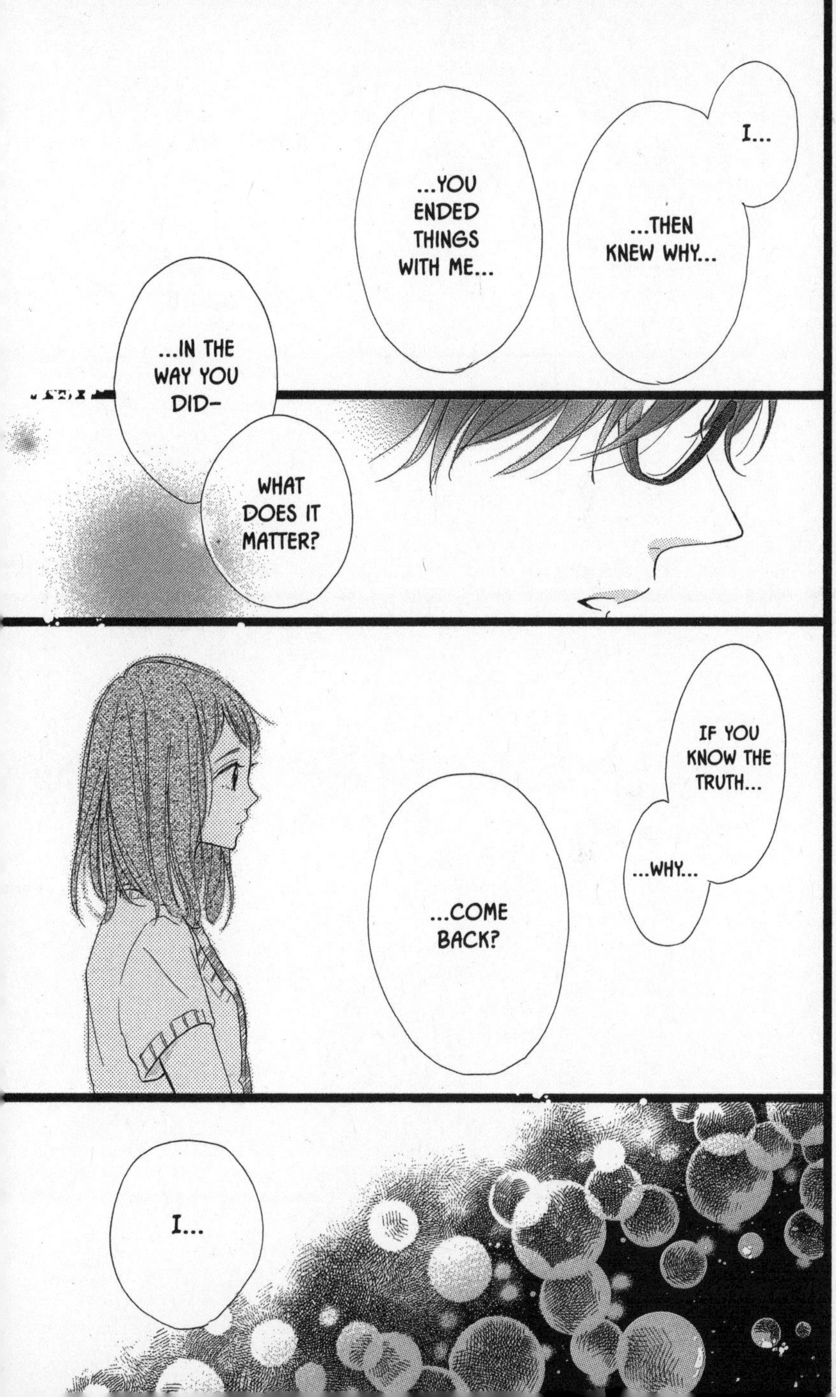
I...
...THEN KNEW WHY...
...YOU ENDED THINGS WITH ME...
...IN THE WAY YOU DID–
WHAT DOES IT MATTER?
IF YOU KNOW THE TRUTH...
...WHY...
...COME BACK?
I...

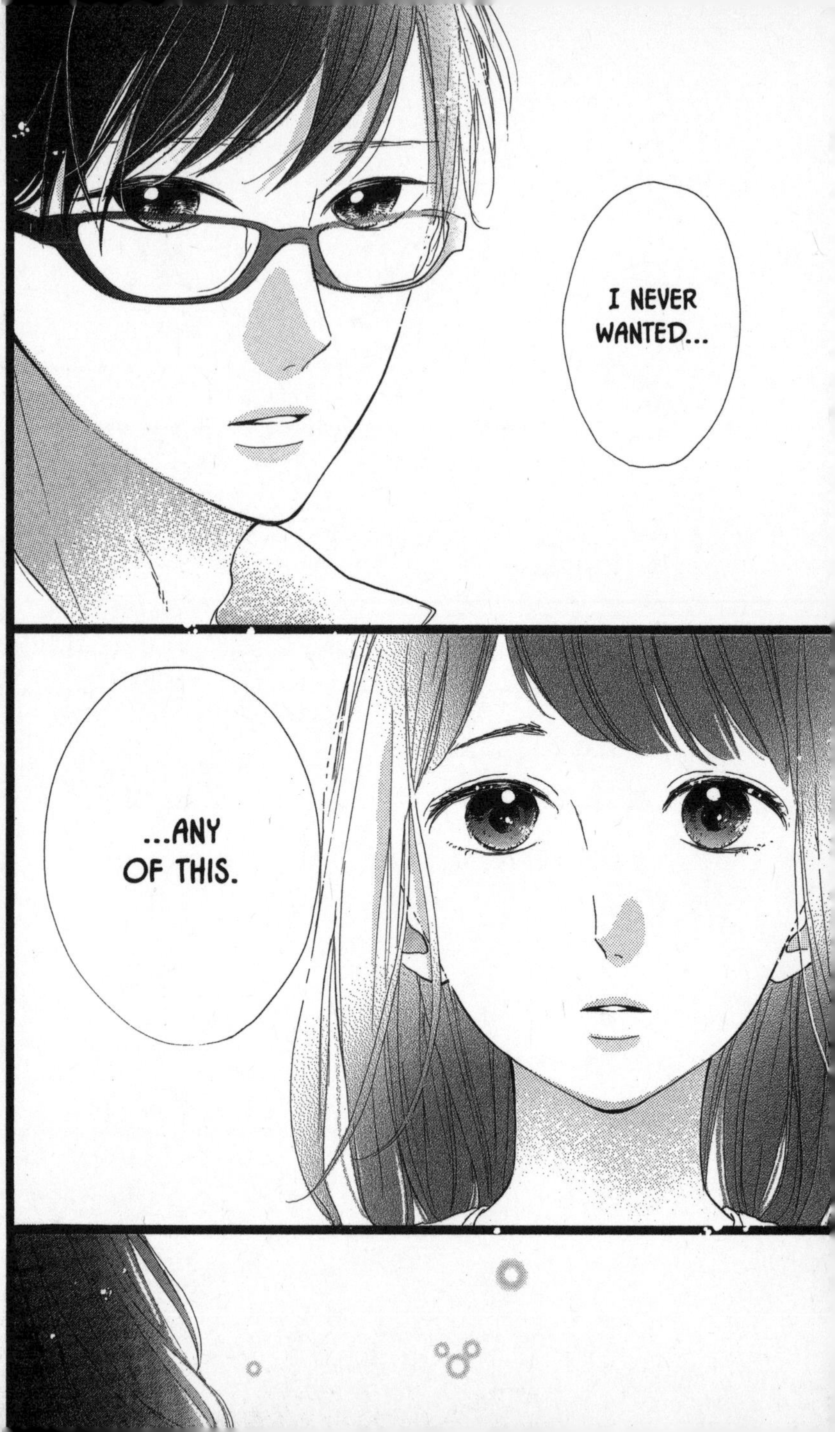
I NEVER WANTED...
...ANY OF THIS.

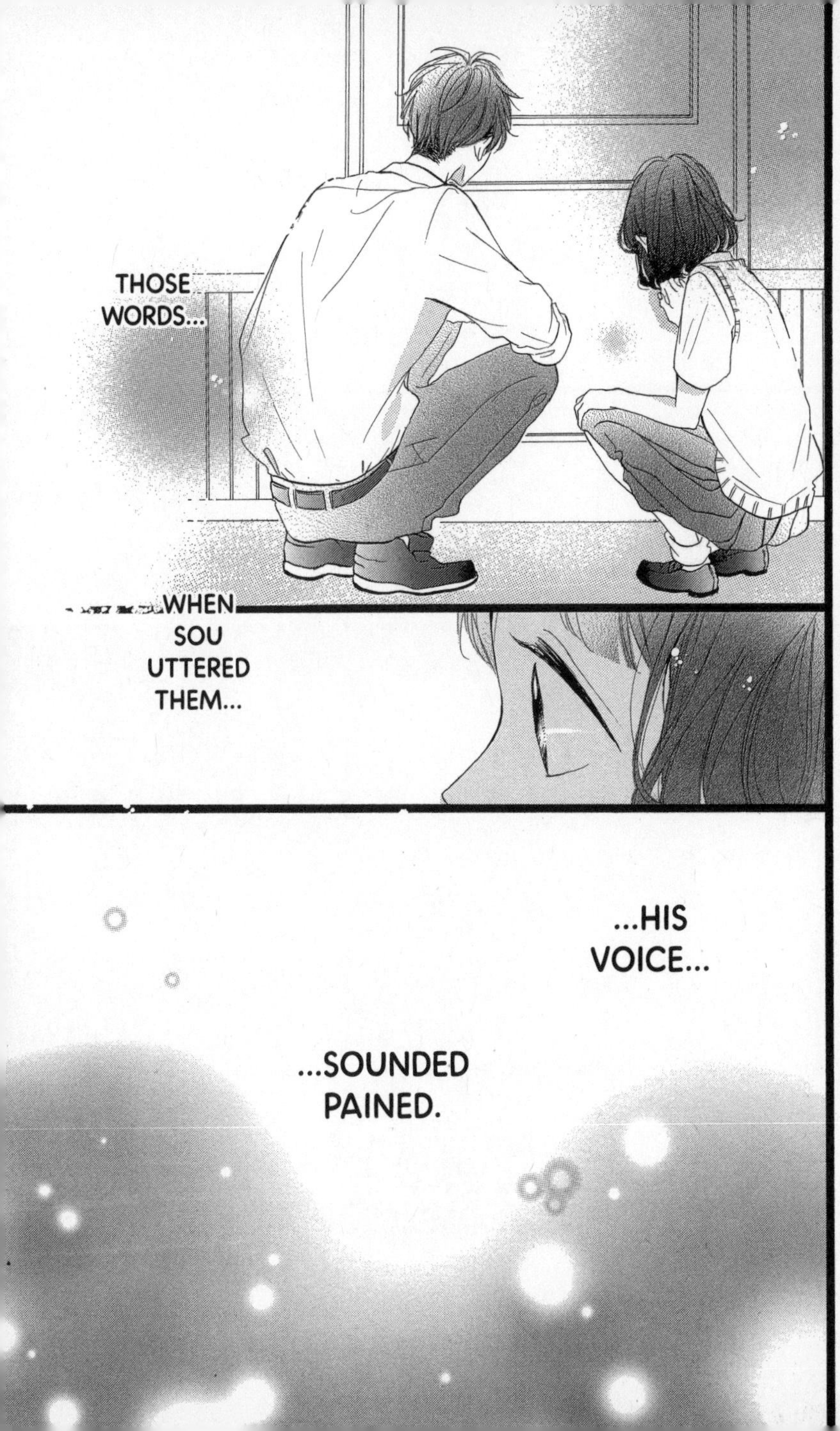
THOSE WORDS...
WHEN SOU UTTERED THEM...
...HIS VOICE...
...SOUNDED PAINED.

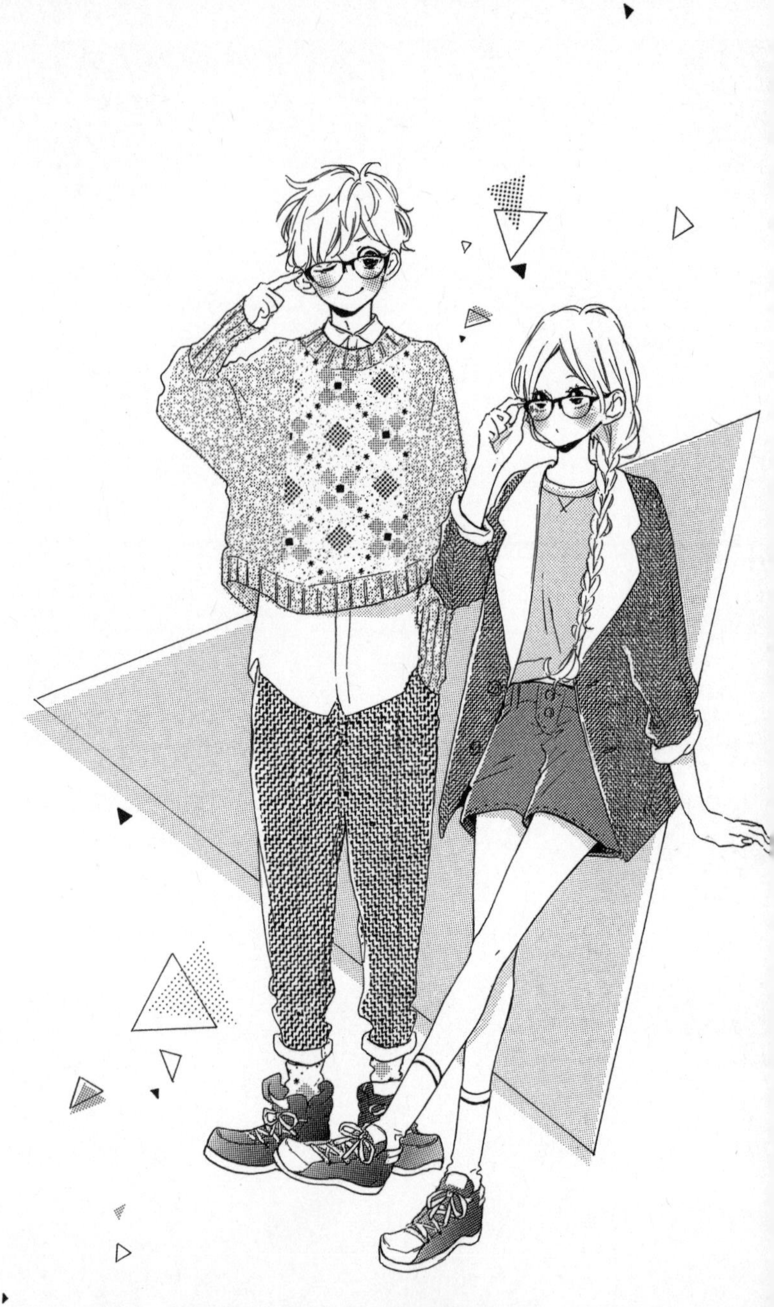

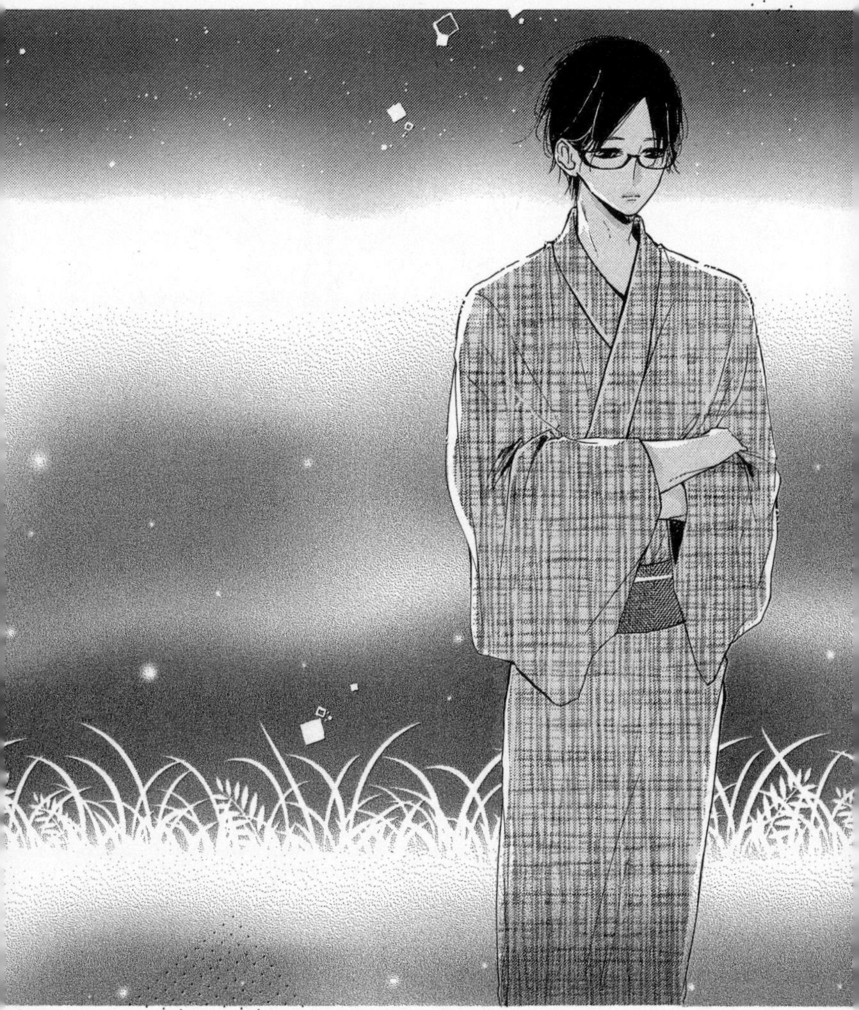

#38 Your Happiness

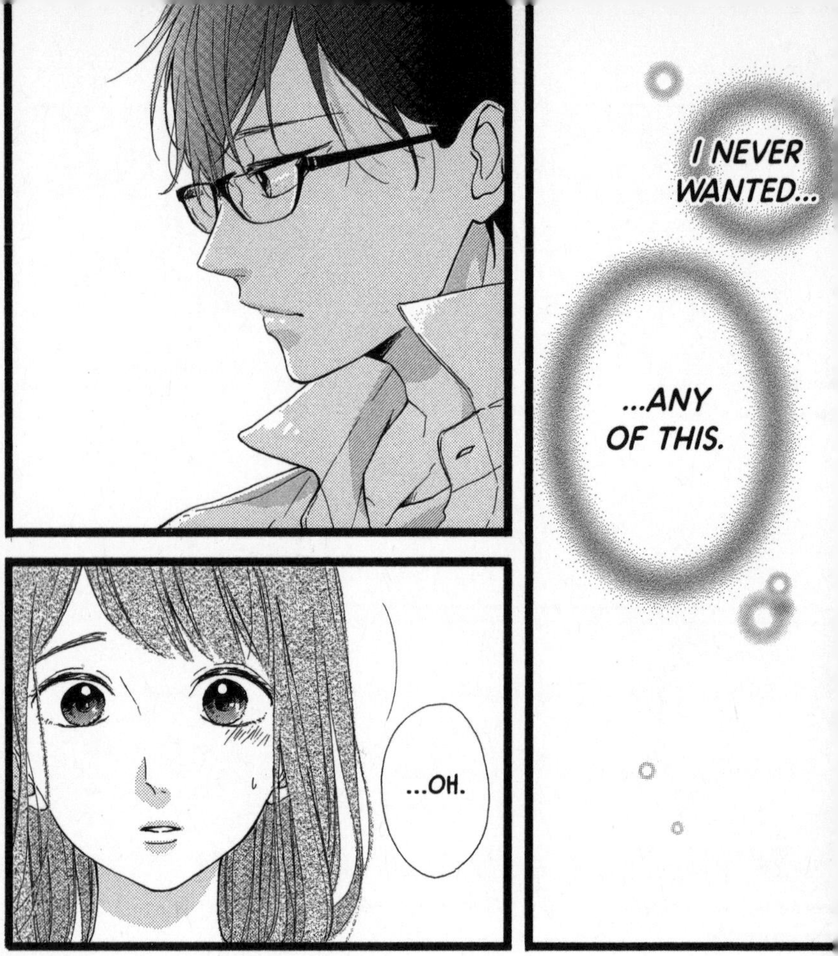
I NEVER WANTED...
...ANY OF THIS.
...OH.

Honey So Sweet

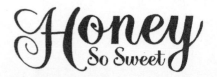

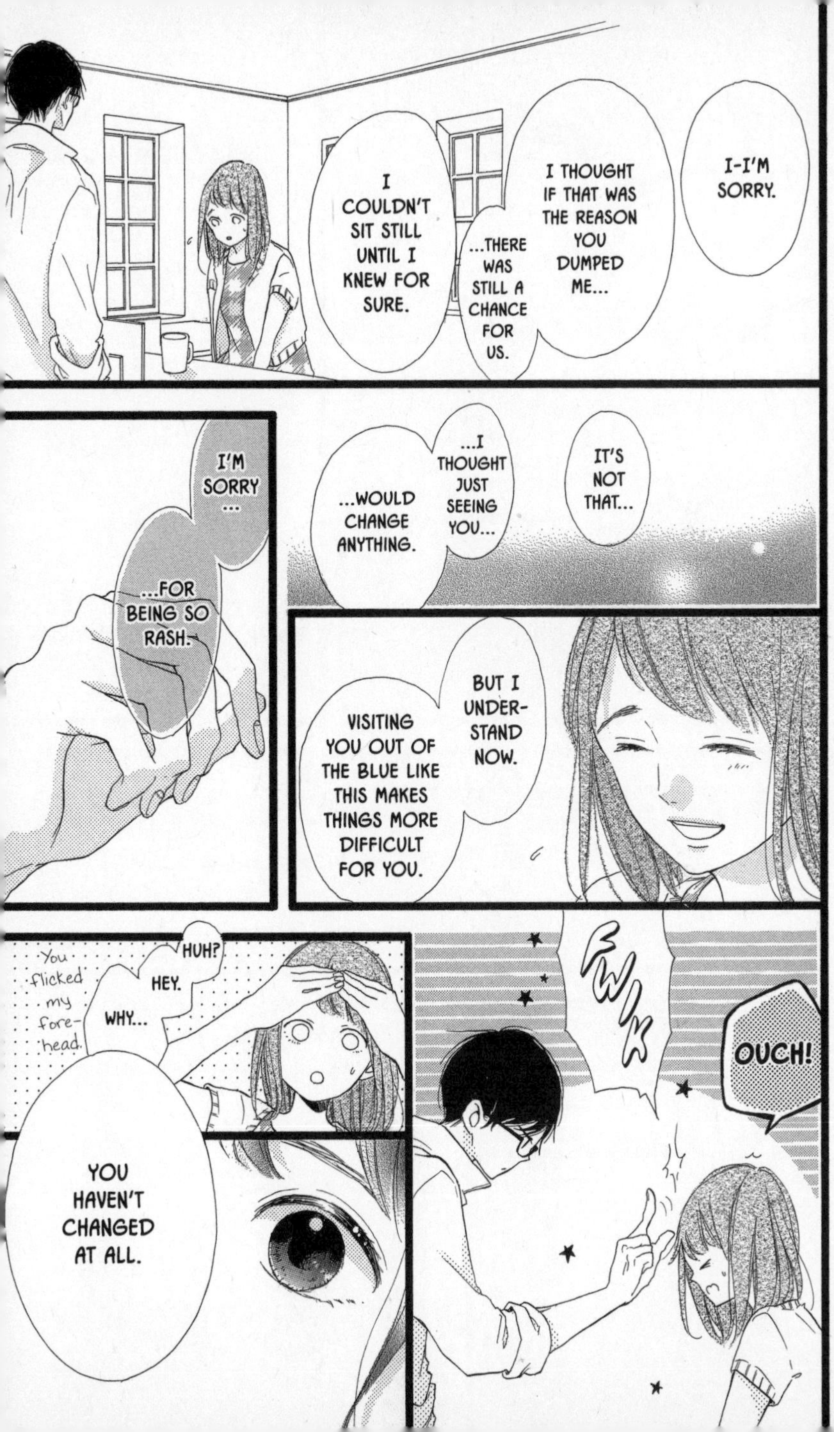
I-I'M SORRY.
I THOUGHT IF THAT WAS THE REASON YOU DUMPED ME...
...THERE WAS STILL A CHANCE FOR US.
I COULDN'T SIT STILL UNTIL I KNEW FOR SURE.
IT'S NOT THAT...
...I THOUGHT JUST SEEING YOU...
...WOULD CHANGE ANYTHING.
BUT I UNDER-STAND NOW.
VISITING YOU OUT OF THE BLUE LIKE THIS MAKES THINGS MORE DIFFICULT FOR YOU.
I'M SORRY...
...FOR BEING SO RASH.
FWIK
OUCH!
HUH?
HEY.
WHY...
You flicked my fore-head.
YOU HAVEN'T CHANGED AT ALL.

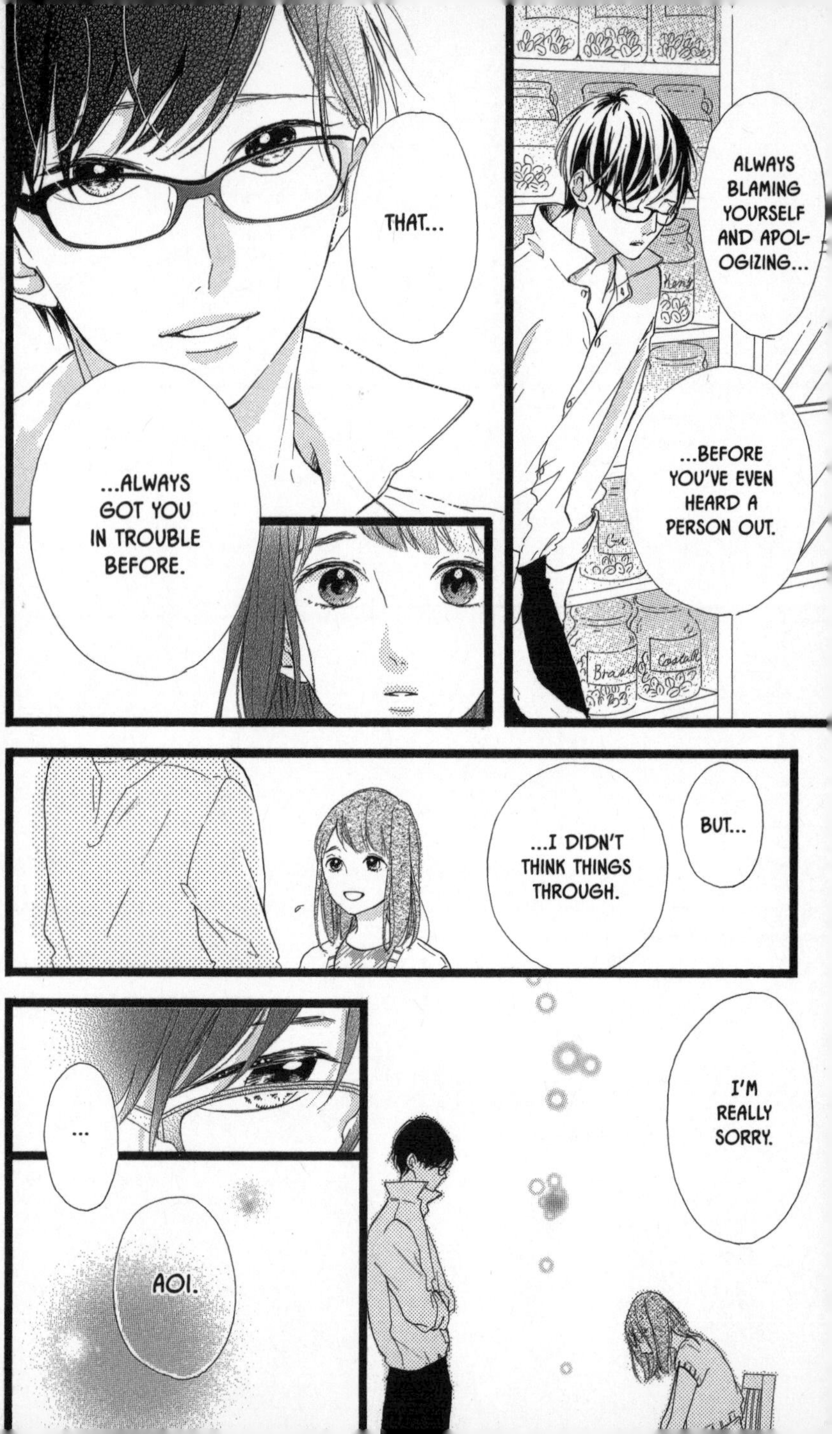
ALWAYS BLAMING YOURSELF AND APOL-OGIZING...
...BEFORE YOU'VE EVEN HEARD A PERSON OUT.
THAT...
...ALWAYS GOT YOU IN TROUBLE BEFORE.
BUT...
...I DIDN'T THINK THINGS THROUGH.
I'M REALLY SORRY.
...
AOI.

HUH?

WHAT I JUST SAID...

...WASN'T ABOUT YOUR COMING HERE TODAY.

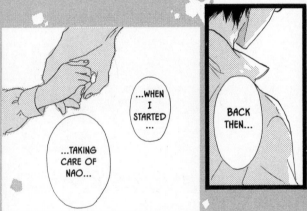

...WHEN I STARTED...

...TAKING CARE OF NAO...

BACK THEN...

...I MADE THE DECISION...

...TO DO EVERYTHING IN MY POWER TO PROTECT HER SMILE.

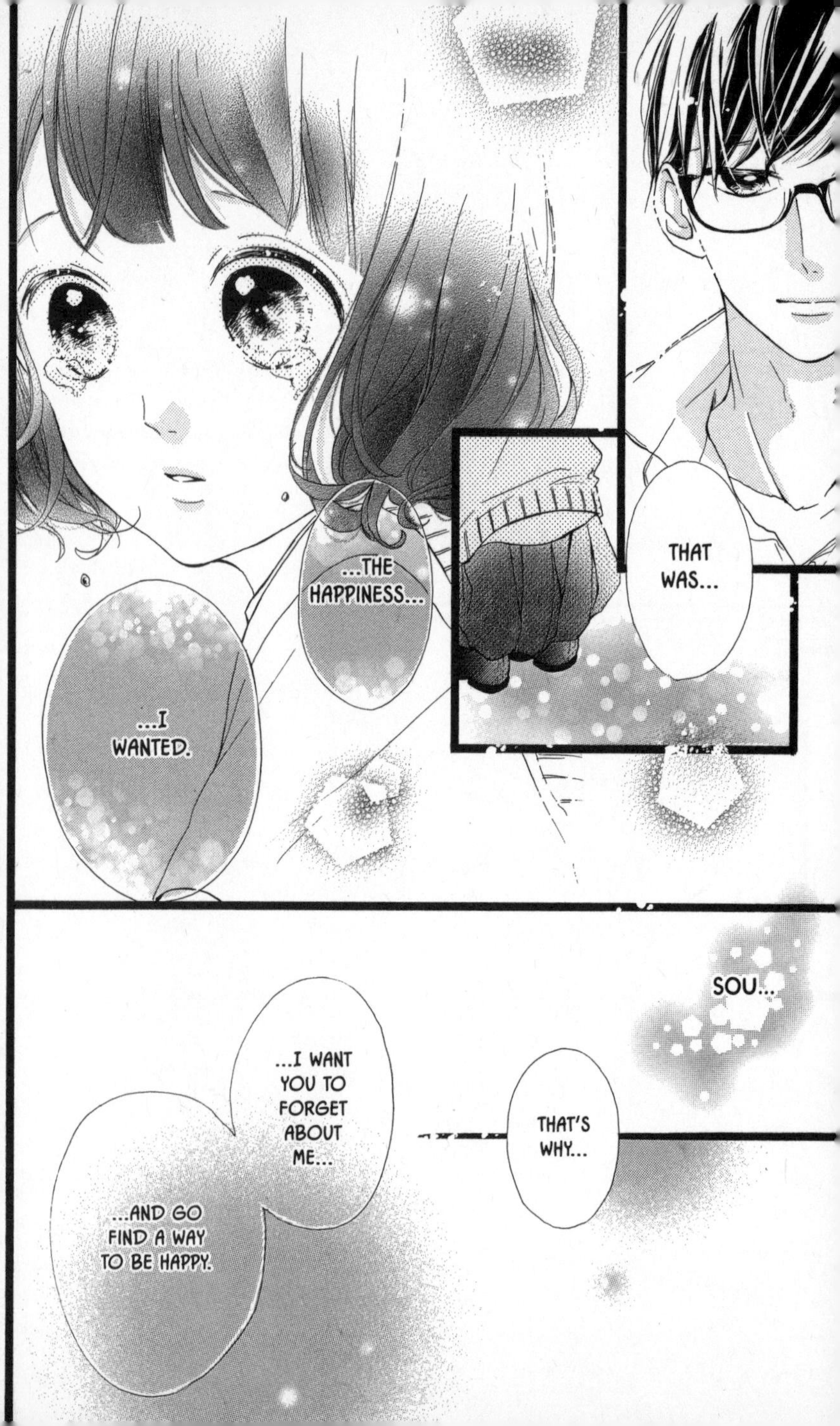
THAT WAS...
...THE HAPPINESS...
...I WANTED.
SOU...
THAT'S WHY...
...I WANT YOU TO FORGET ABOUT ME...
...AND GO FIND A WAY TO BE HAPPY.

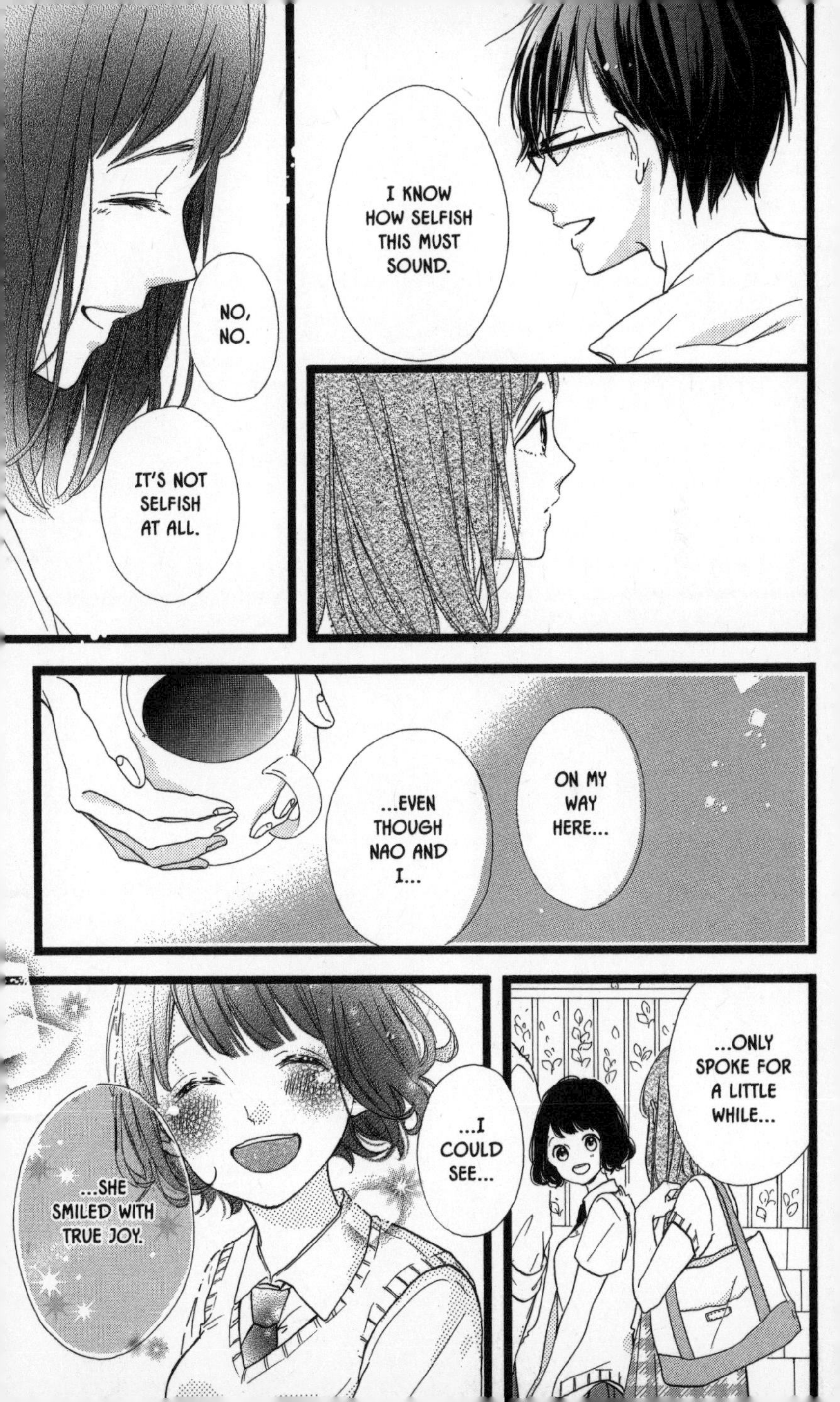
I KNOW HOW SELFISH THIS MUST SOUND.
NO, NO.
IT'S NOT SELFISH AT ALL.
ON MY WAY HERE...
...EVEN THOUGH NAO AND I...
...ONLY SPOKE FOR A LITTLE WHILE...
...I COULD SEE...
...SHE SMILED WITH TRUE JOY.

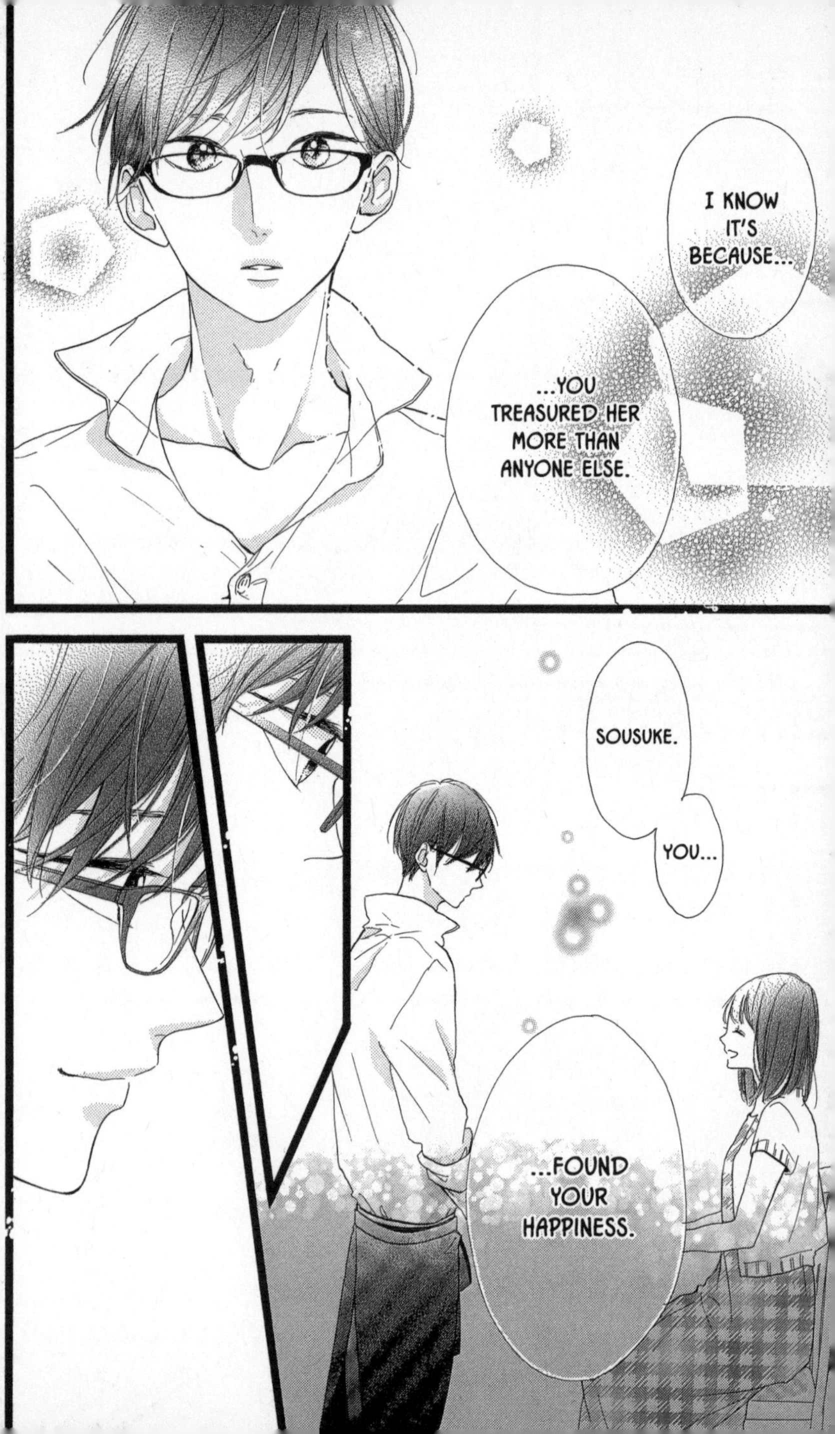
I KNOW IT'S BECAUSE...
...YOU TREASURED HER MORE THAN ANYONE ELSE.
SOUSUKE.
YOU...
...FOUND YOUR HAPPINESS.

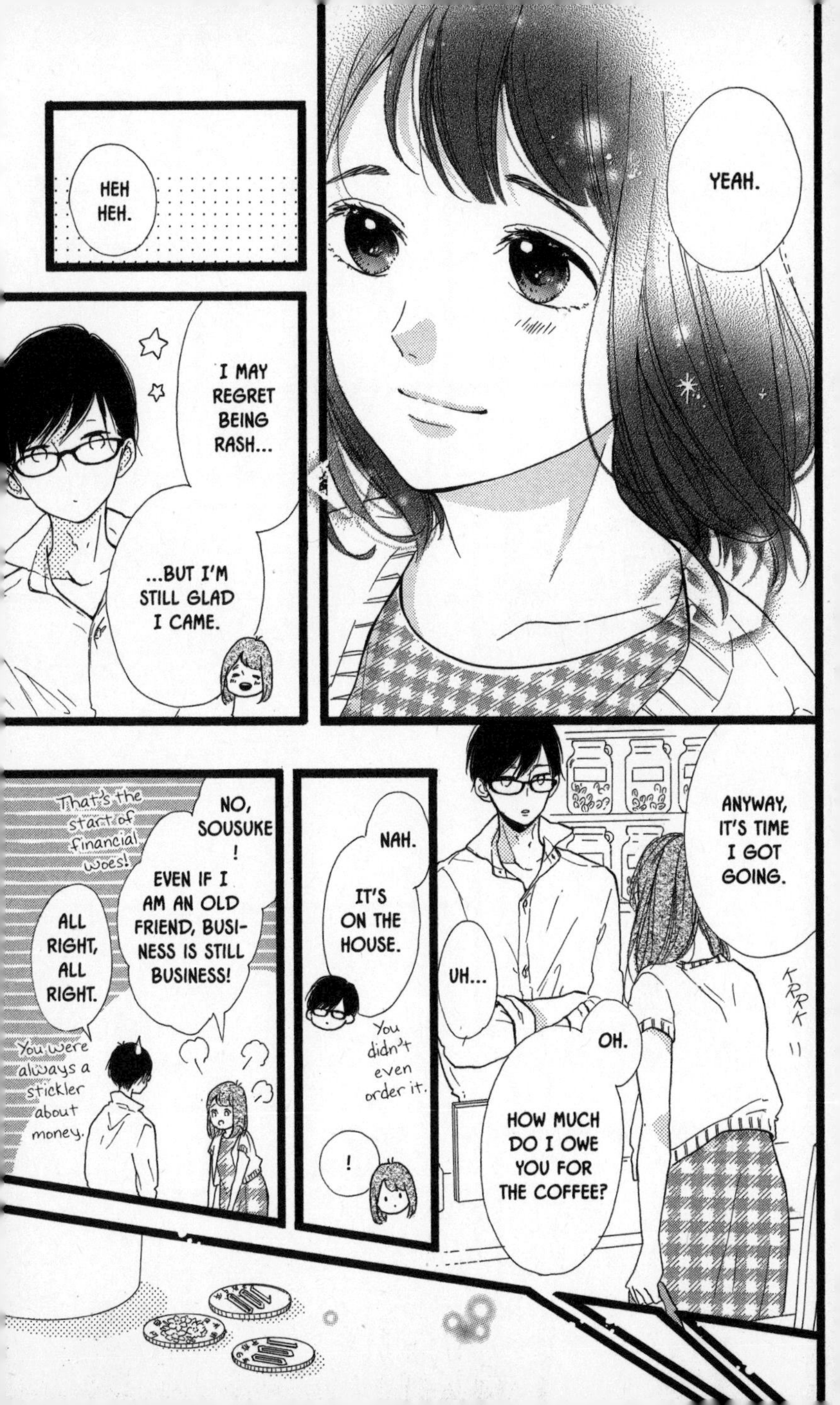
YEAH.
HEH HEH.
I MAY REGRET BEING RASH...
...BUT I'M STILL GLAD I CAME.
ANYWAY, IT'S TIME I GOT GOING.
KRRK
OH.
HOW MUCH DO I OWE YOU FOR THE COFFEE?
UH...
NAH.
IT'S ON THE HOUSE.
You didn't even order it.
!
NO, SOUSUKE!
EVEN IF I AM AN OLD FRIEND, BUSINESS IS STILL BUSINESS!
That's the start of financial woes!
ALL RIGHT, ALL RIGHT.
You were always a stickler about money.

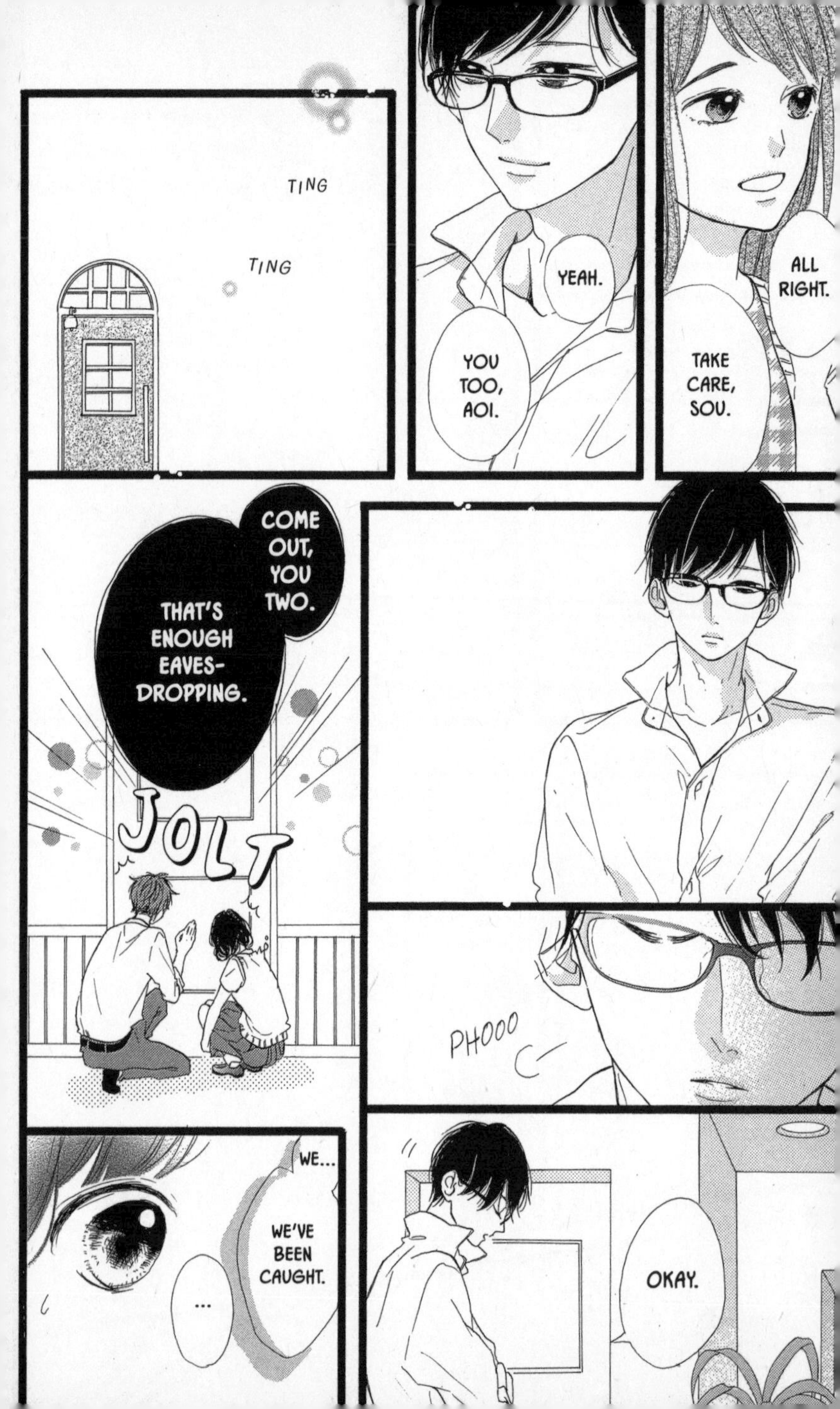
ALL RIGHT.
TAKE CARE, SOU.
YEAH.
YOU TOO, AOI.
TING
TING
PHOOO
COME OUT, YOU TWO.
THAT'S ENOUGH EAVES-DROPPING.
JOLT
OKAY.
WE...
WE'VE BEEN CAUGHT.
...

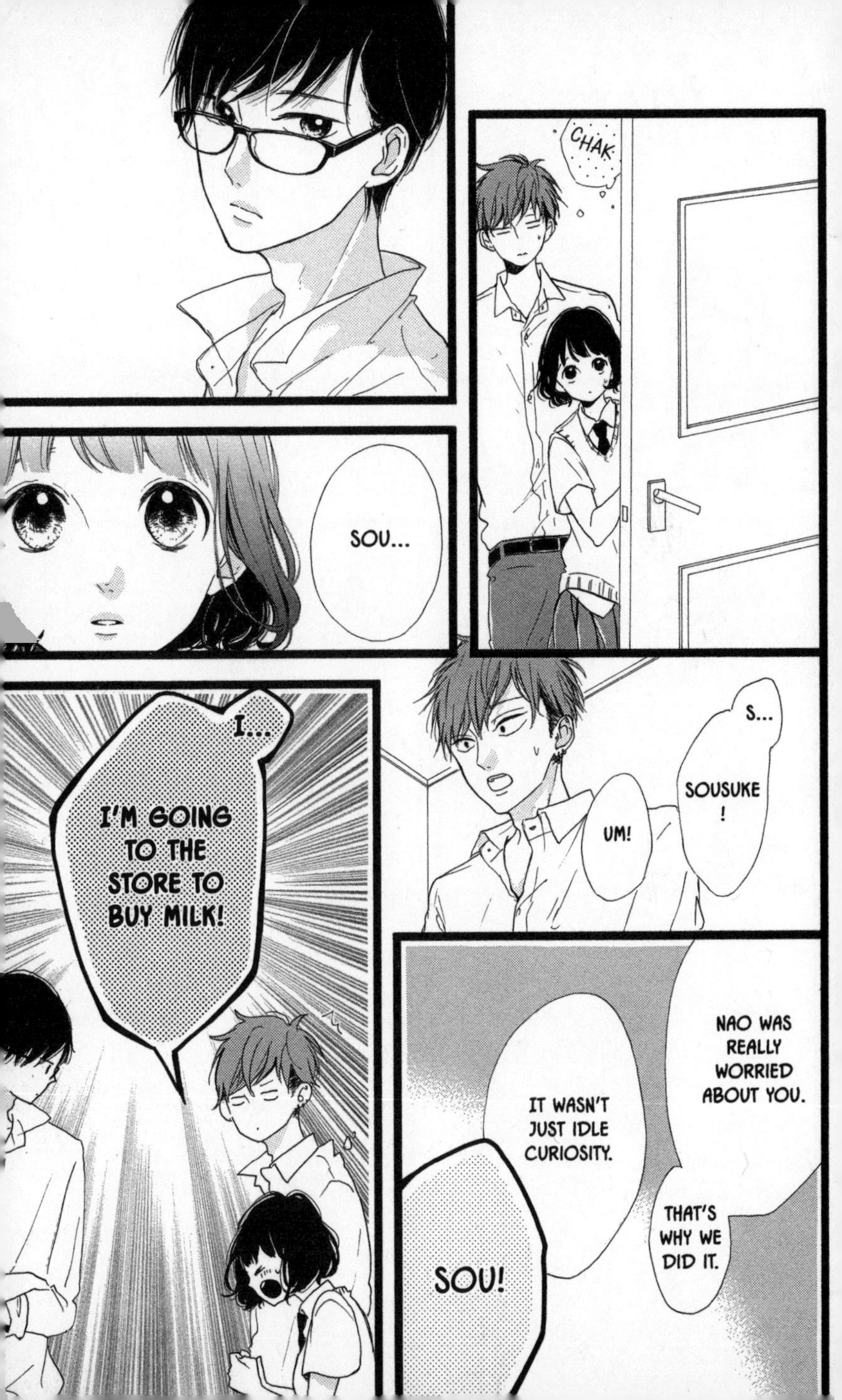
CHAK
SOU...
S...
SOUSUKE!
UM!
NAO WAS REALLY WORRIED ABOUT YOU.
IT WASN'T JUST IDLE CURIOSITY.
THAT'S WHY WE DID IT.
SOU!
I...
I'M GOING TO THE STORE TO BUY MILK!

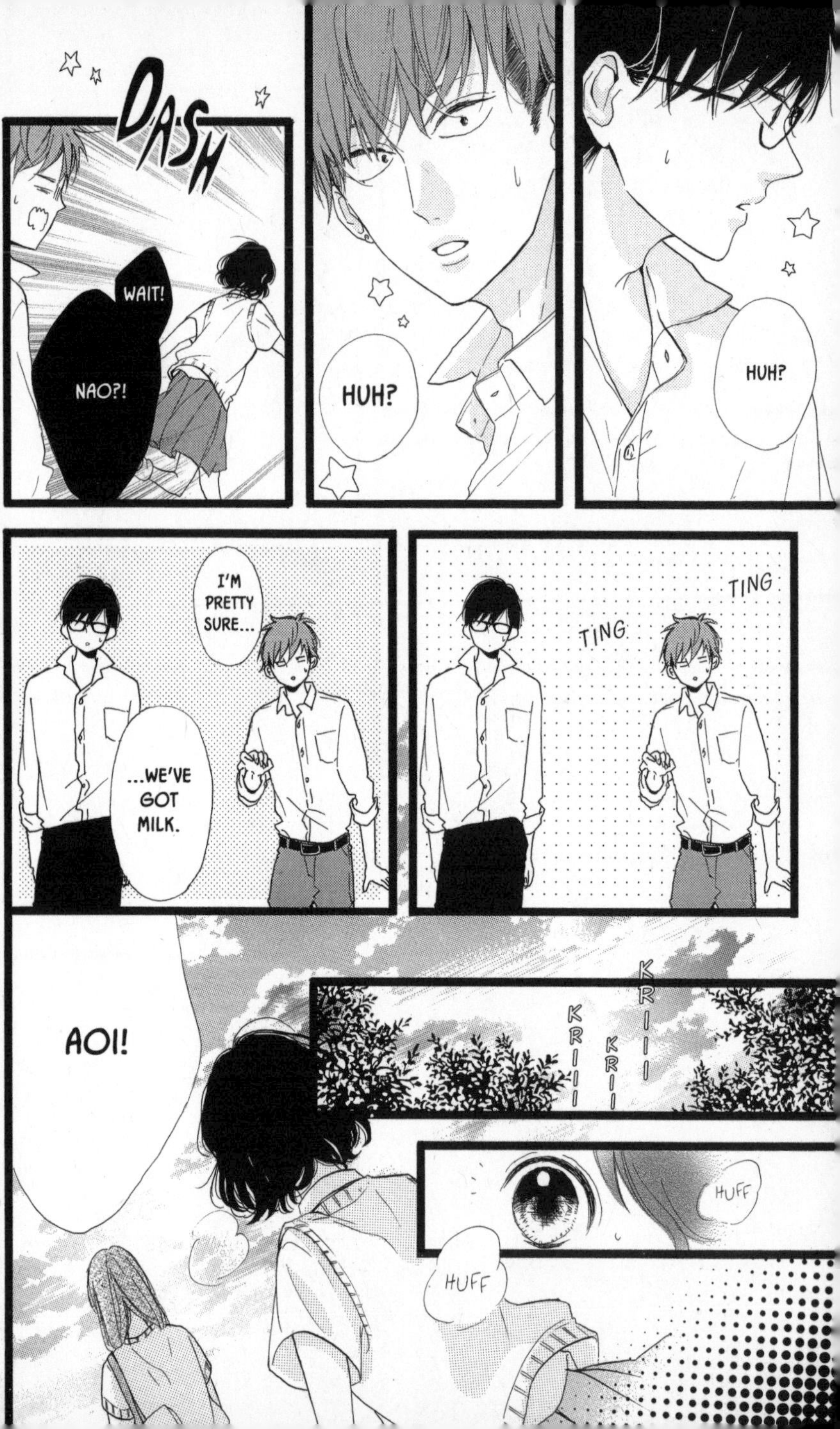
HUH?
HUH?
DASH
WAIT!
NAO?!
TING
TING
I'M PRETTY SURE...
...WE'VE GOT MILK.
KRIII
KRII
KRIII
HUFF
AOI!
HUFF

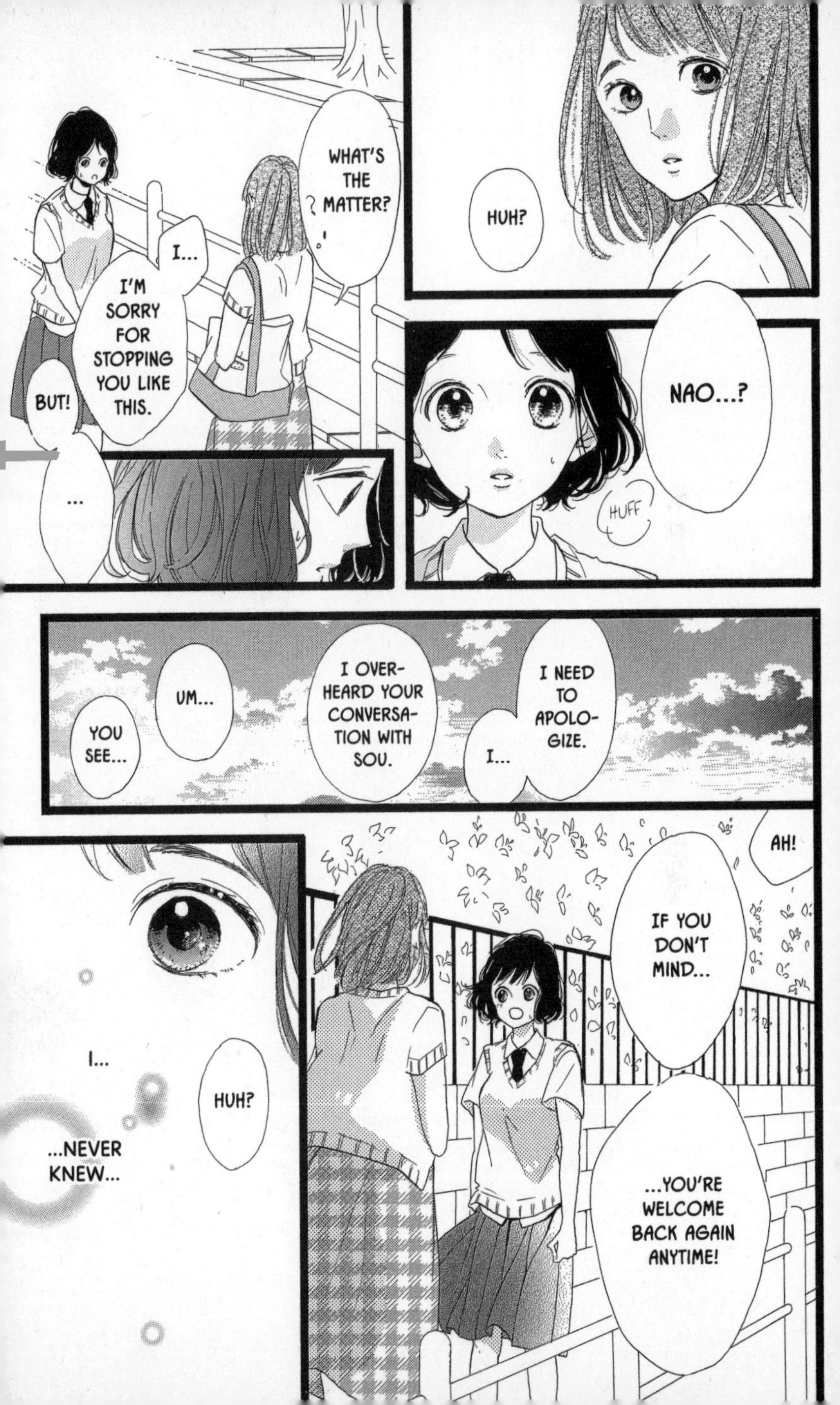
HUH?
NAO...?
HUFF
WHAT'S THE MATTER?
I...
I'M SORRY FOR STOPPING YOU LIKE THIS.
BUT!
...
I NEED TO APOLOGIZE.
I...
I OVER-HEARD YOUR CONVERSA-TION WITH SOU.
UM...
YOU SEE...
AH!
IF YOU DON'T MIND...
...YOU'RE WELCOME BACK AGAIN ANYTIME!
HUH?
I...
...NEVER KNEW...

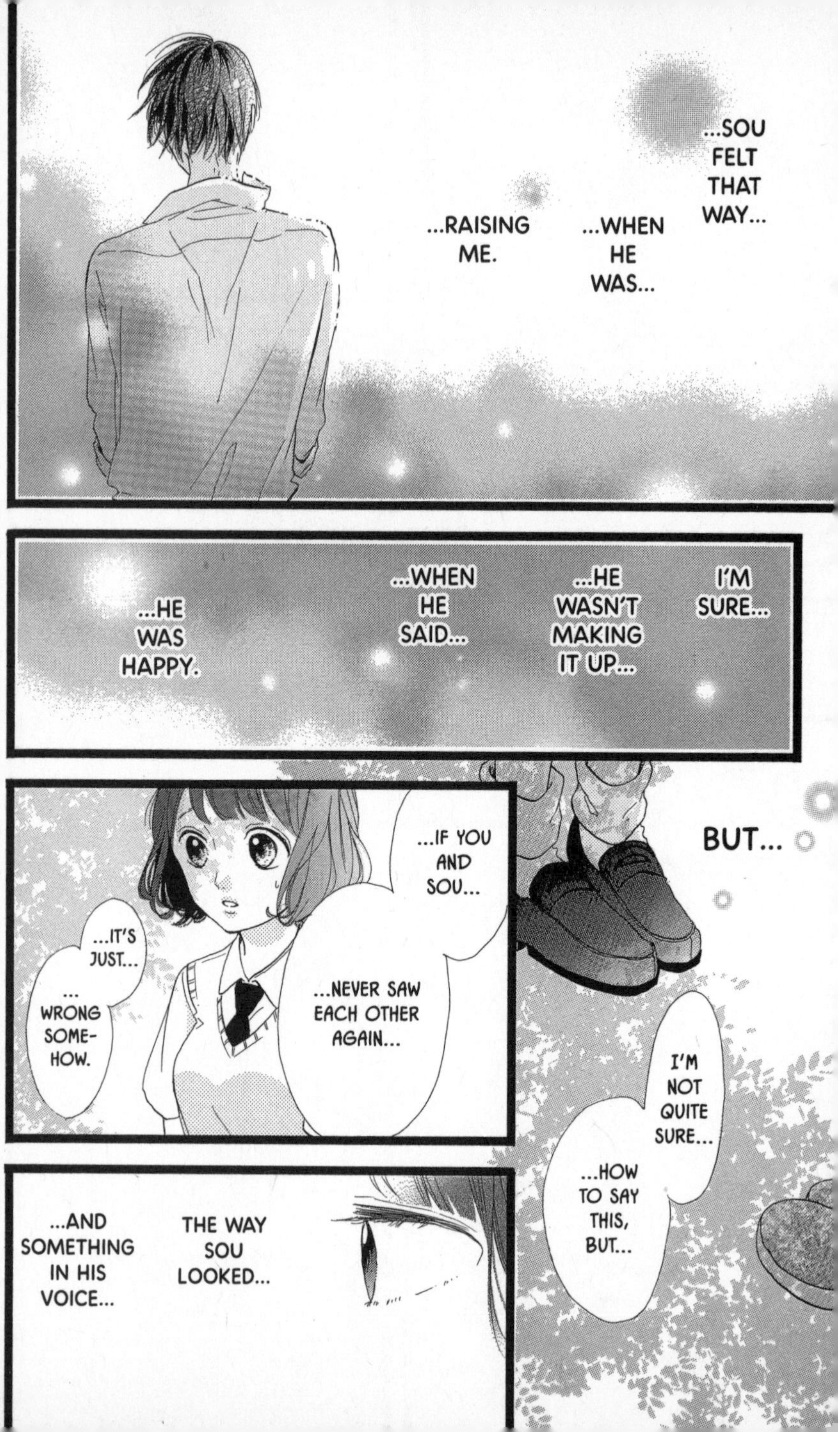
...SOU FELT THAT WAY...
...WHEN HE WAS...
...RAISING ME.
I'M SURE...
...HE WASN'T MAKING IT UP...
...WHEN HE SAID...
...HE WAS HAPPY.
BUT...
I'M NOT QUITE SURE...
...HOW TO SAY THIS, BUT...
...IF YOU AND SOU...
...NEVER SAW EACH OTHER AGAIN...
...IT'S JUST... ...WRONG SOME-HOW.
THE WAY SOU LOOKED...
...AND SOMETHING IN HIS VOICE...

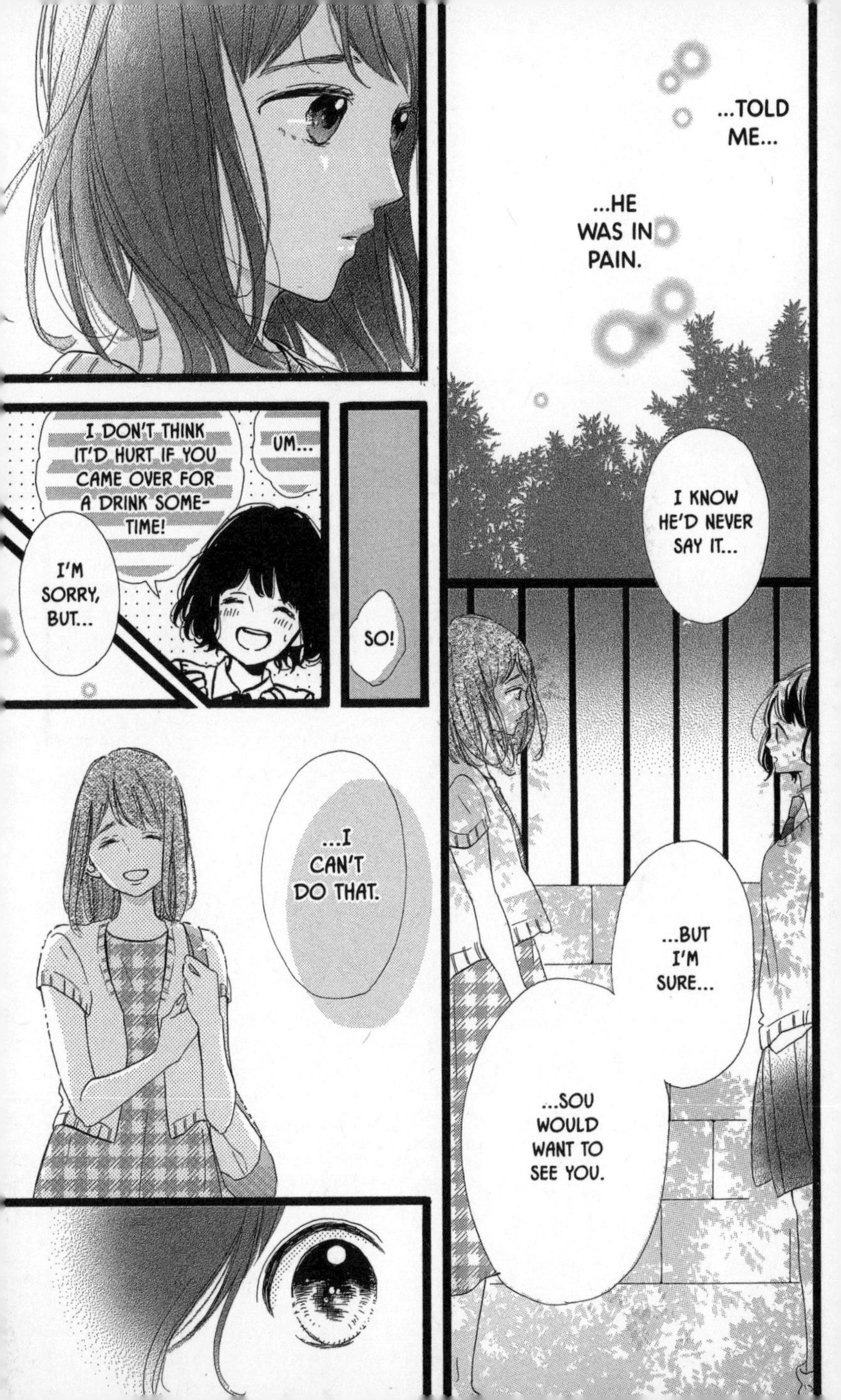
...TOLD ME...
...HE WAS IN PAIN.
I KNOW HE'D NEVER SAY IT...
...BUT I'M SURE...
...SOU WOULD WANT TO SEE YOU.
SO!
UM...
I DON'T THINK IT'D HURT IF YOU CAME OVER FOR A DRINK SOME-TIME!
I'M SORRY, BUT...
...I CAN'T DO THAT.

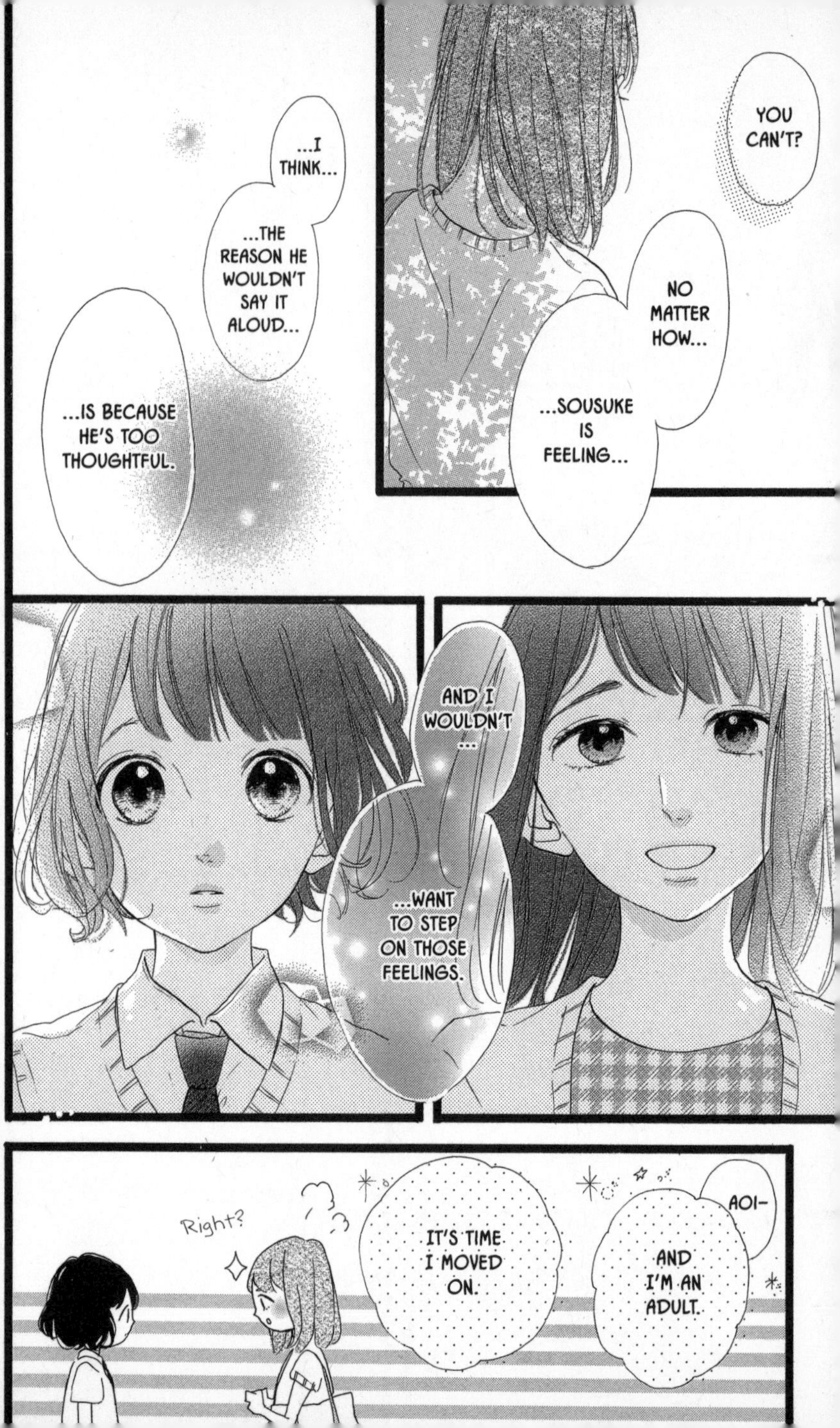
YOU CAN'T?
NO MATTER HOW...
...SOUSUKE IS FEELING...
...I THINK...
...THE REASON HE WOULDN'T SAY IT ALOUD...
...IS BECAUSE HE'S TOO THOUGHTFUL.
AND I WOULDN'T ...
...WANT TO STEP ON THOSE FEELINGS.
AOI-
AND I'M AN ADULT.
IT'S TIME I MOVED ON.
Right?

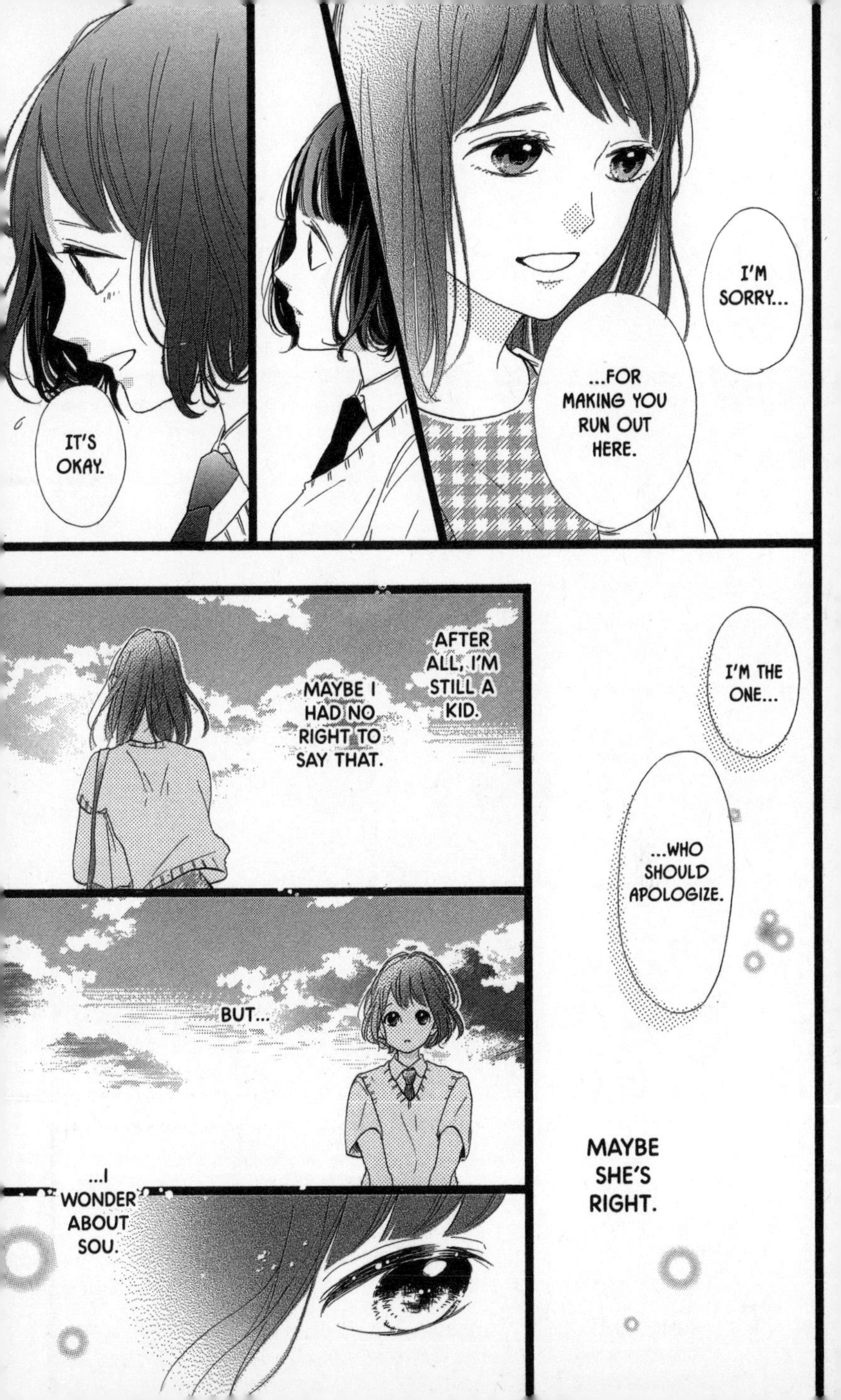

I'M SORRY...
...FOR MAKING YOU RUN OUT HERE.
IT'S OKAY.
I'M THE ONE...
...WHO SHOULD APOLOGIZE.
MAYBE SHE'S RIGHT.
AFTER ALL, I'M STILL A KID.
MAYBE I HAD NO RIGHT TO SAY THAT.
BUT...
...I WONDER ABOUT SOU.

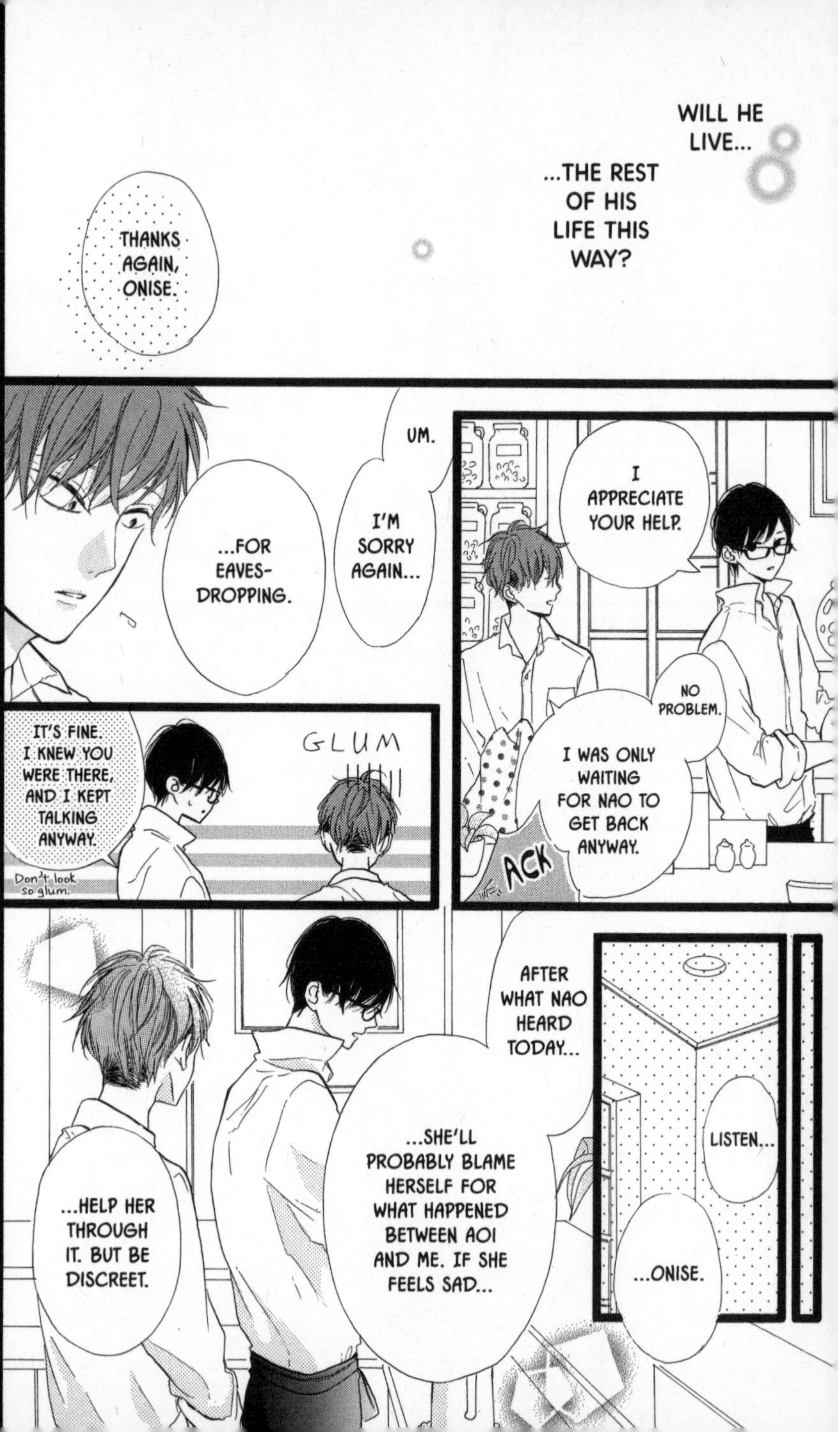
WILL HE LIVE...
...THE REST OF HIS LIFE THIS WAY?
THANKS AGAIN, ONISE.
I APPRECIATE YOUR HELP.
NO PROBLEM.
I WAS ONLY WAITING FOR NAO TO GET BACK ANYWAY.
ACK
UM.
I'M SORRY AGAIN...
...FOR EAVES-DROPPING.
GLUM
IT'S FINE. I KNEW YOU WERE THERE, AND I KEPT TALKING ANYWAY.
Don't look so glum.
LISTEN...
...ONISE.
AFTER WHAT NAO HEARD TODAY...
...SHE'LL PROBABLY BLAME HERSELF FOR WHAT HAPPENED BETWEEN AOI AND ME. IF SHE FEELS SAD...
...HELP HER THROUGH IT. BUT BE DISCREET.

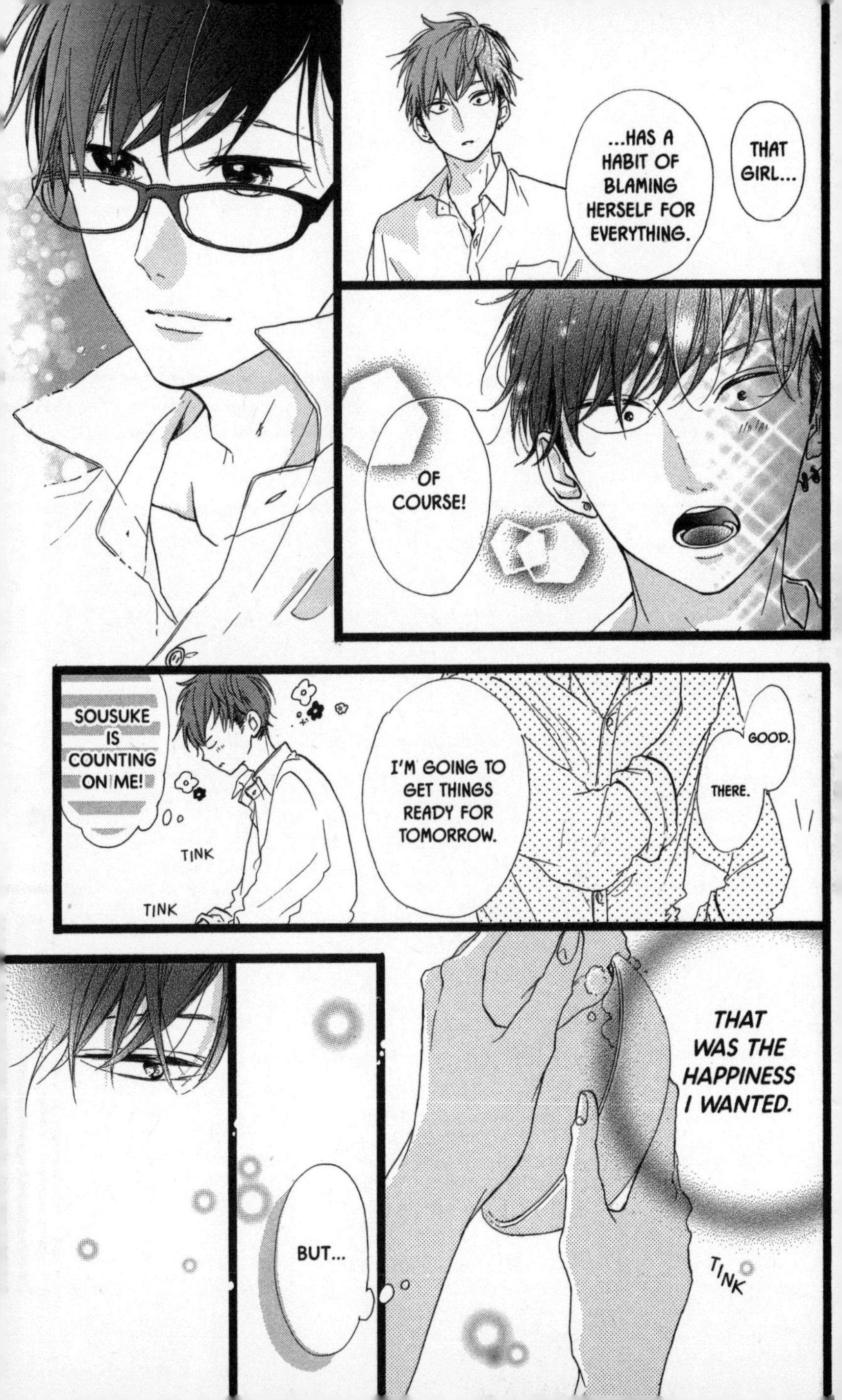
THAT GIRL...
...HAS A HABIT OF BLAMING HERSELF FOR EVERYTHING.
OF COURSE!
GOOD.
THERE.
I'M GOING TO GET THINGS READY FOR TOMORROW.
SOUSUKE IS COUNTING ON ME!
TINK
TINK
THAT WAS THE HAPPINESS I WANTED.
TINK
BUT...

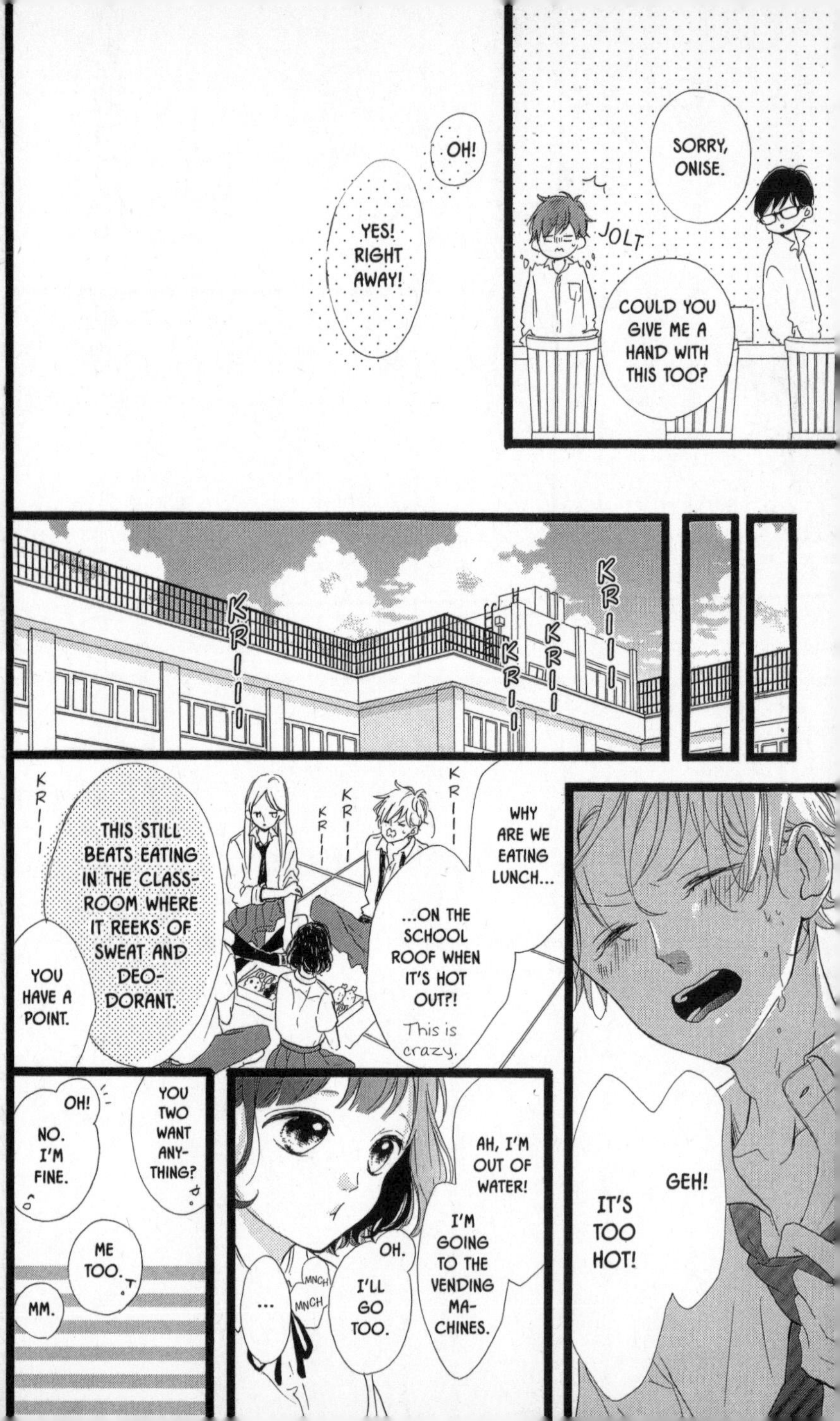
SORRY, ONISE.
JOLT
COULD YOU GIVE ME A HAND WITH THIS TOO?
OH!
YES! RIGHT AWAY!
KRIIII
KRIIII
KRIII
KRIII
KRIII
KRIII
KRIII
WHY ARE WE EATING LUNCH...
...ON THE SCHOOL ROOF WHEN IT'S HOT OUT?!
This is crazy.
THIS STILL BEATS EATING IN THE CLASSROOM WHERE IT REEKS OF SWEAT AND DEODORANT.
YOU HAVE A POINT.
GEH!
IT'S TOO HOT!
AH, I'M OUT OF WATER!
I'M GOING TO THE VENDING MACHINES.
OH.
I'LL GO TOO.
MNCH
MNCH
...
YOU TWO WANT ANYTHING?
OH!
NO. I'M FINE.
ME TOO.
MM.

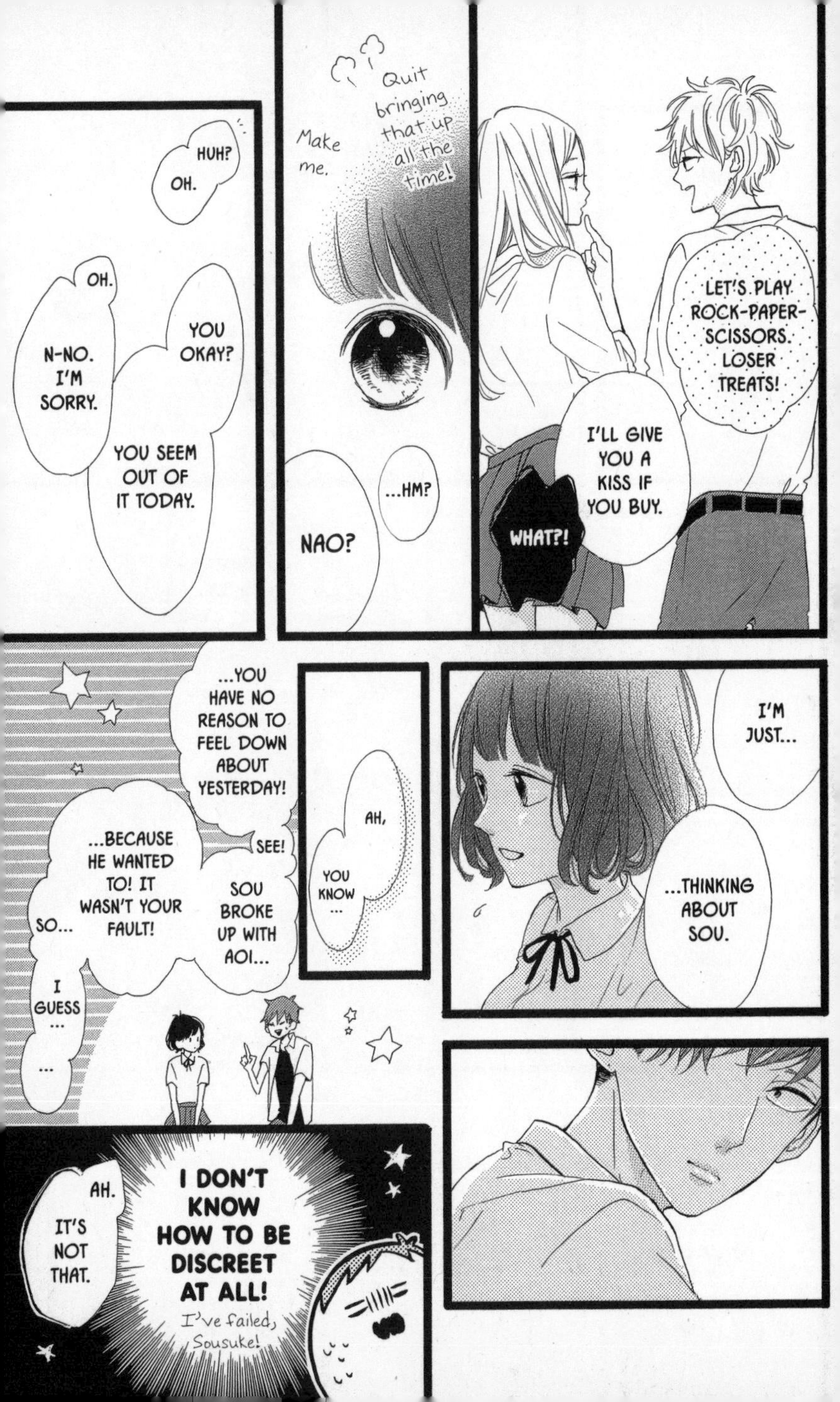

LET'S PLAY ROCK-PAPER-SCISSORS. LOSER TREATS!
I'LL GIVE YOU A KISS IF YOU BUY.
WHAT?!
Quit bringing that up all the time!
Make me.
...HM?
NAO?
HUH? OH.
YOU OKAY?
YOU SEEM OUT OF IT TODAY.
OH.
N-NO. I'M SORRY.
I'M JUST...
...THINKING ABOUT SOU.
AH, YOU KNOW ...
...YOU HAVE NO REASON TO FEEL DOWN ABOUT YESTERDAY!
SEE! SOU BROKE UP WITH AOI...
...BECAUSE HE WANTED TO! IT WASN'T YOUR FAULT!
SO...
I GUESS ...
...
I DON'T KNOW HOW TO BE DISCREET AT ALL!
I've failed, Sousuke!
AH.
IT'S NOT THAT.

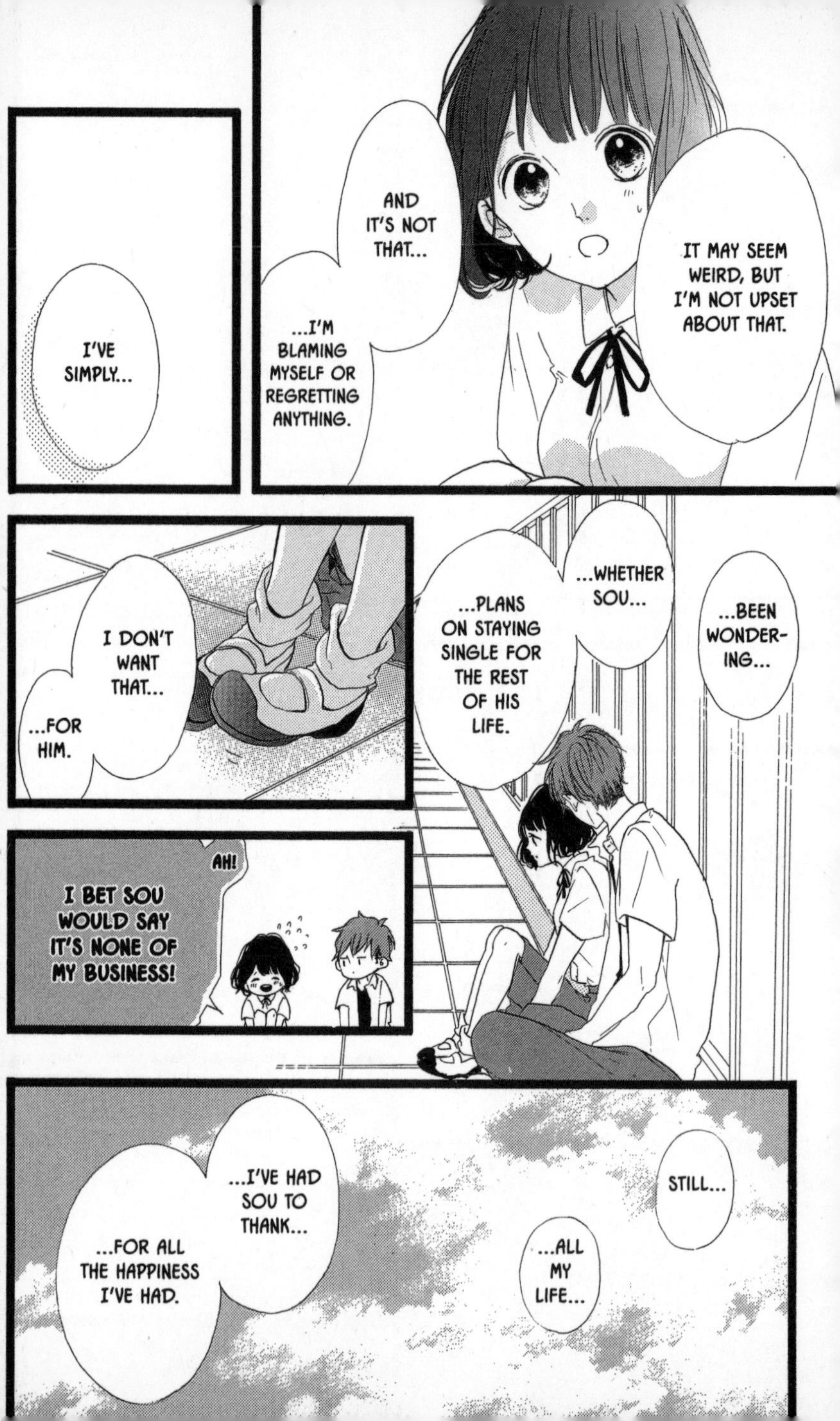
IT MAY SEEM WEIRD, BUT I'M NOT UPSET ABOUT THAT.
AND IT'S NOT THAT...
...I'M BLAMING MYSELF OR REGRETTING ANYTHING.
I'VE SIMPLY...
...BEEN WONDERING...
...WHETHER SOU...
...PLANS ON STAYING SINGLE FOR THE REST OF HIS LIFE.
I DON'T WANT THAT...
...FOR HIM.
AH!
I BET SOU WOULD SAY IT'S NONE OF MY BUSINESS!
STILL...
...ALL MY LIFE...
...I'VE HAD SOU TO THANK...
...FOR ALL THE HAPPINESS I'VE HAD.

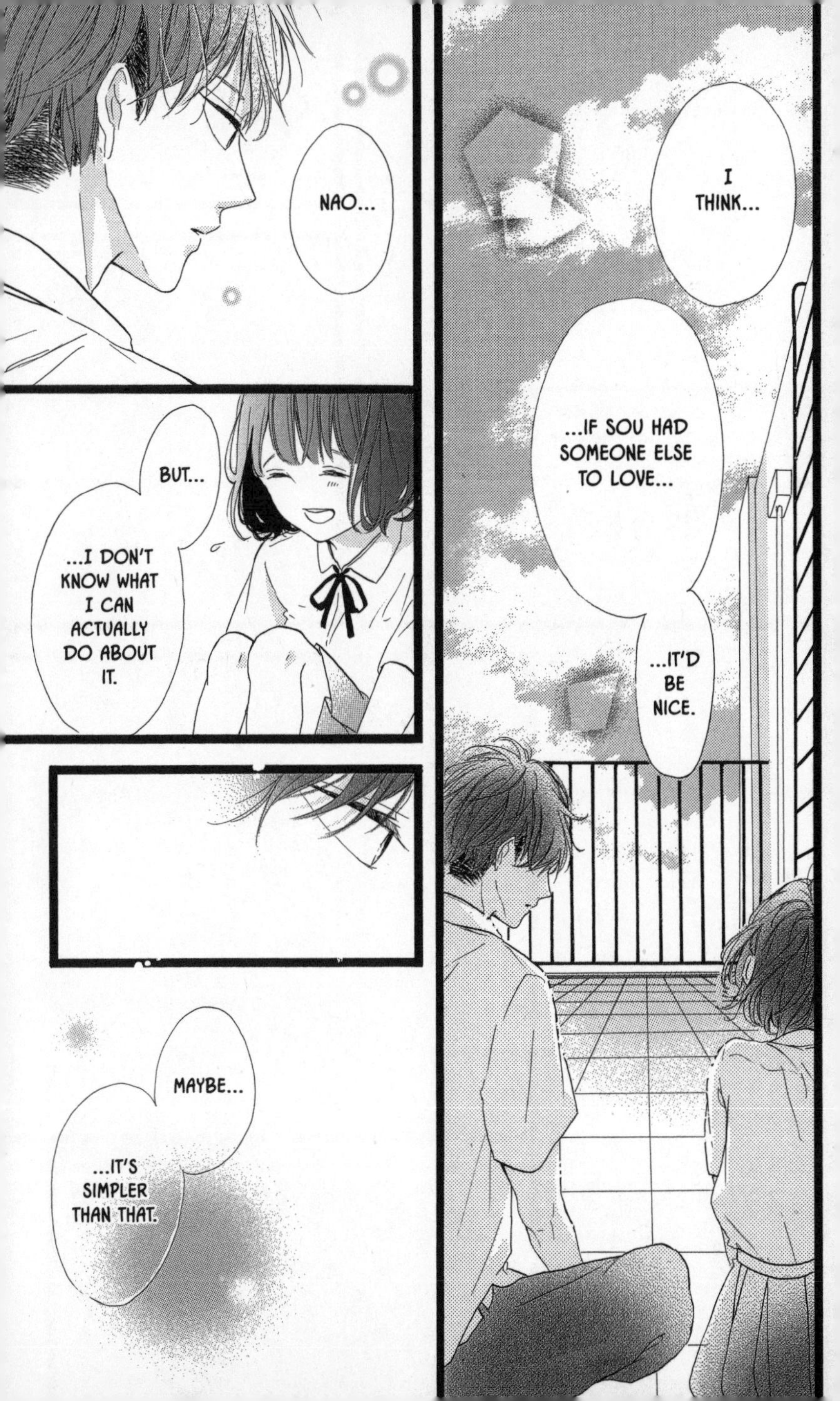
I THINK...
...IF SOU HAD SOMEONE ELSE TO LOVE...
...IT'D BE NICE.
NAO...
BUT...
...I DON'T KNOW WHAT I CAN ACTUALLY DO ABOUT IT.
MAYBE...
...IT'S SIMPLER THAN THAT.

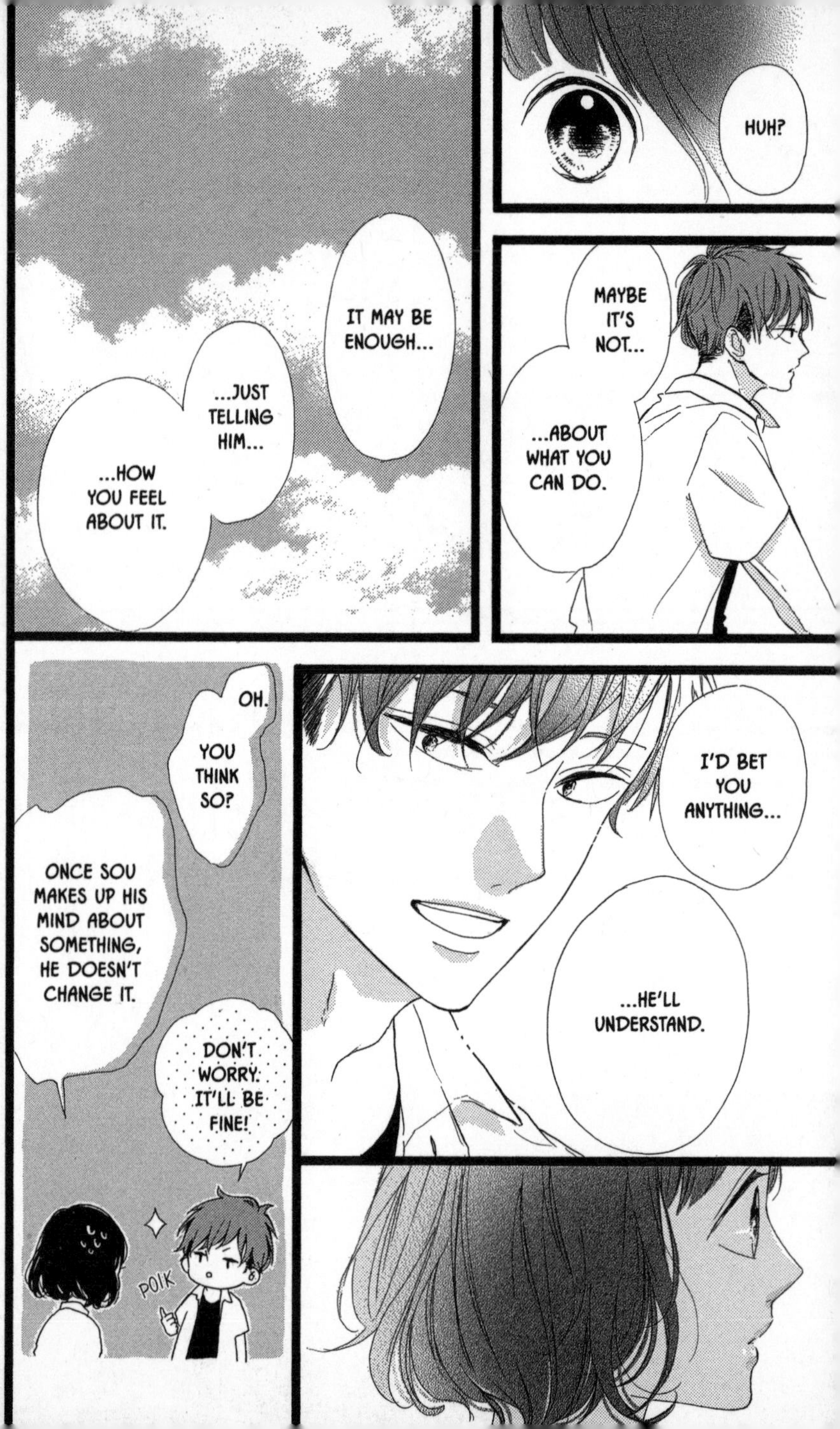
HUH?
MAYBE IT'S NOT...
...ABOUT WHAT YOU CAN DO.
IT MAY BE ENOUGH...
...JUST TELLING HIM...
...HOW YOU FEEL ABOUT IT.
I'D BET YOU ANYTHING...
...HE'LL UNDERSTAND.
OH.
YOU THINK SO?
ONCE SOU MAKES UP HIS MIND ABOUT SOMETHING, HE DOESN'T CHANGE IT.
DON'T WORRY. IT'LL BE FINE!
POIK

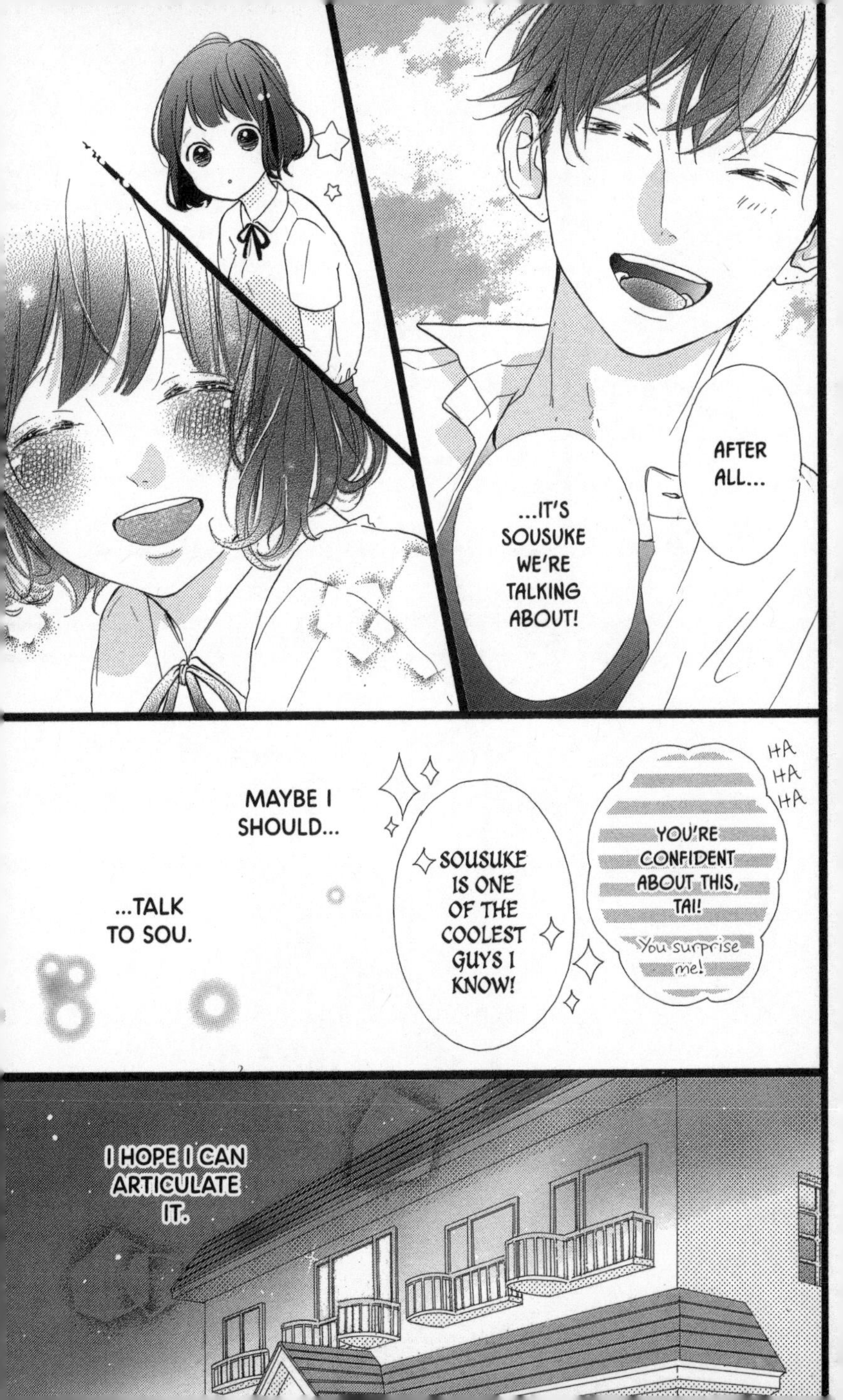
AFTER ALL...
...IT'S SOUSUKE WE'RE TALKING ABOUT!
HA HA HA
YOU'RE CONFIDENT ABOUT THIS, TAI!
You surprise me!
SOUSUKE IS ONE OF THE COOLEST GUYS I KNOW!
MAYBE I SHOULD...
...TALK TO SOU.
I HOPE I CAN ARTICULATE IT.

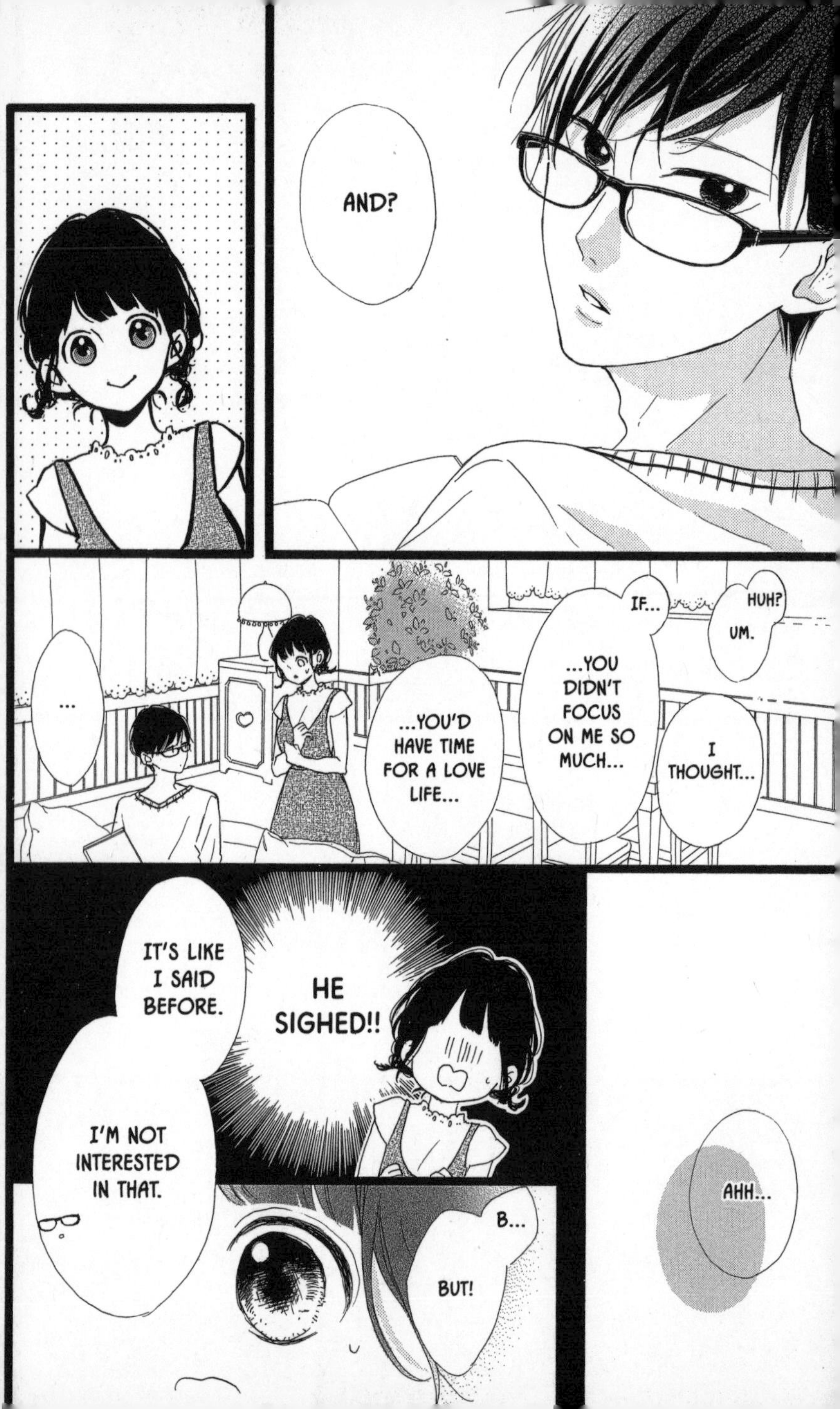
AND?
HUH?
UM.
I THOUGHT...
IF...
...YOU DIDN'T FOCUS ON ME SO MUCH...
...YOU'D HAVE TIME FOR A LOVE LIFE...
...
AHH...
HE SIGHED!!
IT'S LIKE I SAID BEFORE.
I'M NOT INTERESTED IN THAT.
B...
BUT!

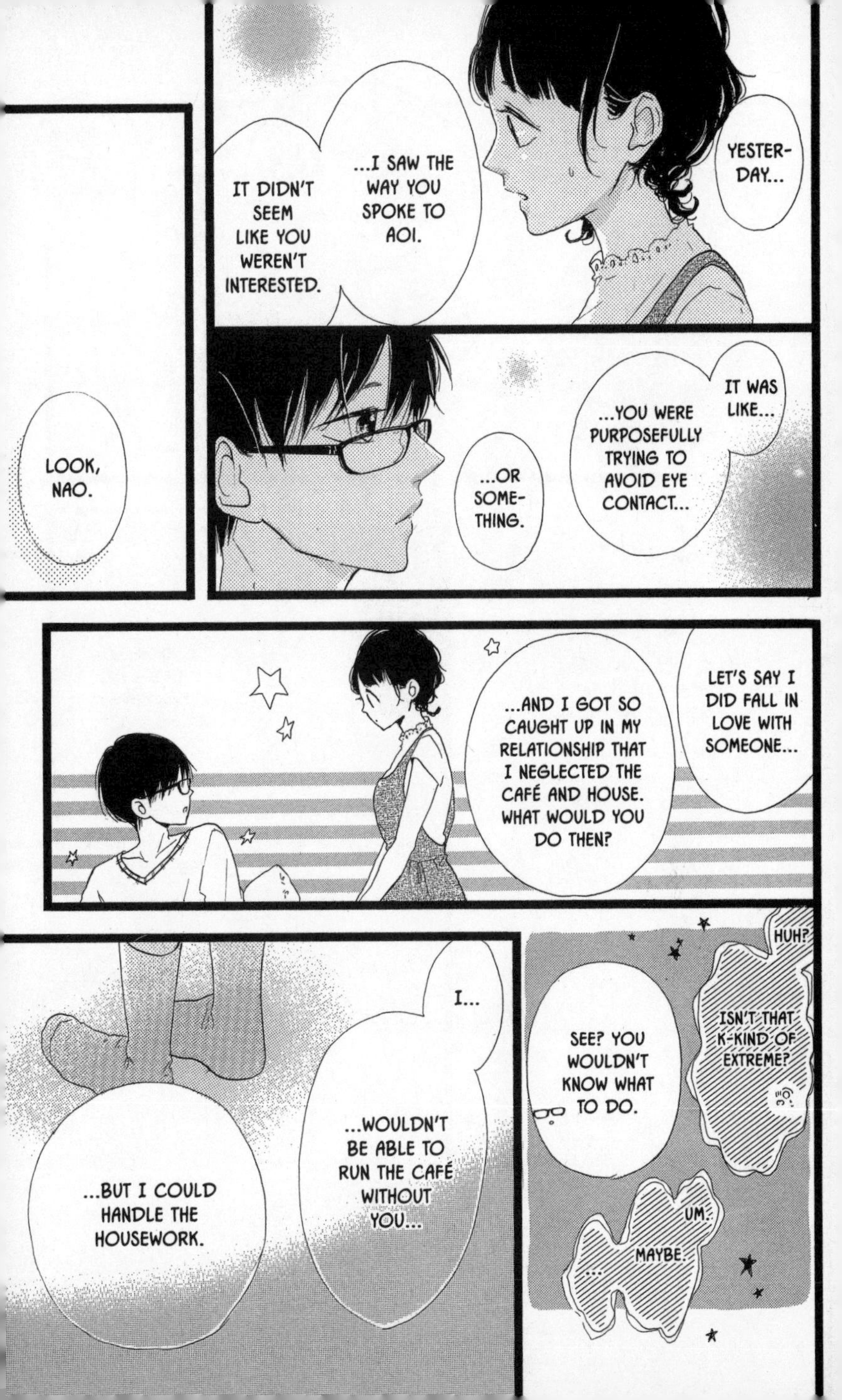
YESTER-DAY...
...I SAW THE WAY YOU SPOKE TO AOI.
IT DIDN'T SEEM LIKE YOU WEREN'T INTERESTED.
IT WAS LIKE...
...YOU WERE PURPOSEFULLY TRYING TO AVOID EYE CONTACT...
...OR SOME-THING.
LOOK, NAO.
LET'S SAY I DID FALL IN LOVE WITH SOMEONE...
...AND I GOT SO CAUGHT UP IN MY RELATIONSHIP THAT I NEGLECTED THE CAFÉ AND HOUSE. WHAT WOULD YOU DO THEN?
HUH?
ISN'T THAT K-KIND OF EXTREME?
SEE? YOU WOULDN'T KNOW WHAT TO DO.
UM.
MAYBE.
...
I...
...WOULDN'T BE ABLE TO RUN THE CAFÉ WITHOUT YOU...
...BUT I COULD HANDLE THE HOUSEWORK.

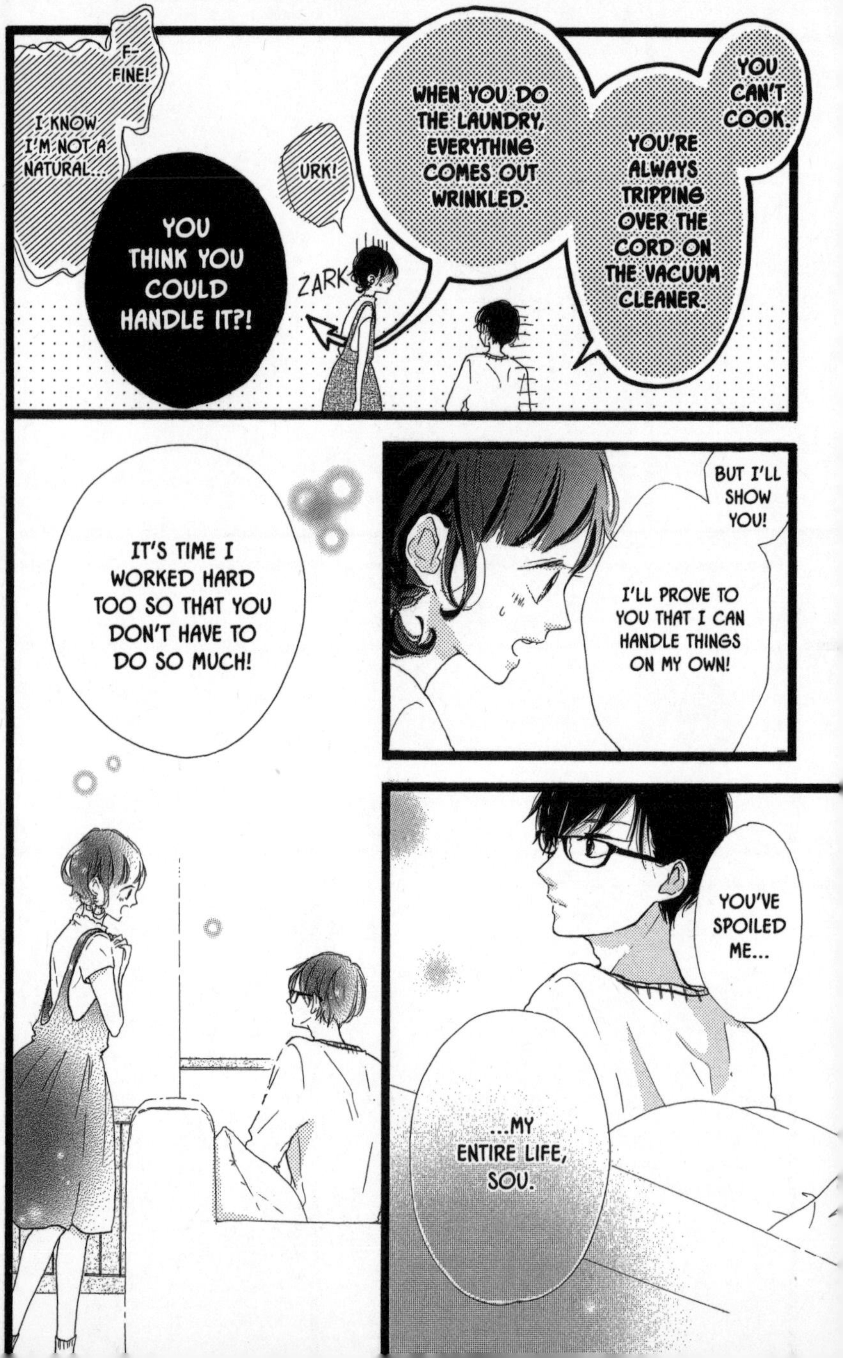
YOU CAN'T COOK.
YOU'RE ALWAYS TRIPPING OVER THE CORD ON THE VACUUM CLEANER.
WHEN YOU DO THE LAUNDRY, EVERYTHING COMES OUT WRINKLED.
URK!
ZARK
YOU THINK YOU COULD HANDLE IT?!
F-FINE!
I KNOW I'M NOT A NATURAL...
BUT I'LL SHOW YOU!
I'LL PROVE TO YOU THAT I CAN HANDLE THINGS ON MY OWN!
YOU'VE SPOILED ME...
...MY ENTIRE LIFE, SOU.
IT'S TIME I WORKED HARD TOO SO THAT YOU DON'T HAVE TO DO SO MUCH!

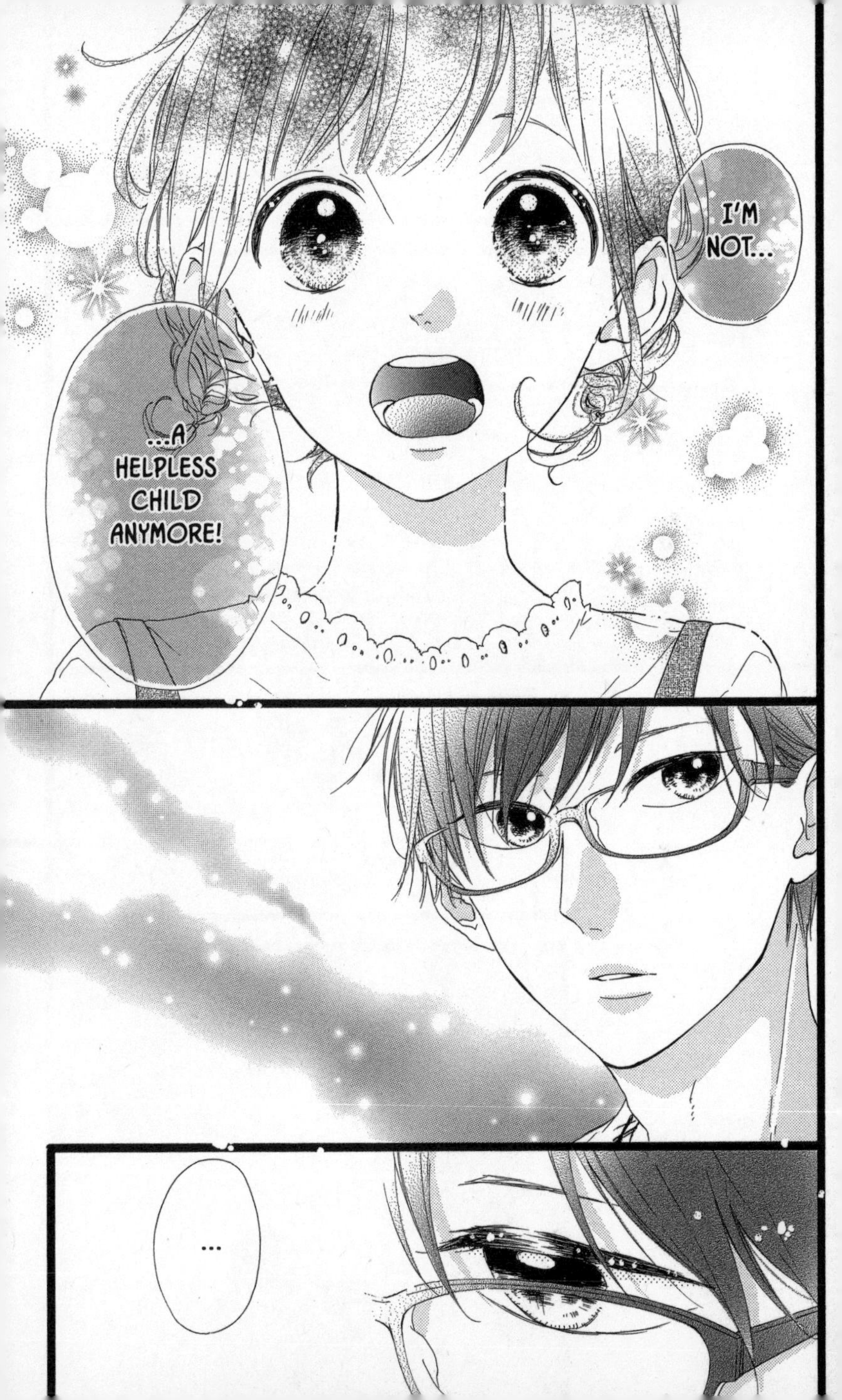
I'M NOT...
...A HELPLESS CHILD ANYMORE!
...

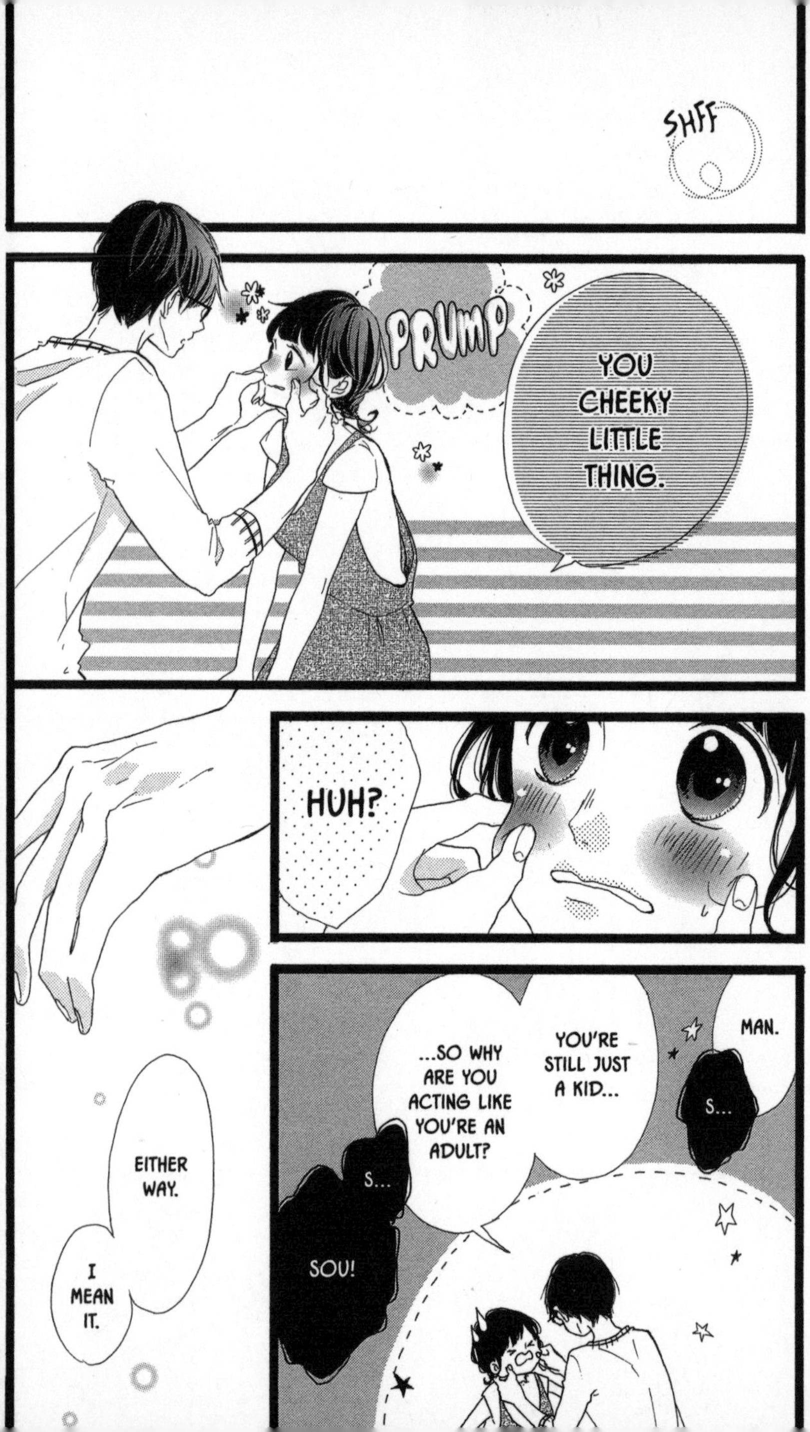
SHFF
PRUMP
YOU CHEEKY LITTLE THING.
HUH?
MAN.
S...
YOU'RE STILL JUST A KID...
...SO WHY ARE YOU ACTING LIKE YOU'RE AN ADULT?
S...
SOU!
EITHER WAY.
I MEAN IT.

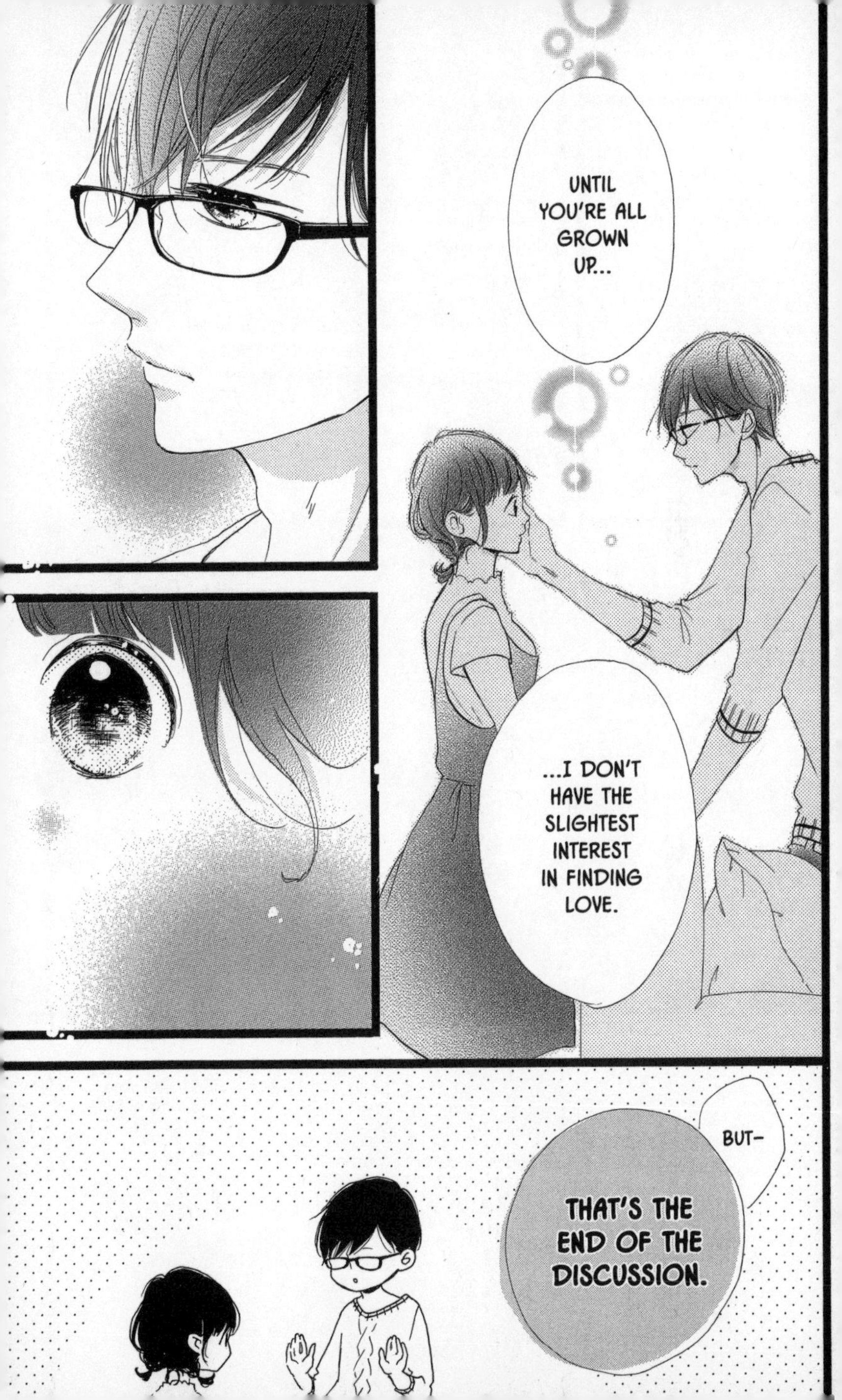
UNTIL YOU'RE ALL GROWN UP...
...I DON'T HAVE THE SLIGHTEST INTEREST IN FINDING LOVE.
BUT-
THAT'S THE END OF THE DISCUSSION.

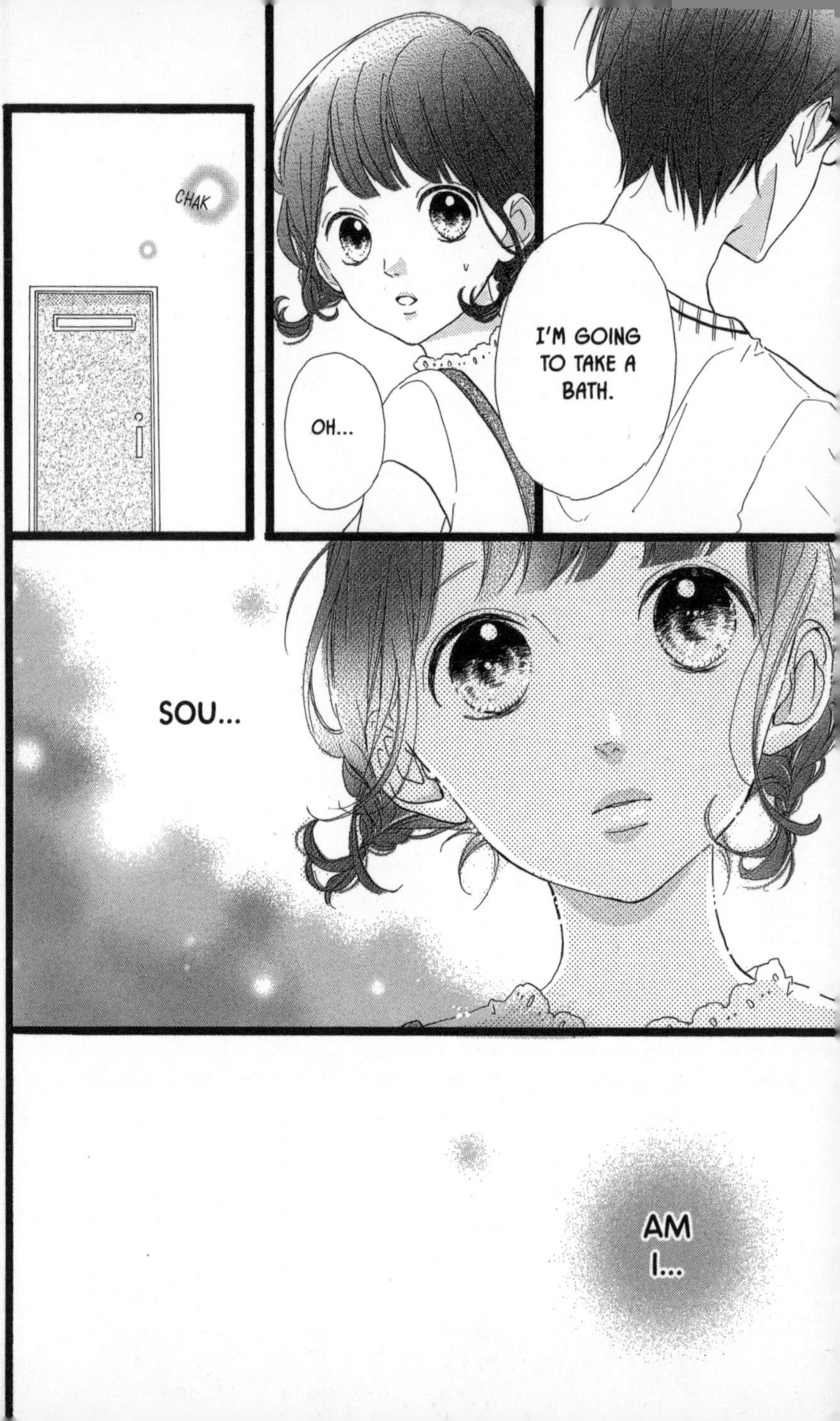
I'M GOING TO TAKE A BATH.
OH...
CHAK
SOU...
AM I...

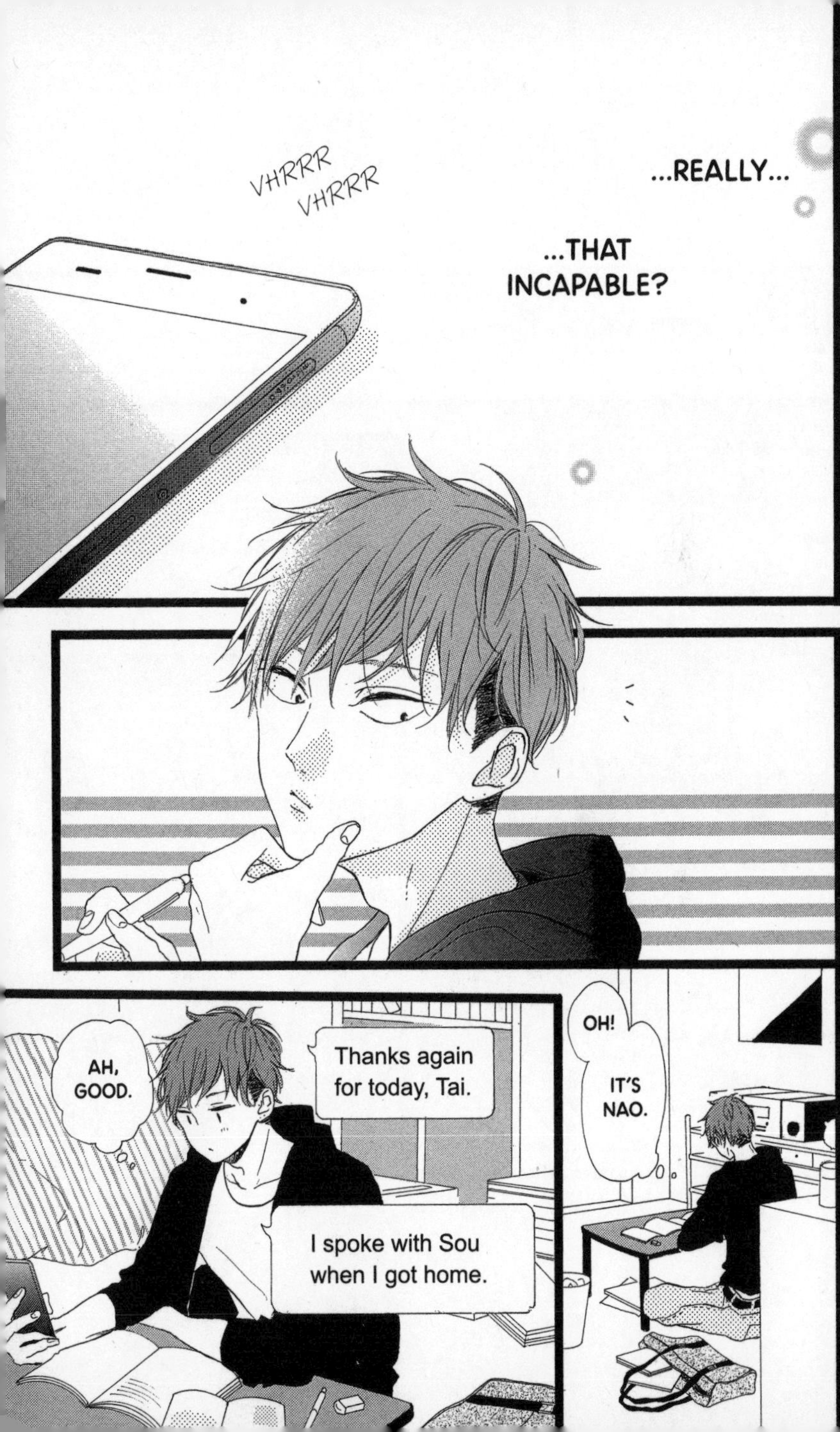
...REALLY...
...THAT INCAPABLE?
VHRRR VHRRR
OH!
IT'S NAO.
Thanks again for today, Tai.
AH, GOOD.
I spoke with Sou when I got home.

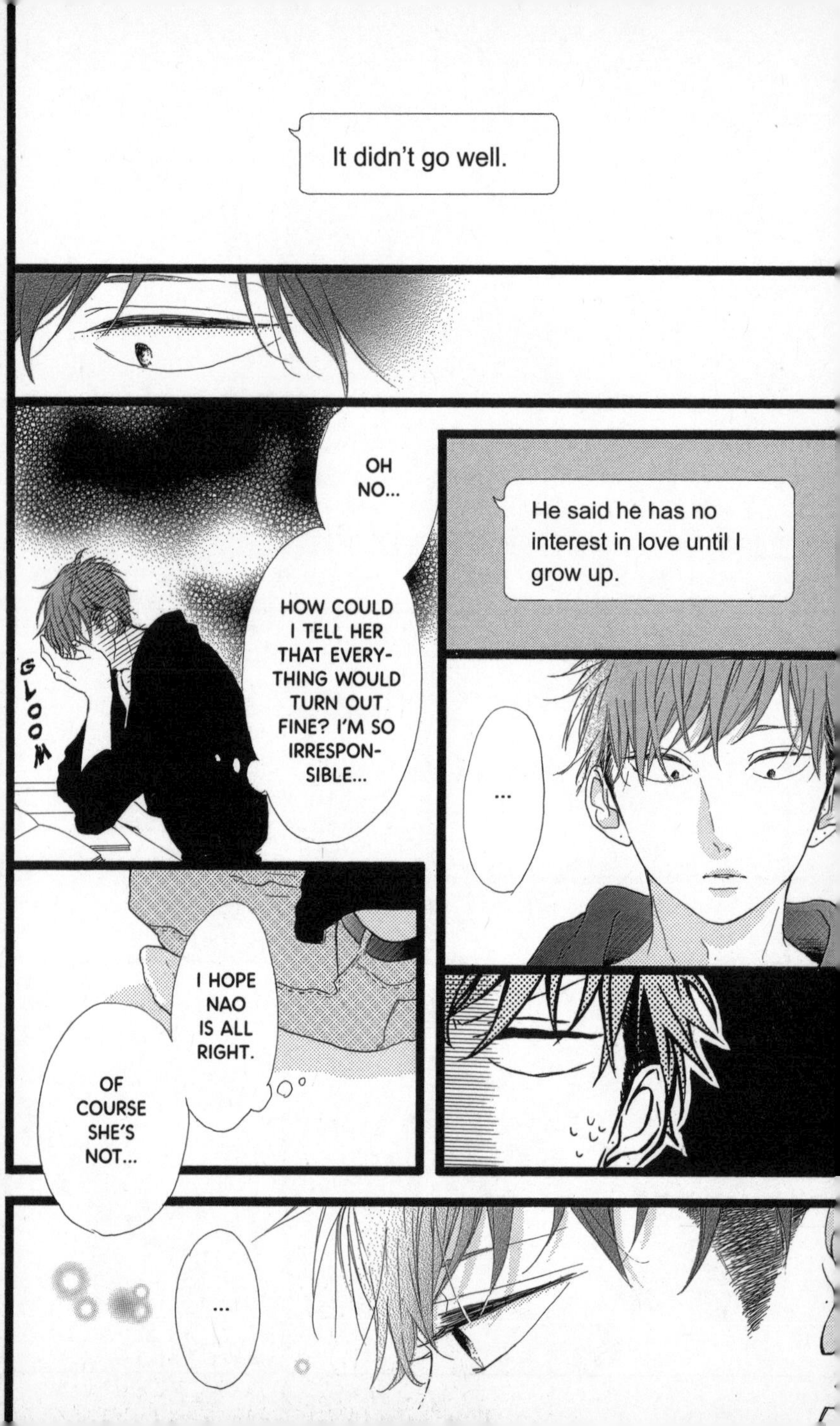

It didn't go well.
He said he has no interest in love until I grow up.
...
OH NO...
HOW COULD I TELL HER THAT EVERY-THING WOULD TURN OUT FINE? I'M SO IRRESPON-SIBLE...
GLOOM
I HOPE NAO IS ALL RIGHT.
OF COURSE SHE'S NOT...
...

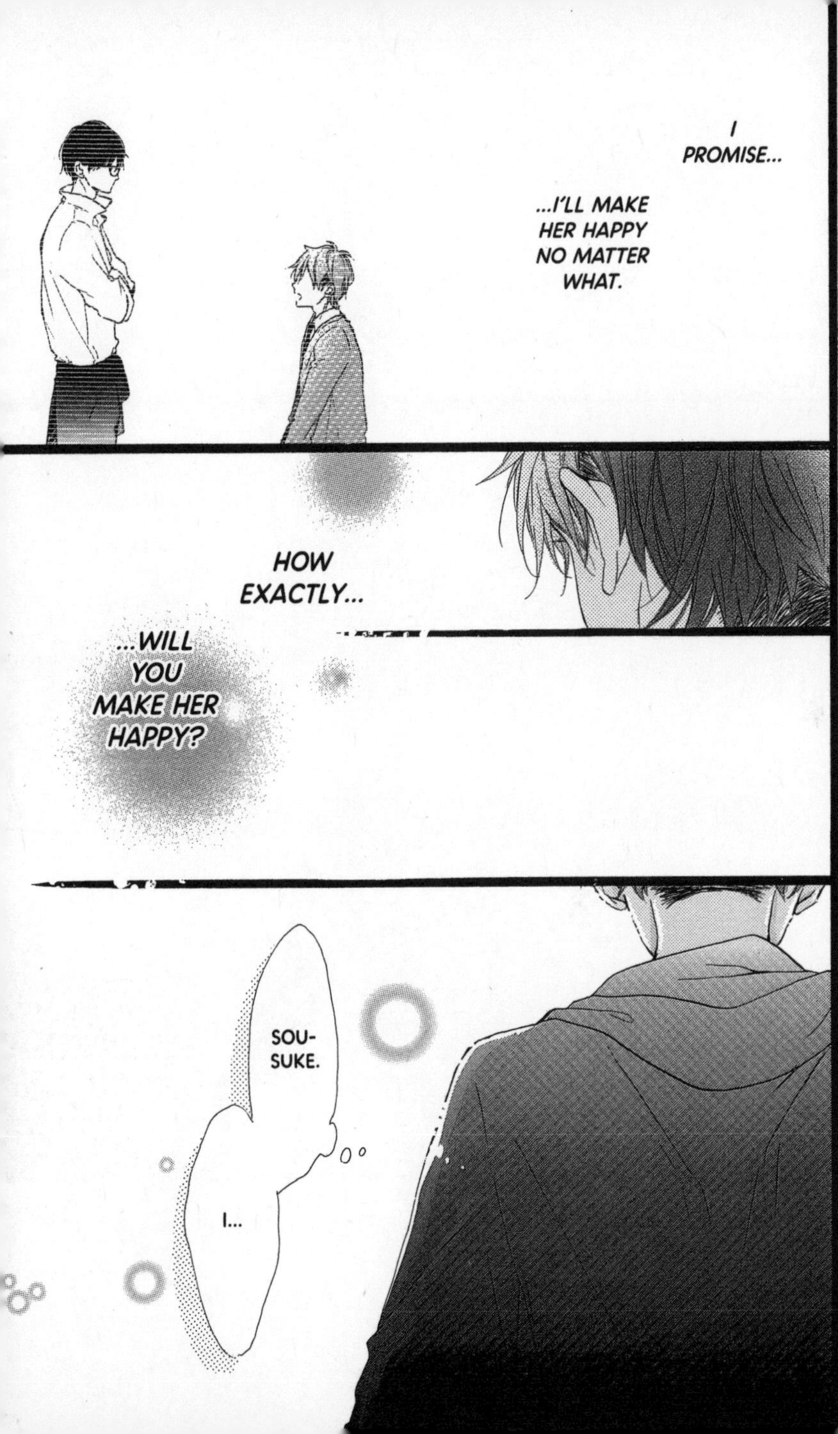
I PROMISE...
...I'LL MAKE HER HAPPY NO MATTER WHAT.
HOW EXACTLY...
...WILL YOU MAKE HER HAPPY?
SOU-SUKE.
I...

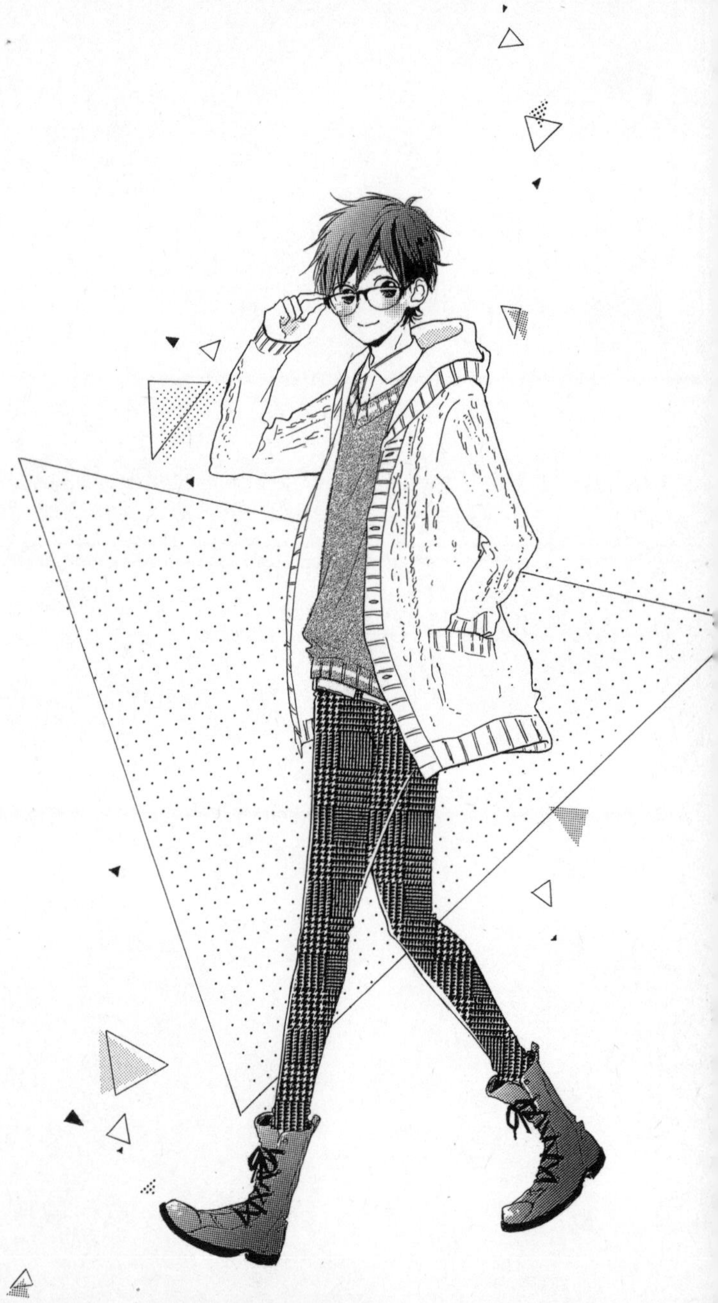

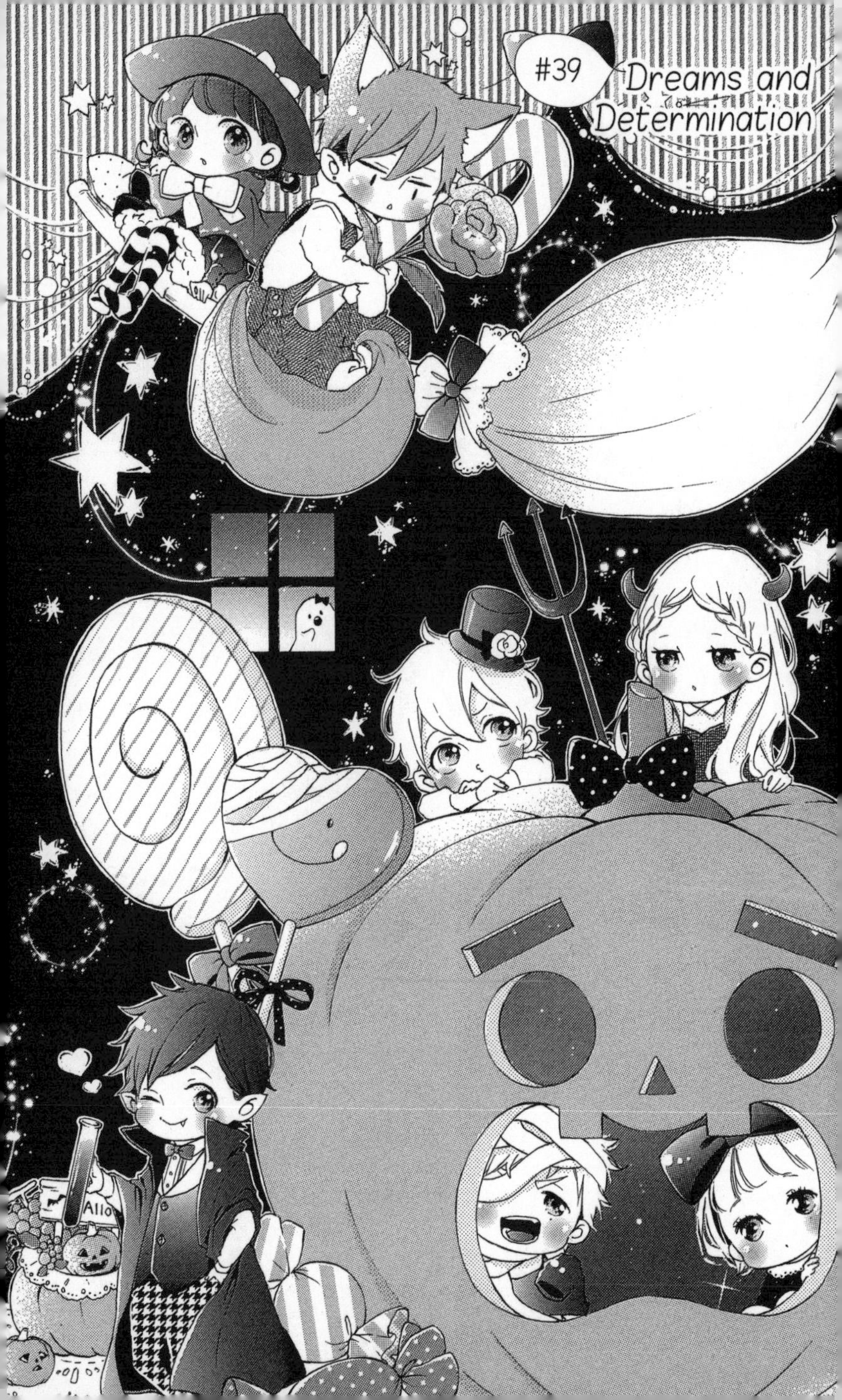
#39
Dreams and Determination

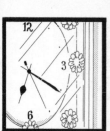

GOOD MORNING, SOU!

Honey
So Sweet

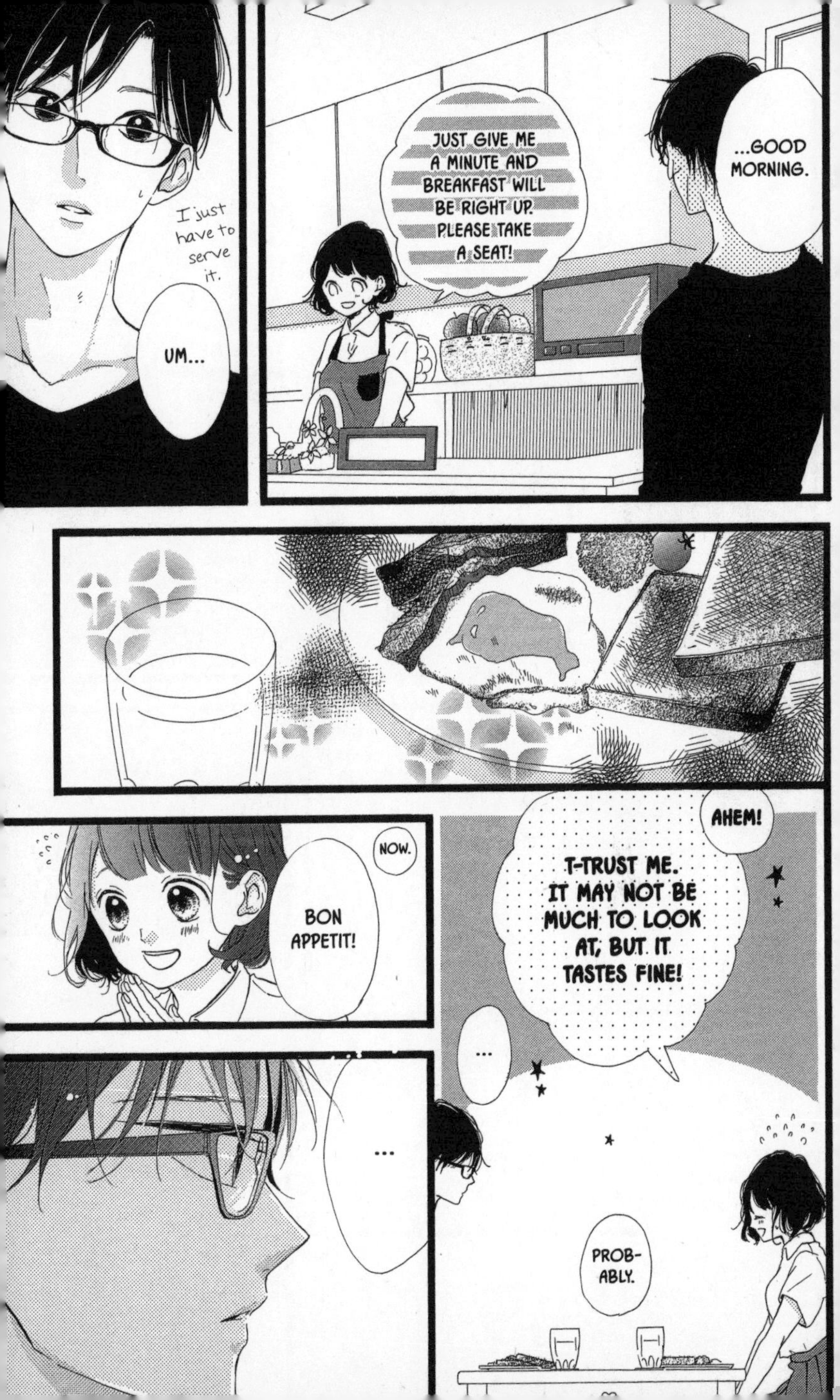
...GOOD MORNING.
JUST GIVE ME A MINUTE AND BREAKFAST WILL BE RIGHT UP. PLEASE TAKE A SEAT!
I just have to serve it.
UM...
AHEM!
T-TRUST ME. IT MAY NOT BE MUCH TO LOOK AT, BUT IT TASTES FINE!
...
PROB-ABLY.
NOW.
BON APPETIT!
...

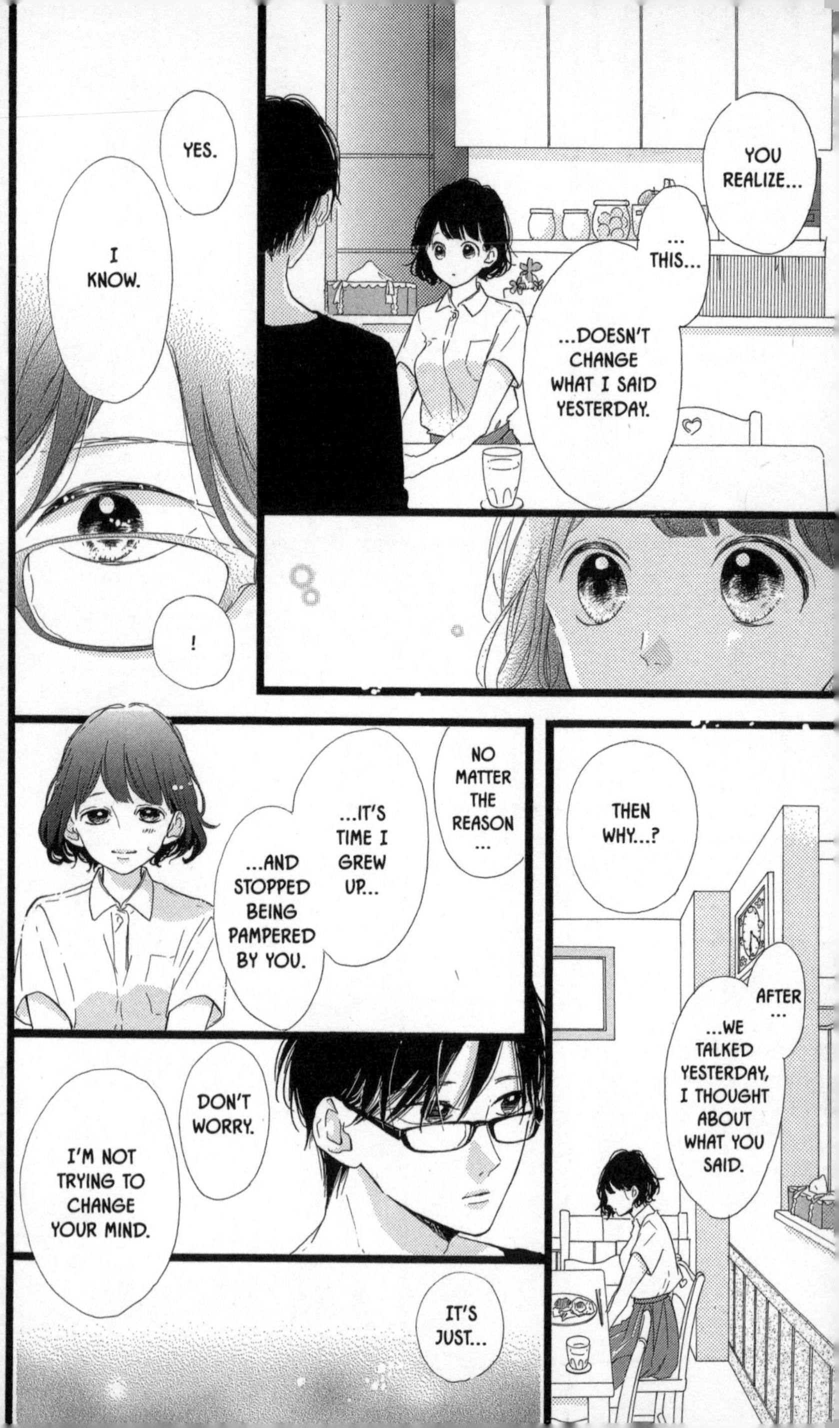
YOU REALIZE...
...THIS...
...DOESN'T CHANGE WHAT I SAID YESTERDAY.
YES.
I KNOW.
!
THEN WHY...?
AFTER...
...WE TALKED YESTERDAY, I THOUGHT ABOUT WHAT YOU SAID.
NO MATTER THE REASON...
...IT'S TIME I GREW UP...
...AND STOPPED BEING PAMPERED BY YOU.
DON'T WORRY.
I'M NOT TRYING TO CHANGE YOUR MIND.
IT'S JUST...

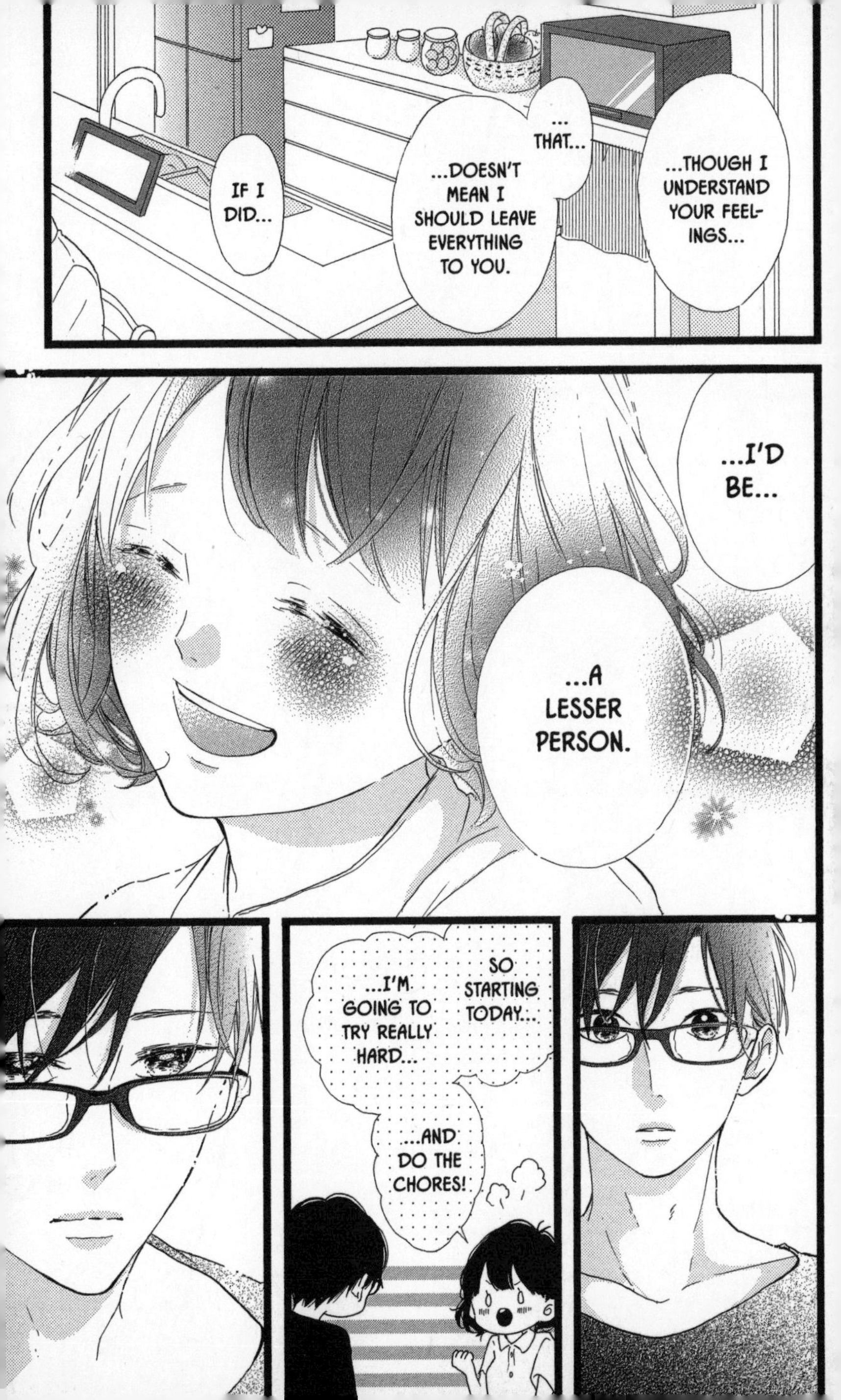
...THOUGH I UNDERSTAND YOUR FEEL-INGS...
...THAT...
...DOESN'T MEAN I SHOULD LEAVE EVERYTHING TO YOU.
IF I DID...
...I'D BE...
...A LESSER PERSON.
SO STARTING TODAY...
...I'M GOING TO TRY REALLY HARD...
...AND DO THE CHORES!

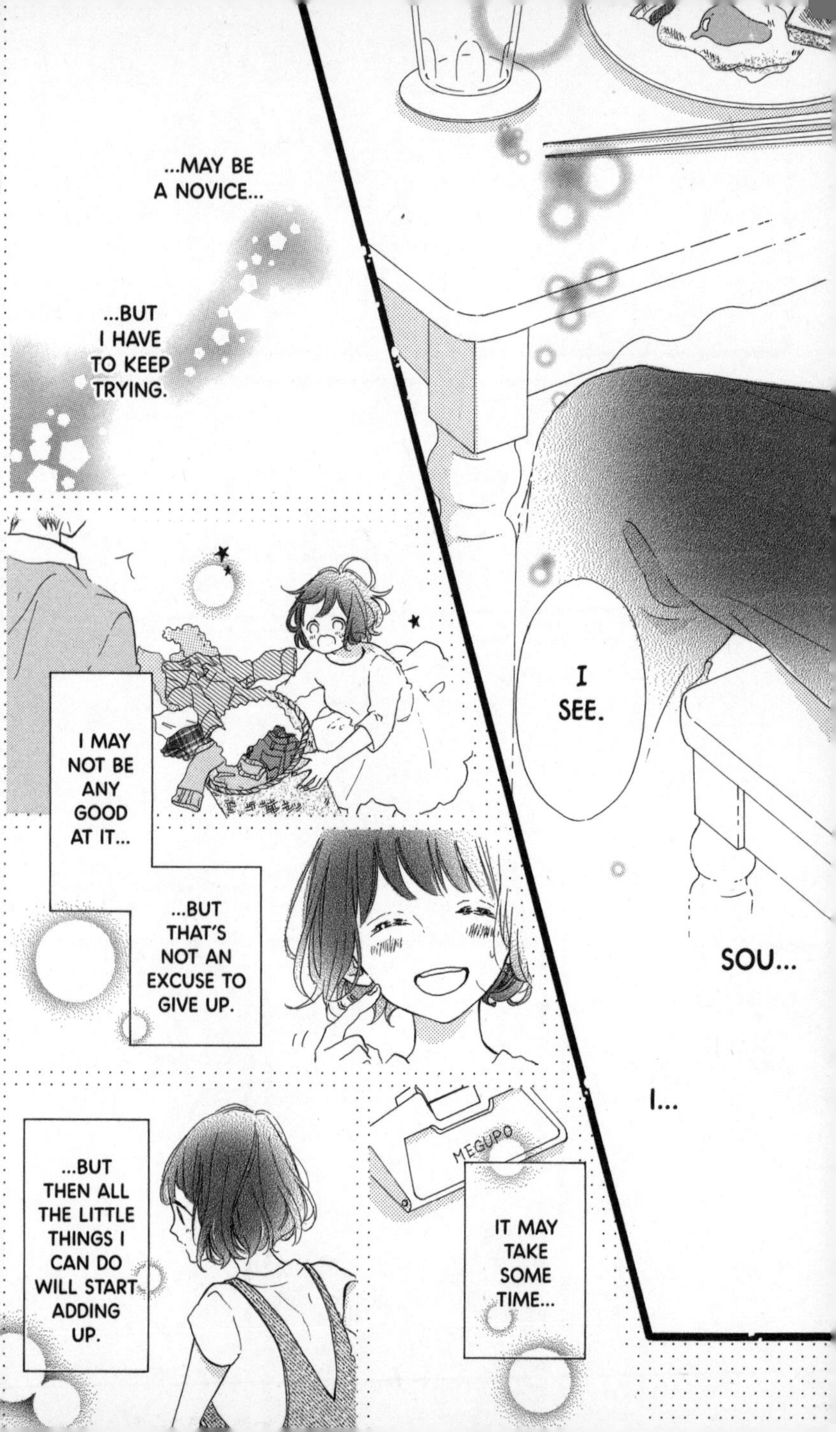
I SEE.
SOU...
I...
...MAY BE A NOVICE...
...BUT I HAVE TO KEEP TRYING.
I MAY NOT BE ANY GOOD AT IT...
...BUT THAT'S NOT AN EXCUSE TO GIVE UP.
MEGUPO
IT MAY TAKE SOME TIME...
...BUT THEN ALL THE LITTLE THINGS I CAN DO WILL START ADDING UP.

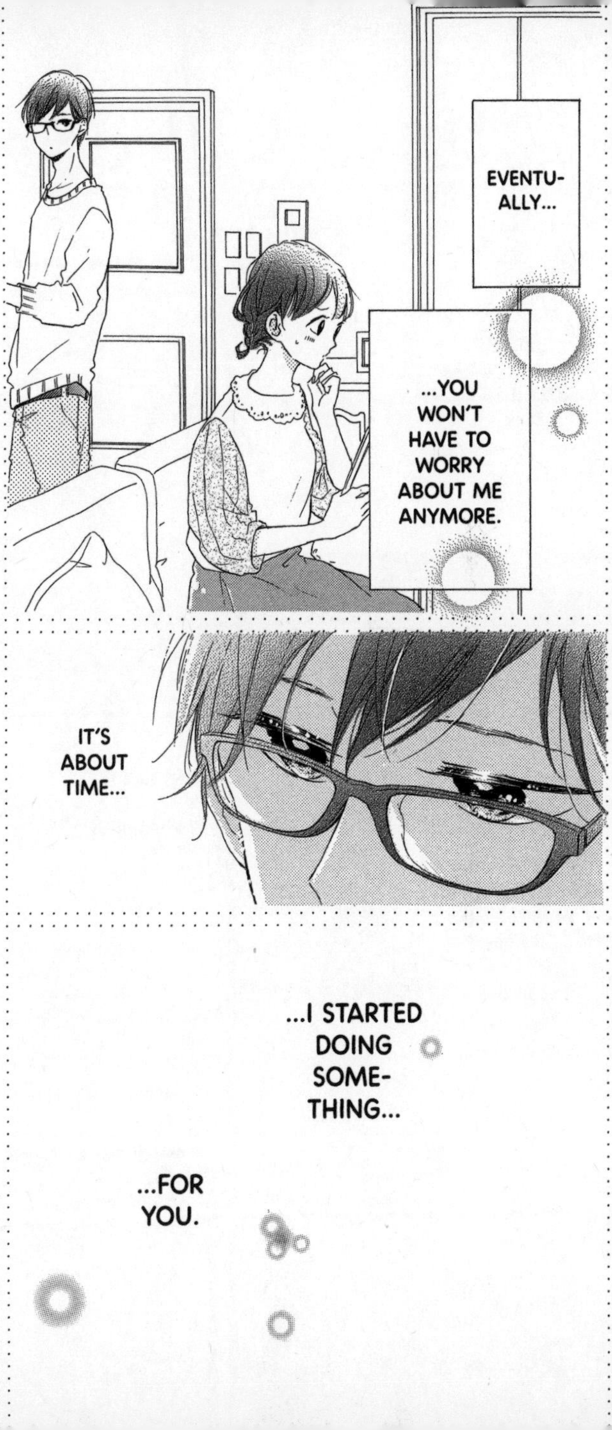
EVENTU-ALLY...
...YOU WON'T HAVE TO WORRY ABOUT ME ANYMORE.
IT'S ABOUT TIME...
...I STARTED DOING SOME-THING...
...FOR YOU.

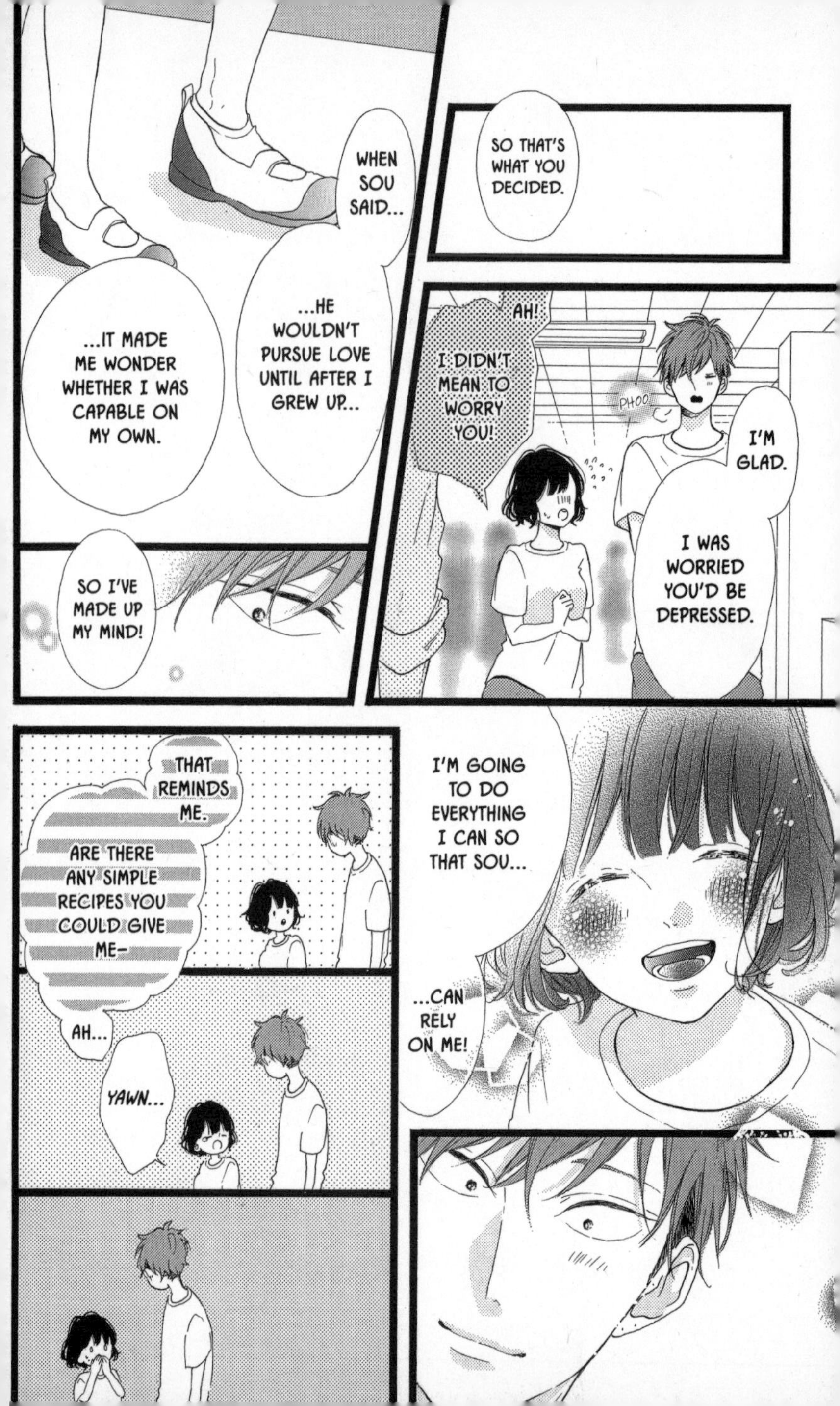
WHEN SOU SAID...
...HE WOULDN'T PURSUE LOVE UNTIL AFTER I GREW UP...
...IT MADE ME WONDER WHETHER I WAS CAPABLE ON MY OWN.
SO I'VE MADE UP MY MIND!
SO THAT'S WHAT YOU DECIDED.
PHOO
I'M GLAD.
I WAS WORRIED YOU'D BE DEPRESSED.
AH!
I DIDN'T MEAN TO WORRY YOU!
I'M GOING TO DO EVERYTHING I CAN SO THAT SOU...
...CAN RELY ON ME!
THAT REMINDS ME.
ARE THERE ANY SIMPLE RECIPES YOU COULD GIVE ME–
AH...
YAWN...

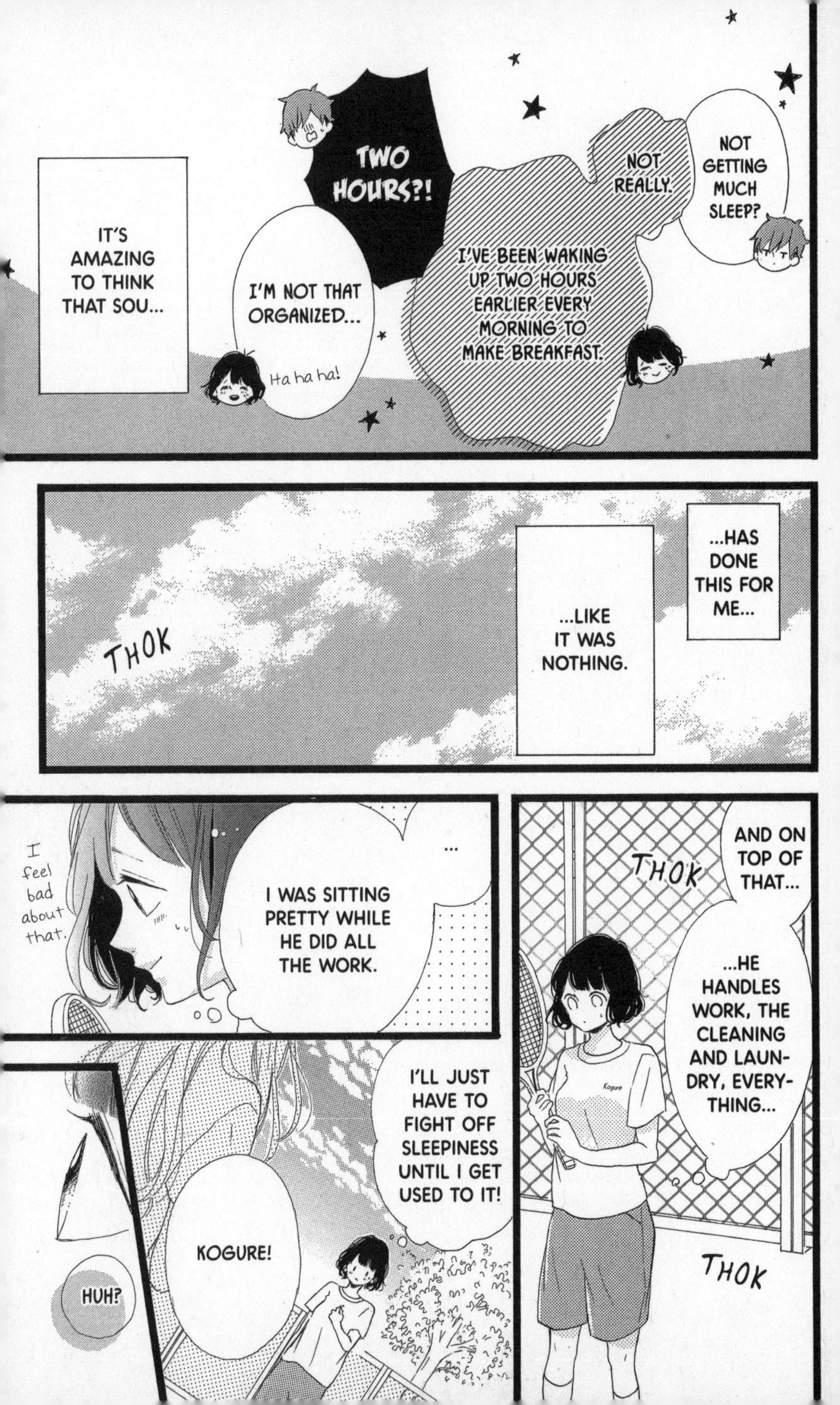
NOT GETTING MUCH SLEEP?
NOT REALLY.
I'VE BEEN WAKING UP TWO HOURS EARLIER EVERY MORNING TO MAKE BREAKFAST.
TWO HOURS?!
I'M NOT THAT ORGANIZED...
Ha ha ha!
IT'S AMAZING TO THINK THAT SOU...
...HAS DONE THIS FOR ME...
...LIKE IT WAS NOTHING.
THOK
THOK
AND ON TOP OF THAT...
...HE HANDLES WORK, THE CLEANING AND LAUN-DRY, EVERY-THING...
Kogure
THOK
...
I WAS SITTING PRETTY WHILE HE DID ALL THE WORK.
I feel bad about that.
I'LL JUST HAVE TO FIGHT OFF SLEEPINESS UNTIL I GET USED TO IT!
KOGURE!
HUH?

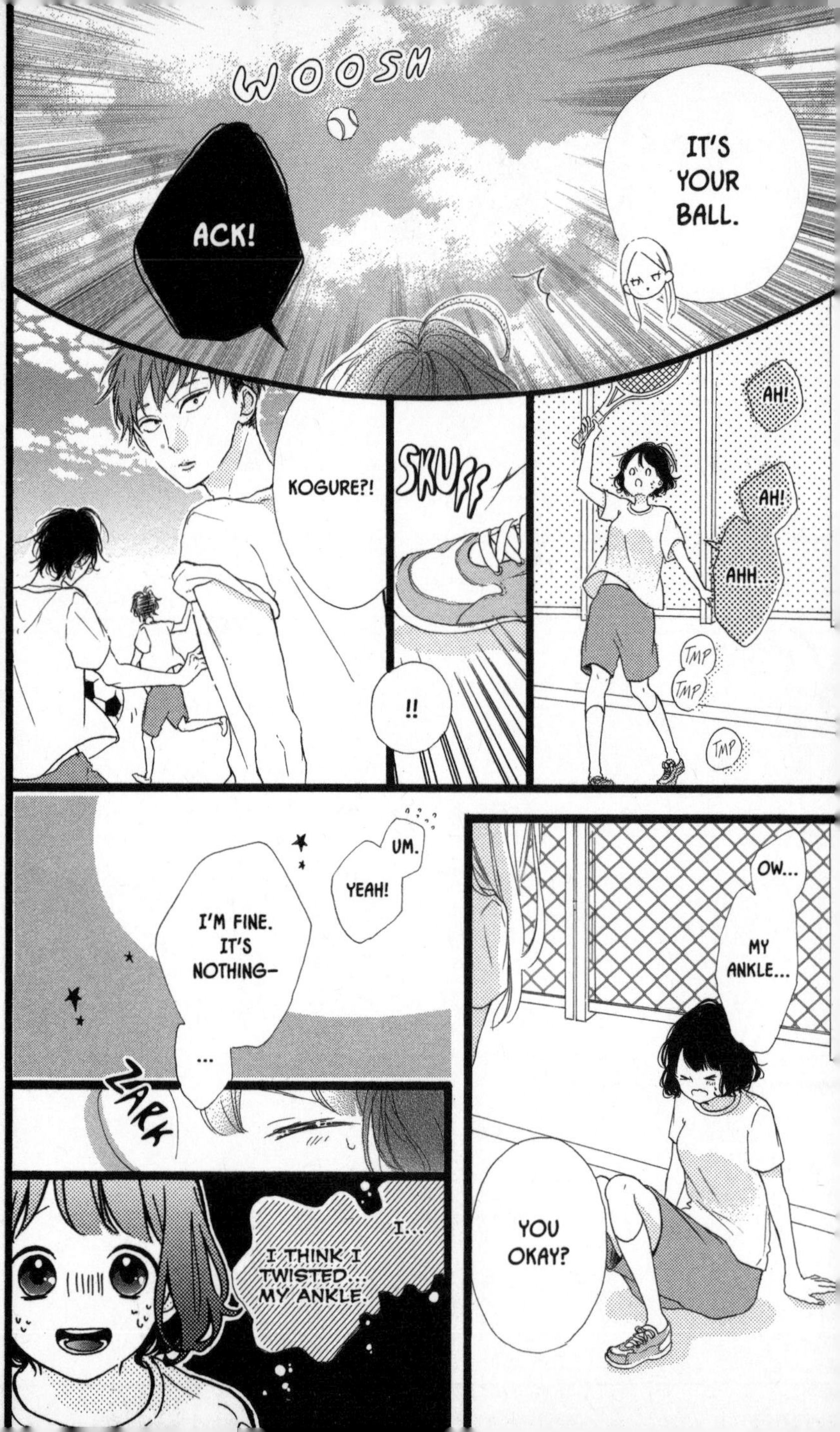
IT'S YOUR BALL.
WOOSH
ACK!
AH!
AH!
AHH...
TMP
TMP
TMP
SKUFF
!!
KOGURE?!
OW...
MY ANKLE...
YOU OKAY?
UM.
YEAH!
I'M FINE. IT'S NOTHING—
...
ZARK
I...
I THINK I TWISTED... MY ANKLE.

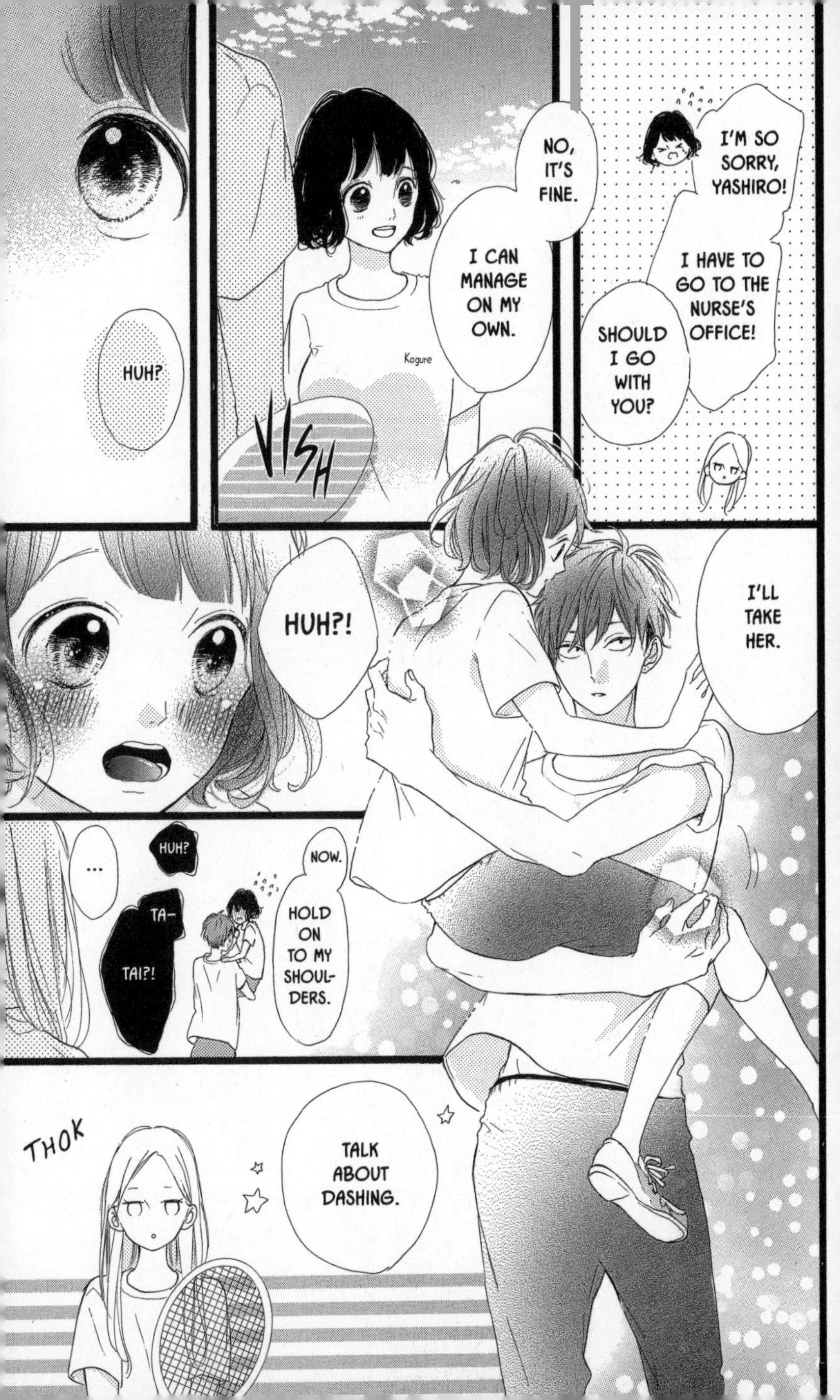

I'M SO SORRY, YASHIRO!
I HAVE TO GO TO THE NURSE'S OFFICE!
SHOULD I GO WITH YOU?
NO, IT'S FINE.
I CAN MANAGE ON MY OWN.
Kogure
VISH
HUH?
I'LL TAKE HER.
HUH?!
NOW.
HOLD ON TO MY SHOULDERS.
HUH?
TA-
TAI?!
...
TALK ABOUT DASHING.
THOK

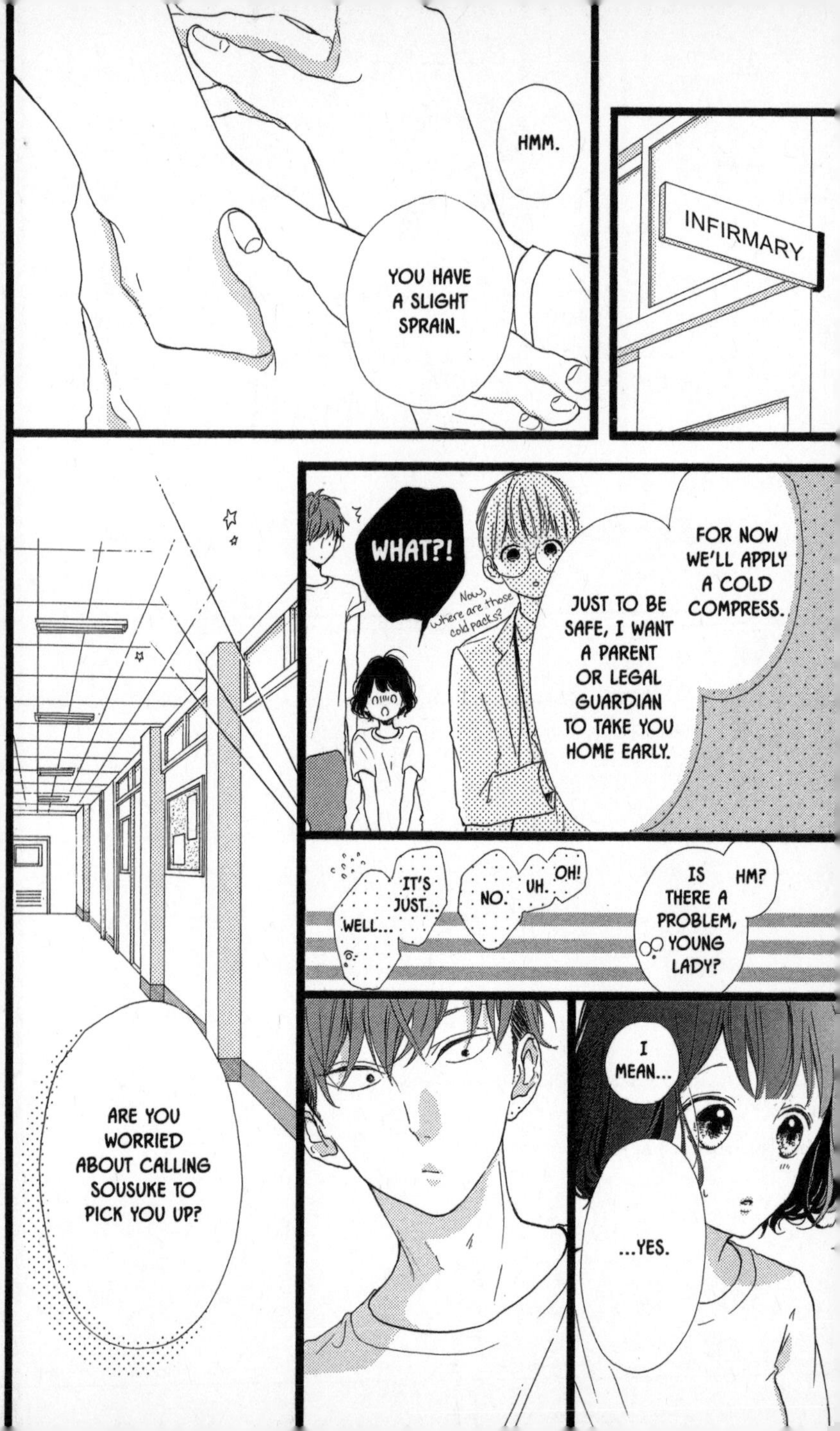
INFIRMARY
HMM.
YOU HAVE A SLIGHT SPRAIN.
FOR NOW WE'LL APPLY A COLD COMPRESS.
JUST TO BE SAFE, I WANT A PARENT OR LEGAL GUARDIAN TO TAKE YOU HOME EARLY.
WHAT?!
Now, where are those cold packs?
HM?
IS THERE A PROBLEM, YOUNG LADY?
OH!
UH.
NO.
IT'S JUST...
WELL...
I MEAN...
...YES.
ARE YOU WORRIED ABOUT CALLING SOUSUKE TO PICK YOU UP?

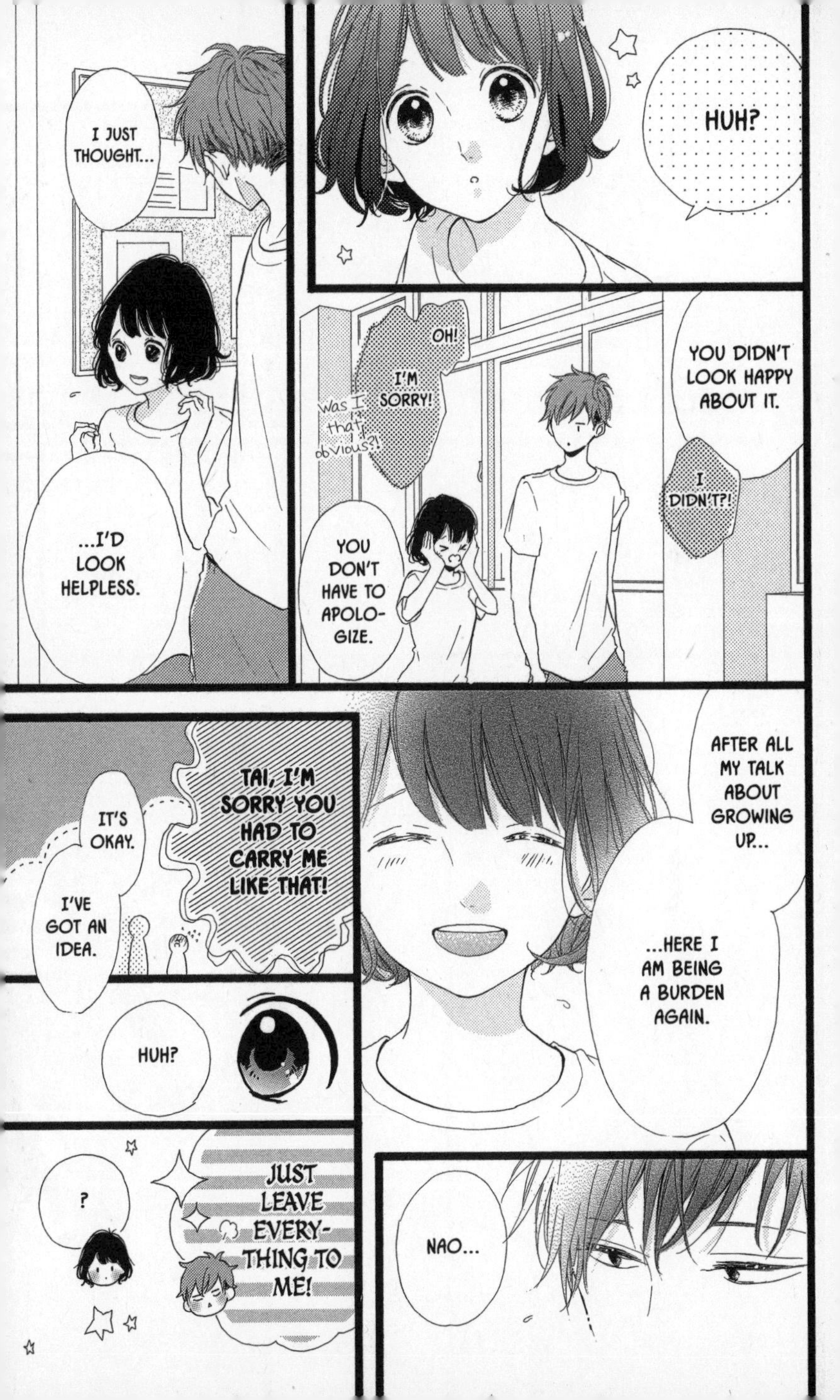
HUH?
YOU DIDN'T LOOK HAPPY ABOUT IT.
I DIDN'T?!
OH! I'M SORRY!
Was I that obvious?!
YOU DON'T HAVE TO APOLOGIZE.
I JUST THOUGHT...
...I'D LOOK HELPLESS.
AFTER ALL MY TALK ABOUT GROWING UP...
...HERE I AM BEING A BURDEN AGAIN.
NAO...
TAI, I'M SORRY YOU HAD TO CARRY ME LIKE THAT!
IT'S OKAY.
I'VE GOT AN IDEA.
HUH?
?
JUST LEAVE EVERYTHING TO ME!

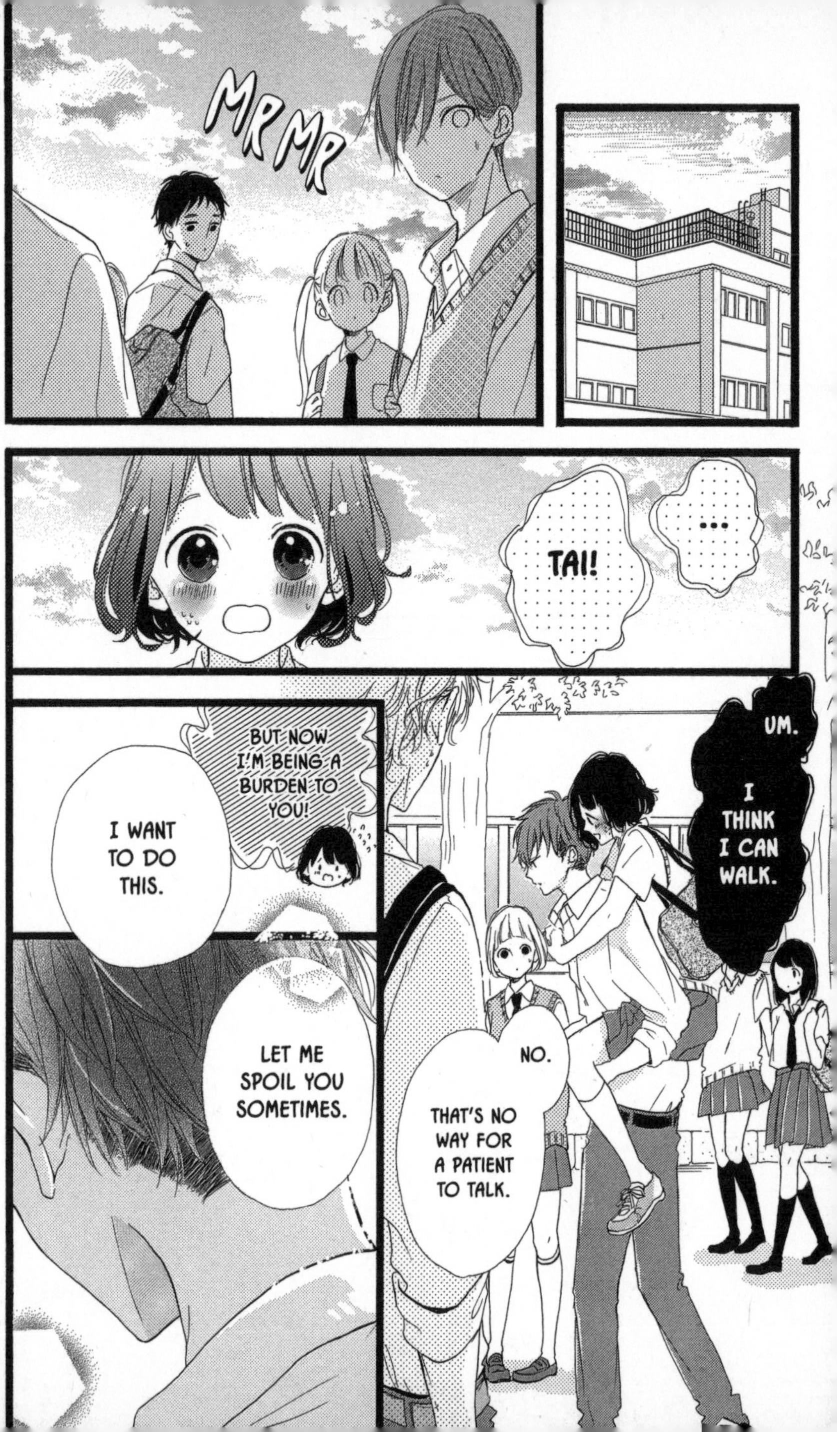
MRMR
...
TAI!
UM.
I THINK I CAN WALK.
NO.
THAT'S NO WAY FOR A PATIENT TO TALK.
BUT NOW I'M BEING A BURDEN TO YOU!
I WANT TO DO THIS.
LET ME SPOIL YOU SOMETIMES.

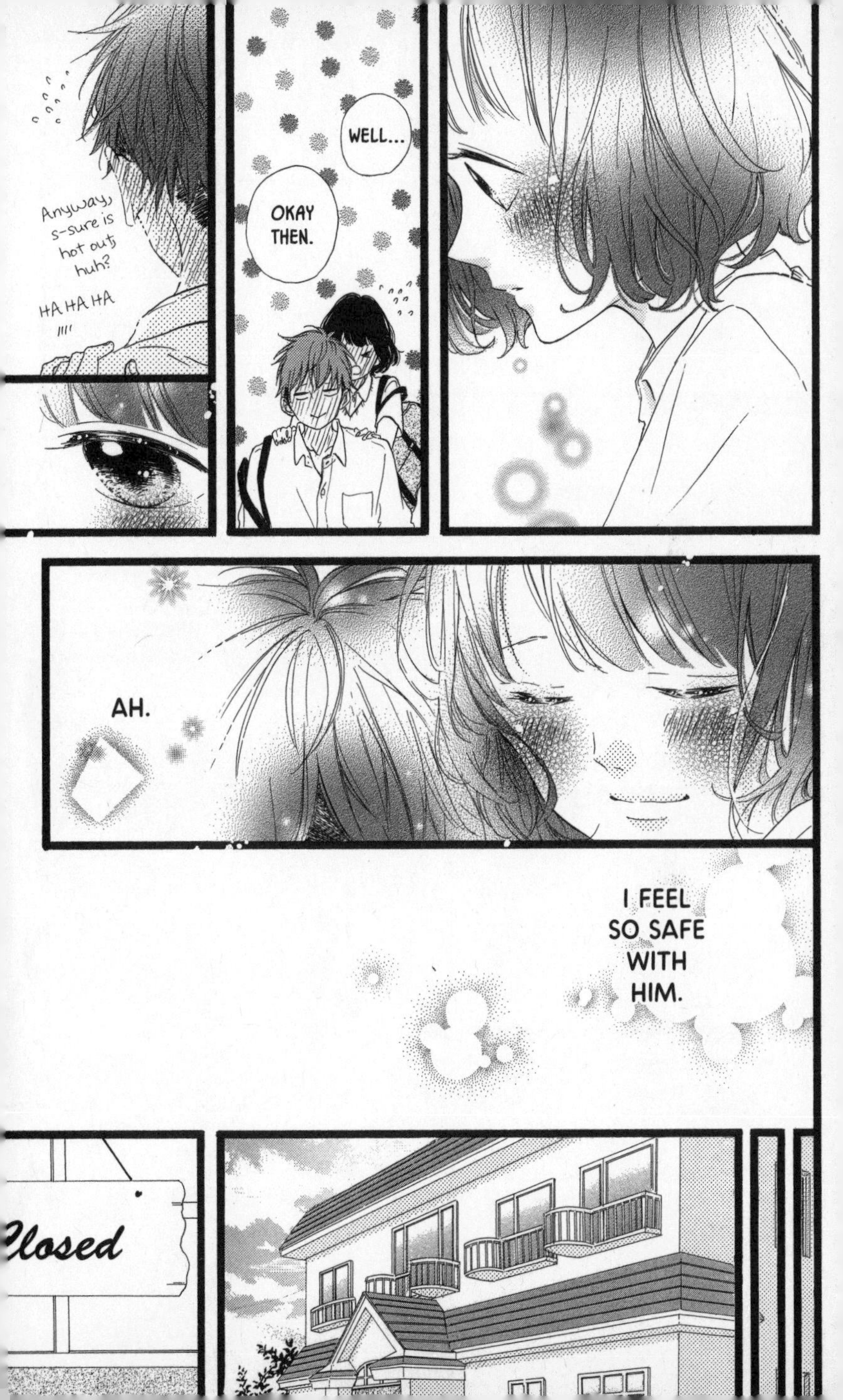
WELL...
OKAY THEN.
Anyway, s-sure is hot out, huh?
HA HA HA
AH.
I FEEL SO SAFE WITH HIM.
Closed

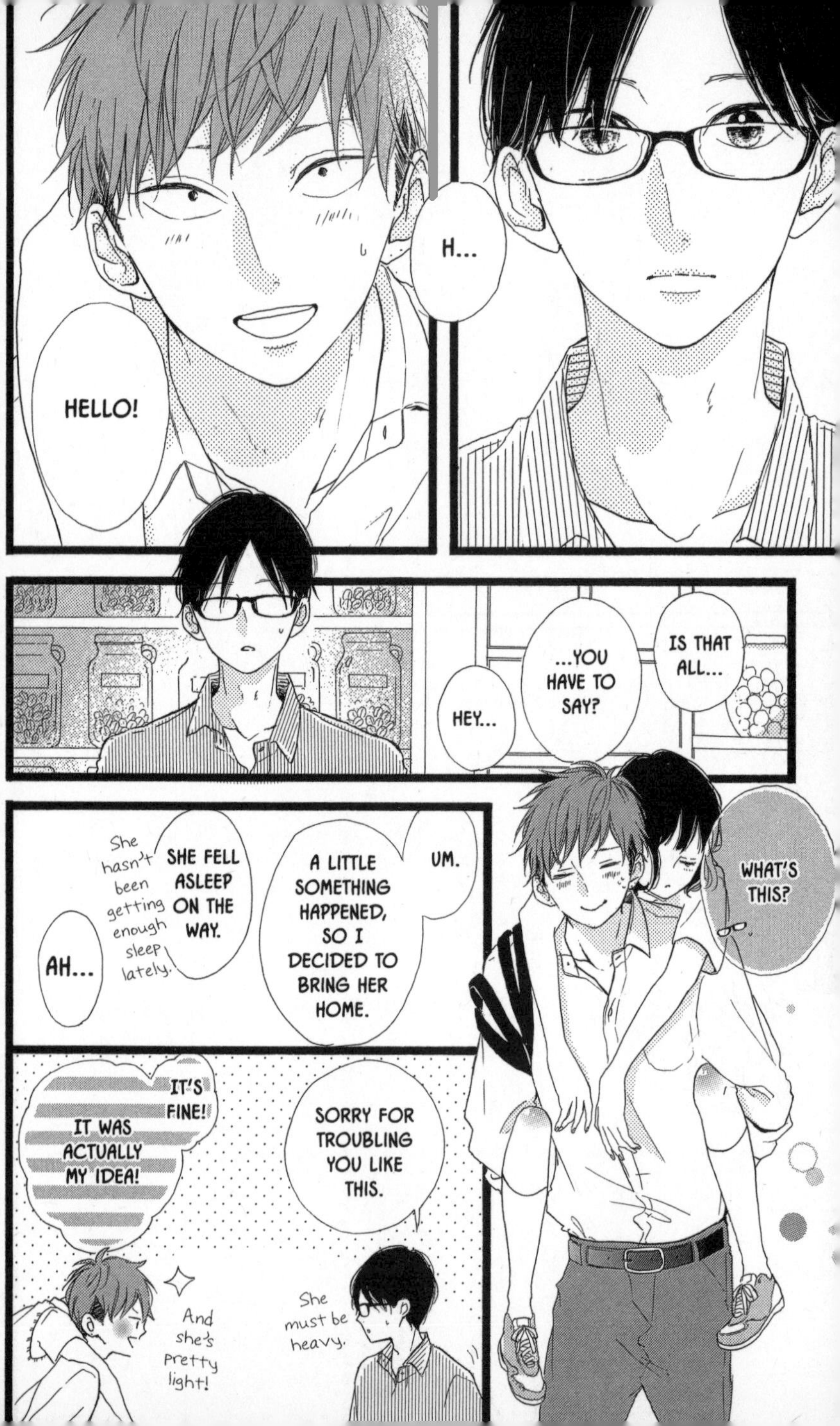
H...
HELLO!
IS THAT ALL...
...YOU HAVE TO SAY?
HEY...
WHAT'S THIS?
UM.
A LITTLE SOMETHING HAPPENED, SO I DECIDED TO BRING HER HOME.
SHE FELL ASLEEP ON THE WAY.
She hasn't been getting enough sleep lately.
AH...
SORRY FOR TROUBLING YOU LIKE THIS.
IT'S FINE!
IT WAS ACTUALLY MY IDEA!
She must be heavy.
And she's pretty light!

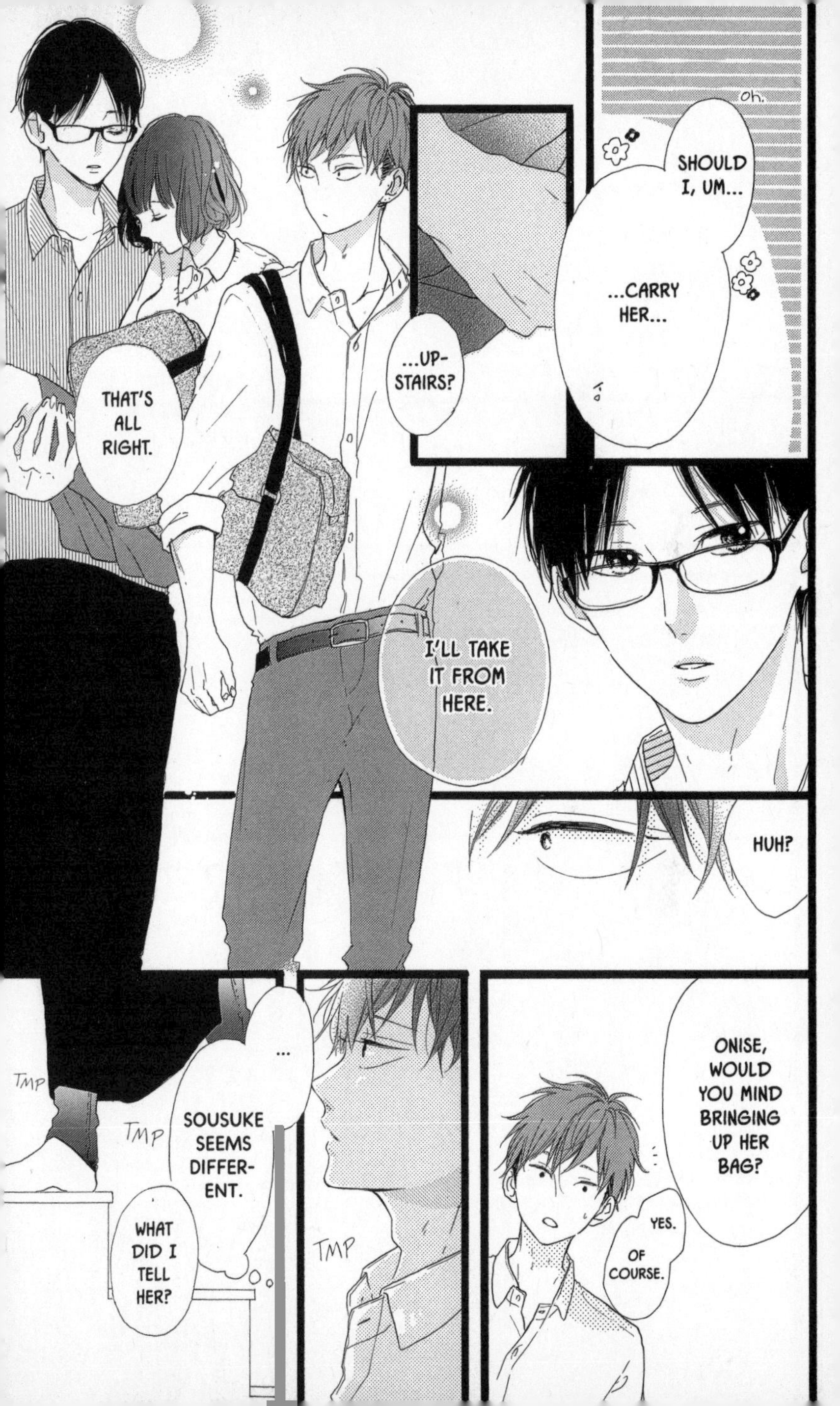
oh.
SHOULD I, UM...
...CARRY HER...
...UP-STAIRS?
I'LL TAKE IT FROM HERE.
HUH?
THAT'S ALL RIGHT.
ONISE, WOULD YOU MIND BRINGING UP HER BAG?
YES.
OF COURSE.
...
TMP
TMP
TMP
SOUSUKE SEEMS DIFFER-ENT.
WHAT DID I TELL HER?

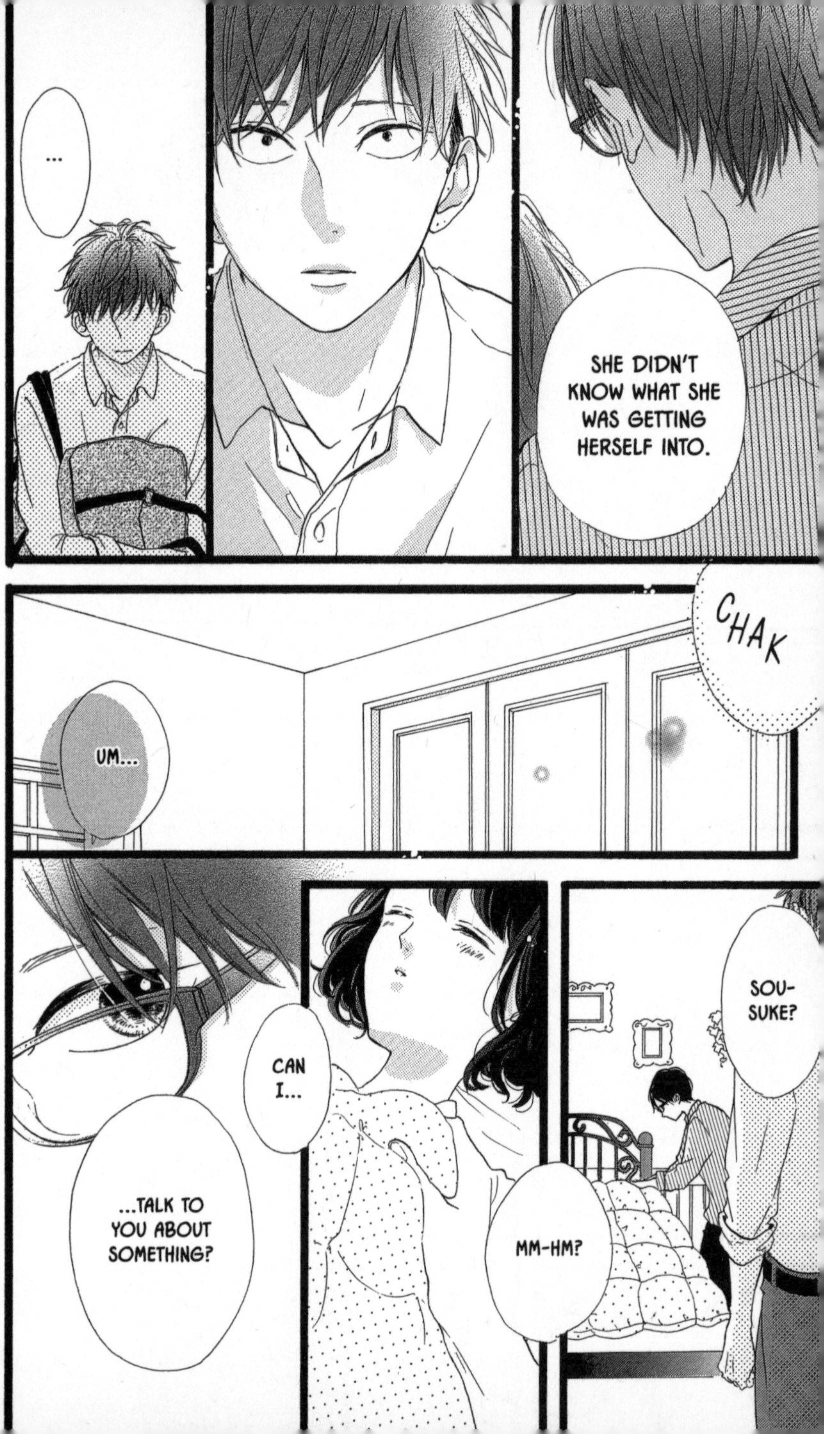
SHE DIDN'T KNOW WHAT SHE WAS GETTING HERSELF INTO.
...
CHAK
UM...
SOU-SUKE?
MM-HM?
CAN I...
...TALK TO YOU ABOUT SOMETHING?

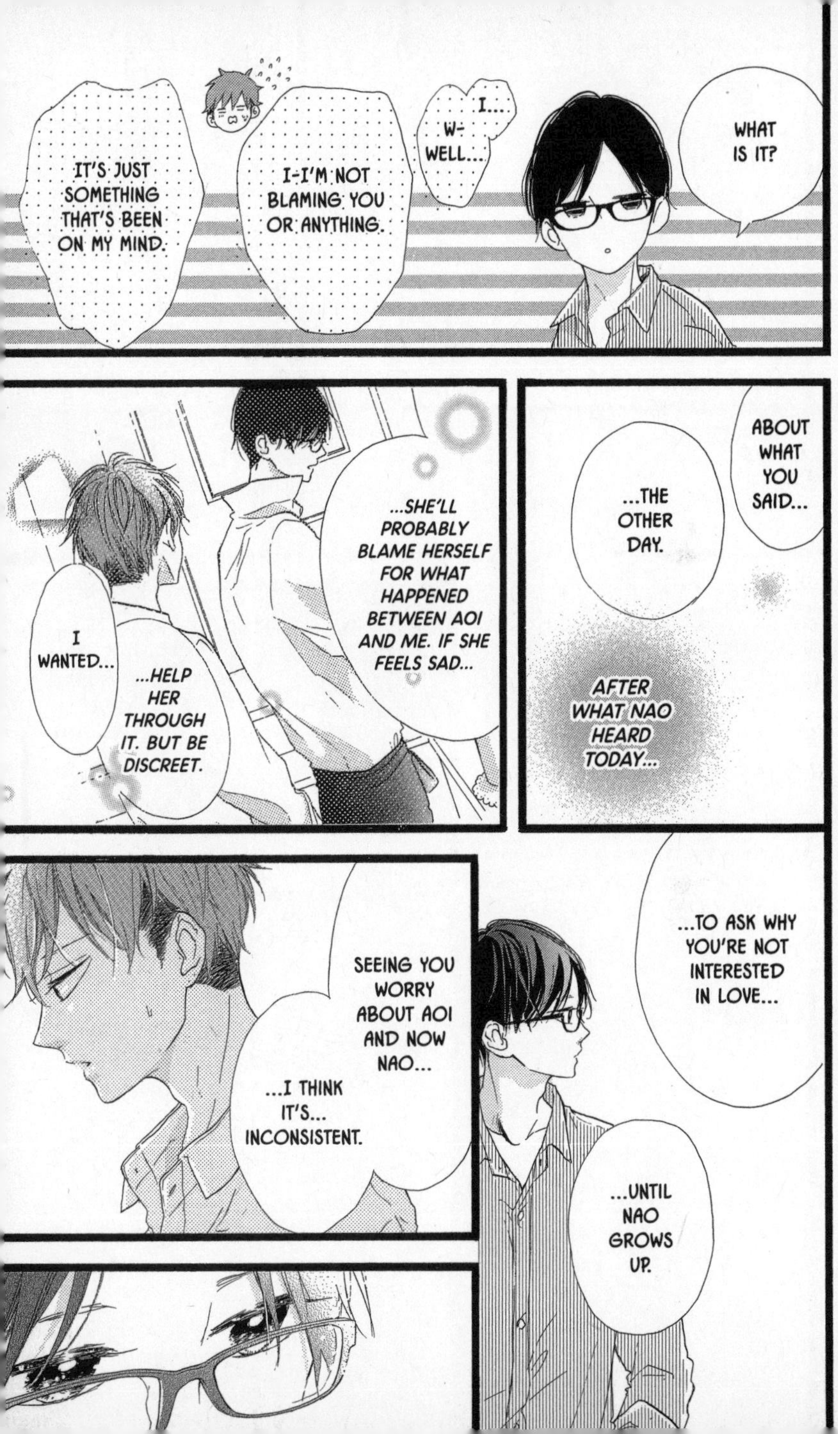
WHAT IS IT?
I... W-WELL...
I-I'M NOT BLAMING YOU OR ANYTHING.
IT'S JUST SOMETHING THAT'S BEEN ON MY MIND.
ABOUT WHAT YOU SAID...
...THE OTHER DAY.
AFTER WHAT NAO HEARD TODAY...
...SHE'LL PROBABLY BLAME HERSELF FOR WHAT HAPPENED BETWEEN AOI AND ME. IF SHE FEELS SAD...
I WANTED...
...HELP HER THROUGH IT. BUT BE DISCREET.
...TO ASK WHY YOU'RE NOT INTERESTED IN LOVE...
...UNTIL NAO GROWS UP.
SEEING YOU WORRY ABOUT AOI AND NOW NAO...
...I THINK IT'S... INCONSISTENT.

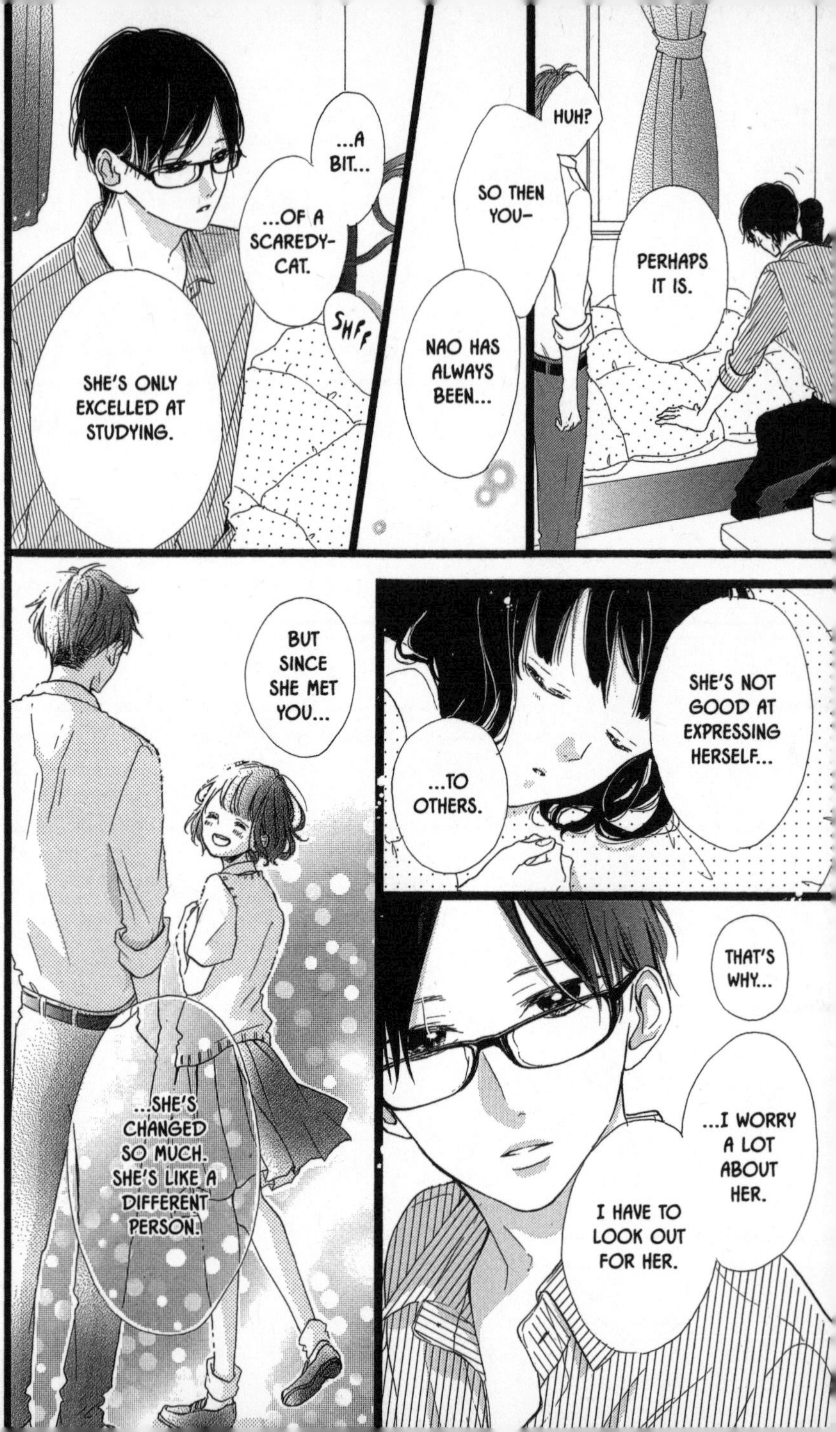
HUH?
SO THEN YOU-
PERHAPS IT IS.
NAO HAS ALWAYS BEEN...
...A BIT...
...OF A SCAREDY-CAT.
SHFF
SHE'S ONLY EXCELLED AT STUDYING.
SHE'S NOT GOOD AT EXPRESSING HERSELF...
...TO OTHERS.
THAT'S WHY...
...I WORRY A LOT ABOUT HER.
I HAVE TO LOOK OUT FOR HER.
BUT SINCE SHE MET YOU...
...SHE'S CHANGED SO MUCH. SHE'S LIKE A DIFFERENT PERSON.

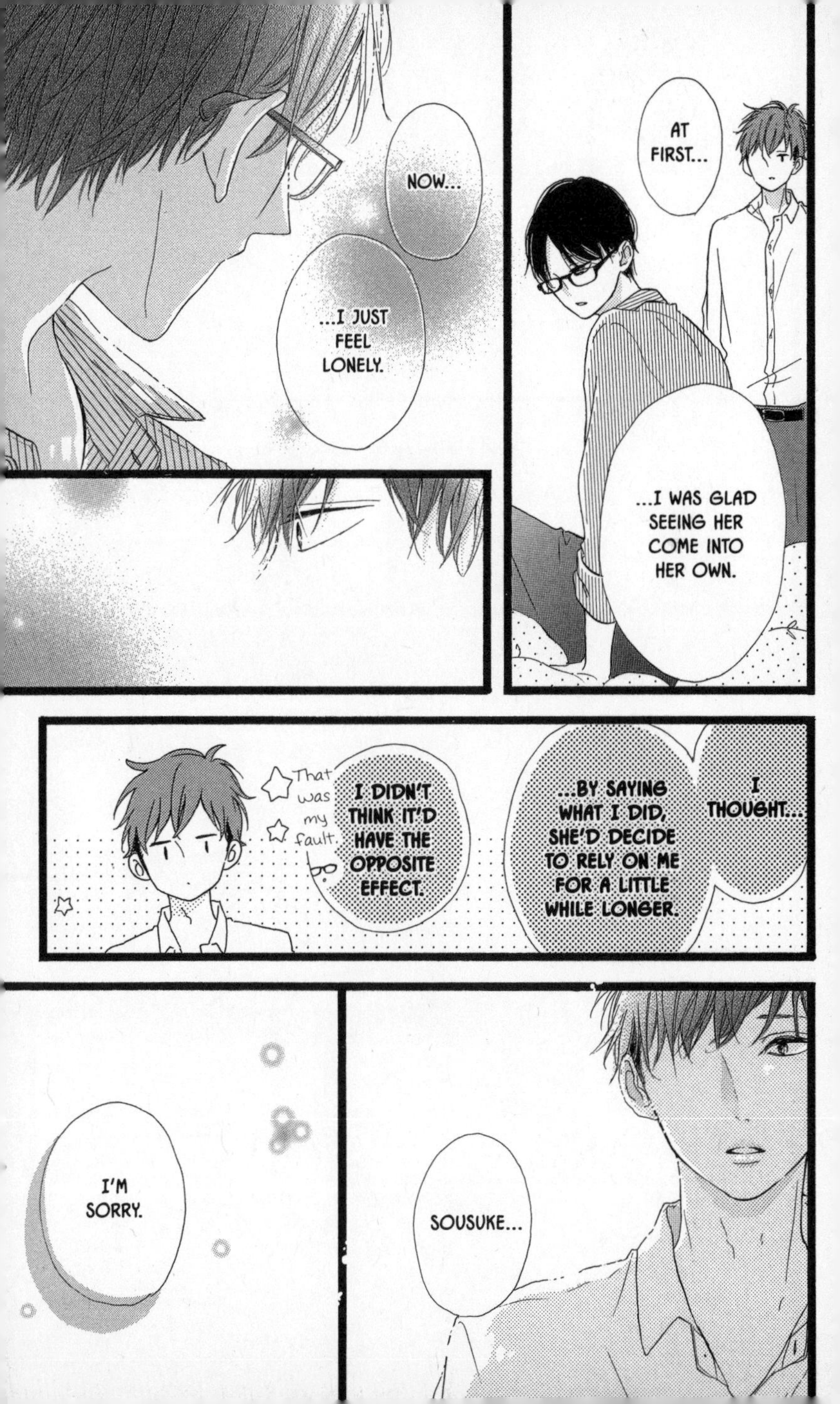

AT FIRST...
...I WAS GLAD SEEING HER COME INTO HER OWN.
NOW...
...I JUST FEEL LONELY.
I THOUGHT...
...BY SAYING WHAT I DID, SHE'D DECIDE TO RELY ON ME FOR A LITTLE WHILE LONGER.
I DIDN'T THINK IT'D HAVE THE OPPOSITE EFFECT.
That was my fault.
SOUSUKE...
I'M SORRY.

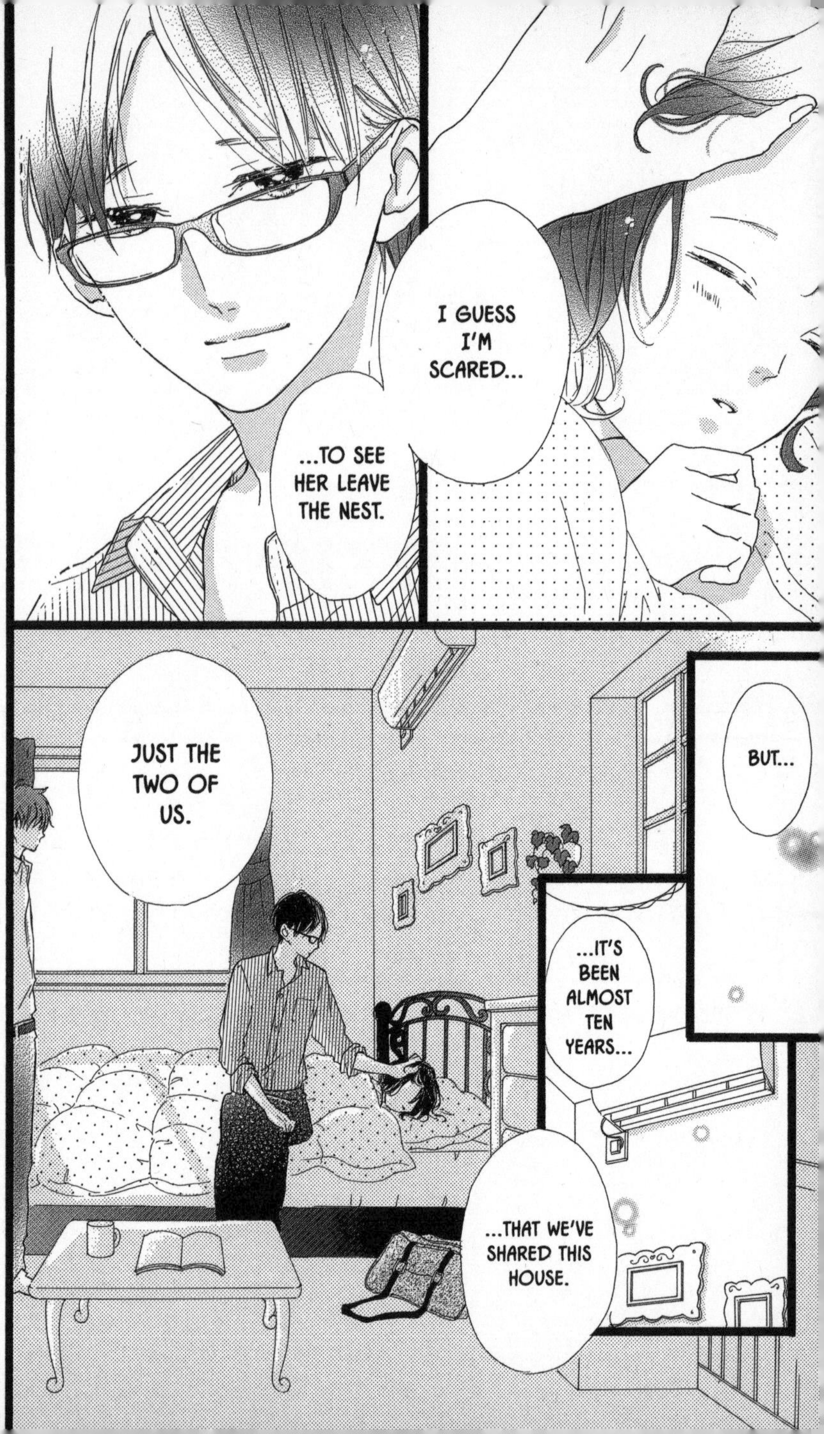
I GUESS I'M SCARED...
...TO SEE HER LEAVE THE NEST.
BUT...
...IT'S BEEN ALMOST TEN YEARS...
...THAT WE'VE SHARED THIS HOUSE.
JUST THE TWO OF US.

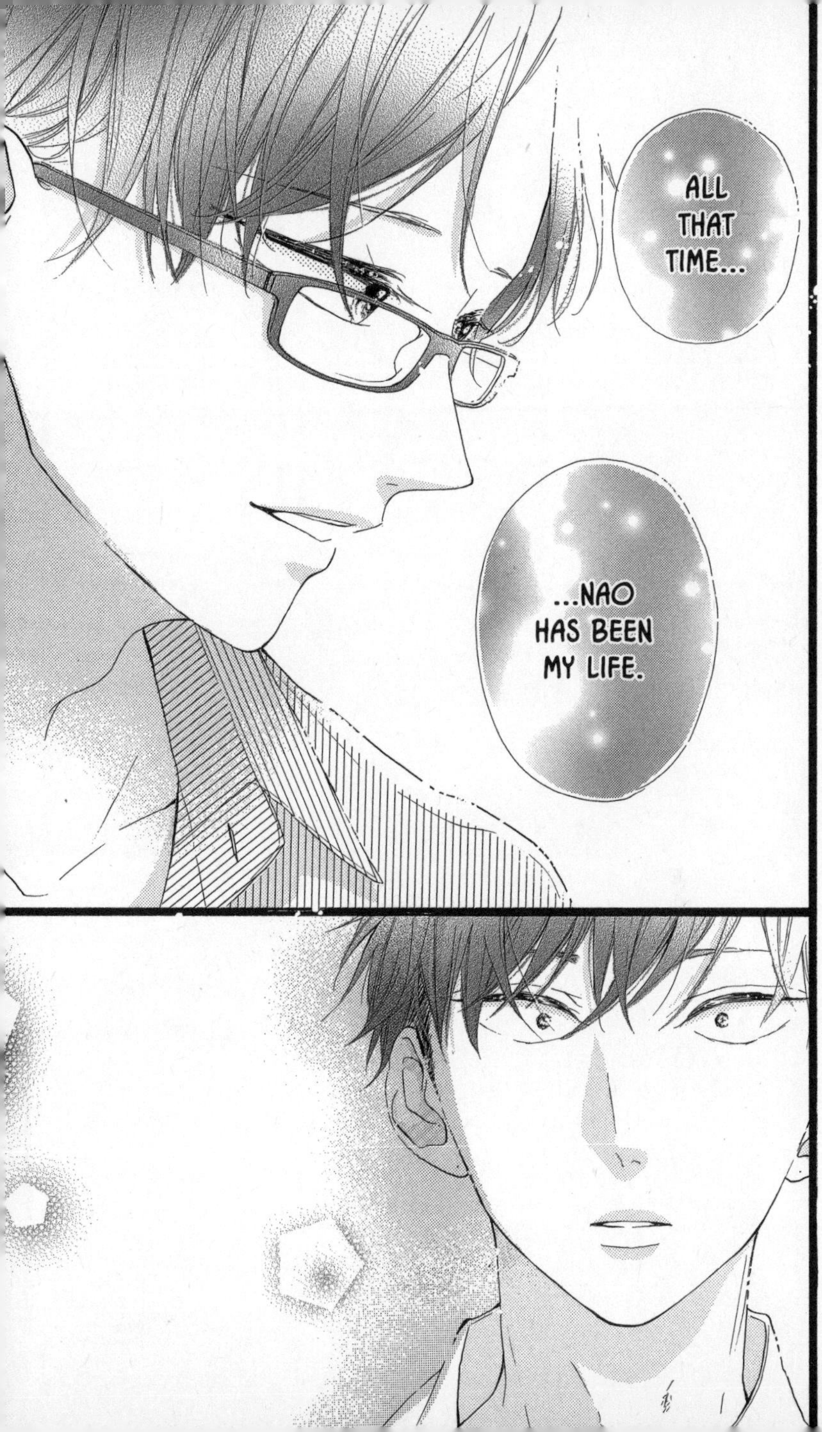
ALL THAT TIME...
...NAO HAS BEEN MY LIFE.

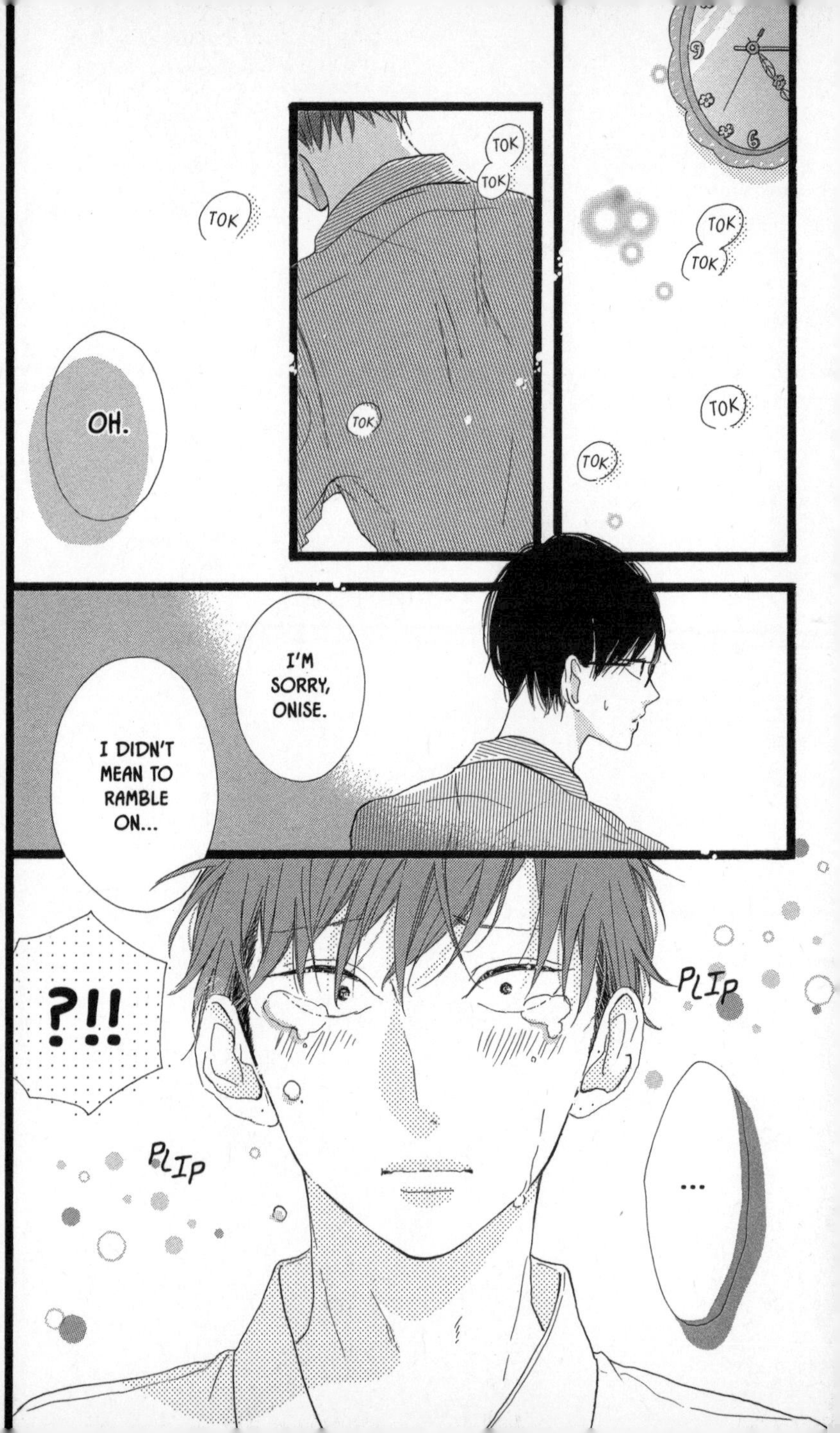
TOK
TOK
TOK
TOK
TOK
TOK
TOK
TOK
OH.
I'M SORRY, ONISE.
I DIDN'T MEAN TO RAMBLE ON...
PLIP
...
?!!
PLIP

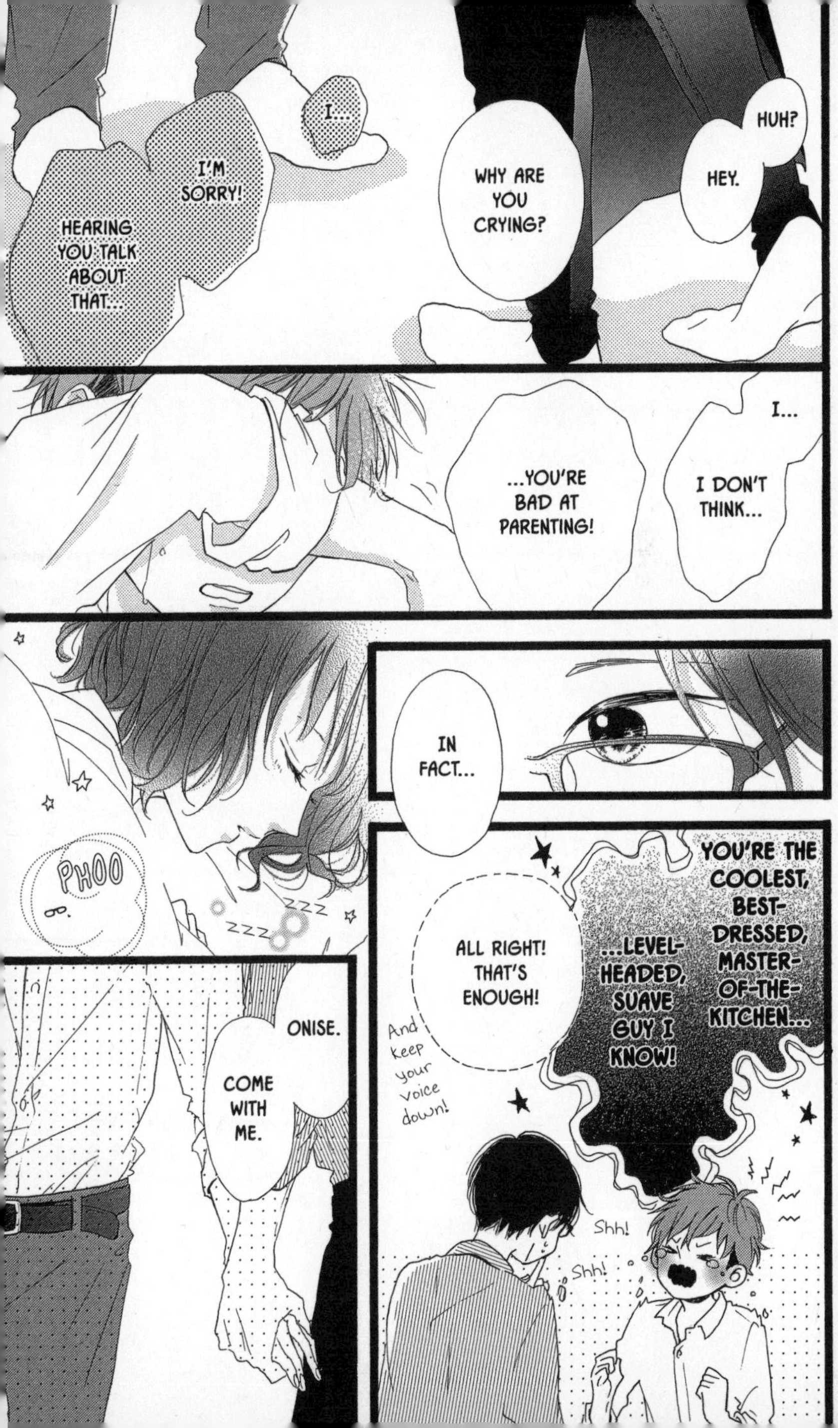
HUH?
HEY.
WHY ARE YOU CRYING?
I...
I'M SORRY!
HEARING YOU TALK ABOUT THAT...
I...
I DON'T THINK...
...YOU'RE BAD AT PARENTING!
IN FACT...
YOU'RE THE COOLEST, BEST-DRESSED, MASTER-OF-THE-KITCHEN...
...LEVEL-HEADED, SUAVE GUY I KNOW!
ALL RIGHT! THAT'S ENOUGH!
And keep your voice down!
Shh!
Shh!
PHOO
ZZZ
ZZZ
ONISE.
COME WITH ME.

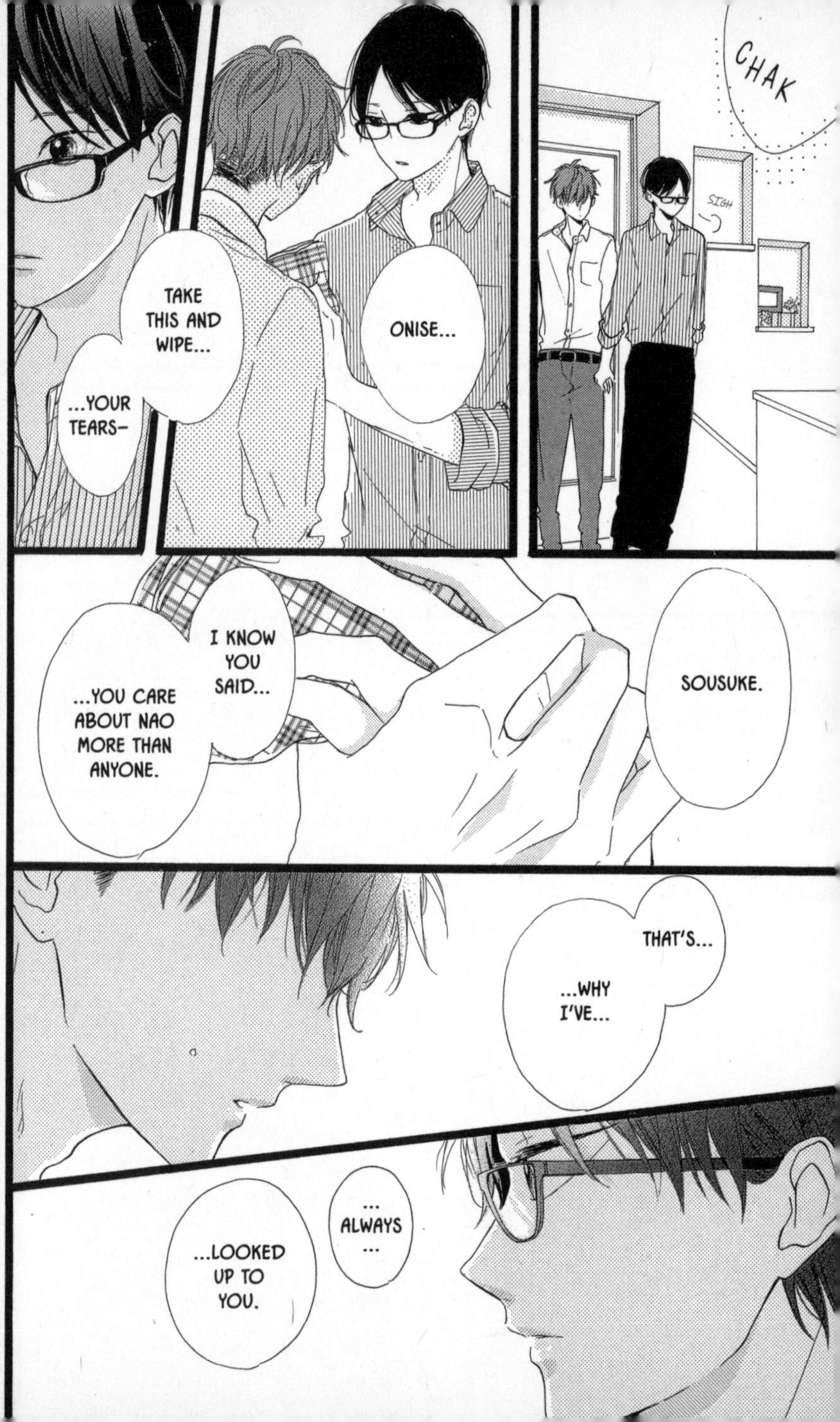
CHAK
SIGH
ONISE...
TAKE THIS AND WIPE...
...YOUR TEARS-
SOUSUKE.
I KNOW YOU SAID...
...YOU CARE ABOUT NAO MORE THAN ANYONE.
THAT'S...
...WHY I'VE...
...ALWAYS...
...LOOKED UP TO YOU.

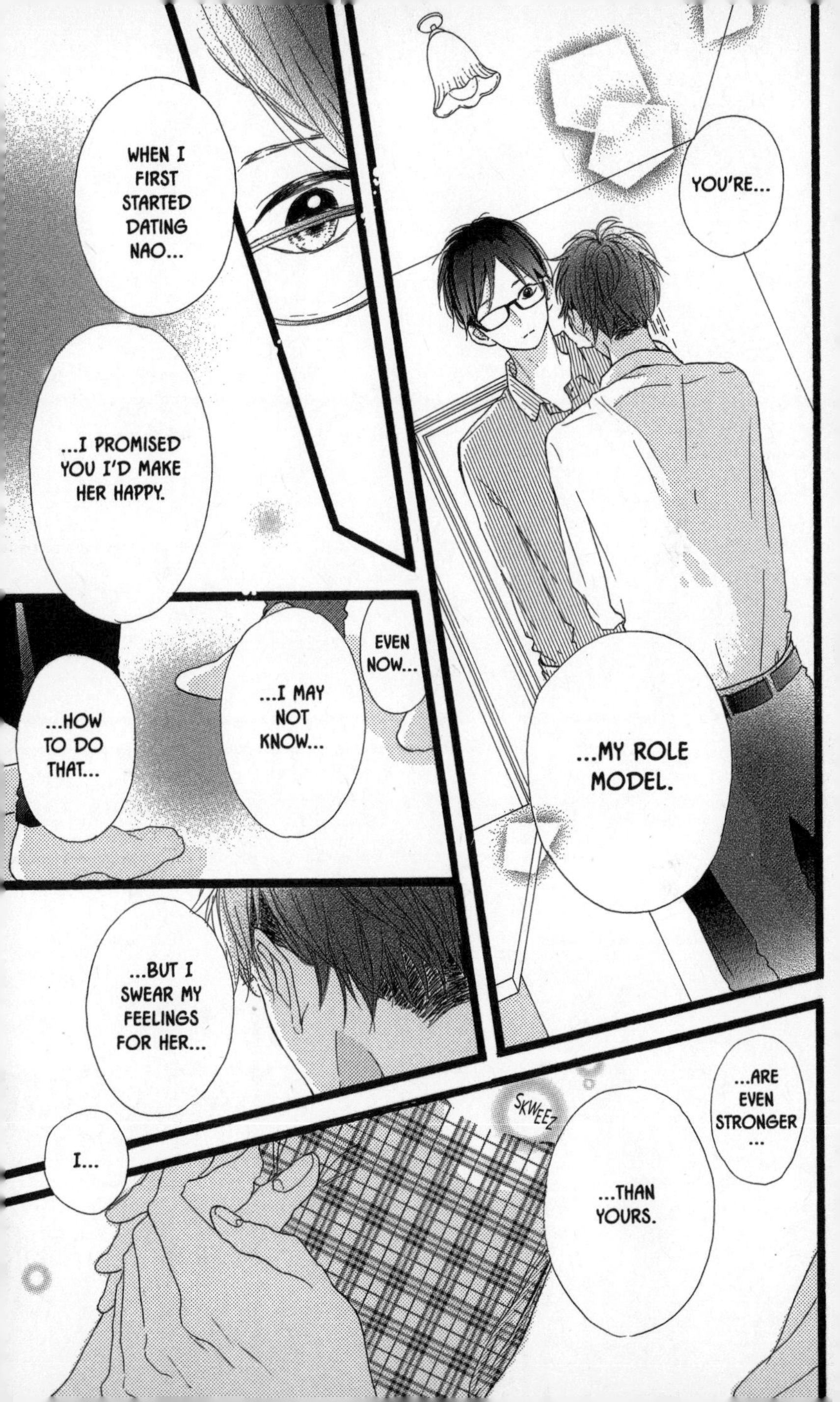
YOU'RE...
...MY ROLE MODEL.
WHEN I FIRST STARTED DATING NAO...
...I PROMISED YOU I'D MAKE HER HAPPY.
EVEN NOW...
...I MAY NOT KNOW...
...HOW TO DO THAT...
...BUT I SWEAR MY FEELINGS FOR HER...
...ARE EVEN STRONGER...
SKWEEZ
...THAN YOURS.
I...

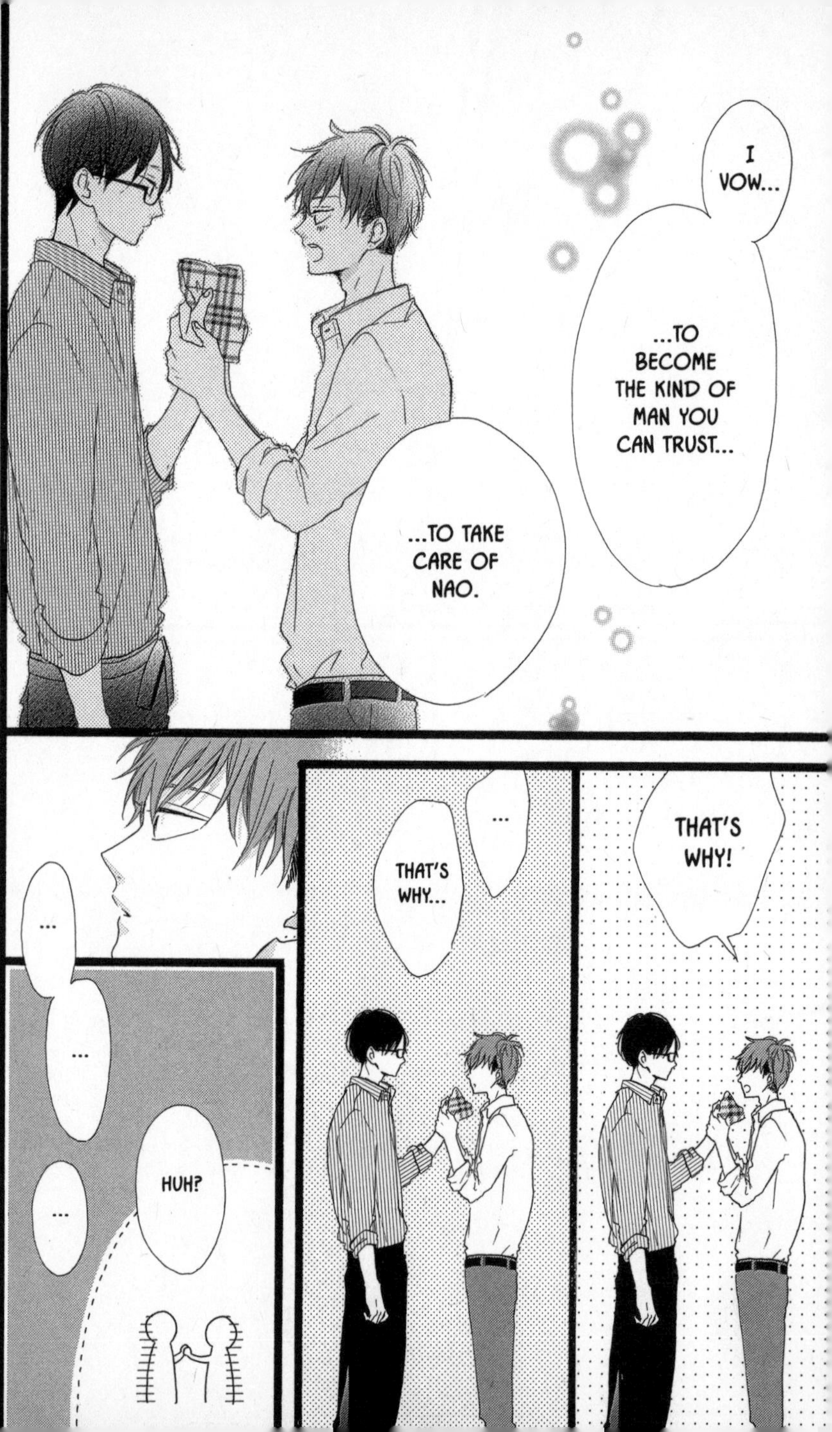
I VOW...
...TO BECOME THE KIND OF MAN YOU CAN TRUST...
...TO TAKE CARE OF NAO.
THAT'S WHY!
...
THAT'S WHY...
...
...
HUH?
...

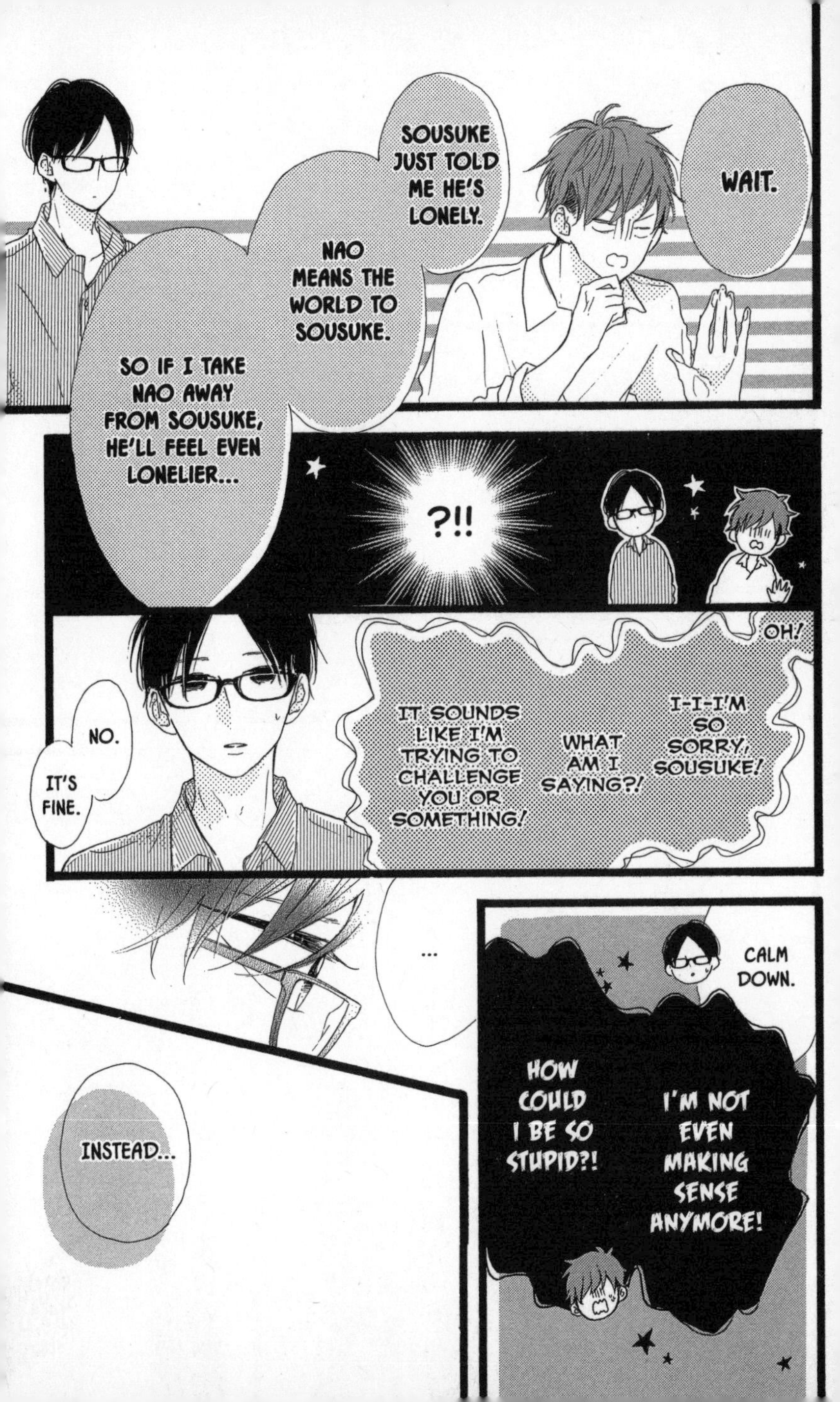
WAIT.
SOUSUKE JUST TOLD ME HE'S LONELY.
NAO MEANS THE WORLD TO SOUSUKE.
SO IF I TAKE NAO AWAY FROM SOUSUKE, HE'LL FEEL EVEN LONELIER...
?!!
OH!
I-I-I'M SO SORRY, SOUSUKE!
WHAT AM I SAYING?!
IT SOUNDS LIKE I'M TRYING TO CHALLENGE YOU OR SOMETHING!
NO.
IT'S FINE.
CALM DOWN.
I'M NOT EVEN MAKING SENSE ANYMORE!
HOW COULD I BE SO STUPID?!
...
INSTEAD...

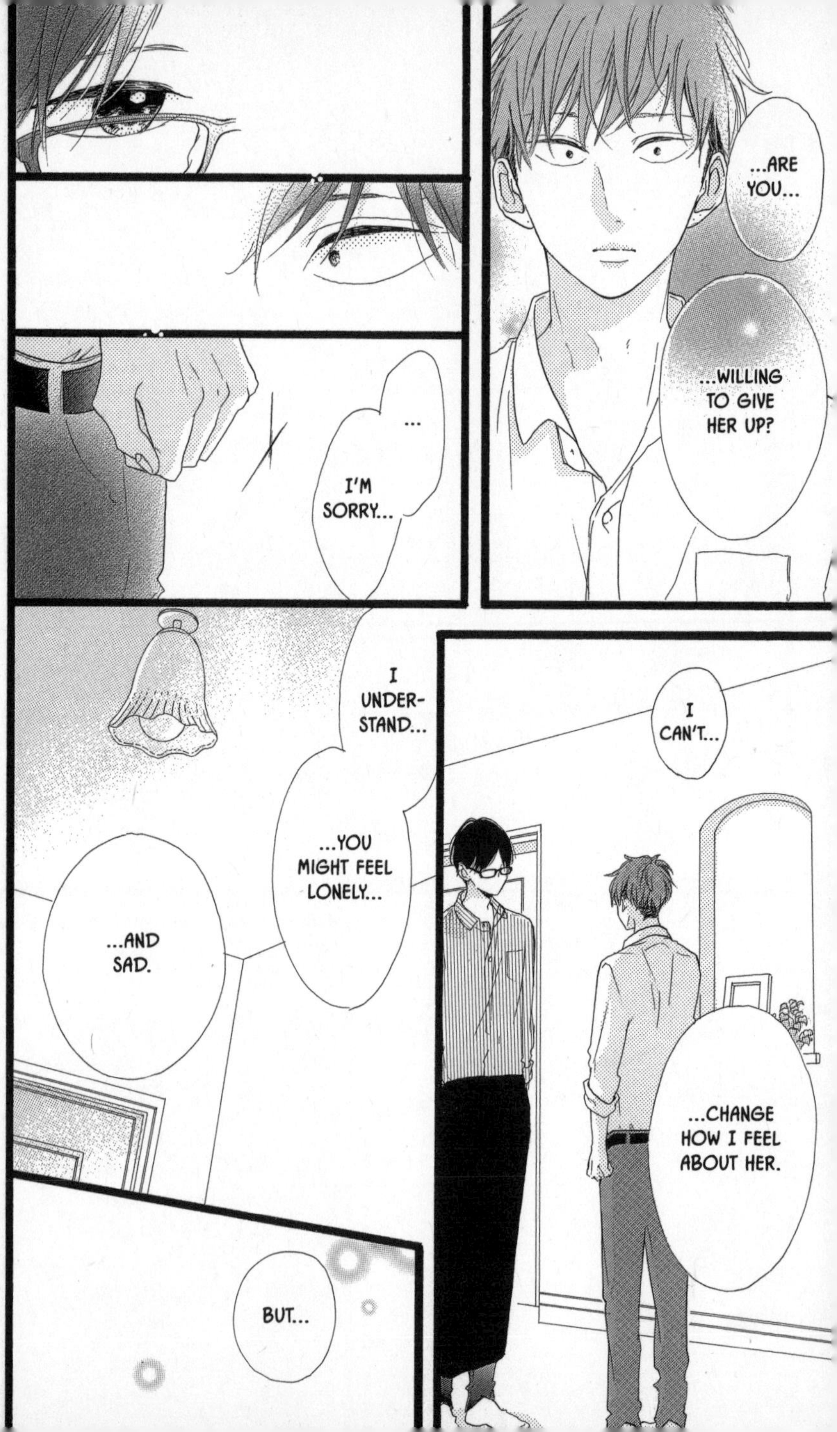
...ARE YOU...
...WILLING TO GIVE HER UP?
...
I'M SORRY...
I CAN'T...
...CHANGE HOW I FEEL ABOUT HER.
I UNDER-STAND...
...YOU MIGHT FEEL LONELY...
...AND SAD.
BUT...

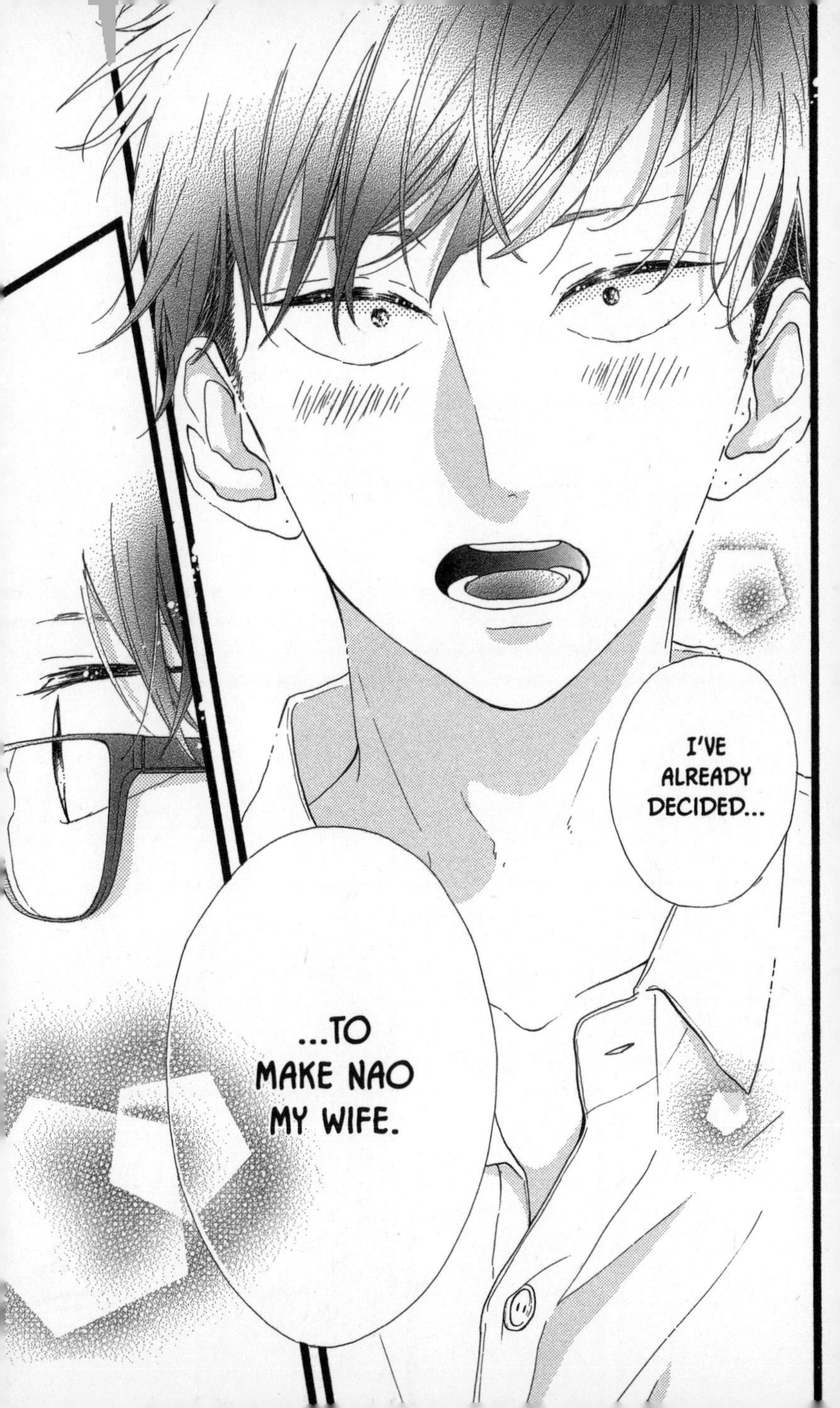
I'VE ALREADY DECIDED...
...TO MAKE NAO MY WIFE.

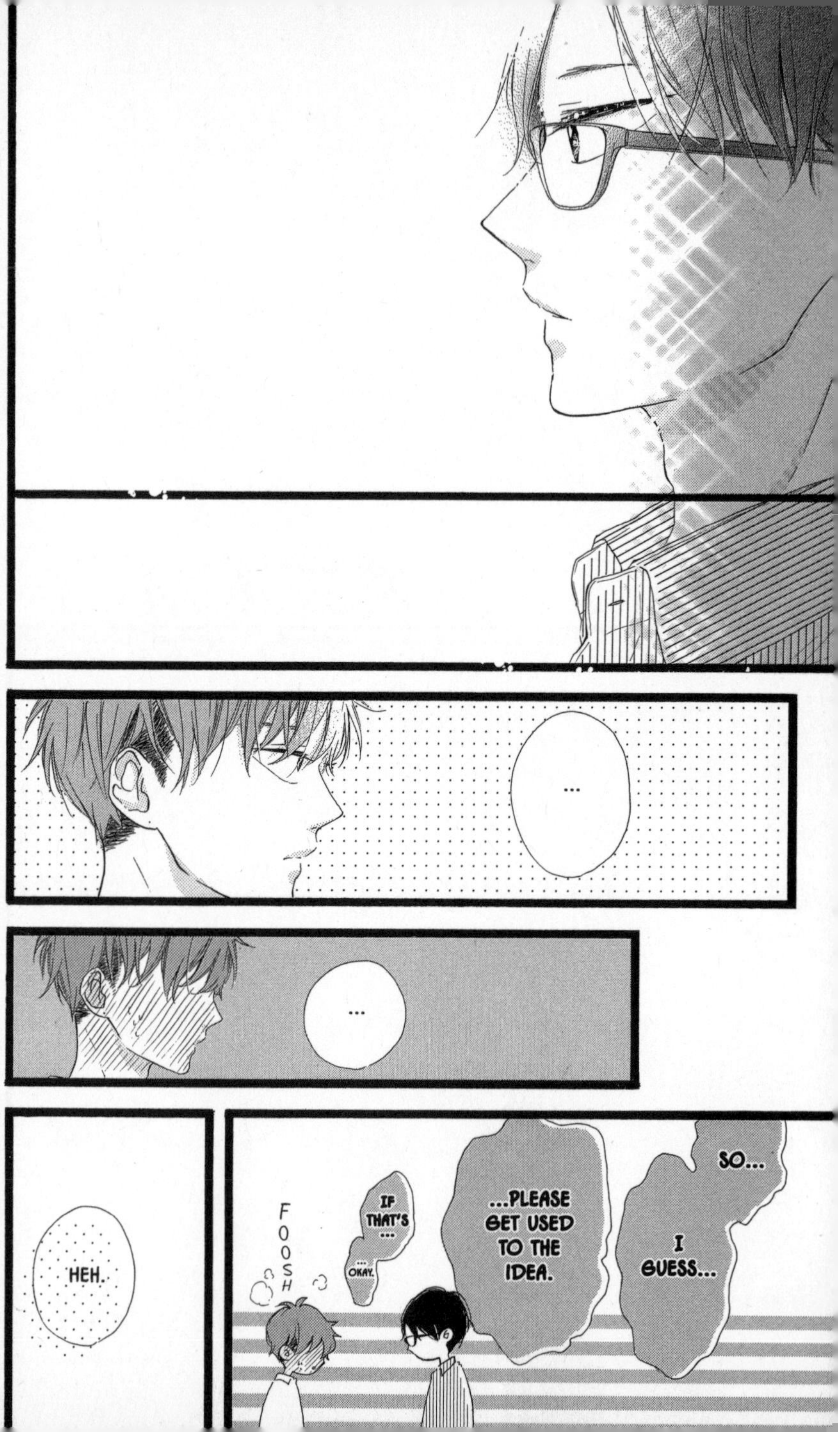
...
...
SO... I GUESS...
...PLEASE GET USED TO THE IDEA.
IF THAT'S...
...OKAY.
FOOSH
HEH.

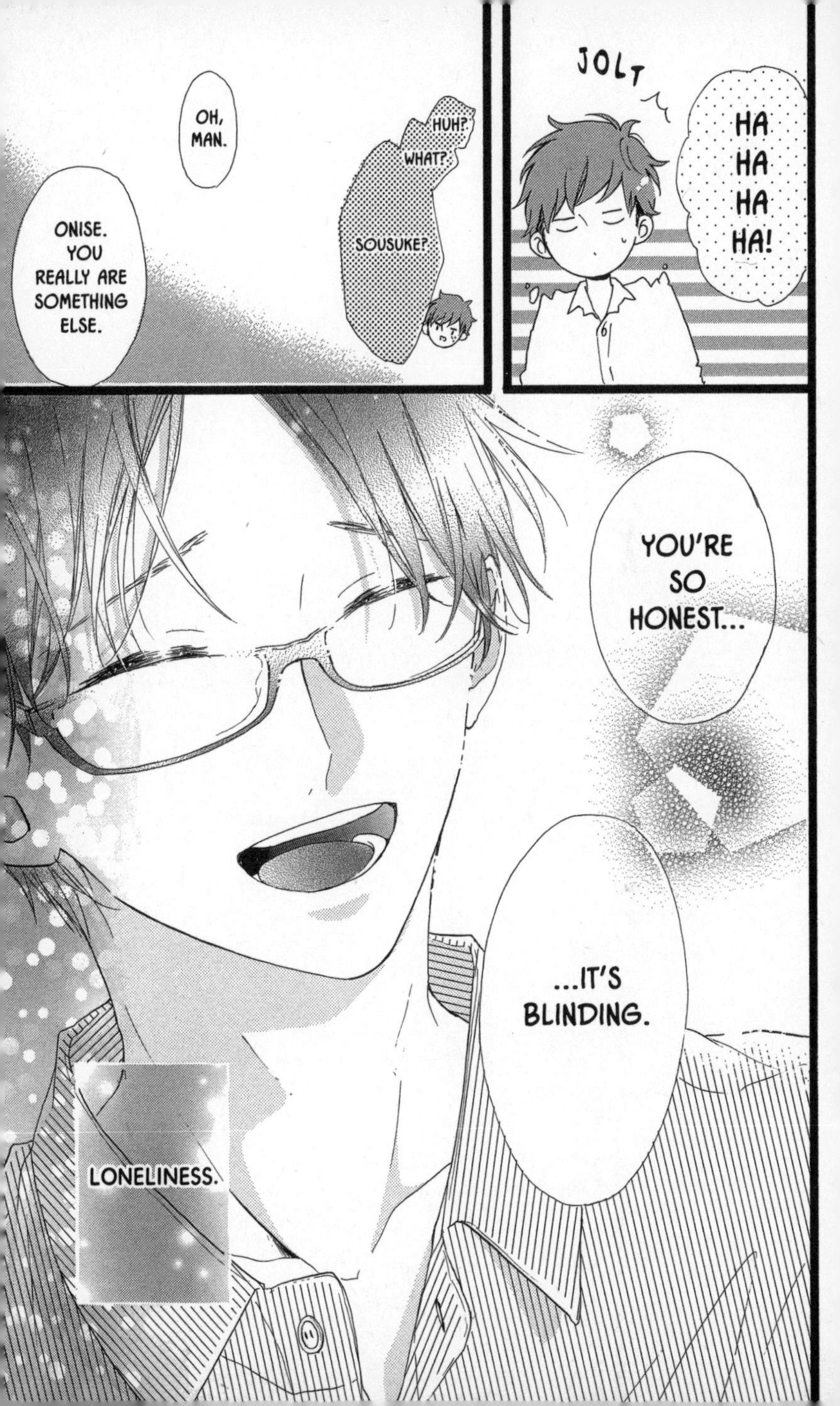
JOLT
HA HA HA HA!
HUH? WHAT?
SOUSUKE?
OH, MAN.
ONISE. YOU REALLY ARE SOMETHING ELSE.
YOU'RE SO HONEST...
...IT'S BLINDING.
LONELINESS.

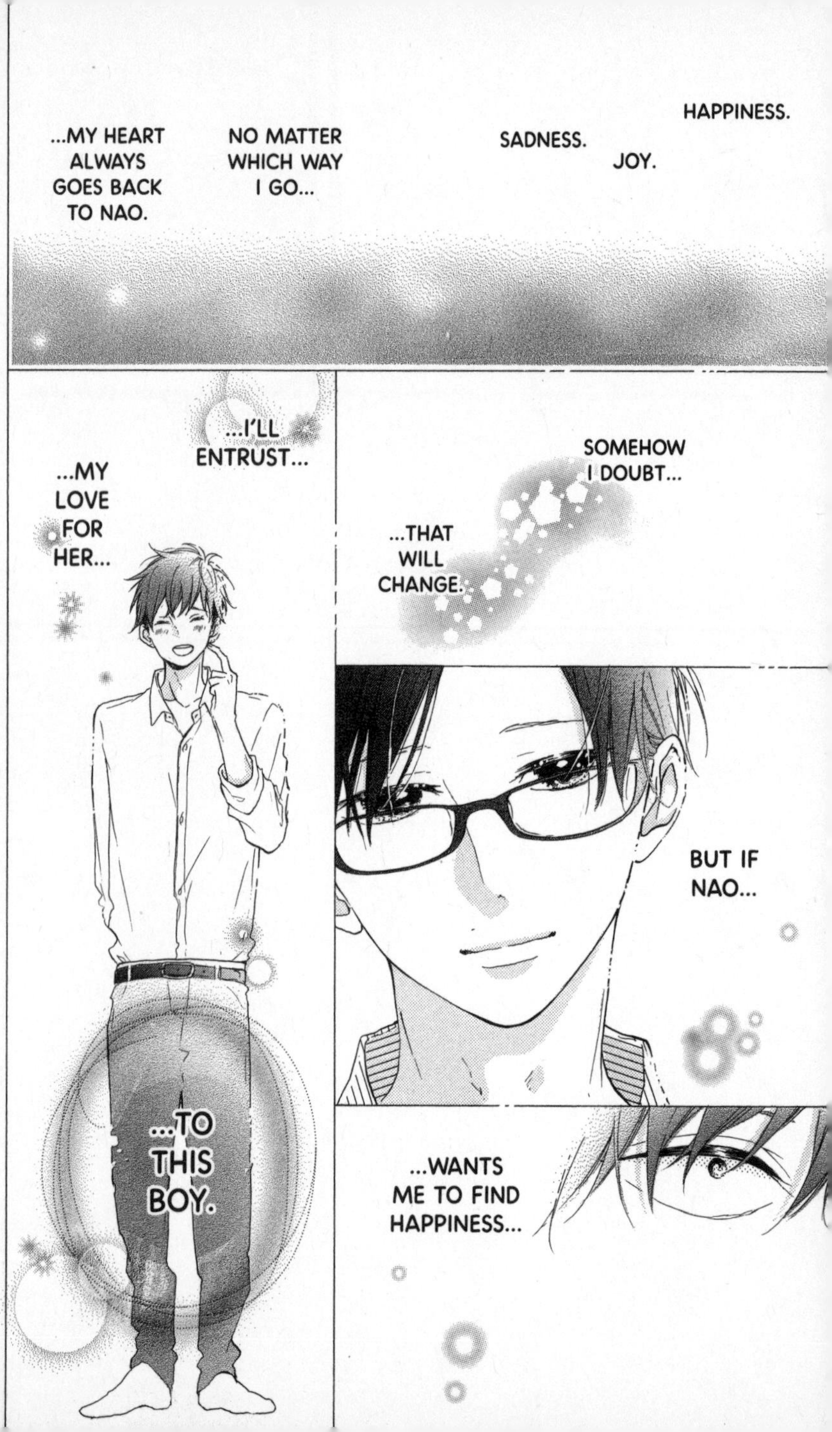
HAPPINESS.
JOY.
SADNESS.
NO MATTER WHICH WAY I GO...
...MY HEART ALWAYS GOES BACK TO NAO.
SOMEHOW I DOUBT...
...THAT WILL CHANGE.
BUT IF NAO...
...WANTS ME TO FIND HAPPINESS...
...I'LL ENTRUST...
...MY LOVE FOR HER...
...TO THIS BOY.

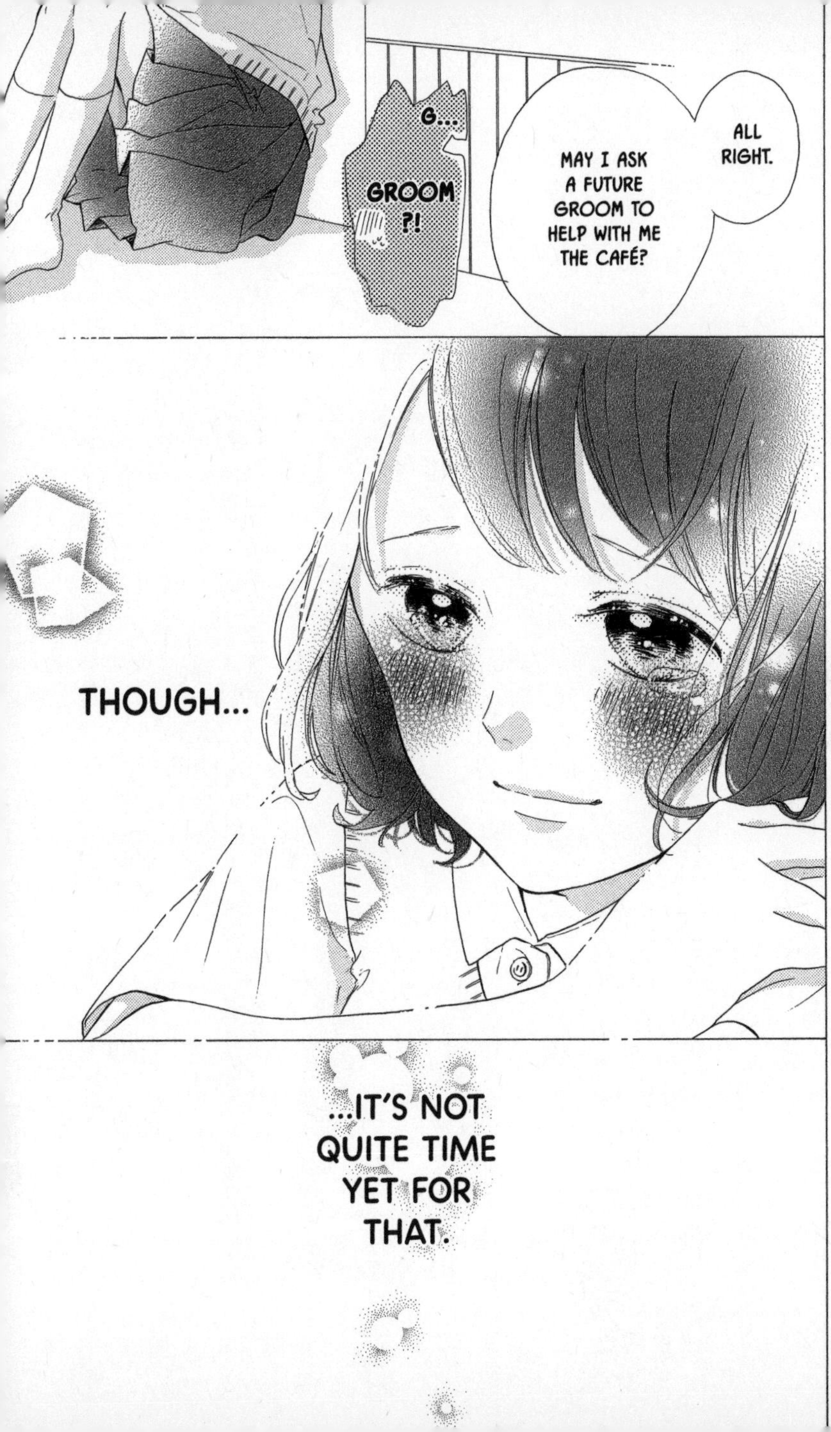
ALL RIGHT.
MAY I ASK A FUTURE GROOM TO HELP WITH ME THE CAFÉ?
G... GROOM ?!
THOUGH...
...IT'S NOT QUITE TIME YET FOR THAT.

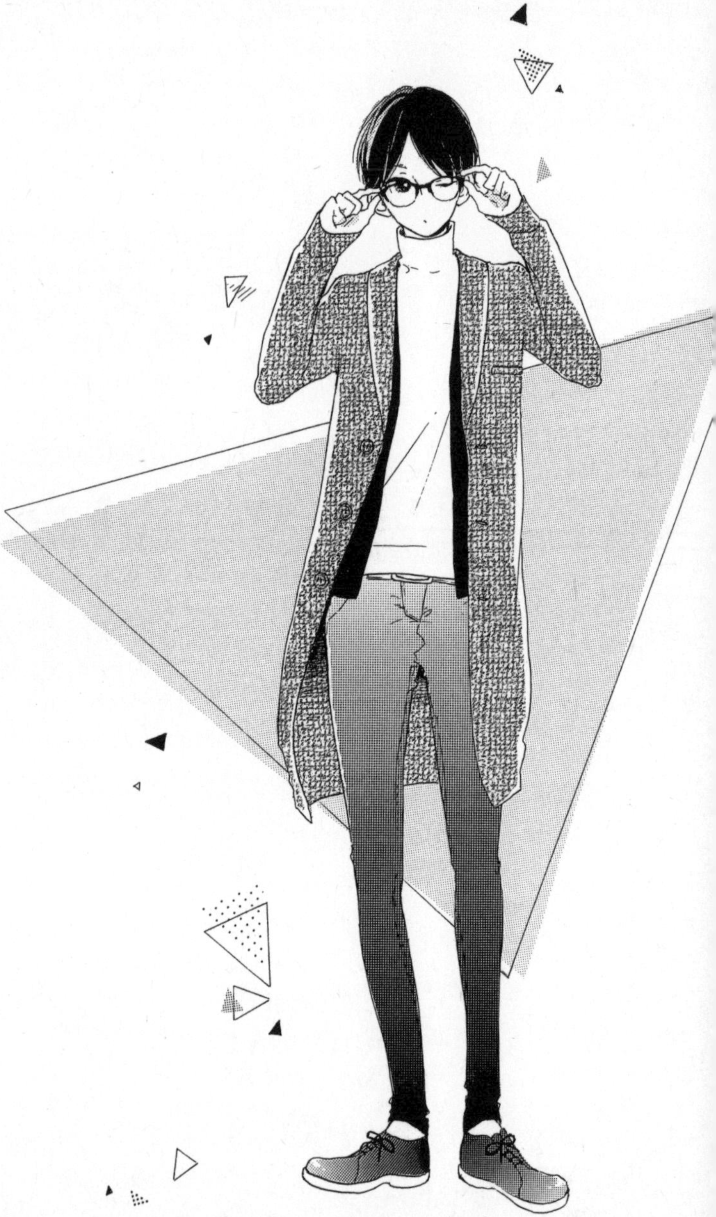

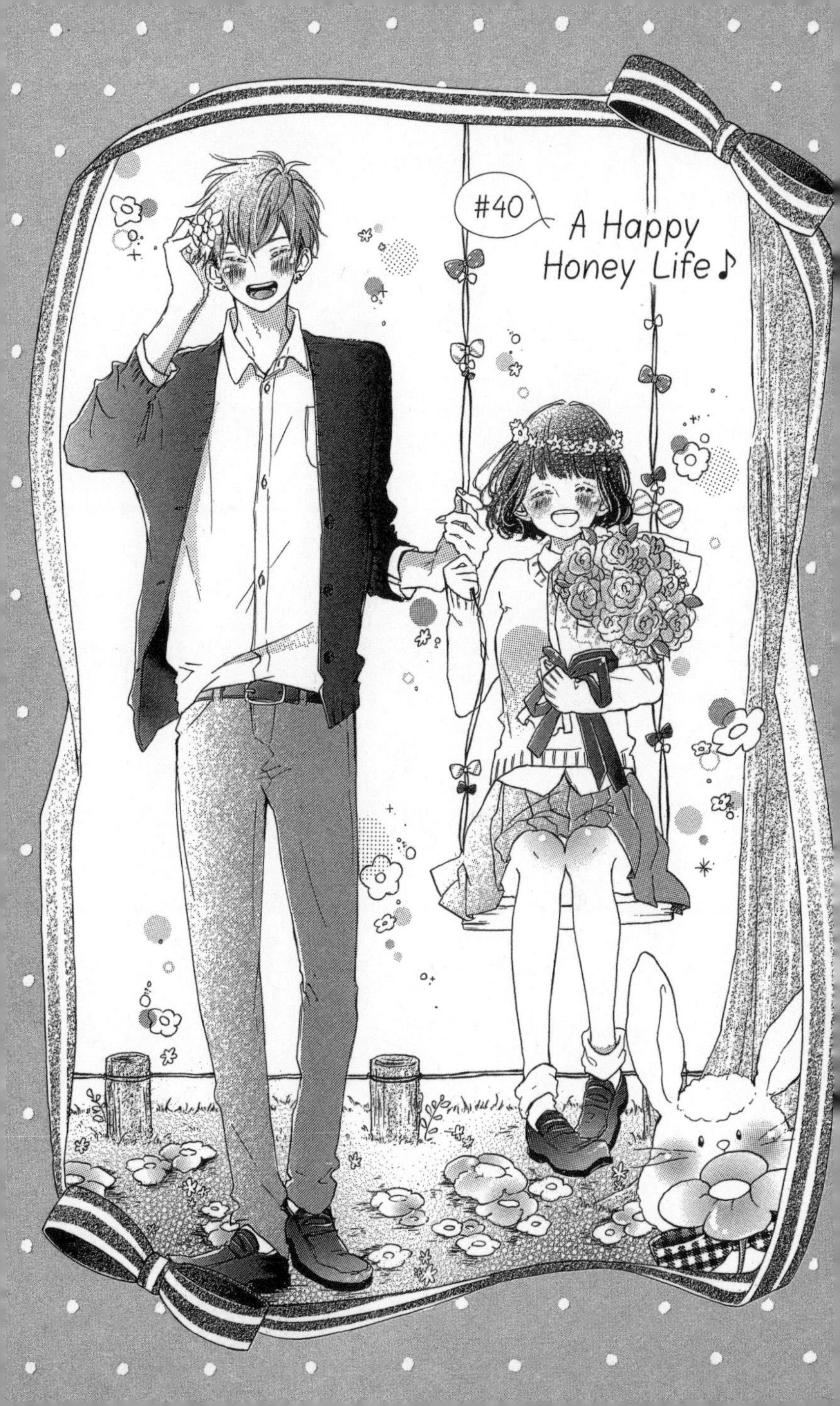
#40
A Happy Honey Life♪

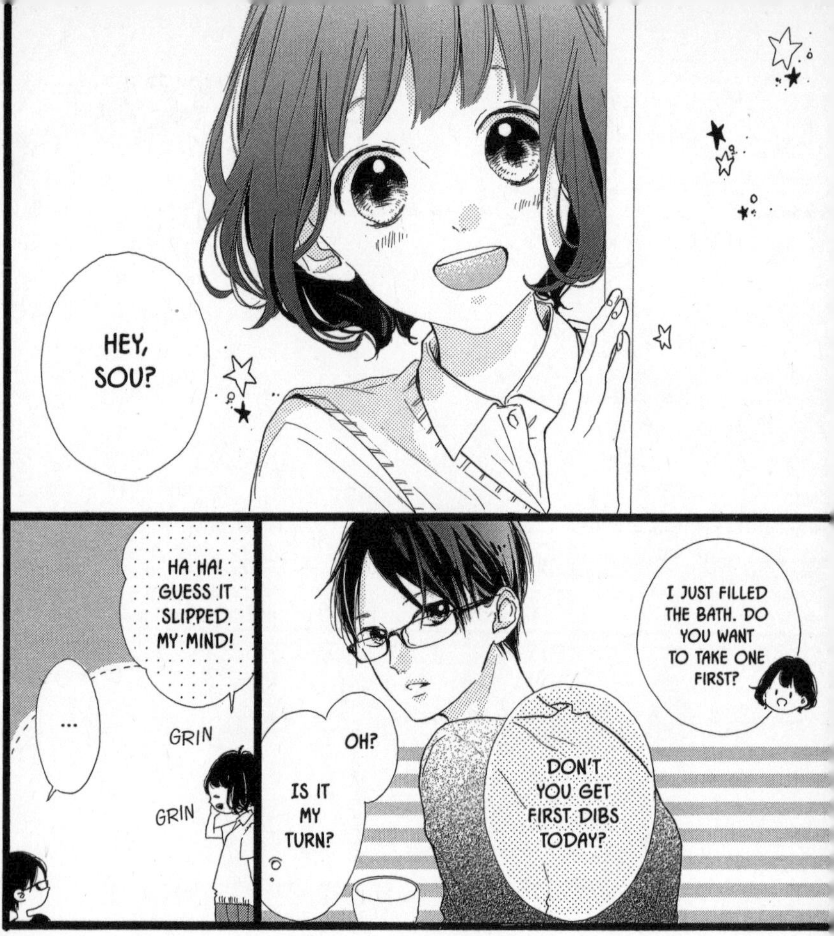
HEY, SOU?
I JUST FILLED THE BATH. DO YOU WANT TO TAKE ONE FIRST?
DON'T YOU GET FIRST DIBS TODAY?
OH? IS IT MY TURN?
HA HA! GUESS IT SLIPPED MY MIND!
GRIN
GRIN
...

Honey So Sweet

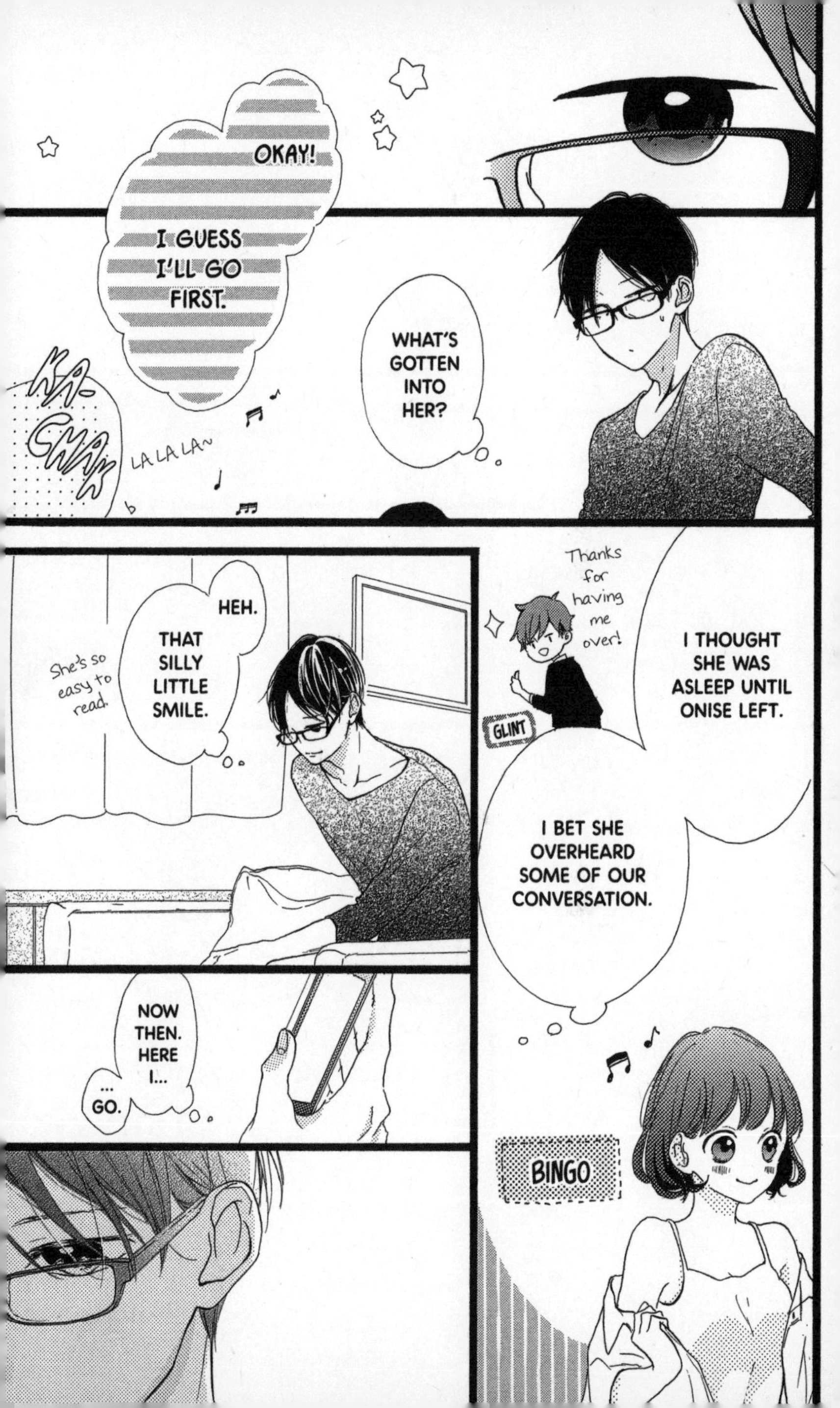
OKAY!
I GUESS I'LL GO FIRST.
KA-CHAK
LA LA LA~
WHAT'S GOTTEN INTO HER?
I THOUGHT SHE WAS ASLEEP UNTIL ONISE LEFT.
Thanks for having me over!
GLINT
I BET SHE OVERHEARD SOME OF OUR CONVERSATION.
BINGO
HEH.
THAT SILLY LITTLE SMILE.
She's so easy to read.
NOW THEN. HERE I...
...GO.

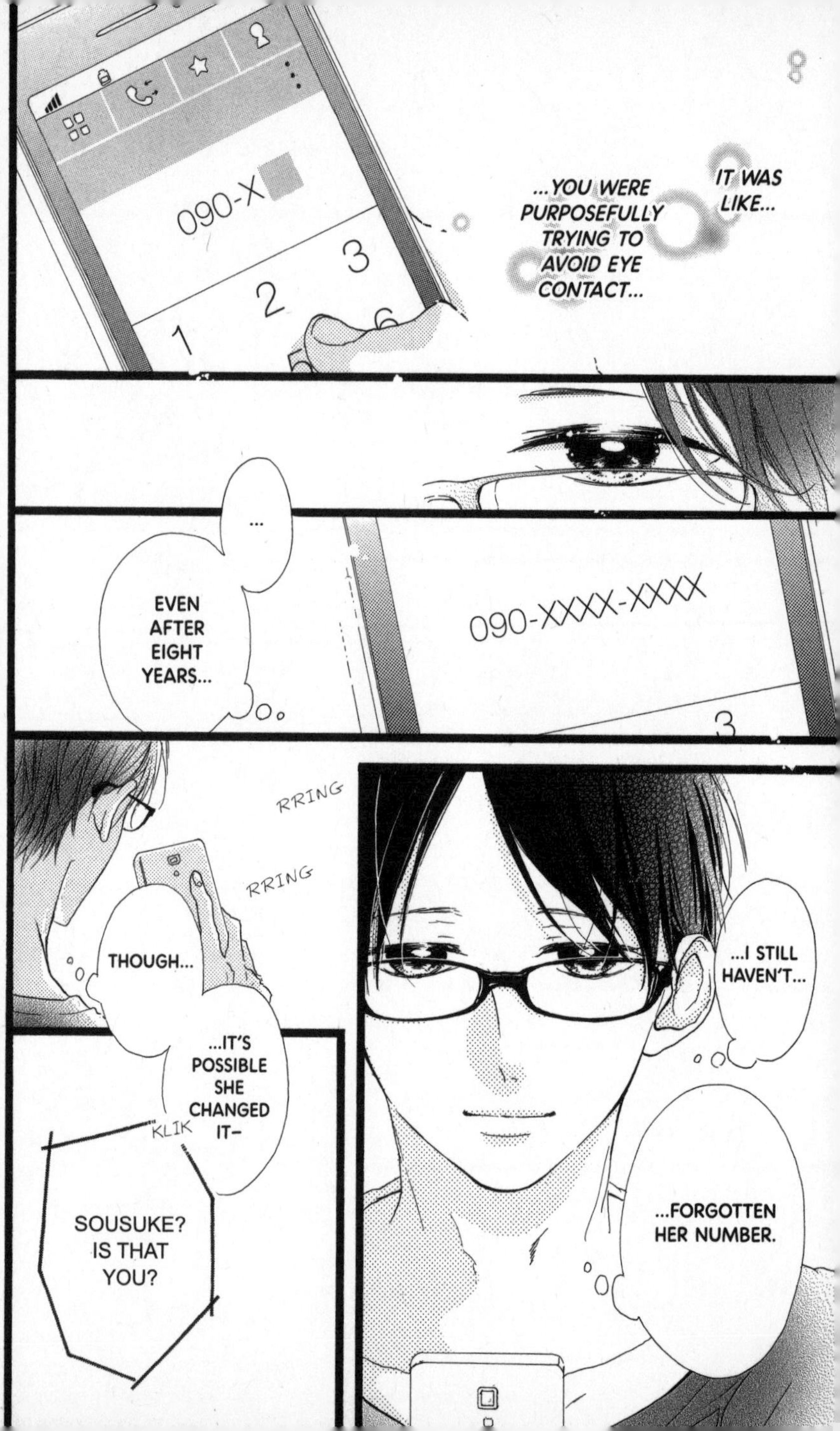
IT WAS LIKE...
...YOU WERE PURPOSEFULLY TRYING TO AVOID EYE CONTACT...
090-X
...
EVEN AFTER EIGHT YEARS...
090-XXXX-XXXX
...I STILL HAVEN'T...
...FORGOTTEN HER NUMBER.
RRING
RRING
THOUGH...
...IT'S POSSIBLE SHE CHANGED IT–
KLIK
SOUSUKE? IS THAT YOU?

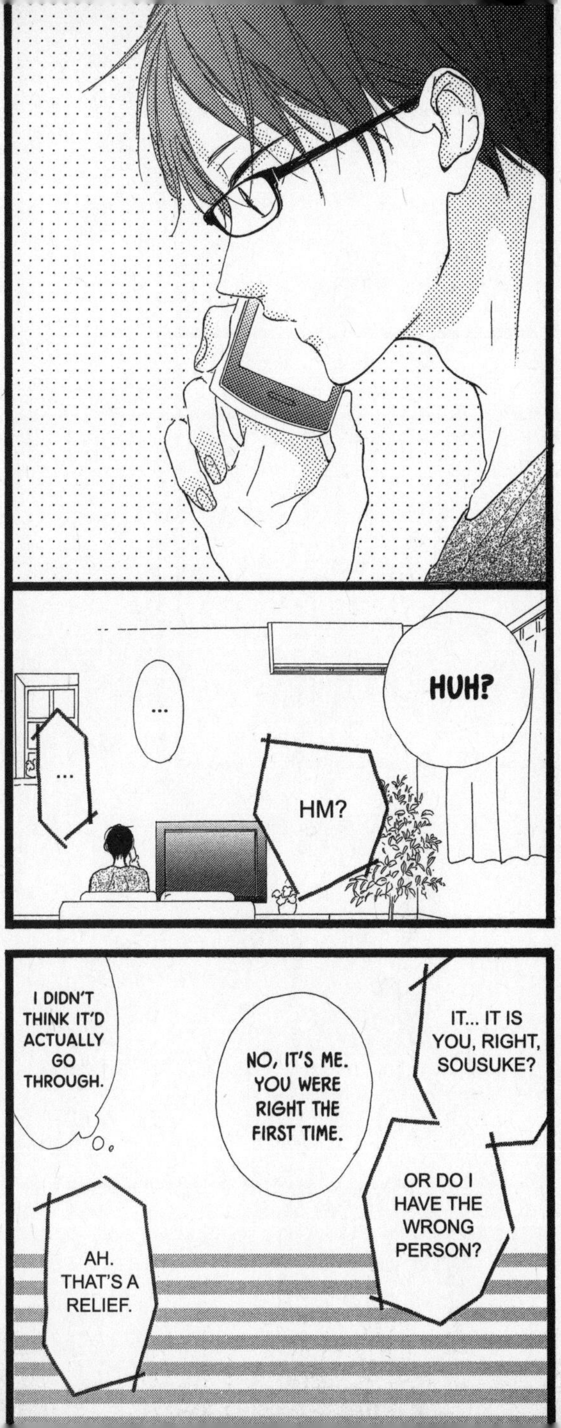
HUH?
...
HM?
...
IT... IT IS YOU, RIGHT, SOUSUKE?
OR DO I HAVE THE WRONG PERSON?
NO, IT'S ME. YOU WERE RIGHT THE FIRST TIME.
I DIDN'T THINK IT'D ACTUALLY GO THROUGH.
AH. THAT'S A RELIEF.
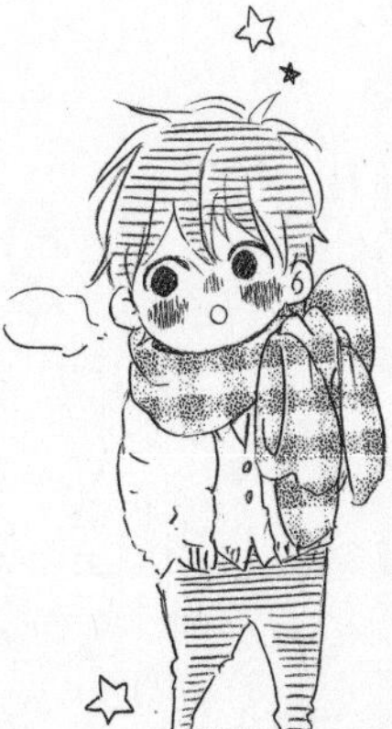

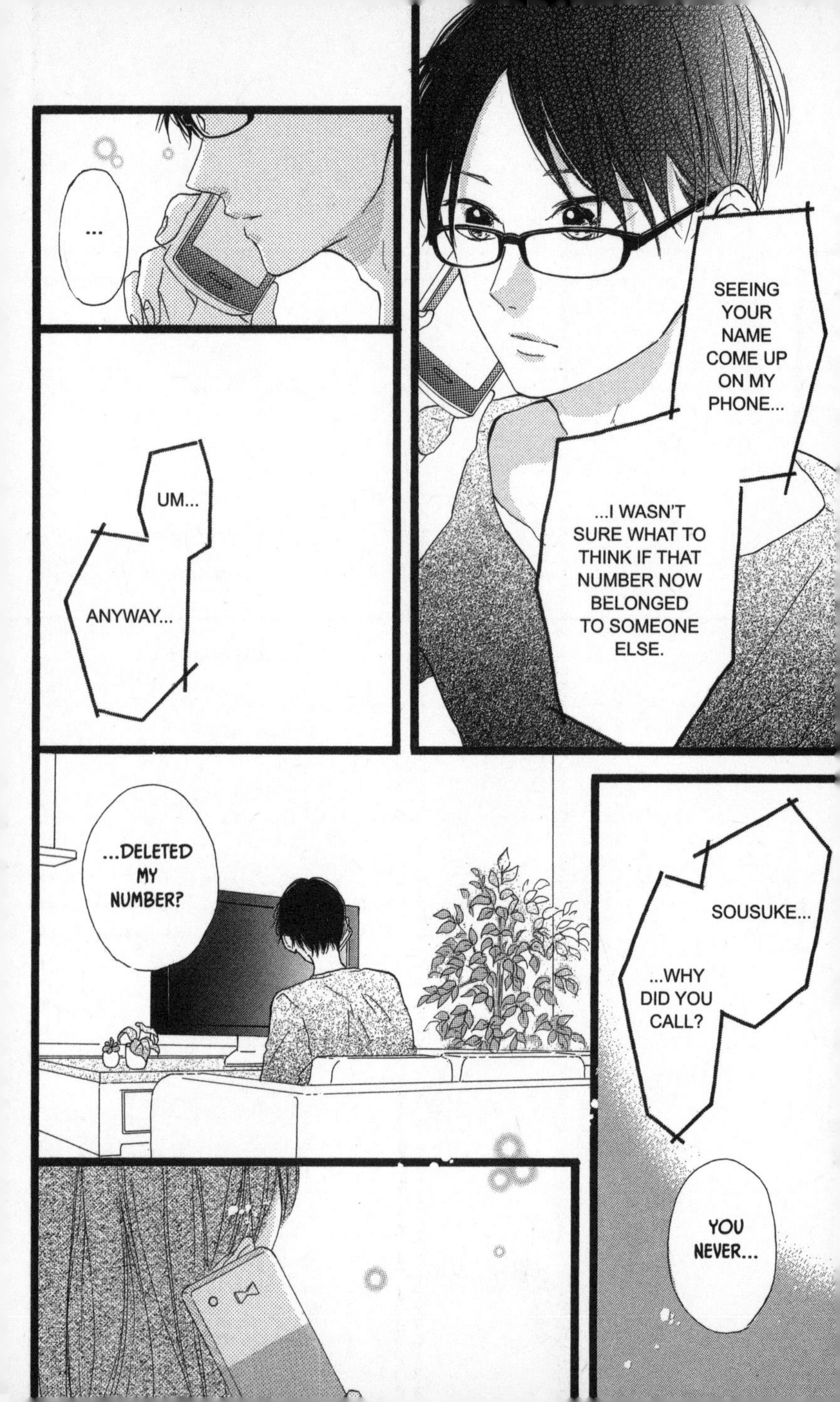
SEEING YOUR NAME COME UP ON MY PHONE...
...I WASN'T SURE WHAT TO THINK IF THAT NUMBER NOW BELONGED TO SOMEONE ELSE.
...
UM...
ANYWAY...
SOUSUKE...
...WHY DID YOU CALL?
YOU NEVER...
...DELETED MY NUMBER?

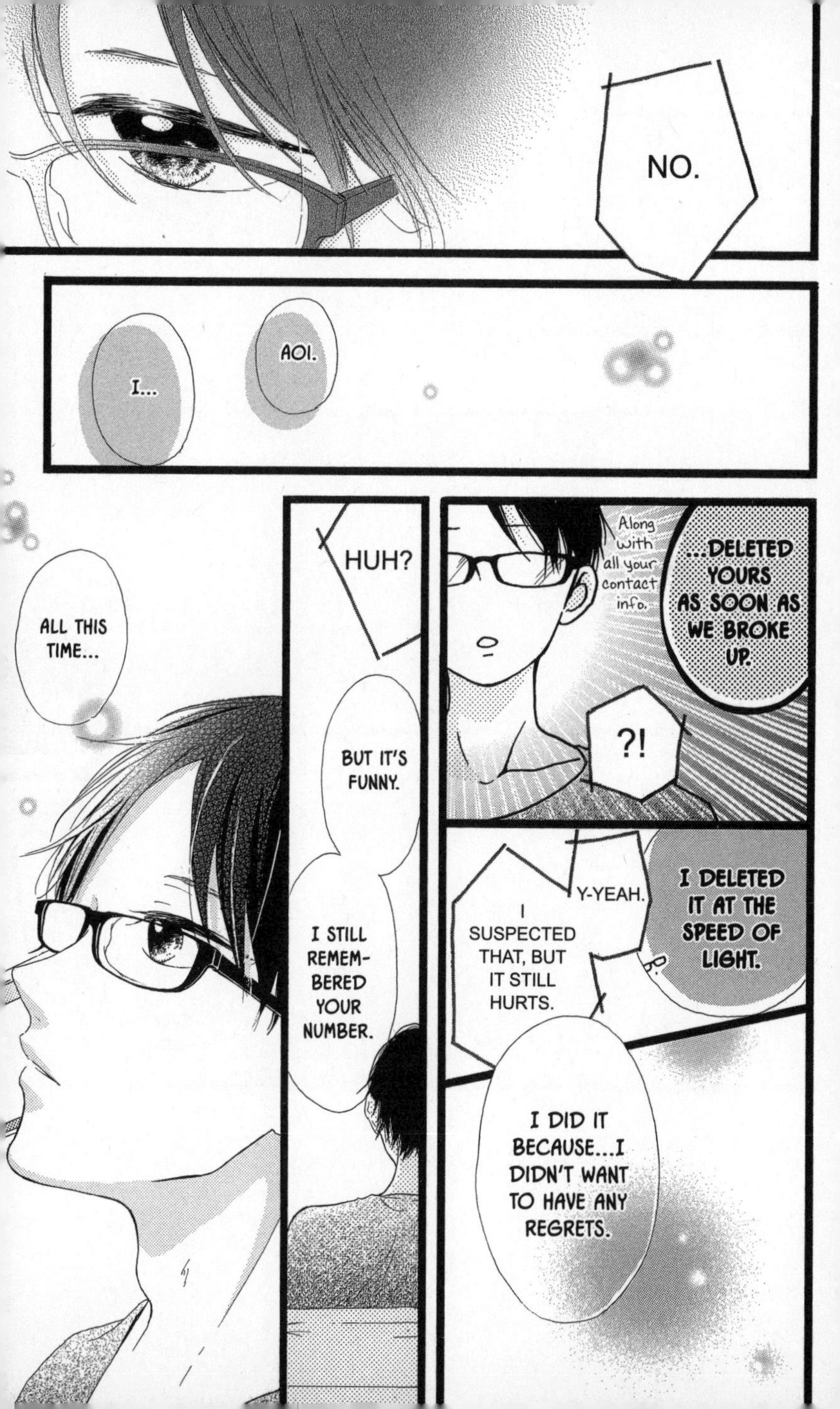
NO.
AOI.
I...
Along with all your contact info.
...DELETED YOURS AS SOON AS WE BROKE UP.
?!
I DELETED IT AT THE SPEED OF LIGHT.
Y-YEAH.
I SUSPECTED THAT, BUT IT STILL HURTS.
I DID IT BECAUSE...I DIDN'T WANT TO HAVE ANY REGRETS.
HUH?
BUT IT'S FUNNY.
I STILL REMEMBERED YOUR NUMBER.
ALL THIS TIME...

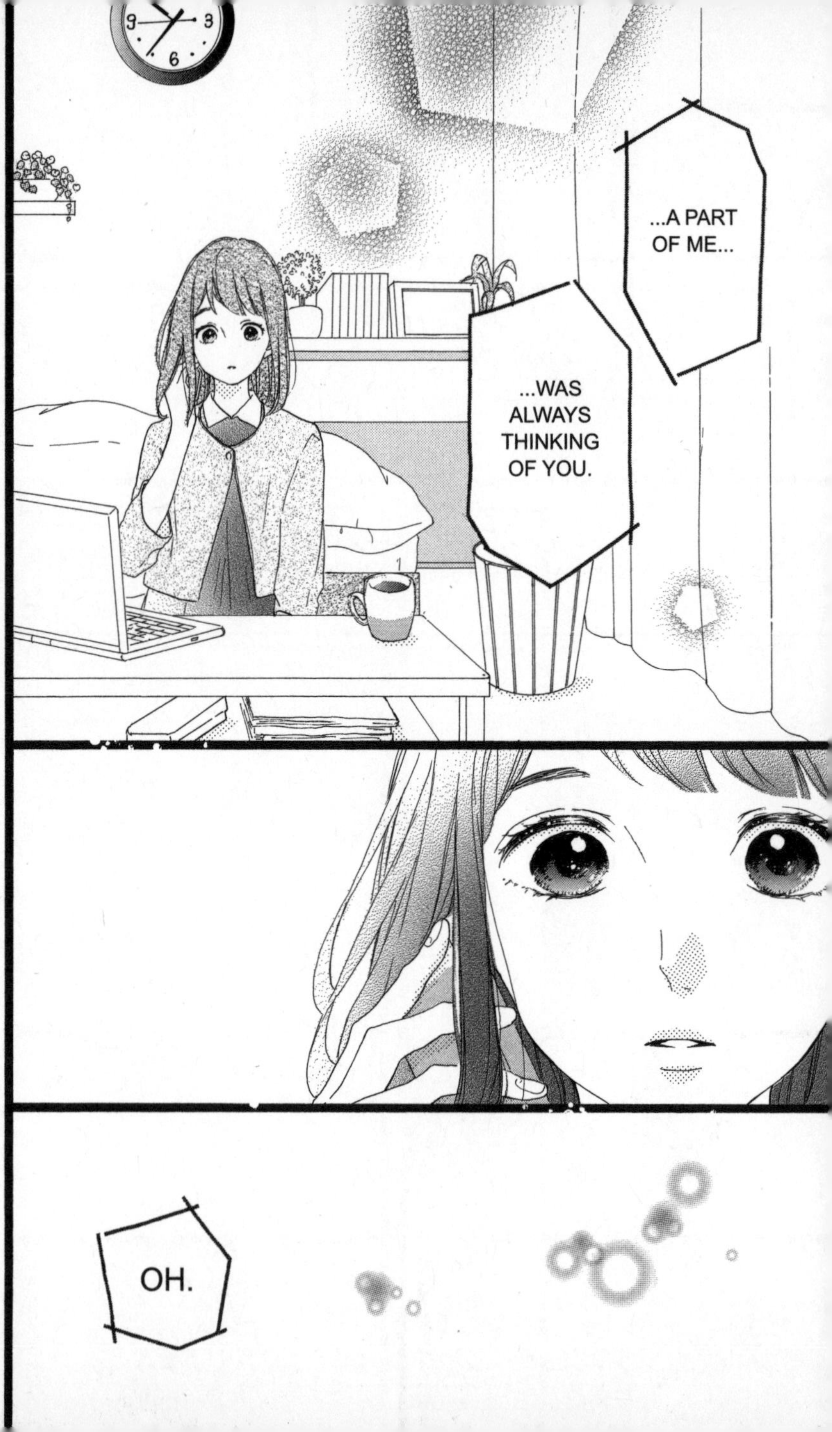
...A PART OF ME...
...WAS ALWAYS THINKING OF YOU.
OH.

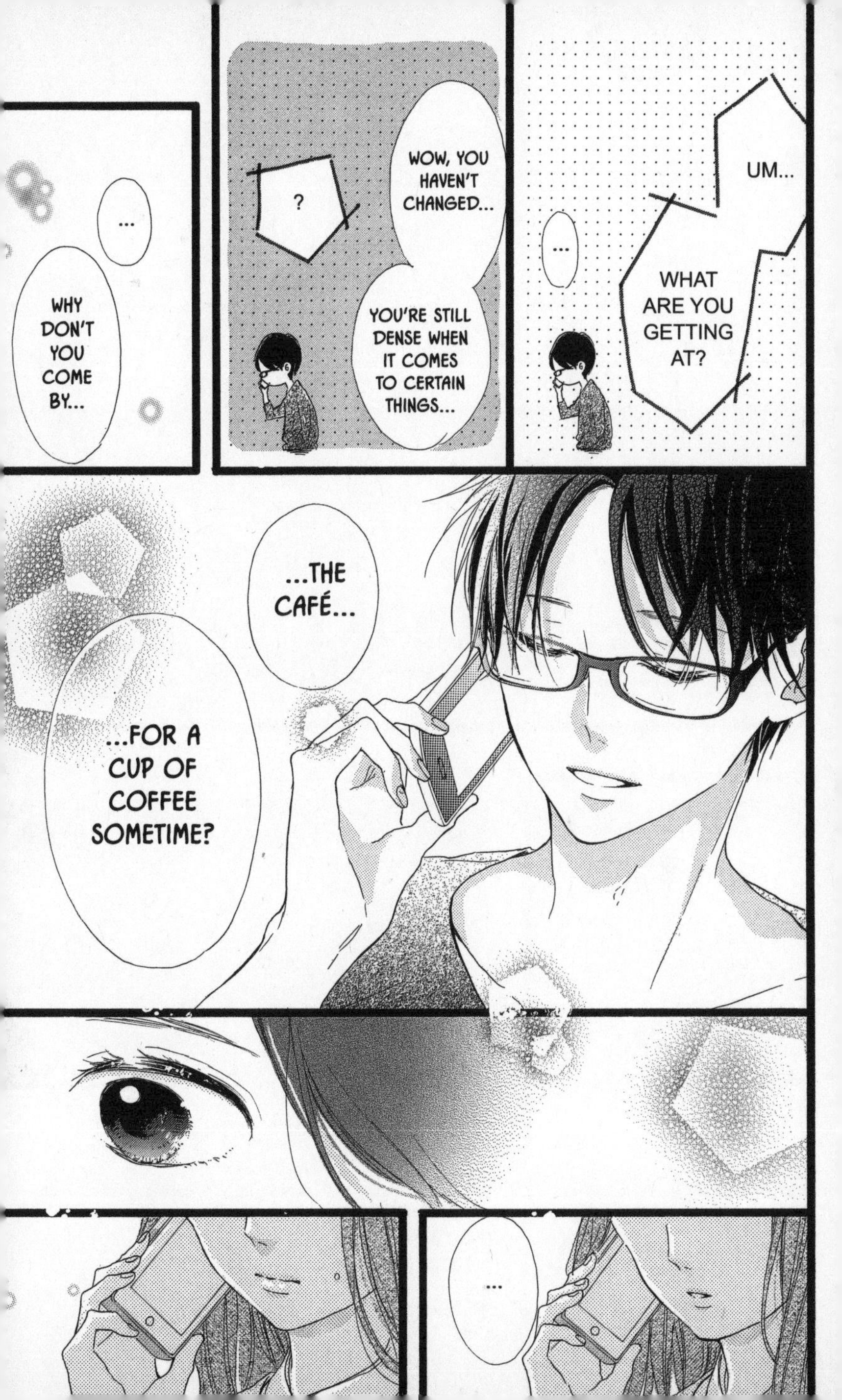
UM...
WHAT ARE YOU GETTING AT?
...
WOW, YOU HAVEN'T CHANGED...
?
YOU'RE STILL DENSE WHEN IT COMES TO CERTAIN THINGS...
...
WHY DON'T YOU COME BY...
...THE CAFÉ...
...FOR A CUP OF COFFEE SOMETIME?
...

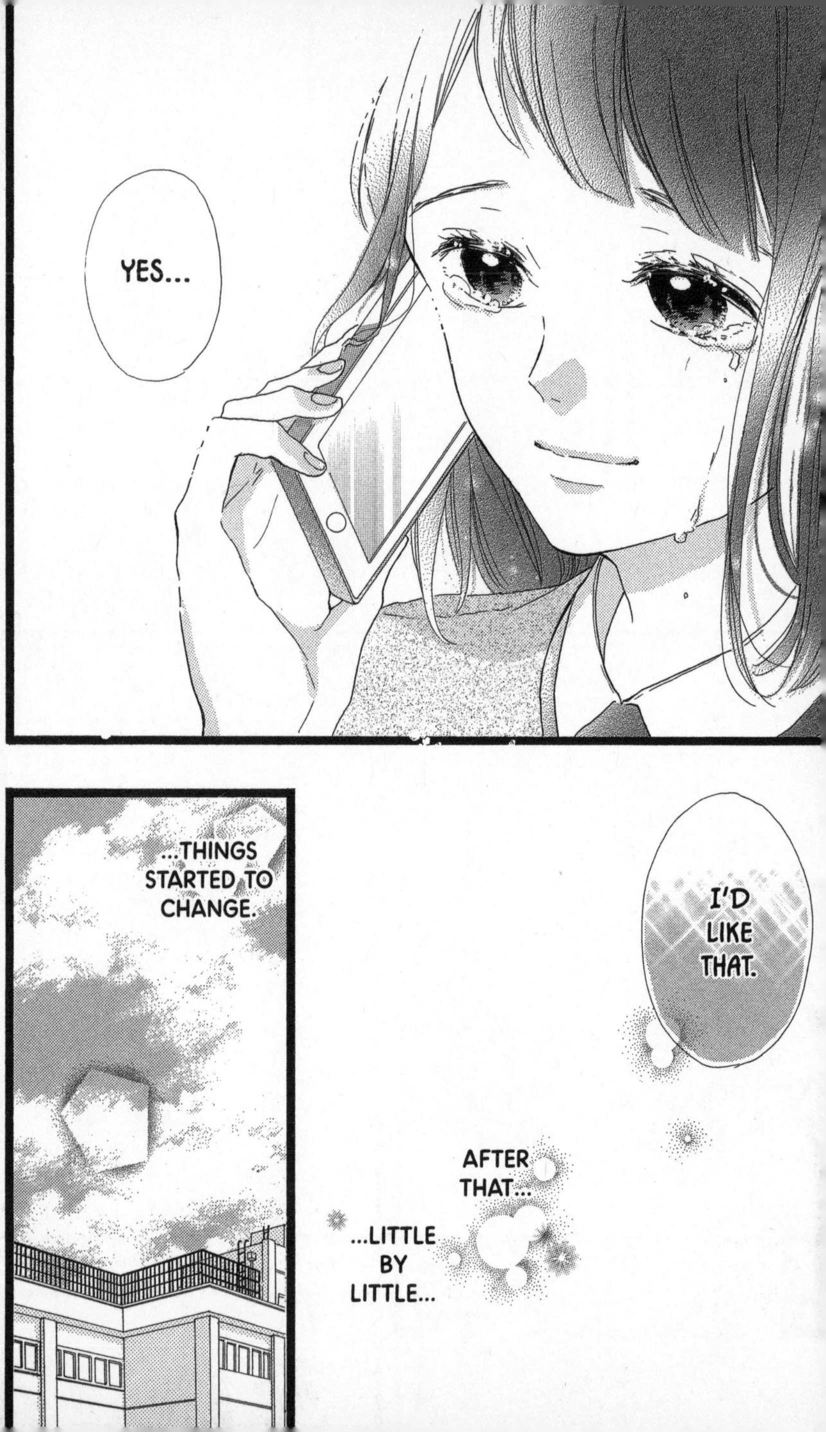
YES...
I'D LIKE THAT.
AFTER THAT...
...LITTLE BY LITTLE...
...THINGS STARTED TO CHANGE.

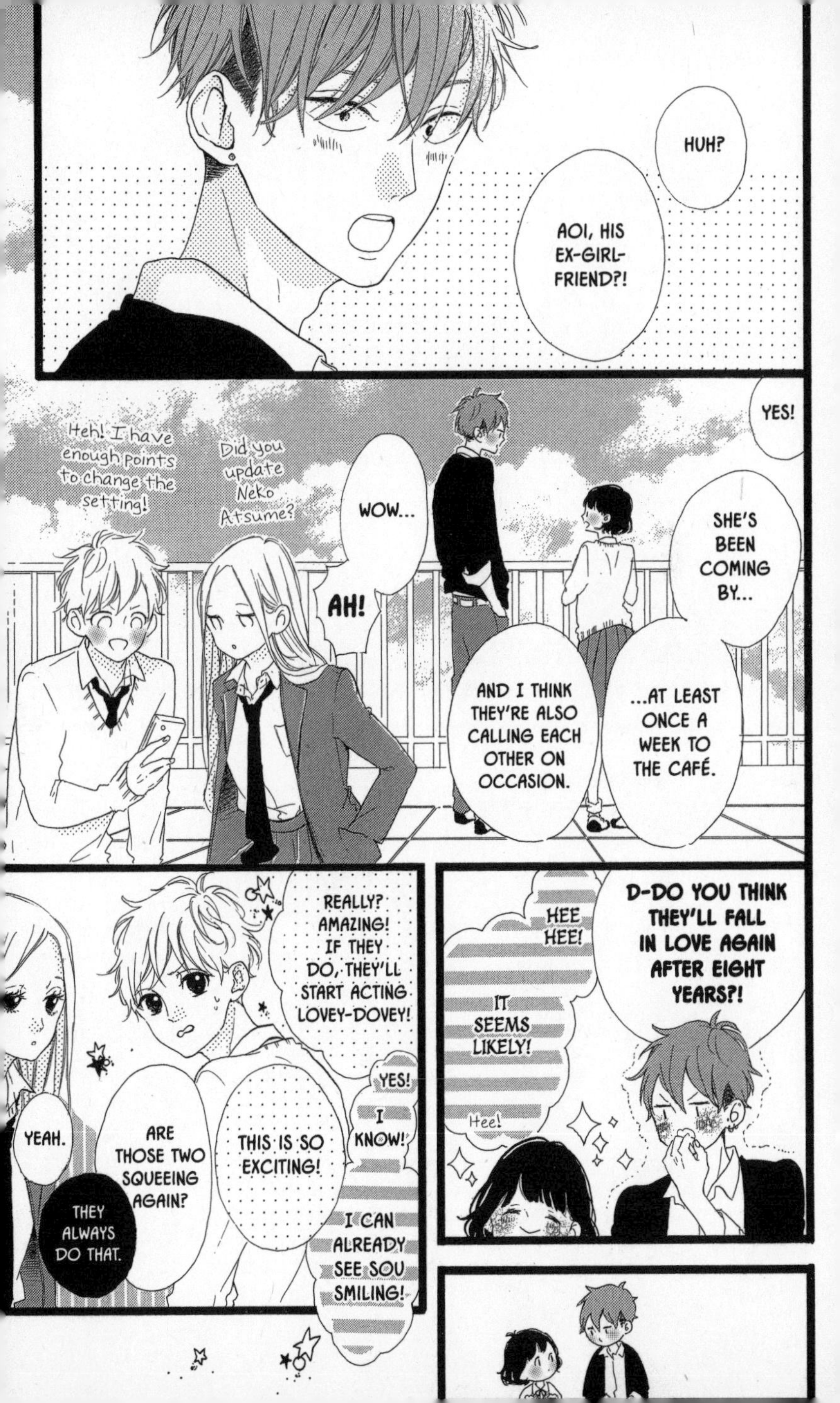
HUH?
AOI, HIS EX-GIRL-FRIEND?!
YES!
SHE'S BEEN COMING BY...
...AT LEAST ONCE A WEEK TO THE CAFÉ.
AND I THINK THEY'RE ALSO CALLING EACH OTHER ON OCCASION.
WOW...
AH!
Did you update Neko Atsume?
Heh! I have enough points to change the setting!
D-DO YOU THINK THEY'LL FALL IN LOVE AGAIN AFTER EIGHT YEARS?!
HEE HEE!
IT SEEMS LIKELY!
Hee!
REALLY? AMAZING! IF THEY DO, THEY'LL START ACTING LOVEY-DOVEY!
YES!
I KNOW!
I CAN ALREADY SEE SOU SMILING!
THIS IS SO EXCITING!
ARE THOSE TWO SQUEEING AGAIN?
YEAH.
THEY ALWAYS DO THAT.

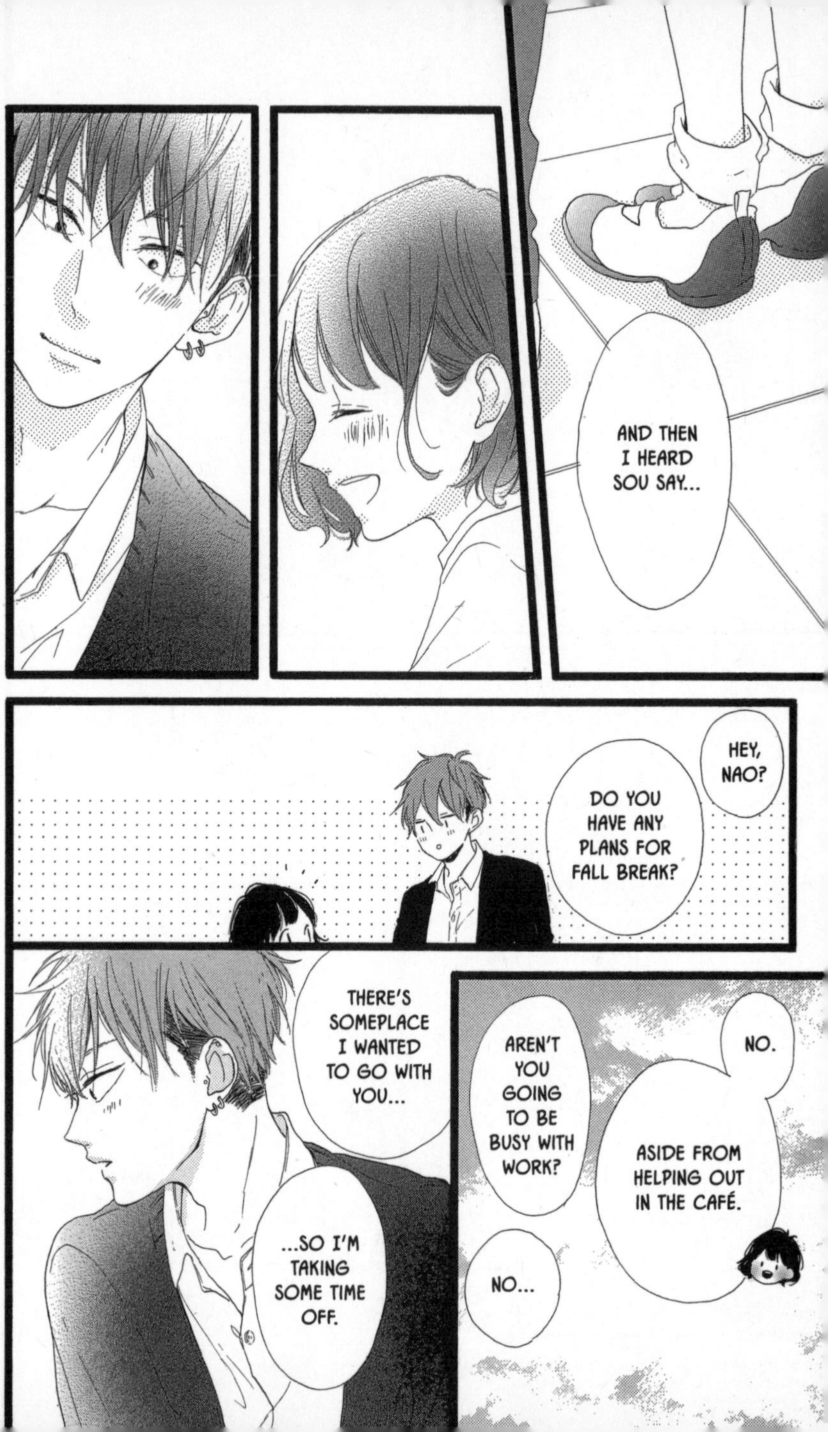

AND THEN I HEARD SOU SAY...
HEY, NAO?
DO YOU HAVE ANY PLANS FOR FALL BREAK?
NO.
ASIDE FROM HELPING OUT IN THE CAFÉ.
AREN'T YOU GOING TO BE BUSY WITH WORK?
NO...
THERE'S SOMEPLACE I WANTED TO GO WITH YOU...
...SO I'M TAKING SOME TIME OFF.

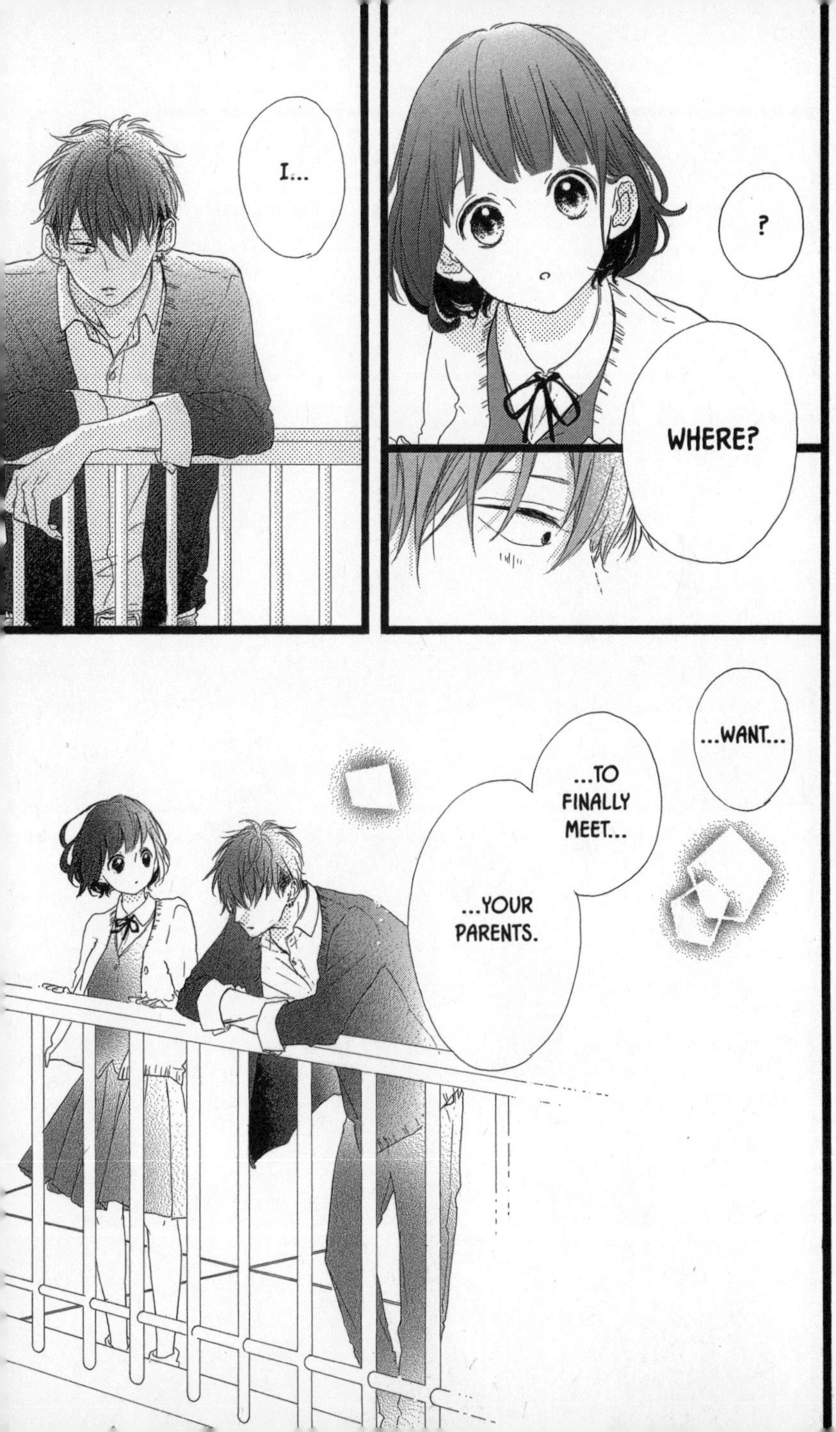
?
WHERE?
I...
...WANT...
...TO FINALLY MEET...
...YOUR PARENTS.

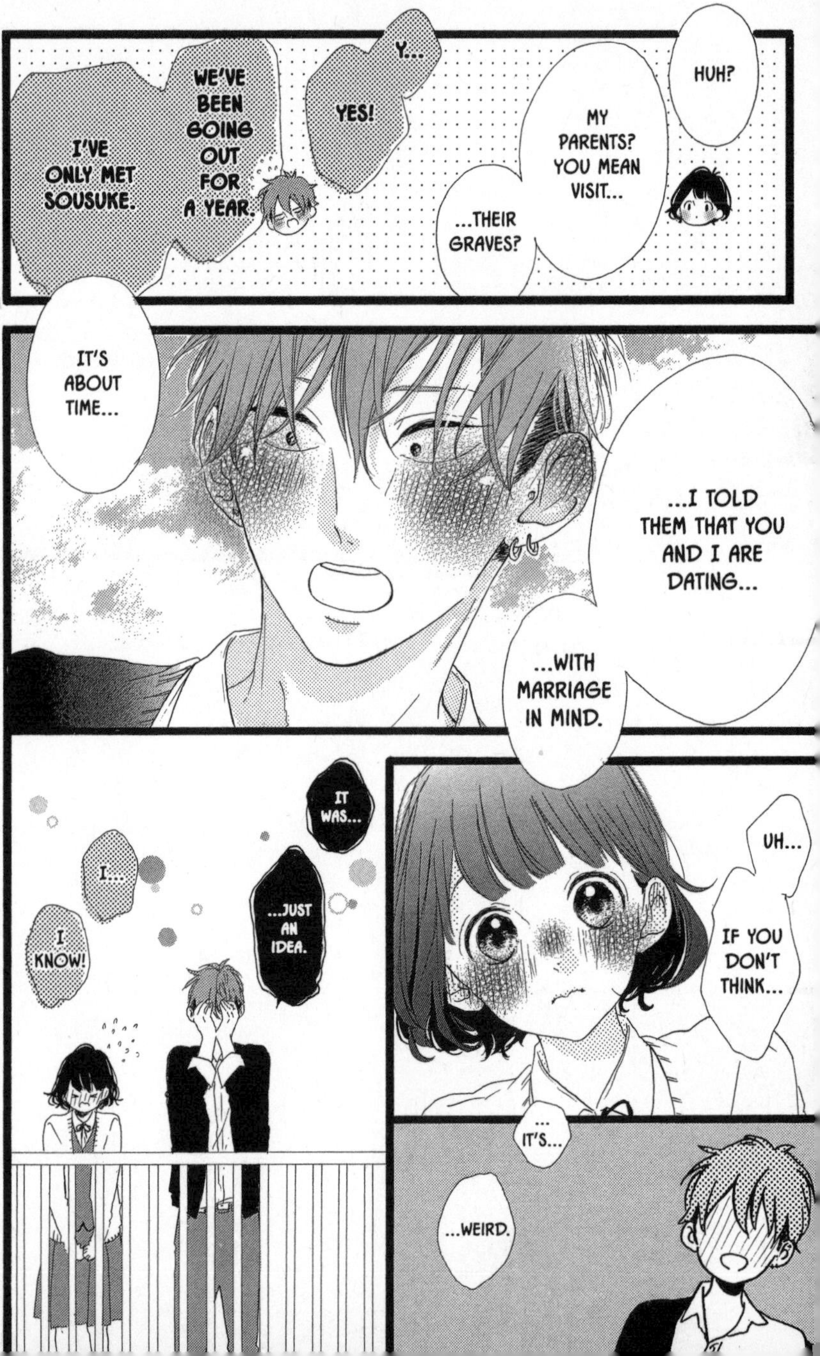

HUH?
MY PARENTS? YOU MEAN VISIT...
...THEIR GRAVES?
Y...
YES!
WE'VE BEEN GOING OUT FOR A YEAR.
I'VE ONLY MET SOUSUKE.
IT'S ABOUT TIME...
...I TOLD THEM THAT YOU AND I ARE DATING...
...WITH MARRIAGE IN MIND.
UH...
IF YOU DON'T THINK...
... IT'S...
...WEIRD.
IT WAS...
...JUST AN IDEA.
I...
I KNOW!

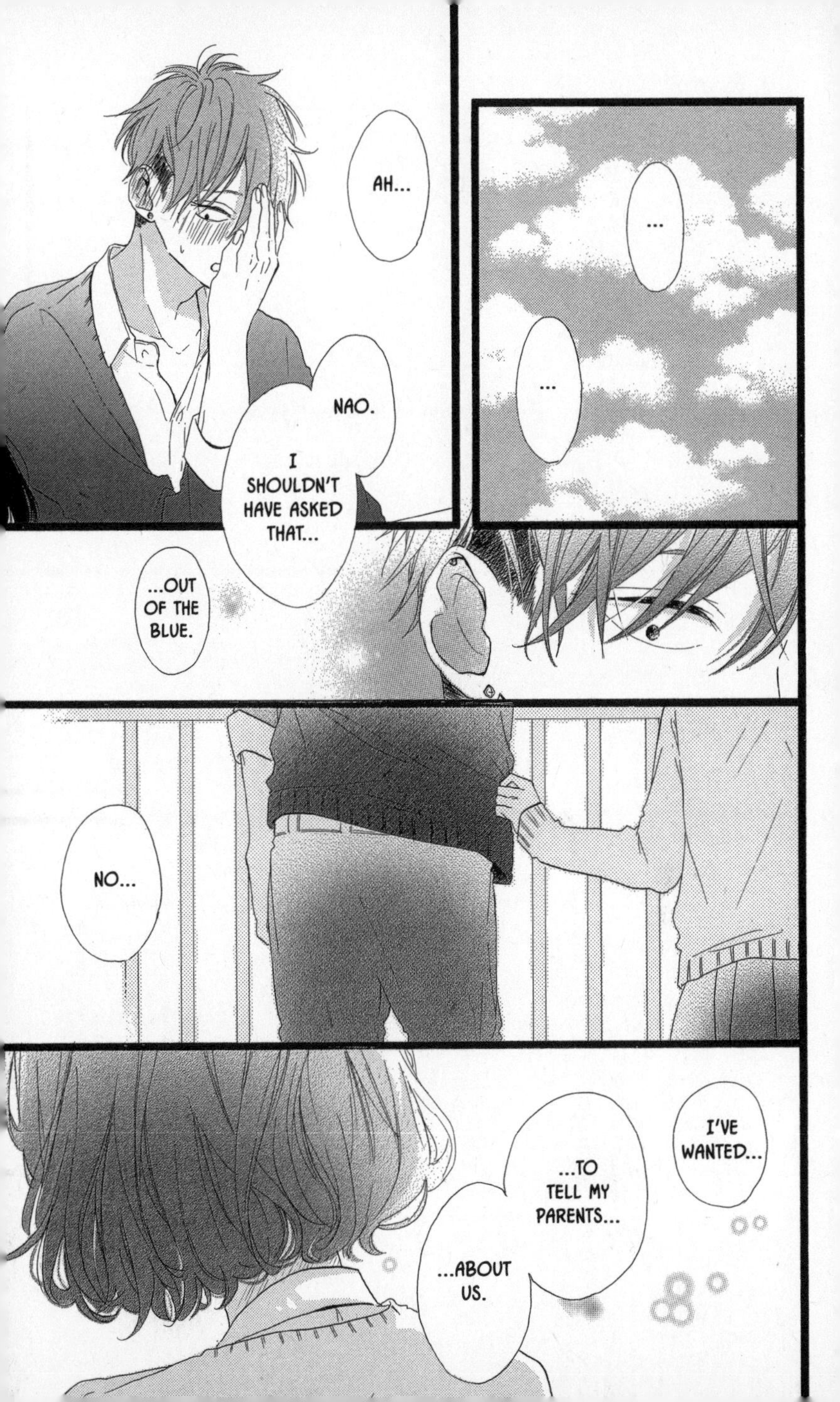
...
...
AH...
NAO.
I SHOULDN'T HAVE ASKED THAT...
...OUT OF THE BLUE.
NO...
I'VE WANTED...
...TO TELL MY PARENTS...
...ABOUT US.

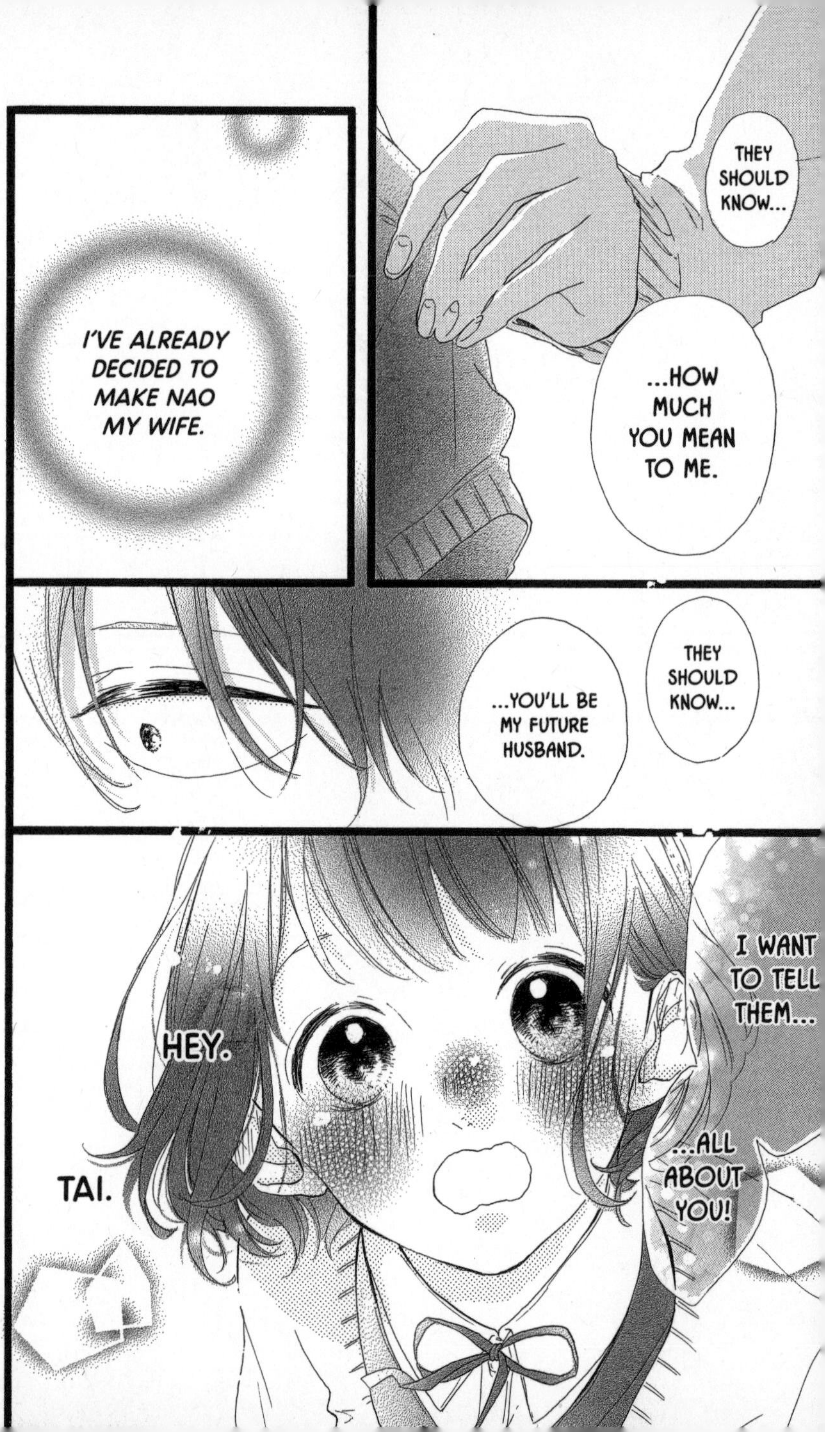
THEY SHOULD KNOW...
...HOW MUCH YOU MEAN TO ME.
I'VE ALREADY DECIDED TO MAKE NAO MY WIFE.
THEY SHOULD KNOW...
...YOU'LL BE MY FUTURE HUSBAND.
I WANT TO TELL THEM...
...ALL ABOUT YOU!
HEY.
TAI.

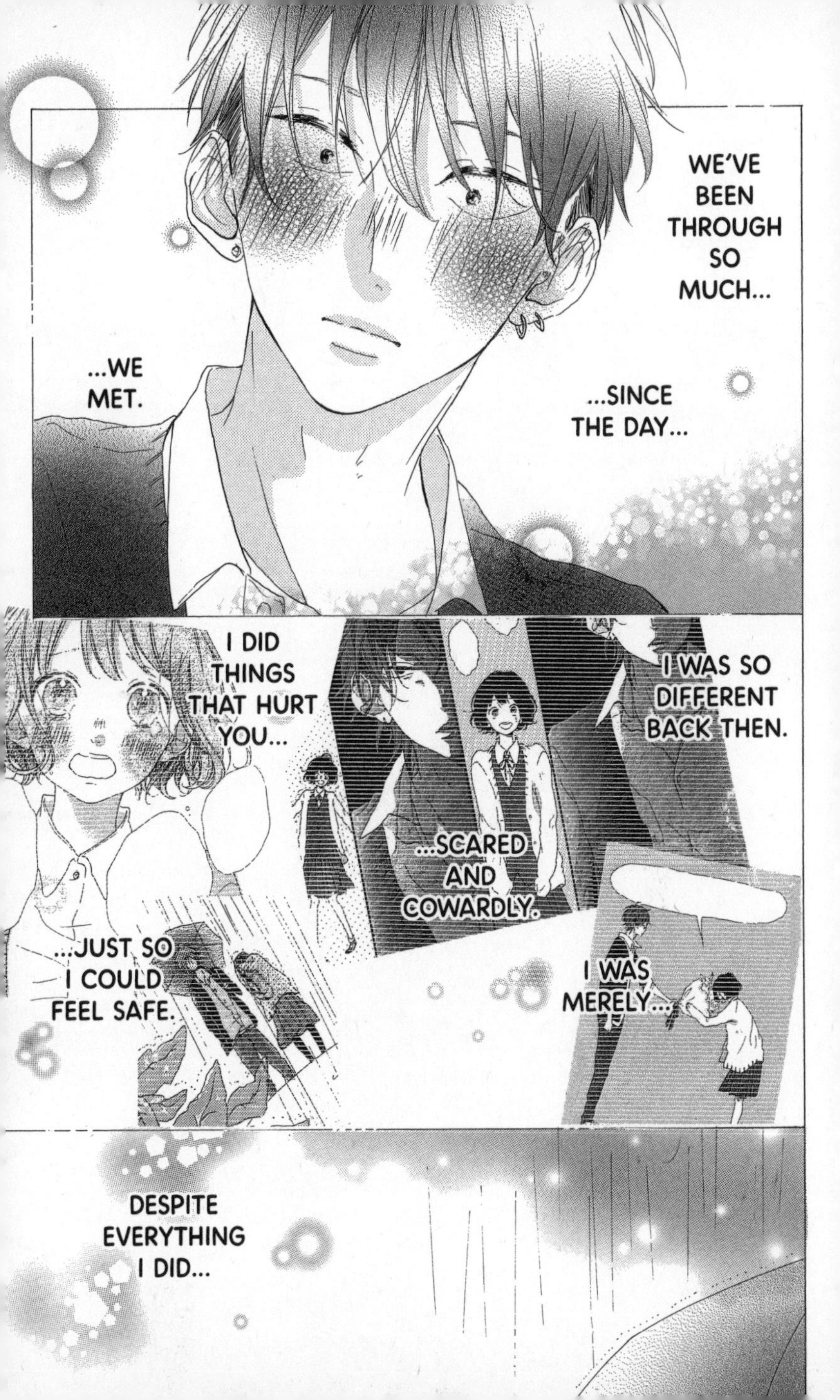
WE'VE BEEN THROUGH SO MUCH...
...SINCE THE DAY...
...WE MET.
I WAS SO DIFFERENT BACK THEN.
...SCARED AND COWARDLY.
I WAS MERELY...
I DID THINGS THAT HURT YOU...
...JUST SO I COULD FEEL SAFE.
DESPITE EVERYTHING I DID...

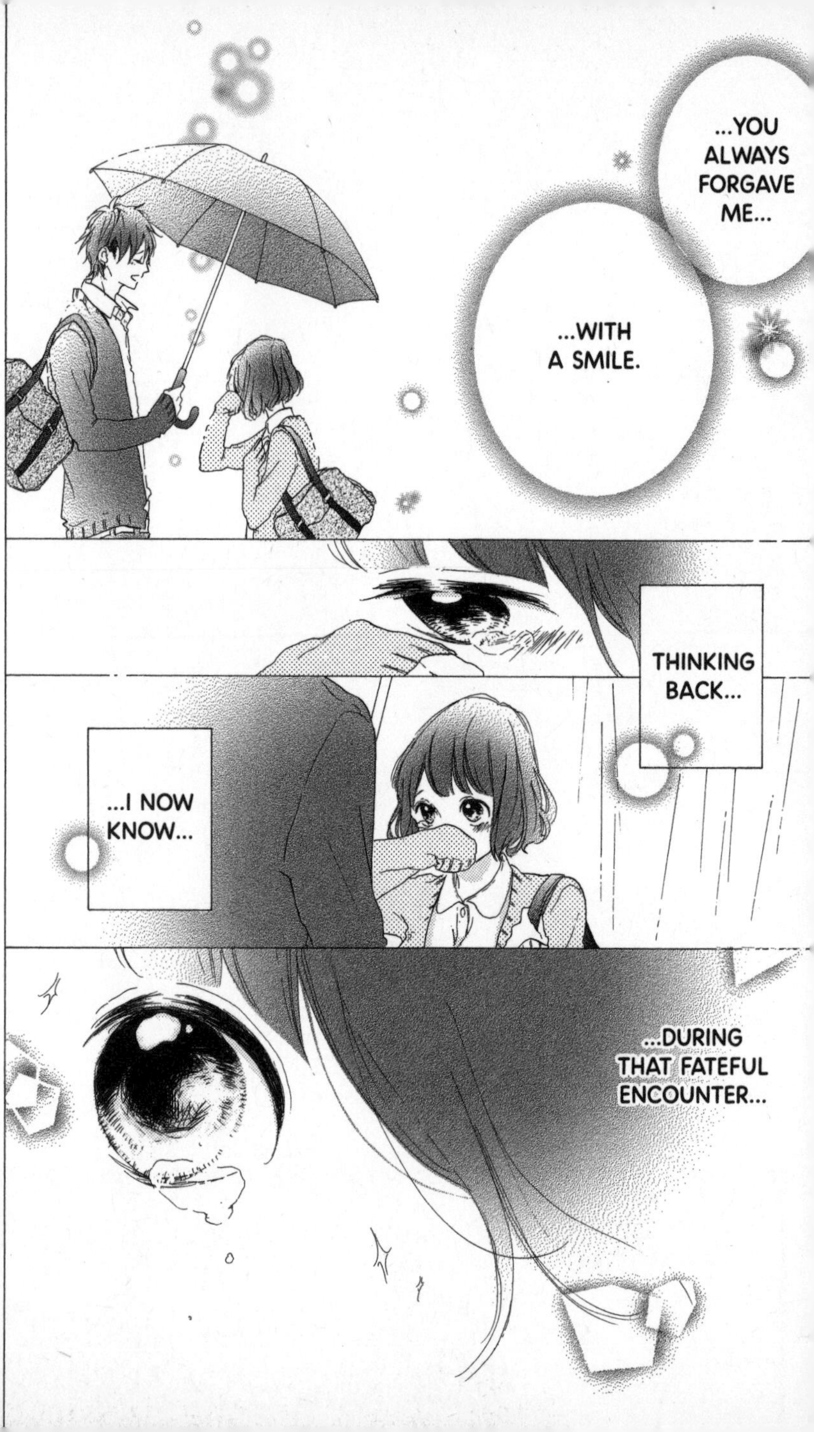
...YOU ALWAYS FORGAVE ME...
...WITH A SMILE.
THINKING BACK...
...I NOW KNOW...
...DURING THAT FATEFUL ENCOUNTER...

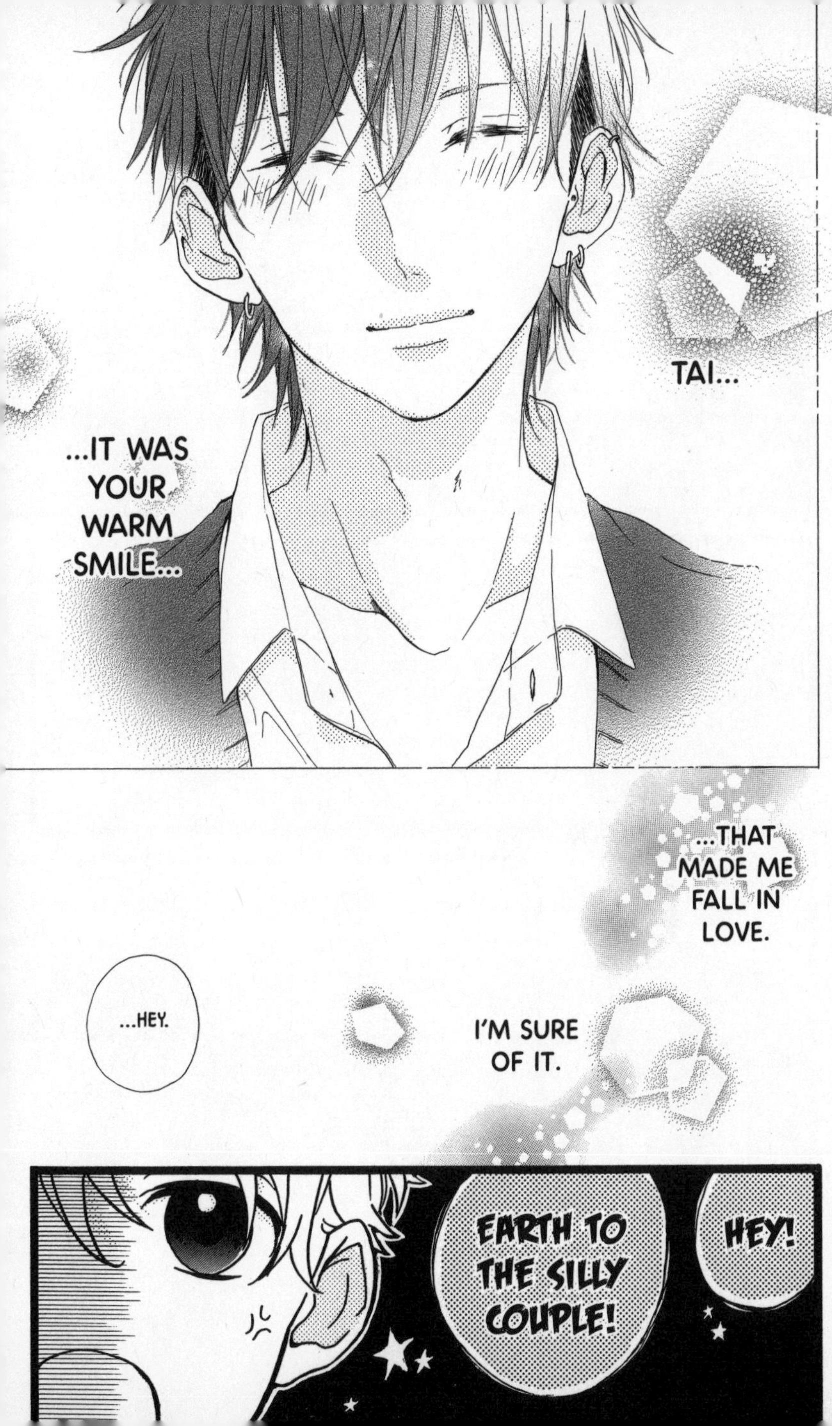
TAI...
...IT WAS YOUR WARM SMILE...
...THAT MADE ME FALL IN LOVE.
I'M SURE OF IT.
...HEY.
HEY!
EARTH TO THE SILLY COUPLE!

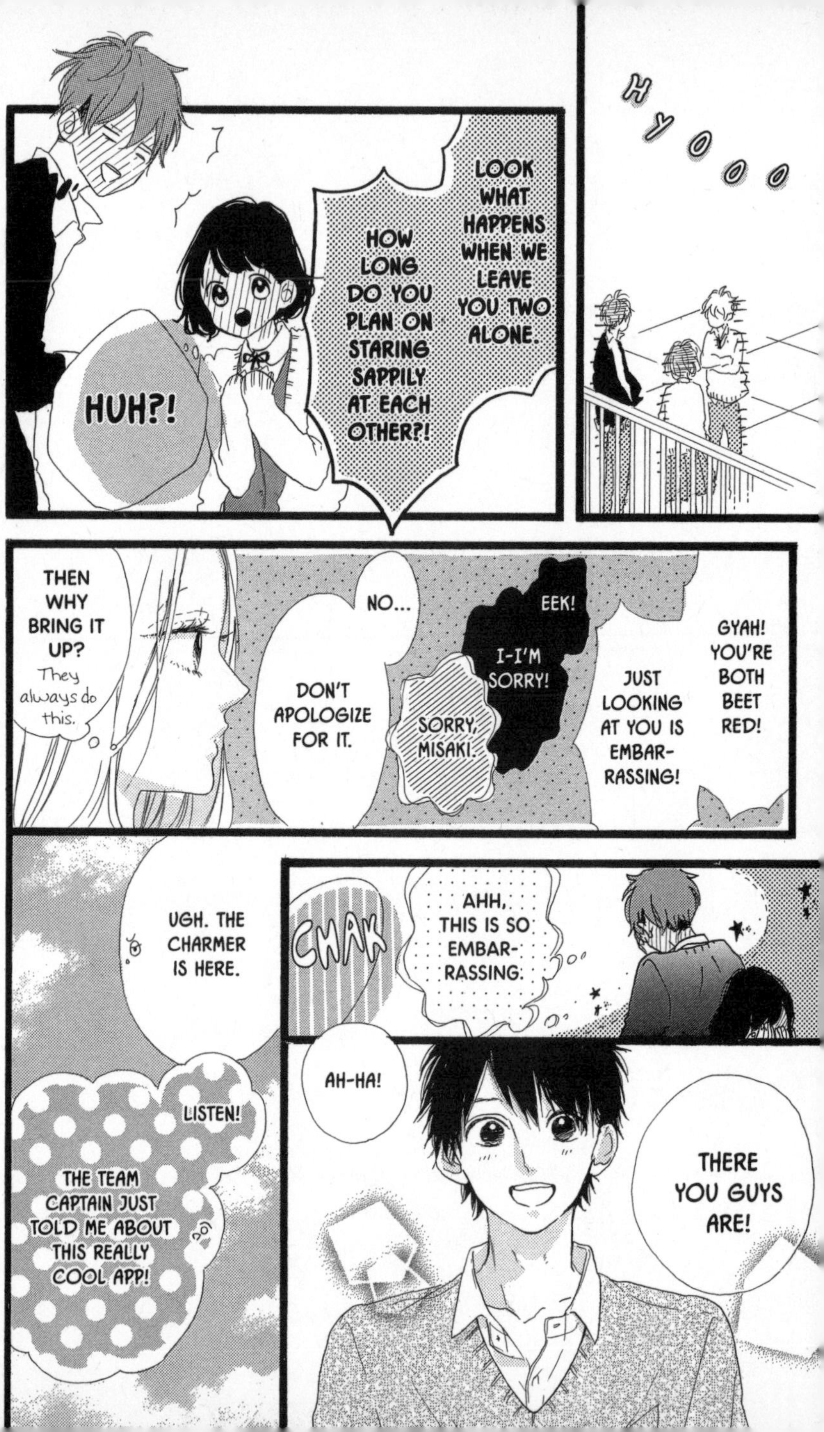
HYOOO
LOOK WHAT HAPPENS WHEN WE LEAVE YOU TWO ALONE.
HOW LONG DO YOU PLAN ON STARING SAPPILY AT EACH OTHER?!
HUH?!
GYAH! YOU'RE BOTH BEET RED!
JUST LOOKING AT YOU IS EMBARRASSING!
EEK!
I-I'M SORRY!
SORRY, MISAKI.
NO...
DON'T APOLOGIZE FOR IT.
THEN WHY BRING IT UP?
They always do this.
AHH, THIS IS SO EMBARRASSING.
CHAK
THERE YOU GUYS ARE!
AH-HA!
UGH. THE CHARMER IS HERE.
LISTEN!
THE TEAM CAPTAIN JUST TOLD ME ABOUT THIS REALLY COOL APP!

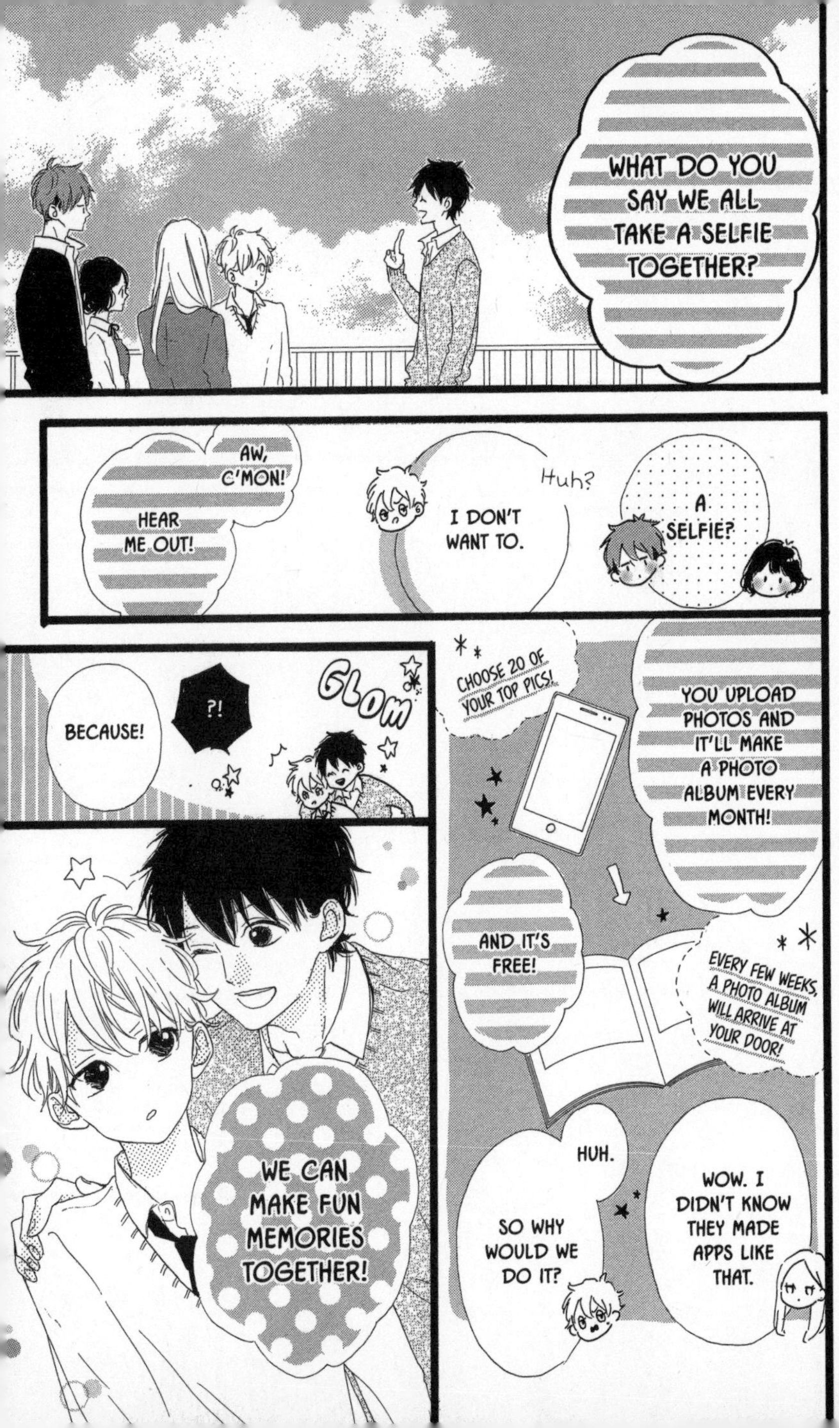
WHAT DO YOU SAY WE ALL TAKE A SELFIE TOGETHER?
A SELFIE?
Huh?
I DON'T WANT TO.
AW, C'MON!
HEAR ME OUT!
YOU UPLOAD PHOTOS AND IT'LL MAKE A PHOTO ALBUM EVERY MONTH!
CHOOSE 20 OF YOUR TOP PICS!
EVERY FEW WEEKS, A PHOTO ALBUM WILL ARRIVE AT YOUR DOOR!
AND IT'S FREE!
WOW. I DIDN'T KNOW THEY MADE APPS LIKE THAT.
HUH.
SO WHY WOULD WE DO IT?
BECAUSE!
?!
GLOM
WE CAN MAKE FUN MEMORIES TOGETHER!

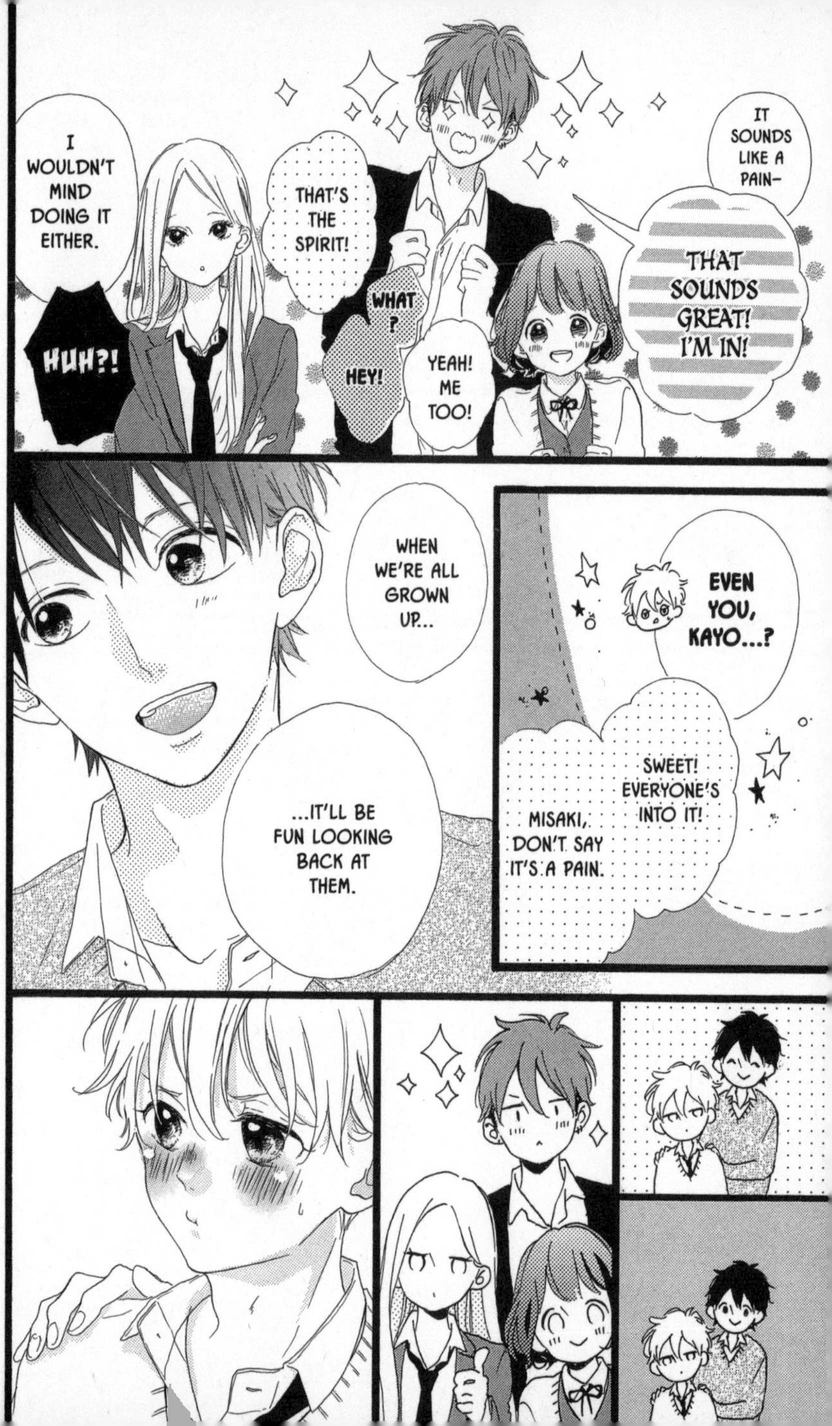

IT SOUNDS LIKE A PAIN—
THAT SOUNDS GREAT! I'M IN!
YEAH! ME TOO!
WHAT?
HEY!
THAT'S THE SPIRIT!
I WOULDN'T MIND DOING IT EITHER.
HUH?!
EVEN YOU, KAYO...?
SWEET! EVERYONE'S INTO IT!
MISAKI, DON'T SAY IT'S A PAIN.
WHEN WE'RE ALL GROWN UP...
...IT'LL BE FUN LOOKING BACK AT THEM.

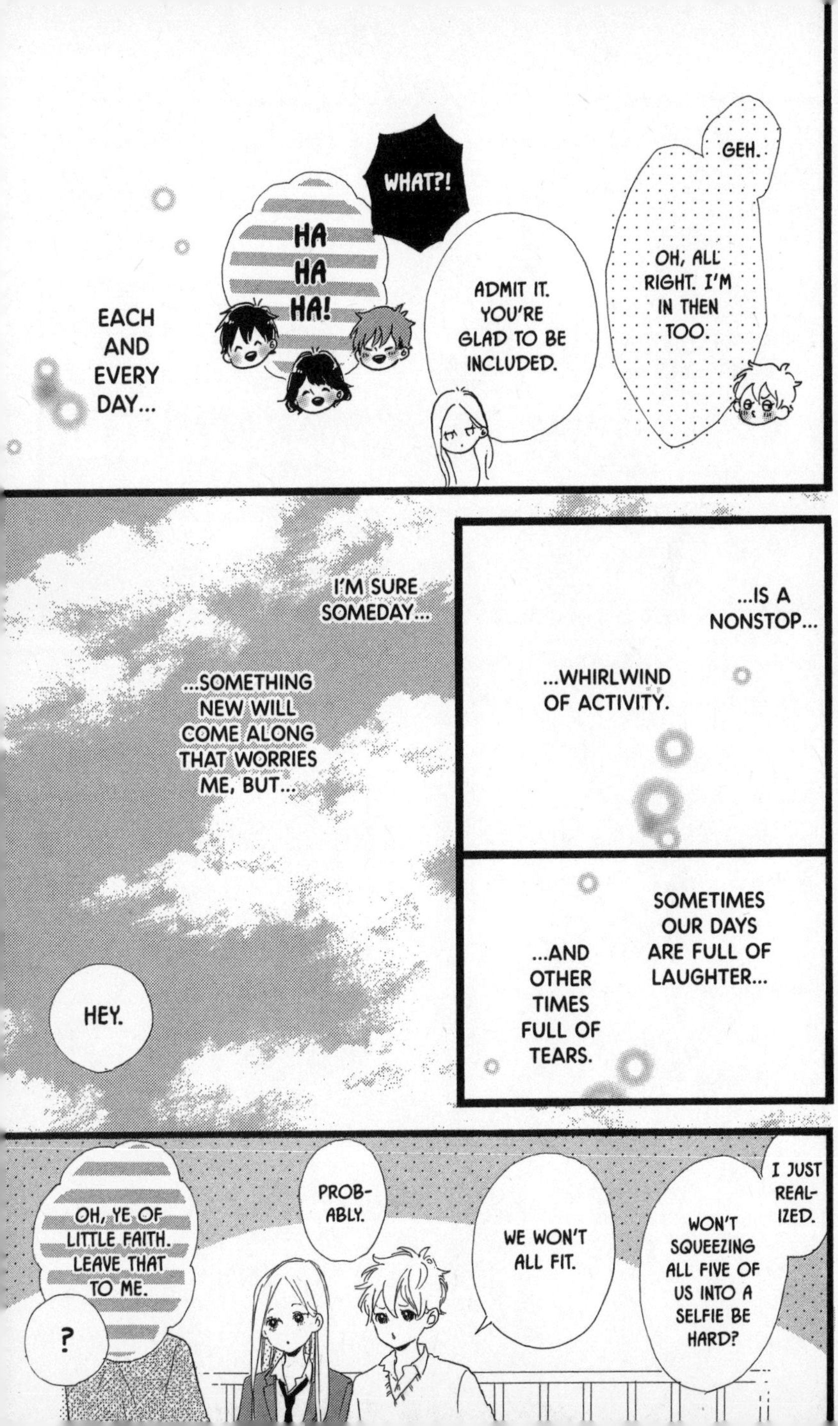
GEH.
OH, ALL RIGHT. I'M IN THEN TOO.
ADMIT IT. YOU'RE GLAD TO BE INCLUDED.
WHAT?!
HA HA HA!
EACH AND EVERY DAY...
...IS A NONSTOP...
...WHIRLWIND OF ACTIVITY.
SOMETIMES OUR DAYS ARE FULL OF LAUGHTER...
...AND OTHER TIMES FULL OF TEARS.
I'M SURE SOMEDAY...
...SOMETHING NEW WILL COME ALONG THAT WORRIES ME, BUT...
HEY.
I JUST REAL-IZED.
WON'T SQUEEZING ALL FIVE OF US INTO A SELFIE BE HARD?
WE WON'T ALL FIT.
PROB-ABLY.
OH, YE OF LITTLE FAITH. LEAVE THAT TO ME.
?

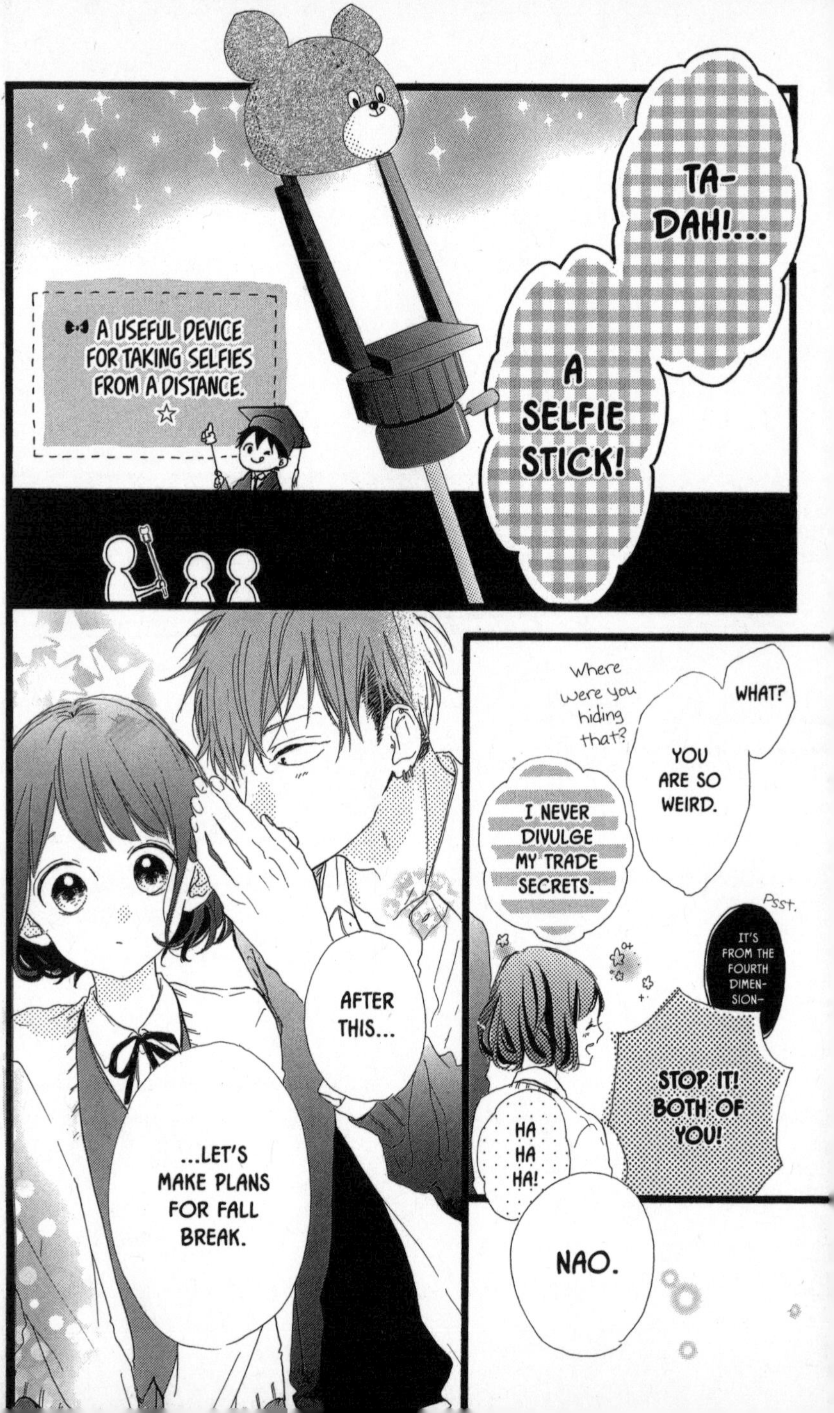
TA-DAH!...
A SELFIE STICK!
A USEFUL DEVICE FOR TAKING SELFIES FROM A DISTANCE. ☆
WHAT?
Where were you hiding that?
YOU ARE SO WEIRD.
I NEVER DIVULGE MY TRADE SECRETS.
Psst.
IT'S FROM THE FOURTH DIMEN-SION-
STOP IT! BOTH OF YOU!
HA HA HA!
NAO.
AFTER THIS...
...LET'S MAKE PLANS FOR FALL BREAK.

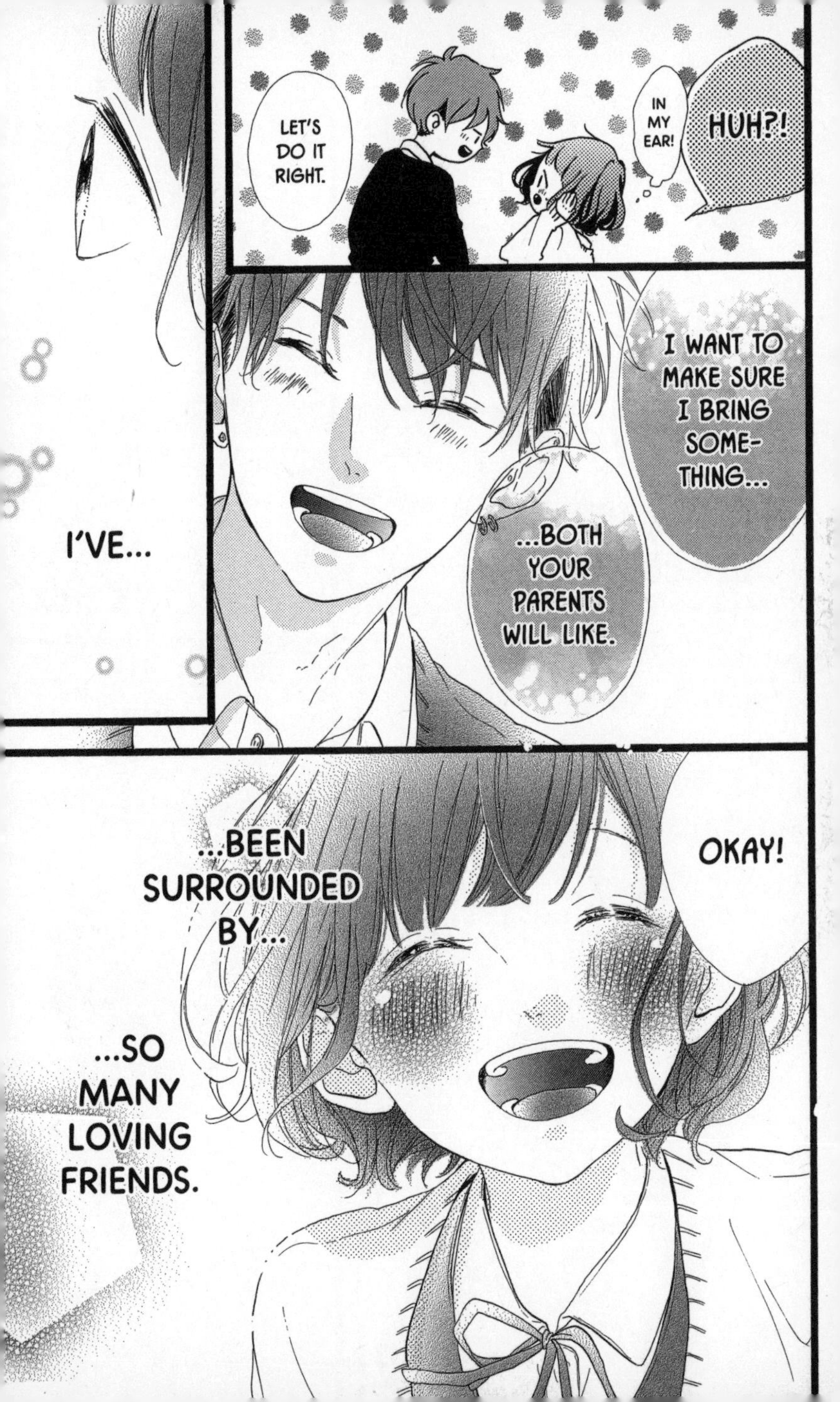
HUH?!
IN MY EAR!
LET'S DO IT RIGHT.
I WANT TO MAKE SURE I BRING SOME-THING...
...BOTH YOUR PARENTS WILL LIKE.
I'VE...
OKAY!
...BEEN SURROUNDED BY...
...SO MANY LOVING FRIENDS.

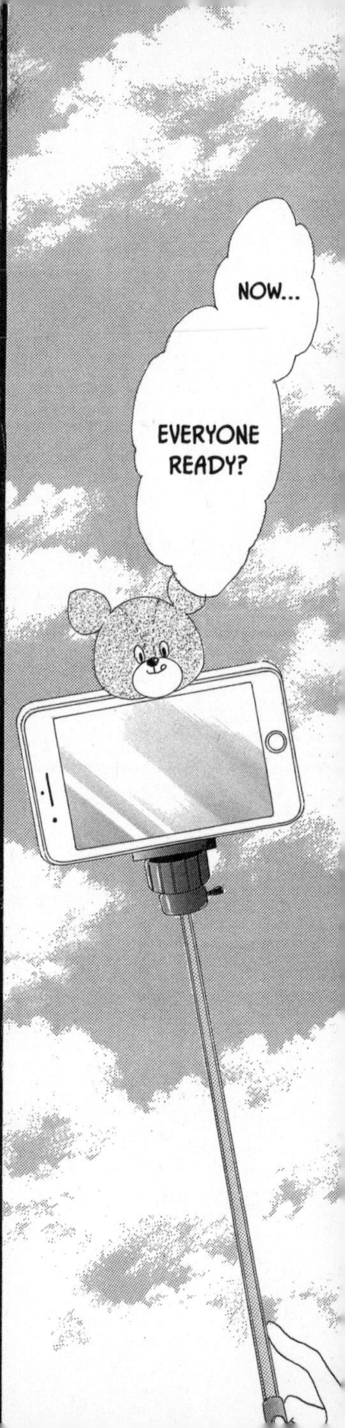
NOW...
EVERYONE READY?

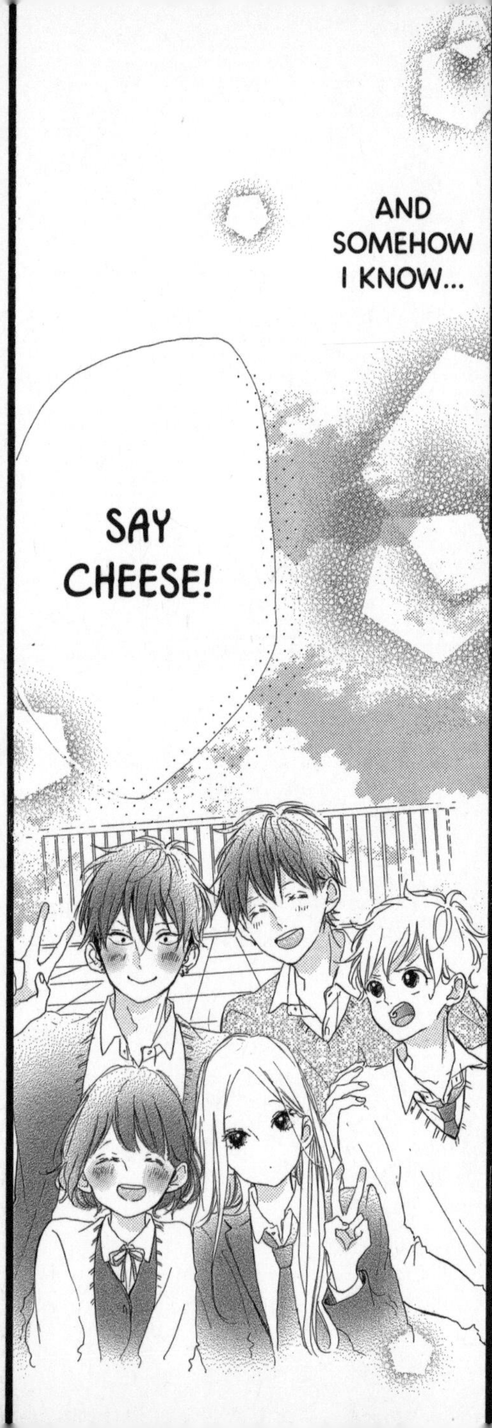
AND SOMEHOW I KNOW...
SAY CHEESE!

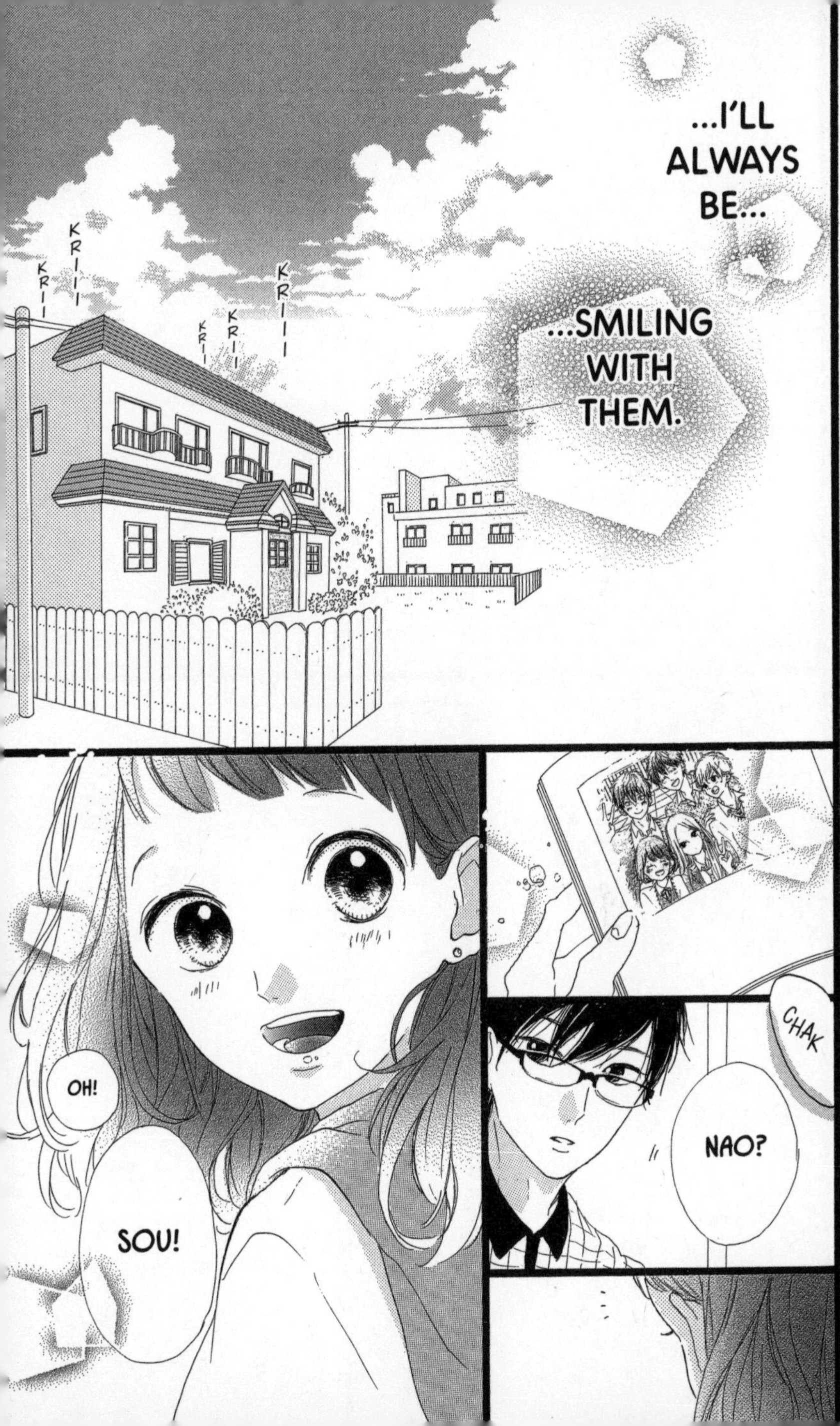
...I'LL ALWAYS BE...
...SMILING WITH THEM.
KRIII
KRII
KRI
KRIII
KRII
CHAK
NAO?
...
OH!
SOU!

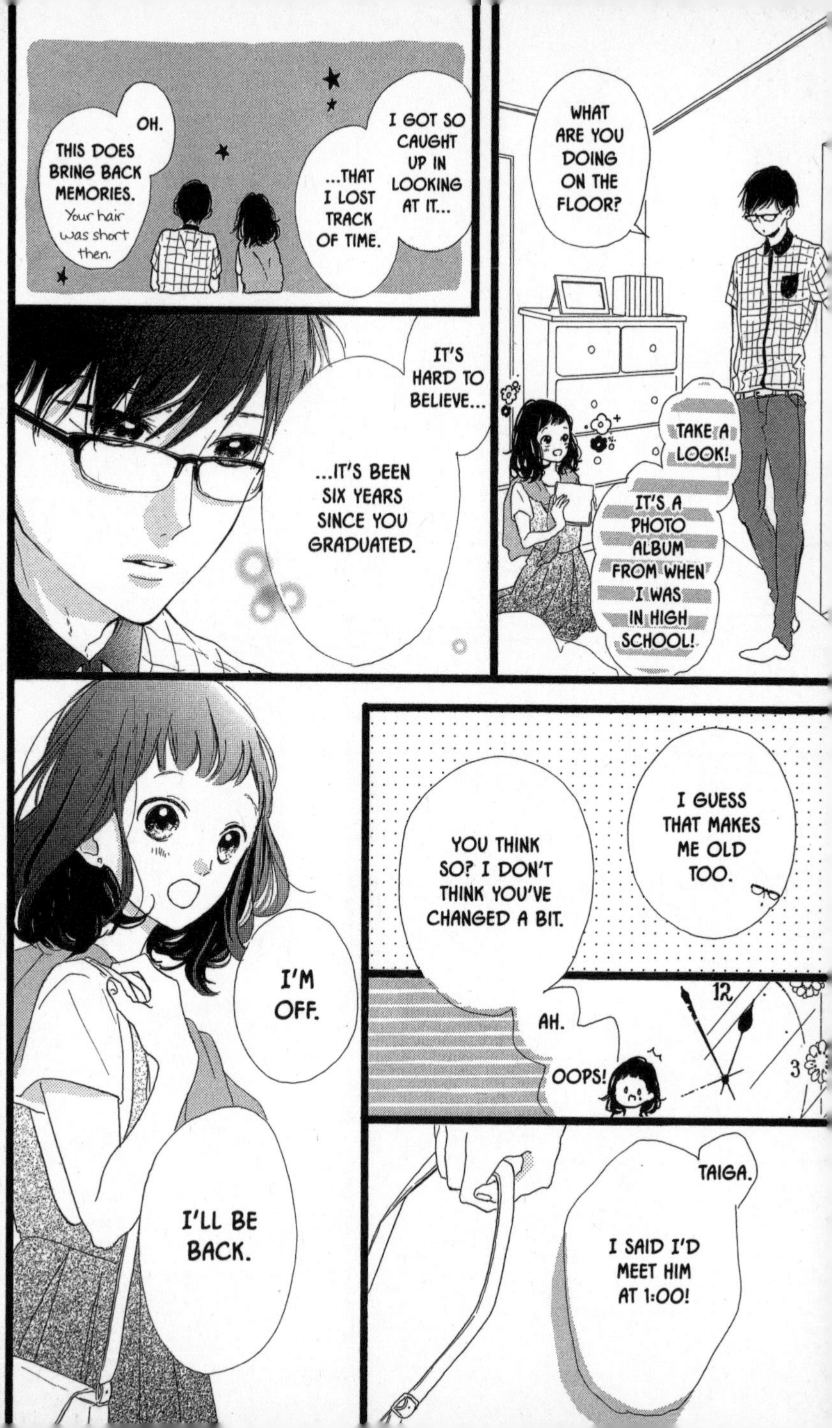
WHAT ARE YOU DOING ON THE FLOOR?
TAKE A LOOK!
IT'S A PHOTO ALBUM FROM WHEN I WAS IN HIGH SCHOOL!
I GOT SO CAUGHT UP IN LOOKING AT IT...
...THAT I LOST TRACK OF TIME.
OH.
THIS DOES BRING BACK MEMORIES.
Your hair was short then.
IT'S HARD TO BELIEVE...
...IT'S BEEN SIX YEARS SINCE YOU GRADUATED.
I GUESS THAT MAKES ME OLD TOO.
YOU THINK SO? I DON'T THINK YOU'VE CHANGED A BIT.
AH.
OOPS!
TAIGA.
I SAID I'D MEET HIM AT 1:00!
I'M OFF.
I'LL BE BACK.

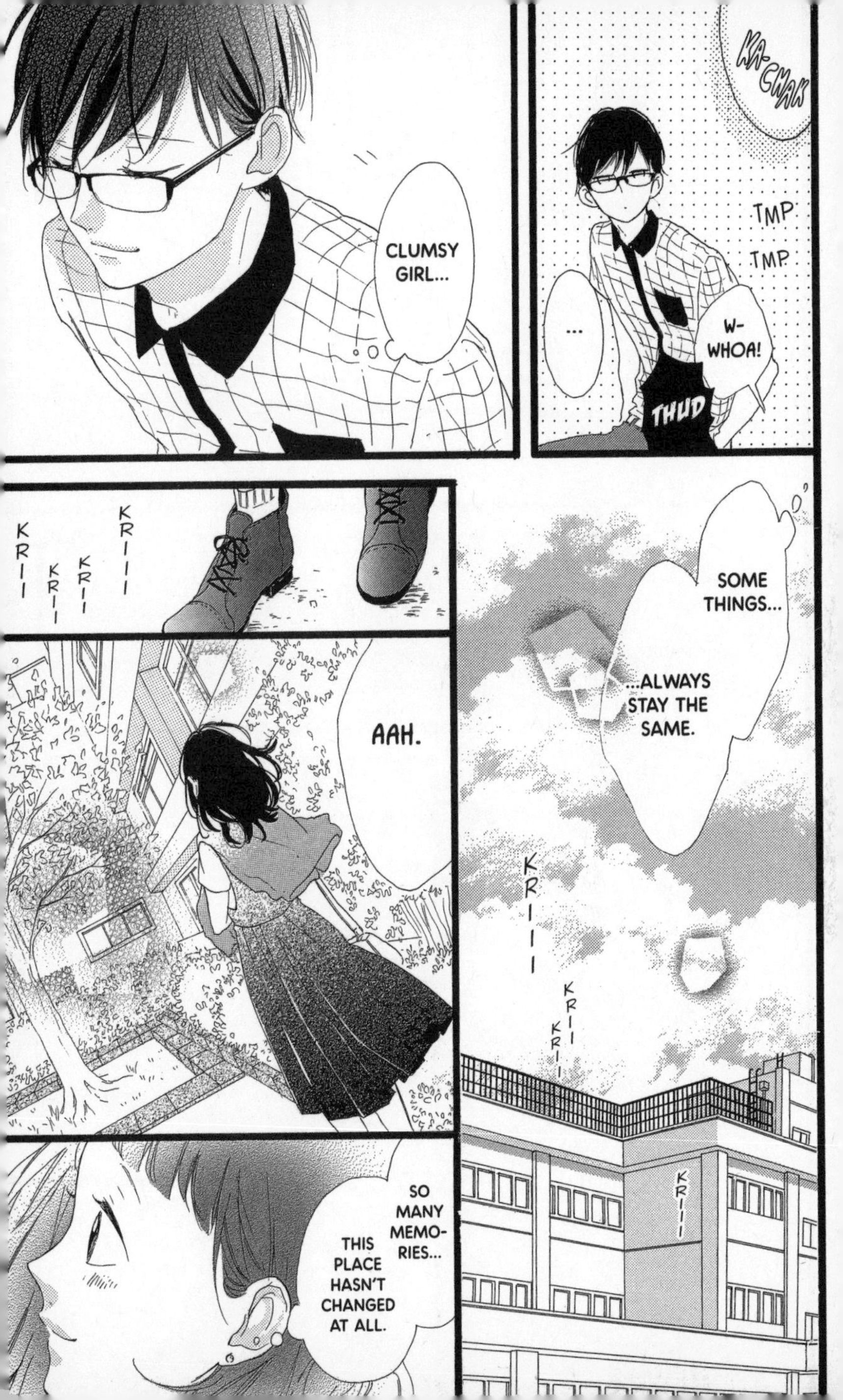
KA-CHAK
TMP
TMP
W-WHOA!
THUD
...
CLUMSY GIRL...
SOME THINGS...
...ALWAYS STAY THE SAME.
KRIII
KRII
KRII
KRIII
KRIII
KRIII
KRII
KRII
KRII
AAH.
SO MANY MEMORIES...
THIS PLACE HASN'T CHANGED AT ALL.

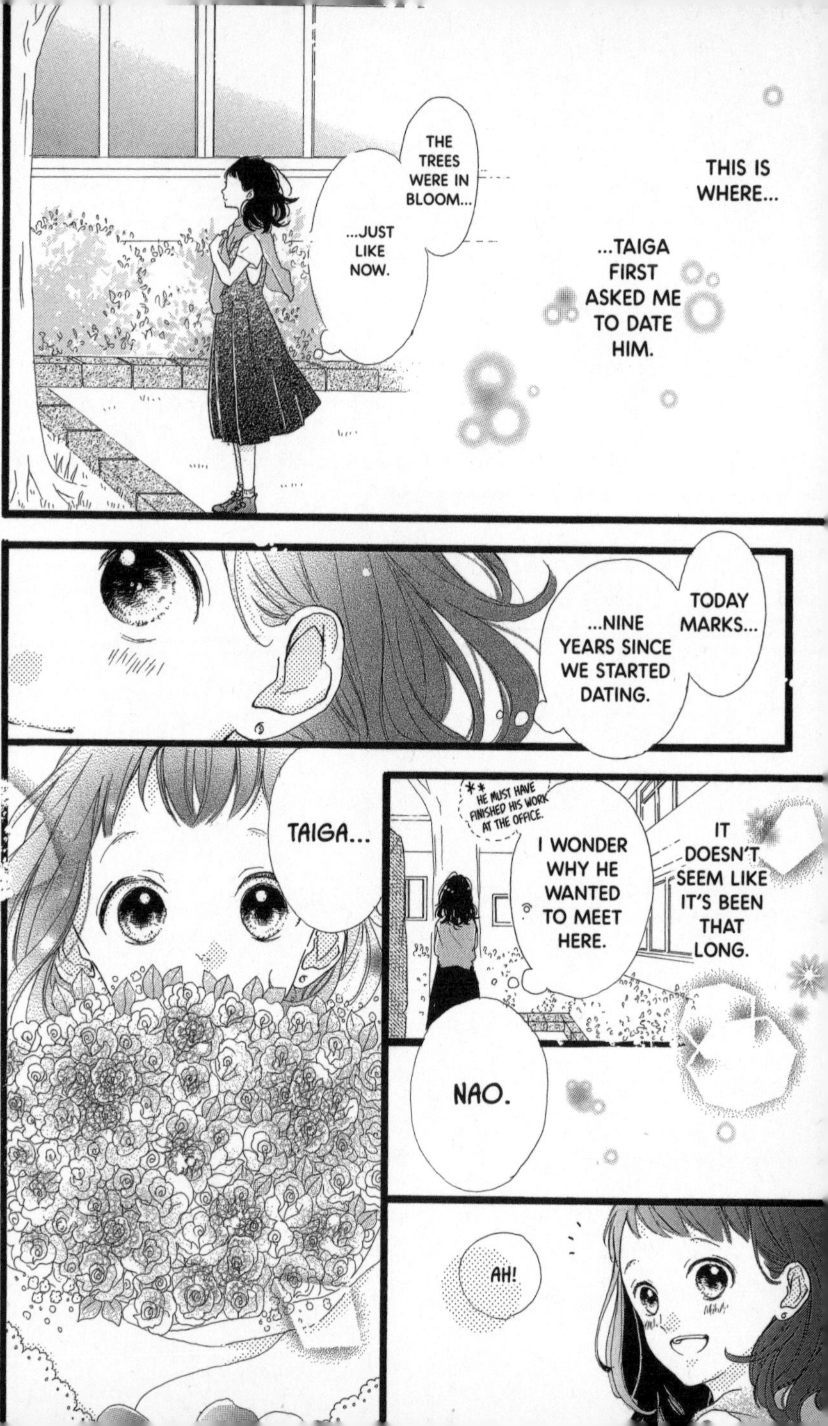
THIS IS WHERE...
...TAIGA FIRST ASKED ME TO DATE HIM.
THE TREES WERE IN BLOOM...
...JUST LIKE NOW.
TODAY MARKS...
...NINE YEARS SINCE WE STARTED DATING.
IT DOESN'T SEEM LIKE IT'S BEEN THAT LONG.
I WONDER WHY HE WANTED TO MEET HERE.
** HE MUST HAVE FINISHED HIS WORK AT THE OFFICE.
NAO.
AH!
TAIGA...

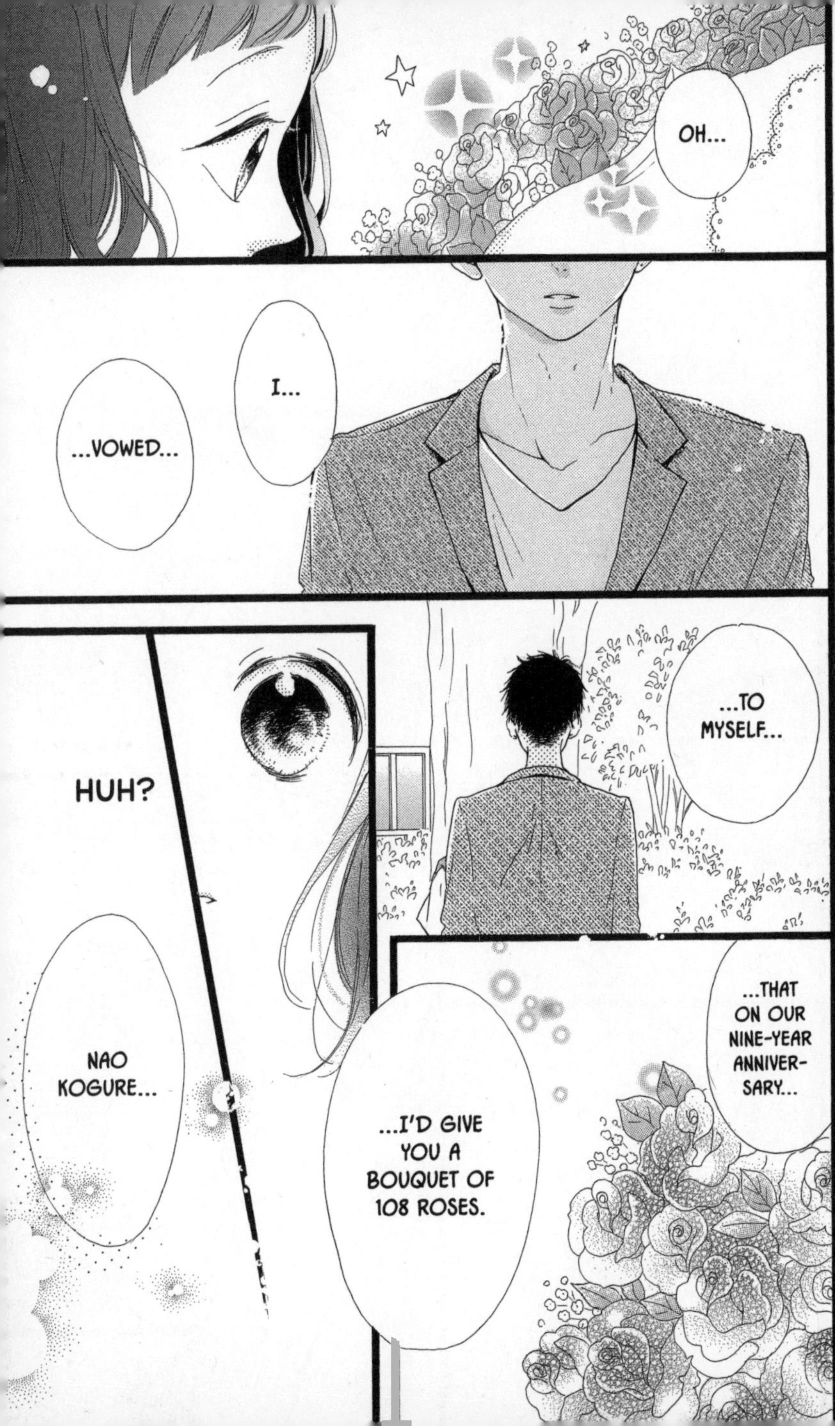
OH...
I...
...VOWED...
...TO MYSELF...
...THAT ON OUR NINE-YEAR ANNIVERSARY...
...I'D GIVE YOU A BOUQUET OF 108 ROSES.
HUH?
NAO KOGURE...

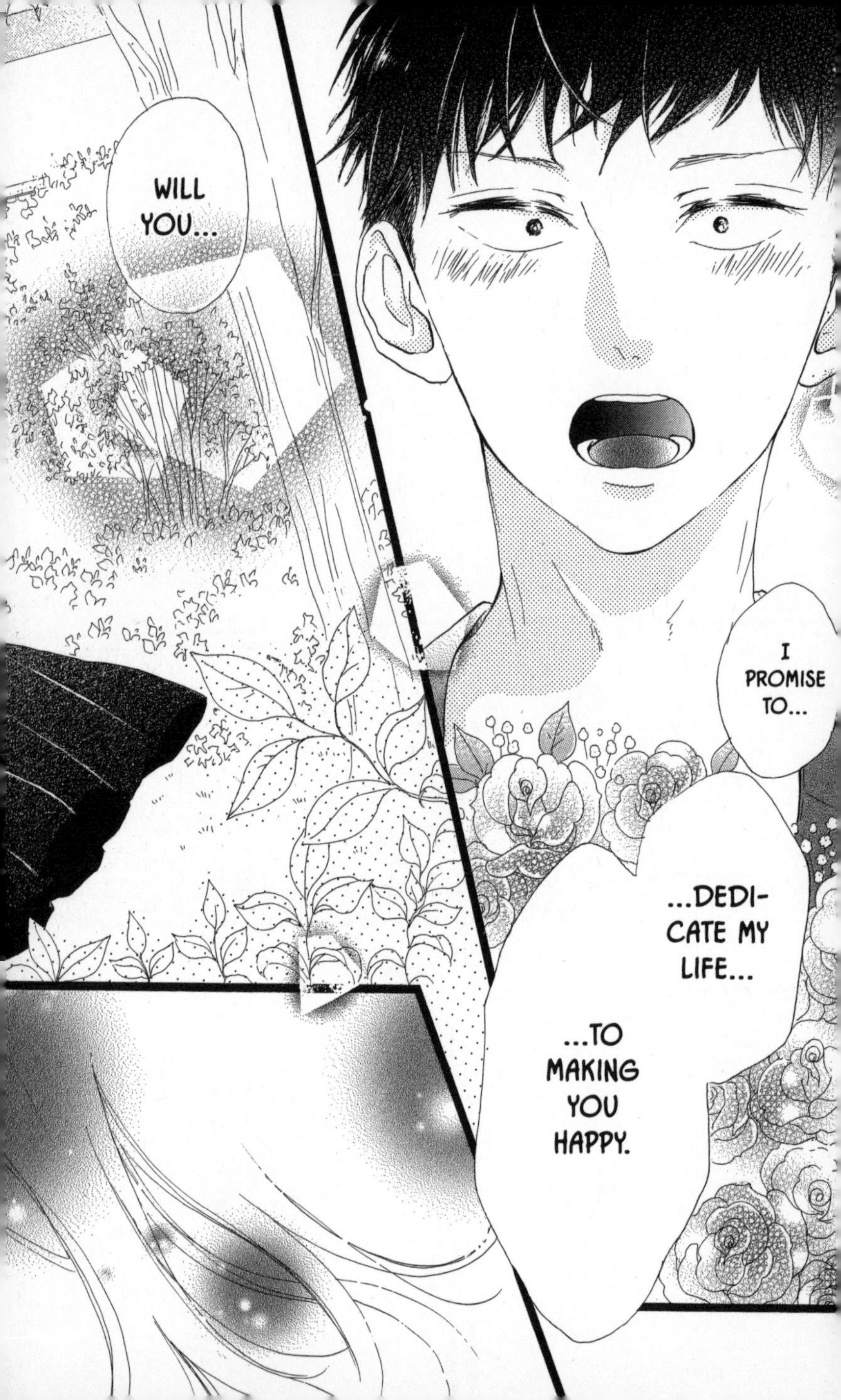
I PROMISE TO...
...DEDI-CATE MY LIFE...
...TO MAKING YOU HAPPY.
WILL YOU...

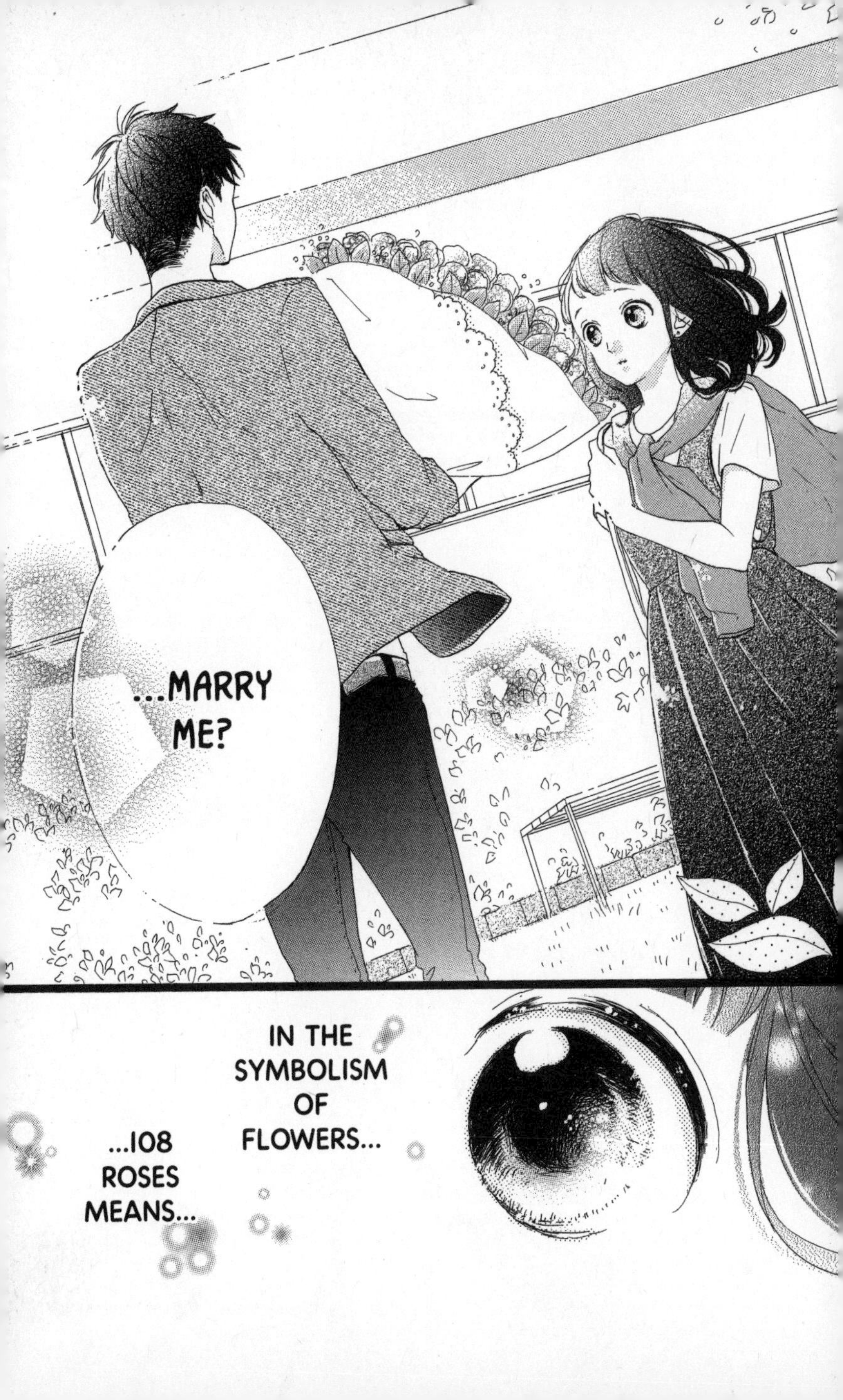
...MARRY ME?
IN THE SYMBOLISM OF FLOWERS...
...108 ROSES MEANS...

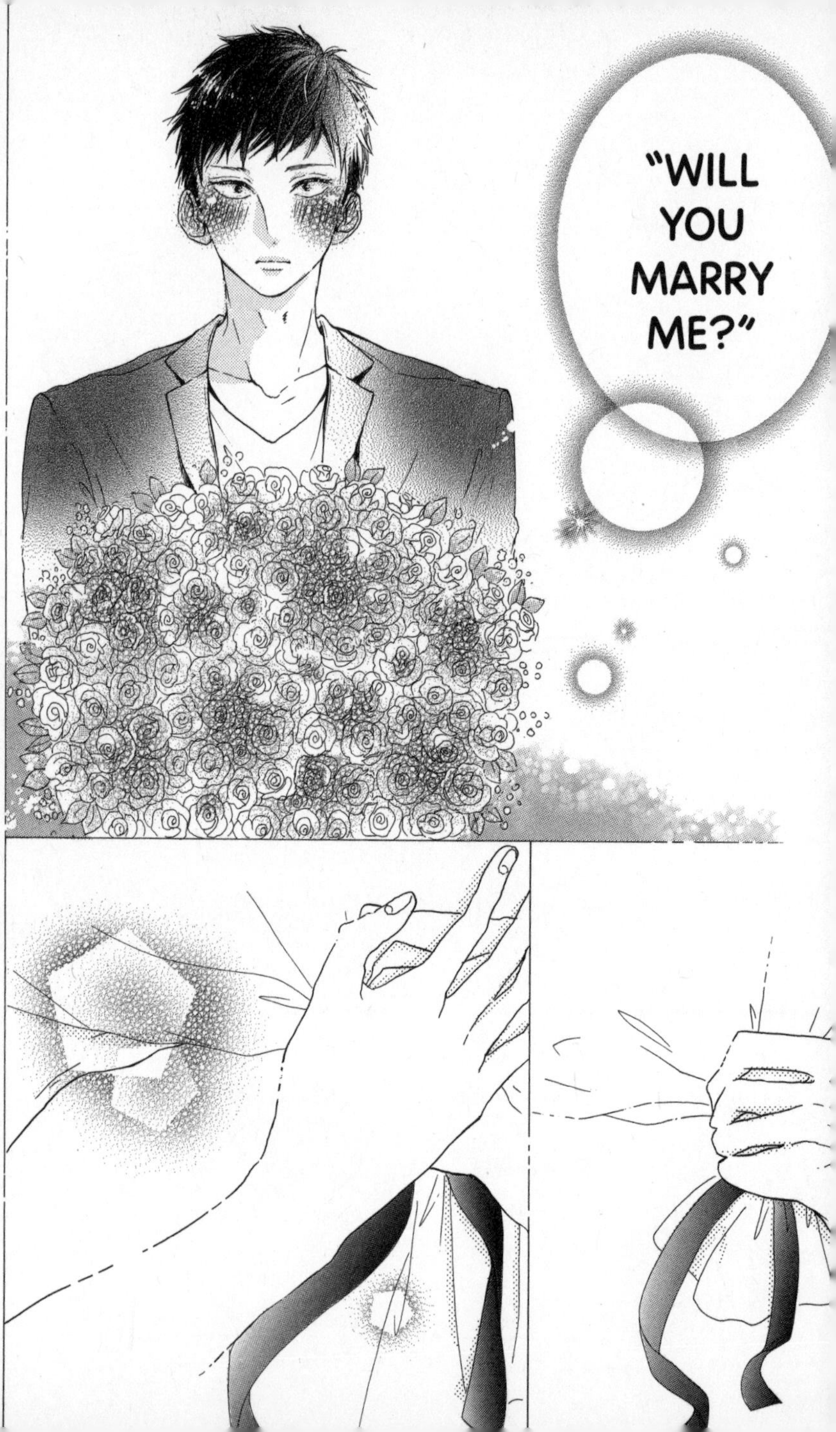
"WILL YOU MARRY ME?"

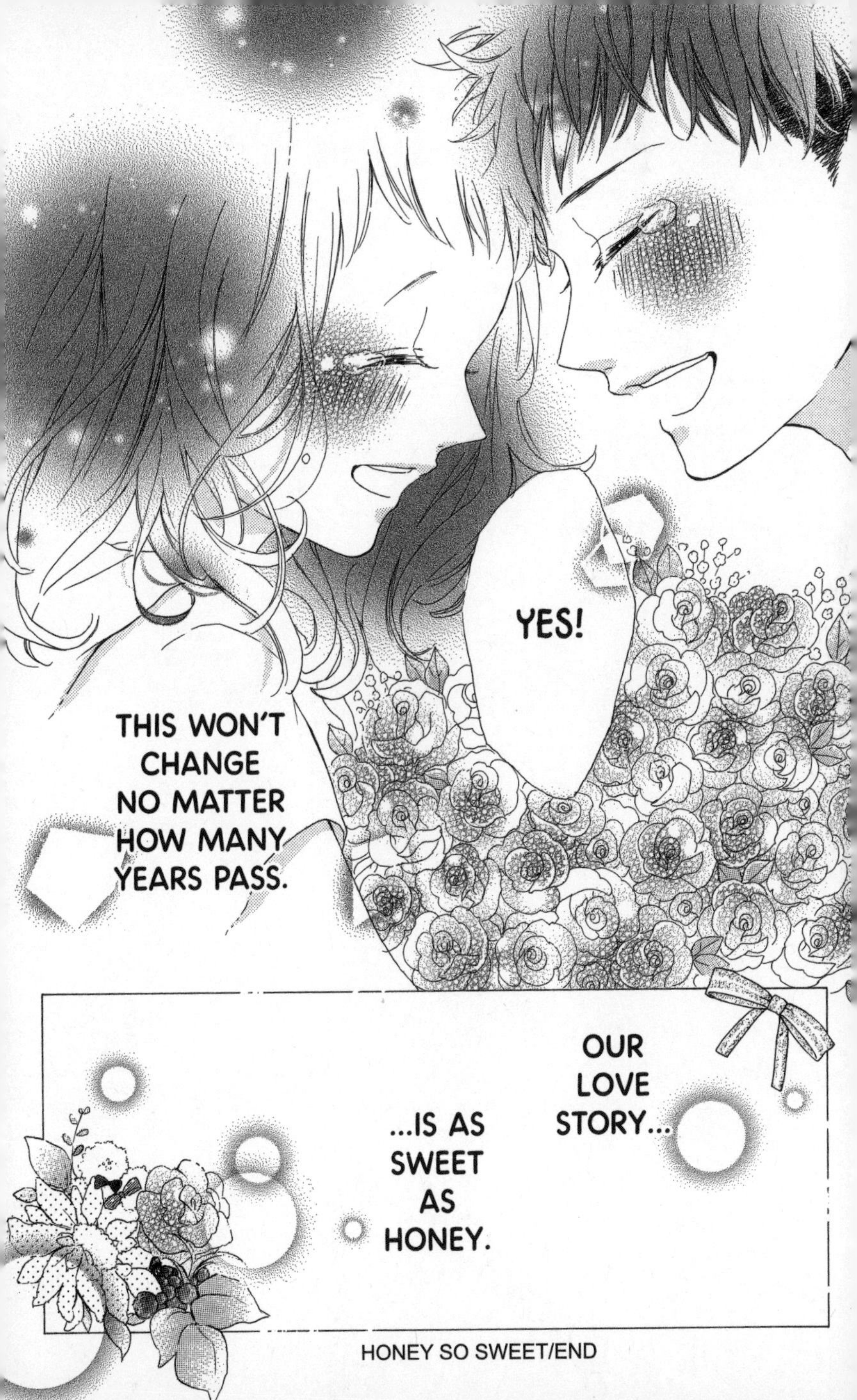
YES!
THIS WON'T CHANGE NO MATTER HOW MANY YEARS PASS.
OUR LOVE STORY...
...IS AS SWEET AS HONEY.

HONEY SO SWEET/END

On the next page starts "Sugar," a 16-page short story that was the basis for what would eventually become *Honey So Sweet*. The artwork is three years old, so it's really hard to even look at... But my friends insisted I show it in its original form. So there you have it.

I hope you enjoy it!

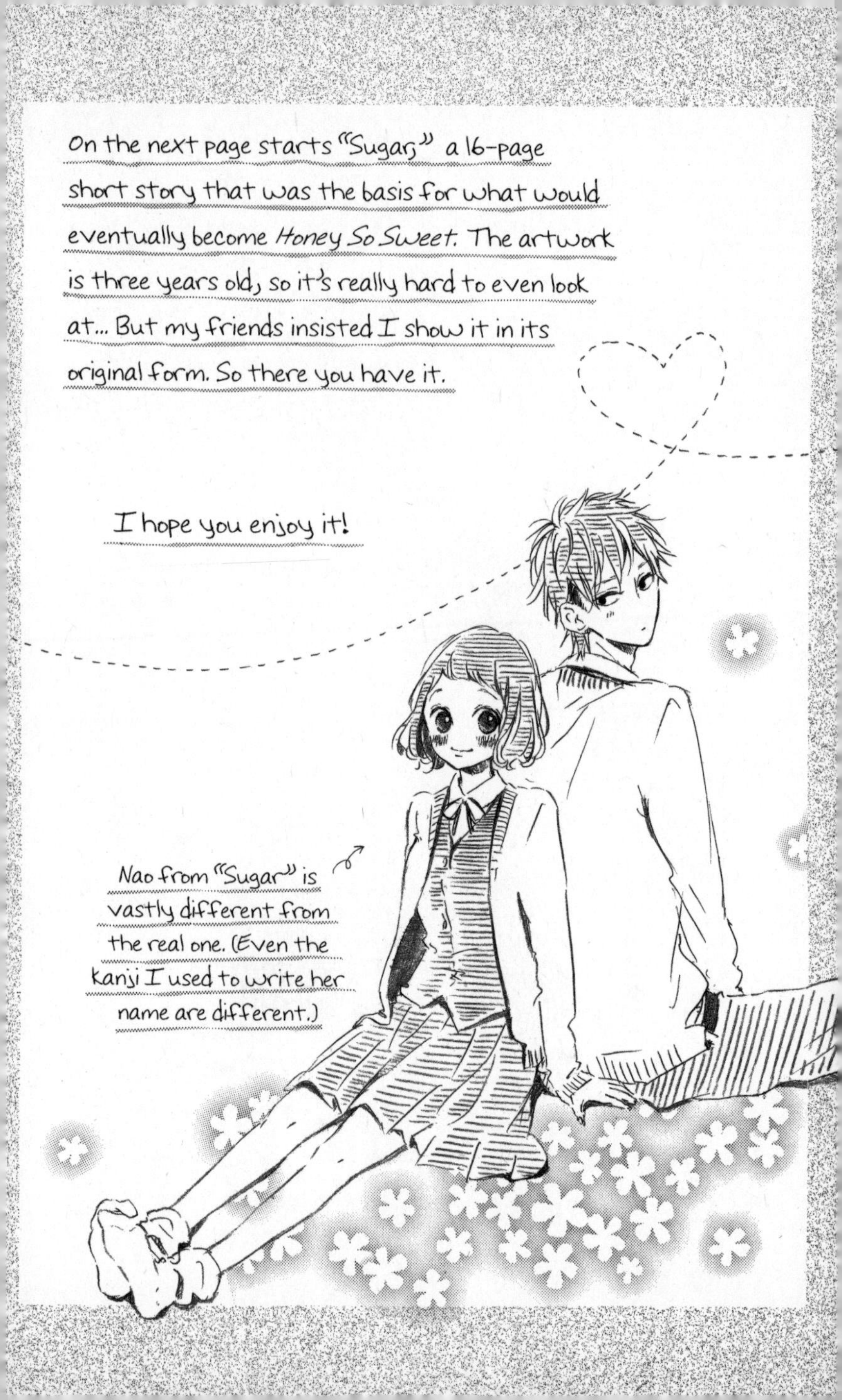

Nao from "Sugar" is vastly different from the real one. (Even the kanji I used to write her name are different.)

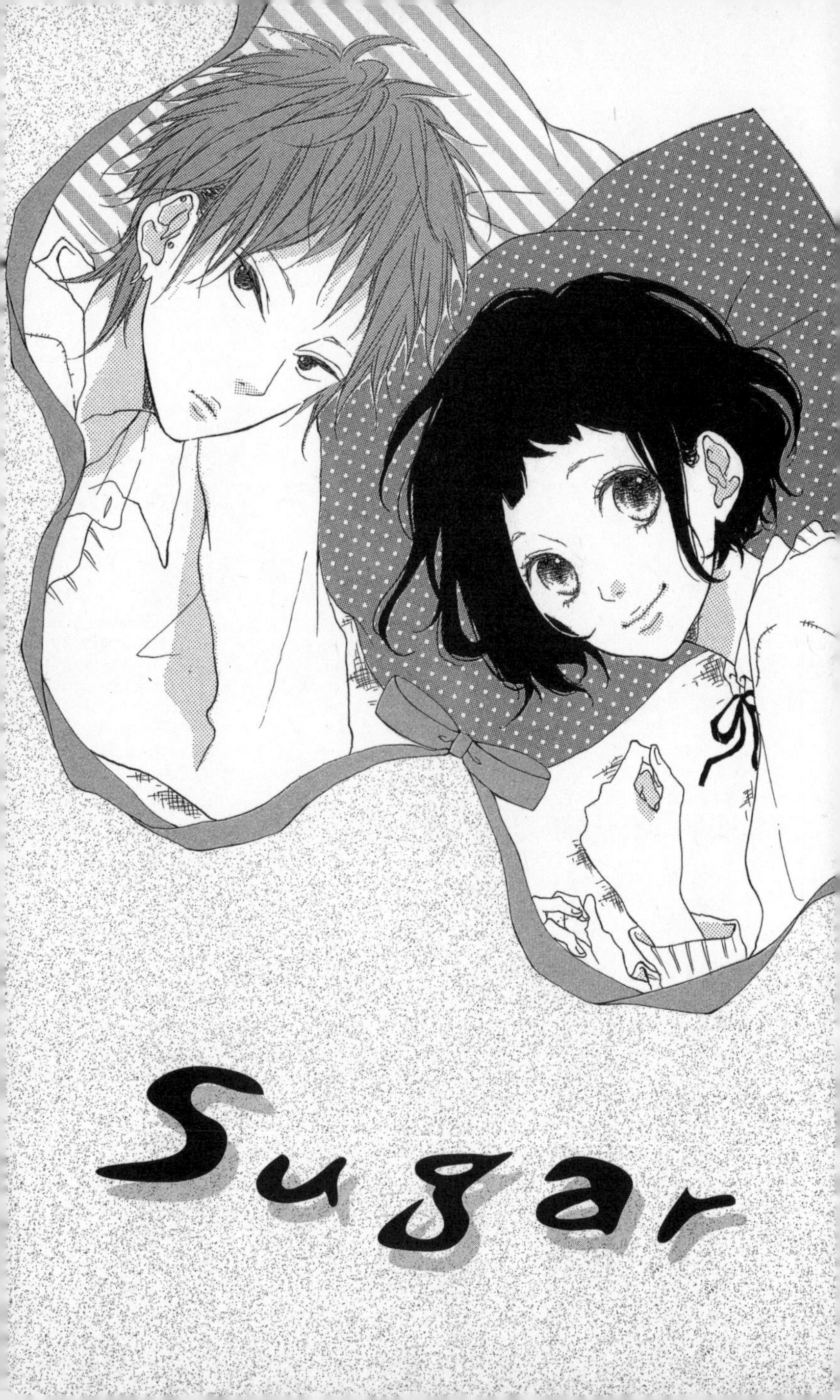
Sugar

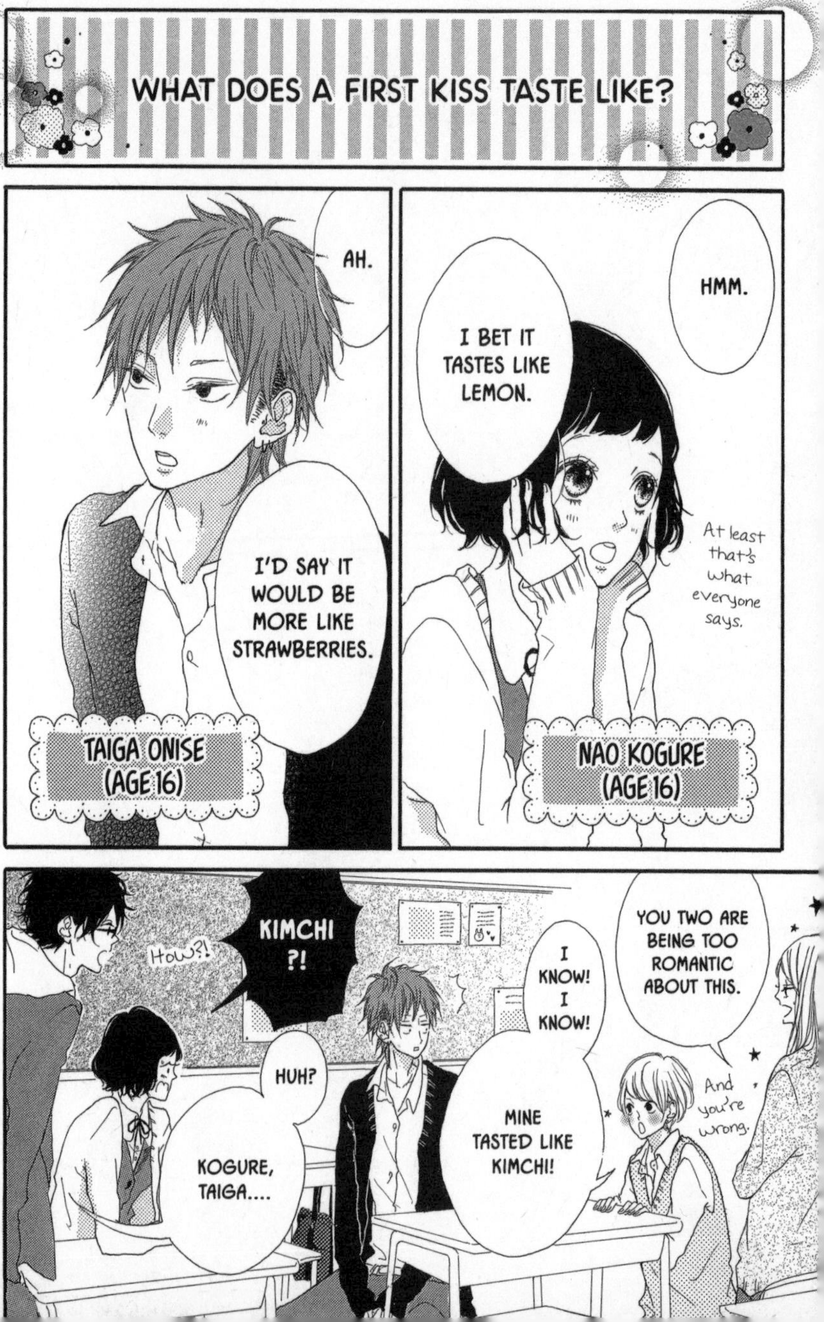
WHAT DOES A FIRST KISS TASTE LIKE?
HMM.
I BET IT TASTES LIKE LEMON.
At least that's what everyone says.
NAO KOGURE (AGE 16)
AH.
I'D SAY IT WOULD BE MORE LIKE STRAWBERRIES.
TAIGA ONISE (AGE 16)
YOU TWO ARE BEING TOO ROMANTIC ABOUT THIS.
And you're wrong.
I KNOW! I KNOW!
MINE TASTED LIKE KIMCHI!
HUH?
KIMCHI?!
How?!
KOGURE, TAIGA....

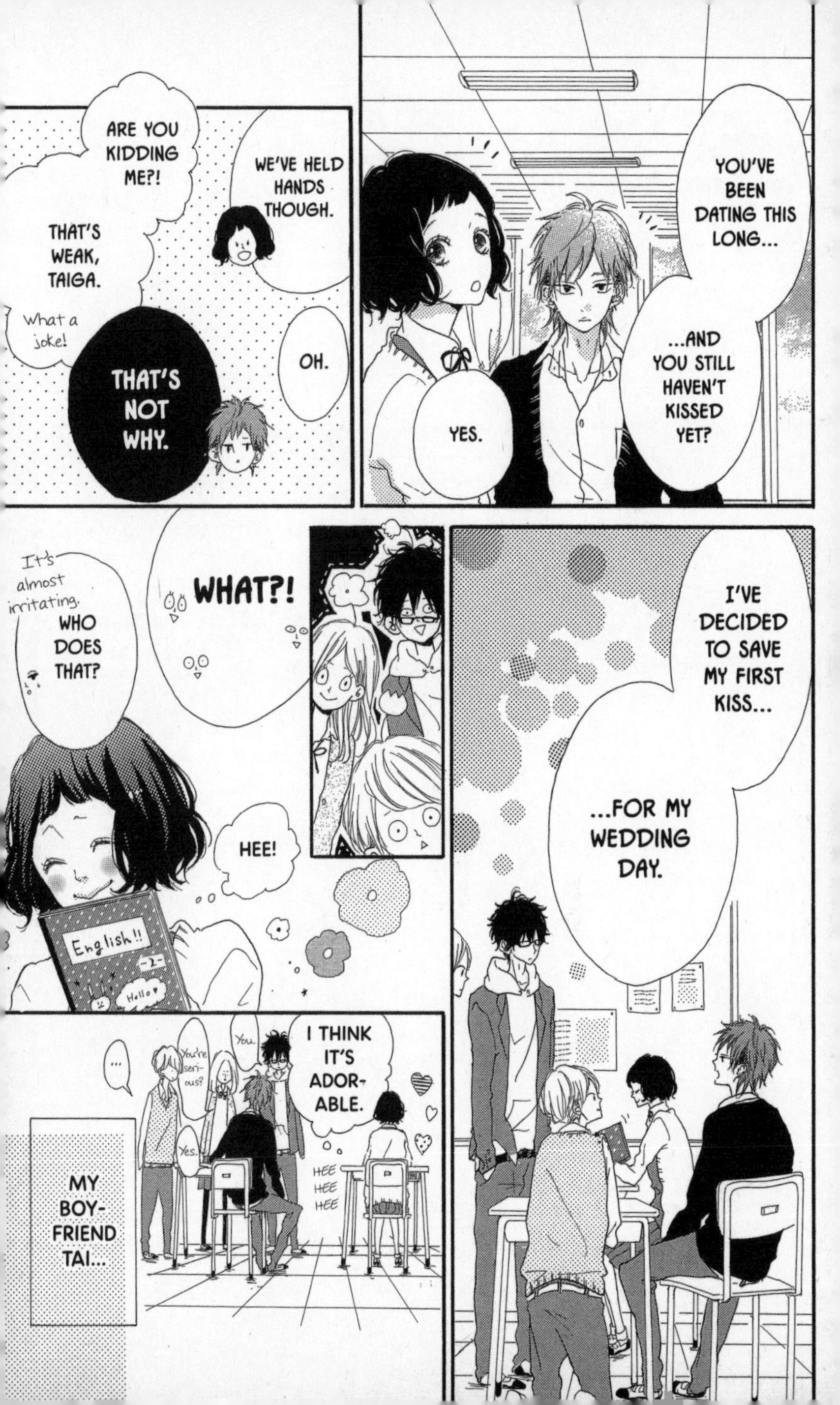
YOU'VE BEEN DATING THIS LONG...
...AND YOU STILL HAVEN'T KISSED YET?
YES.
WE'VE HELD HANDS THOUGH.
OH.
ARE YOU KIDDING ME?!
THAT'S WEAK, TAIGA.
What a joke!
THAT'S NOT WHY.
I'VE DECIDED TO SAVE MY FIRST KISS...
...FOR MY WEDDING DAY.
WHAT?!
It's almost irritating.
WHO DOES THAT?
HEE!
English!!
Hello
I THINK IT'S ADOR-ABLE.
You.
You're seri-ous?
Yes.
...
HEE HEE HEE
MY BOY-FRIEND TAI...

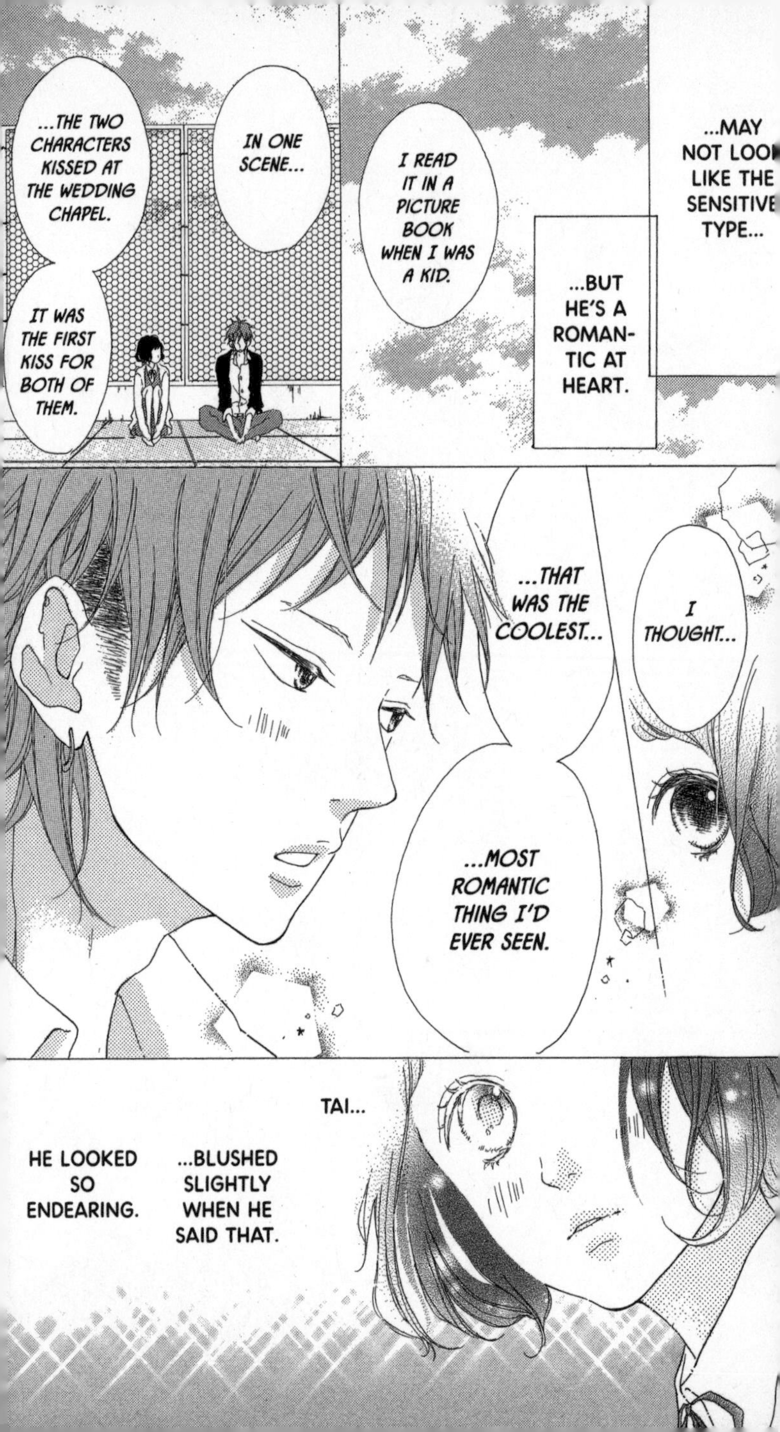
...MAY NOT LOOK LIKE THE SENSITIVE TYPE...
...BUT HE'S A ROMAN-TIC AT HEART.
I READ IT IN A PICTURE BOOK WHEN I WAS A KID.
IN ONE SCENE...
...THE TWO CHARACTERS KISSED AT THE WEDDING CHAPEL.
IT WAS THE FIRST KISS FOR BOTH OF THEM.
I THOUGHT...
...THAT WAS THE COOLEST...
...MOST ROMANTIC THING I'D EVER SEEN.
TAI...
...BLUSHED SLIGHTLY WHEN HE SAID THAT.
HE LOOKED SO ENDEARING.

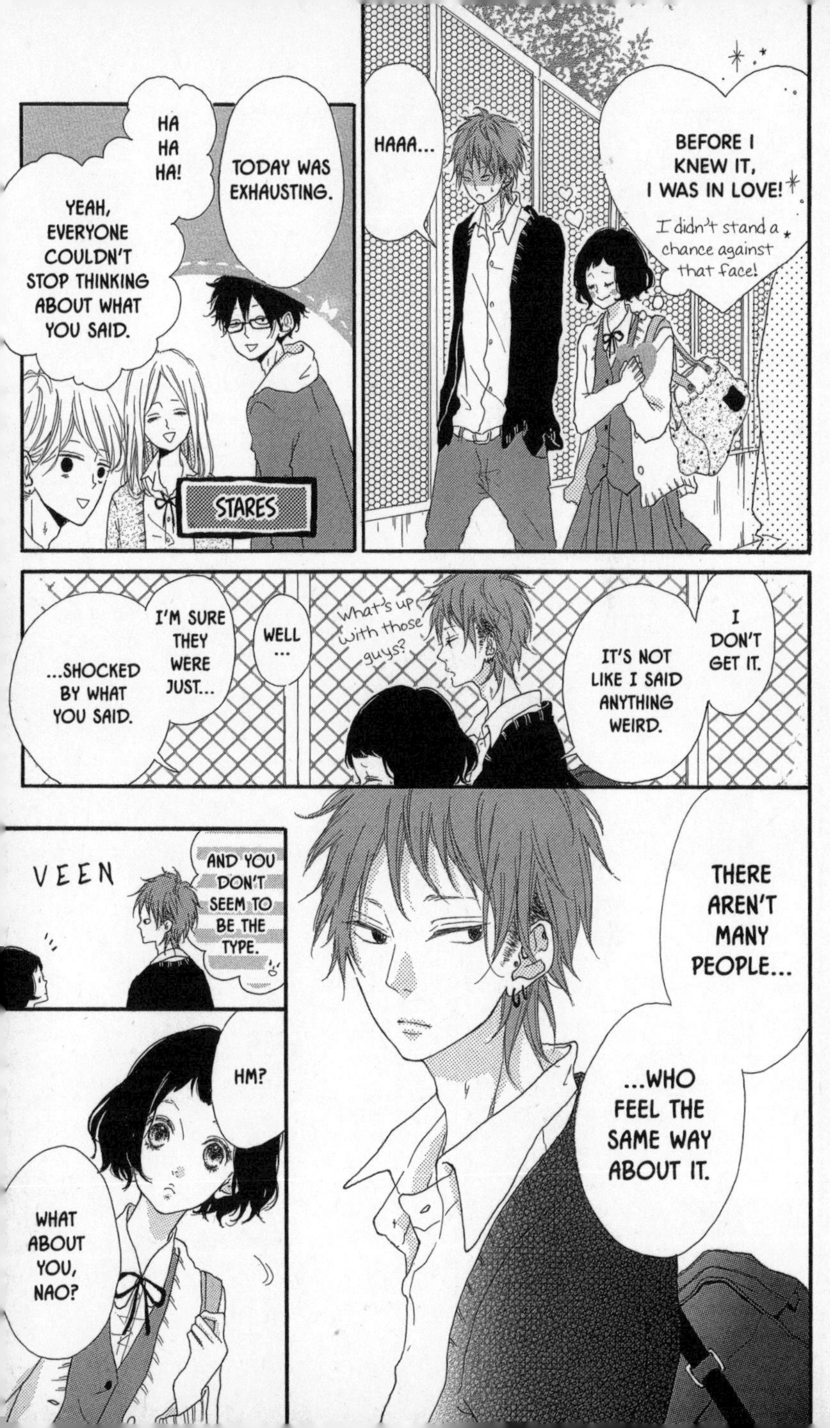
BEFORE I KNEW IT, I WAS IN LOVE!
I didn't stand a chance against that face!
HAAA...
TODAY WAS EXHAUSTING.
HA HA HA!
YEAH, EVERYONE COULDN'T STOP THINKING ABOUT WHAT YOU SAID.
STARES
I DON'T GET IT.
IT'S NOT LIKE I SAID ANYTHING WEIRD.
What's up with those guys?
WELL...
I'M SURE THEY WERE JUST...
...SHOCKED BY WHAT YOU SAID.
THERE AREN'T MANY PEOPLE...
...WHO FEEL THE SAME WAY ABOUT IT.
AND YOU DON'T SEEM TO BE THE TYPE.
VEEN
HM?
WHAT ABOUT YOU, NAO?

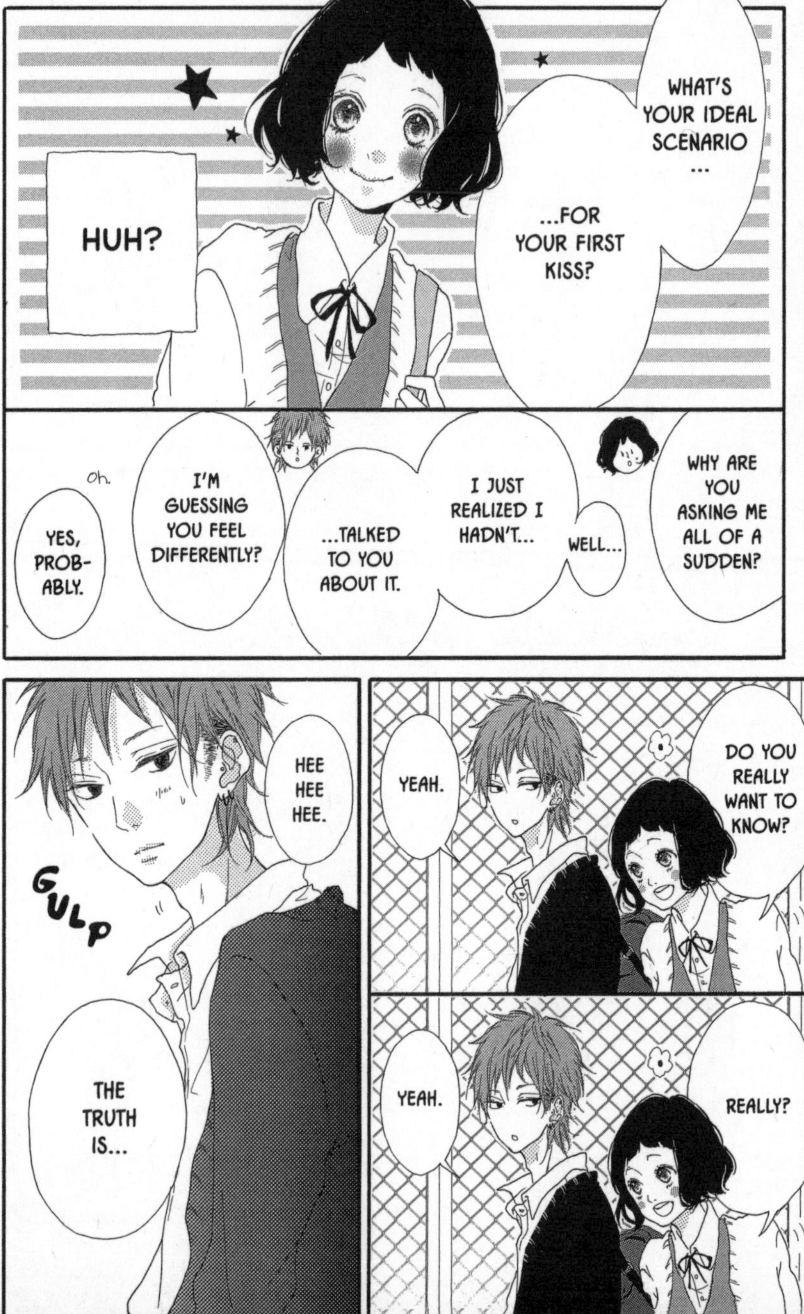
WHAT'S YOUR IDEAL SCENARIO ...
...FOR YOUR FIRST KISS?
HUH?
WHY ARE YOU ASKING ME ALL OF A SUDDEN?
WELL...
I JUST REALIZED I HADN'T...
...TALKED TO YOU ABOUT IT.
I'M GUESSING YOU FEEL DIFFERENTLY?
Oh.
YES, PROB-ABLY.
DO YOU REALLY WANT TO KNOW?
YEAH.
REALLY?
YEAH.
HEE HEE HEE.
GULP
THE TRUTH IS...

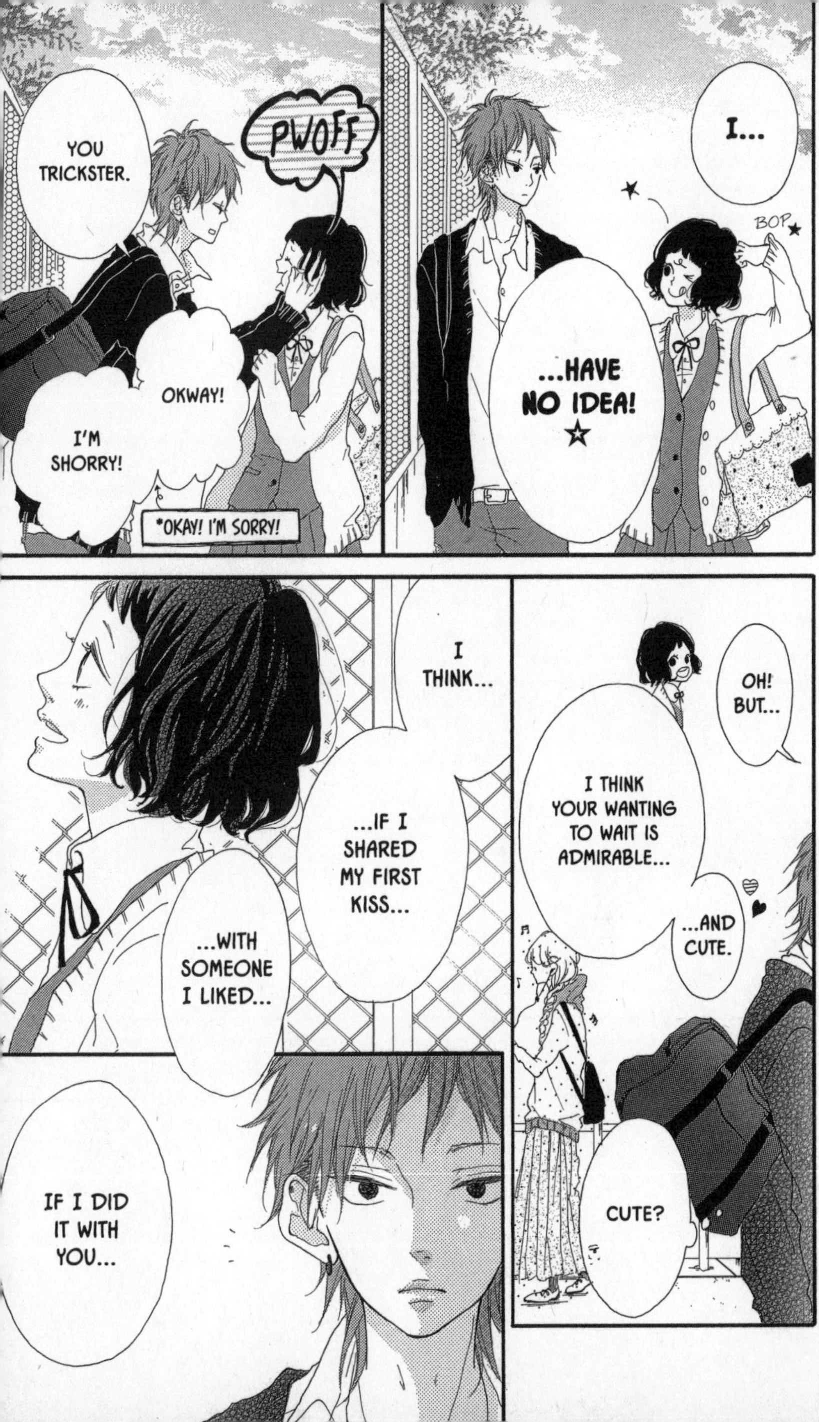
I...
BOP
...HAVE NO IDEA! ☆
PWOFF
YOU TRICKSTER.
OKWAY!
I'M SHORRY!
*OKAY! I'M SORRY!
OH! BUT...
I THINK YOUR WANTING TO WAIT IS ADMIRABLE...
...AND CUTE.
CUTE?
I THINK...
...IF I SHARED MY FIRST KISS...
...WITH SOMEONE I LIKED...
IF I DID IT WITH YOU...

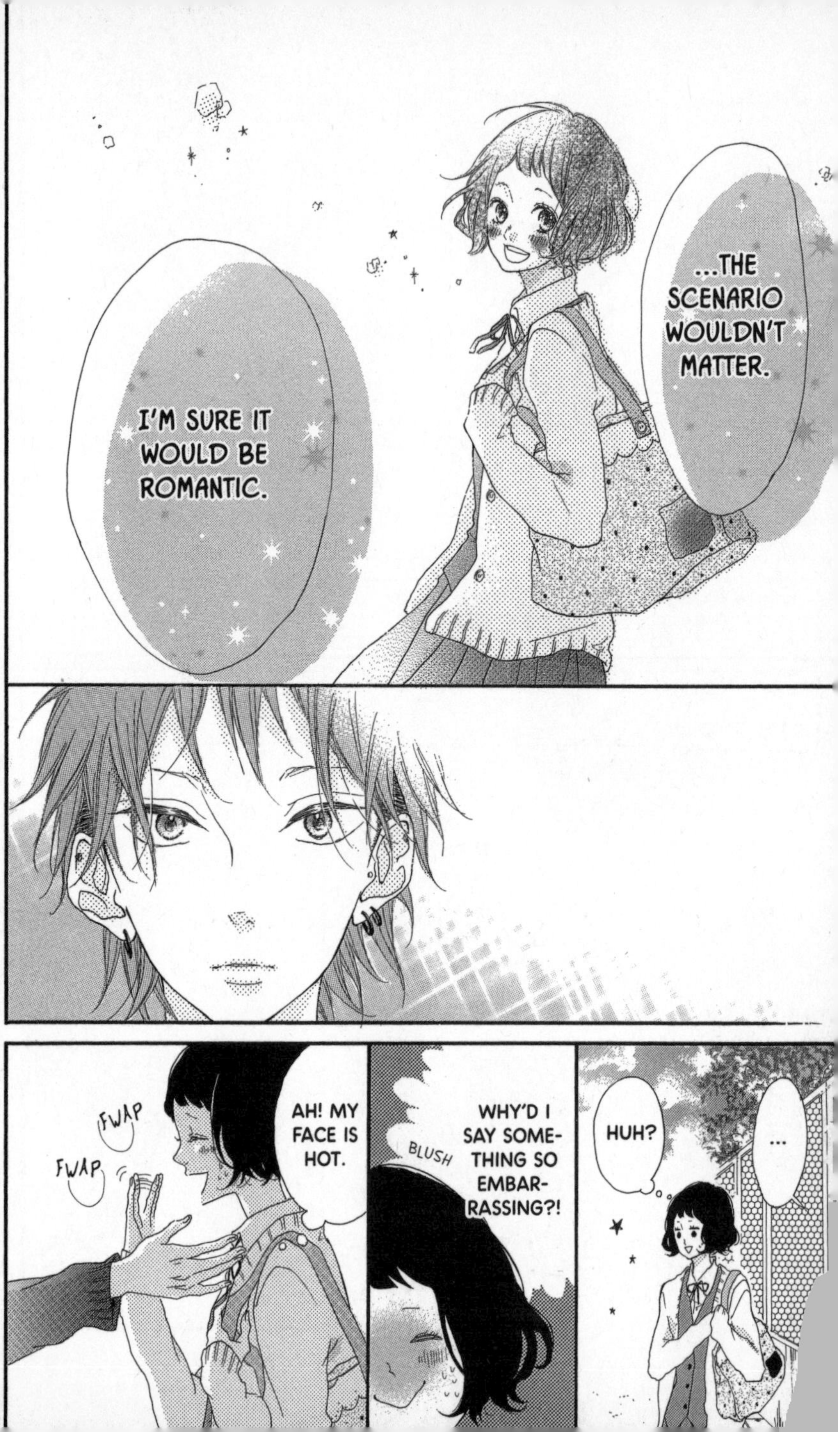
...THE SCENARIO WOULDN'T MATTER.
I'M SURE IT WOULD BE ROMANTIC.
...
HUH?
WHY'D I SAY SOME-THING SO EMBAR-RASSING?!
BLUSH
AH! MY FACE IS HOT.
FWAP
FWAP

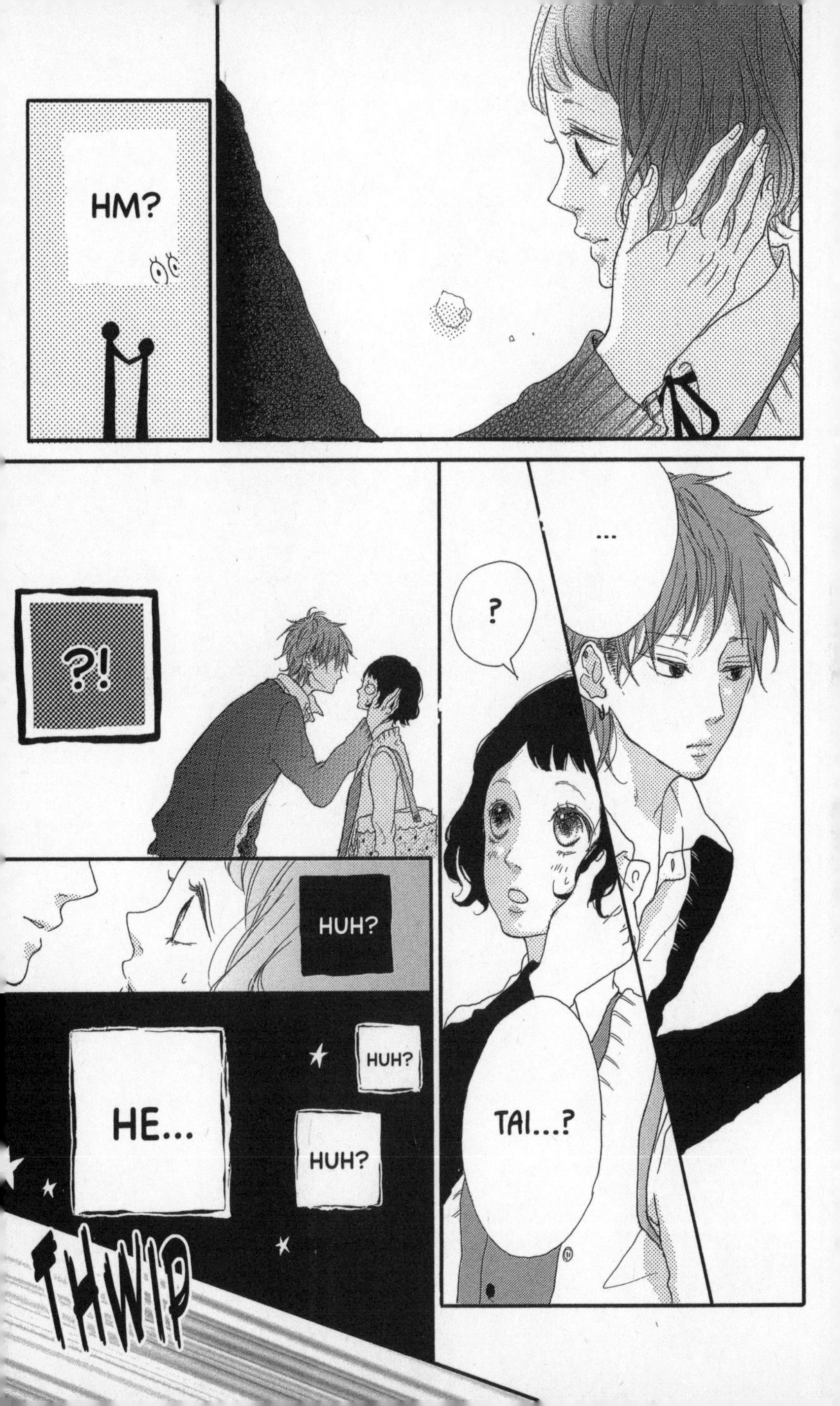
HM?
...
?
TAI...?
?!
HUH?
HUH?
HUH?
HE...
THWIP

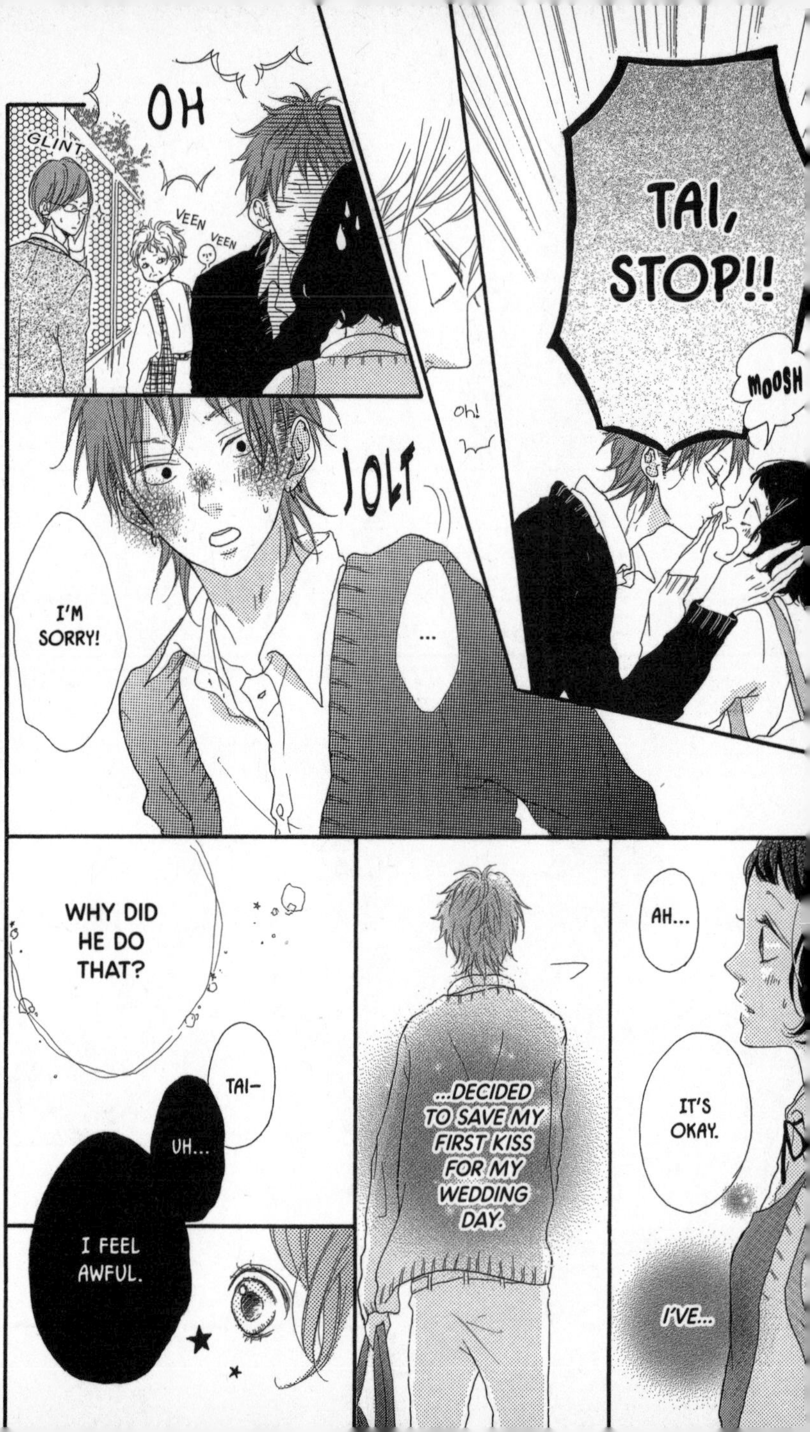
TAI, STOP!!
MOOSH
Oh!
OH
GLINT
VEEN
VEEN
JOLT
...
I'M SORRY!
AH...
IT'S OKAY.
I'VE...
...DECIDED TO SAVE MY FIRST KISS FOR MY WEDDING DAY.
WHY DID HE DO THAT?
TAI—
UH...
I FEEL AWFUL.

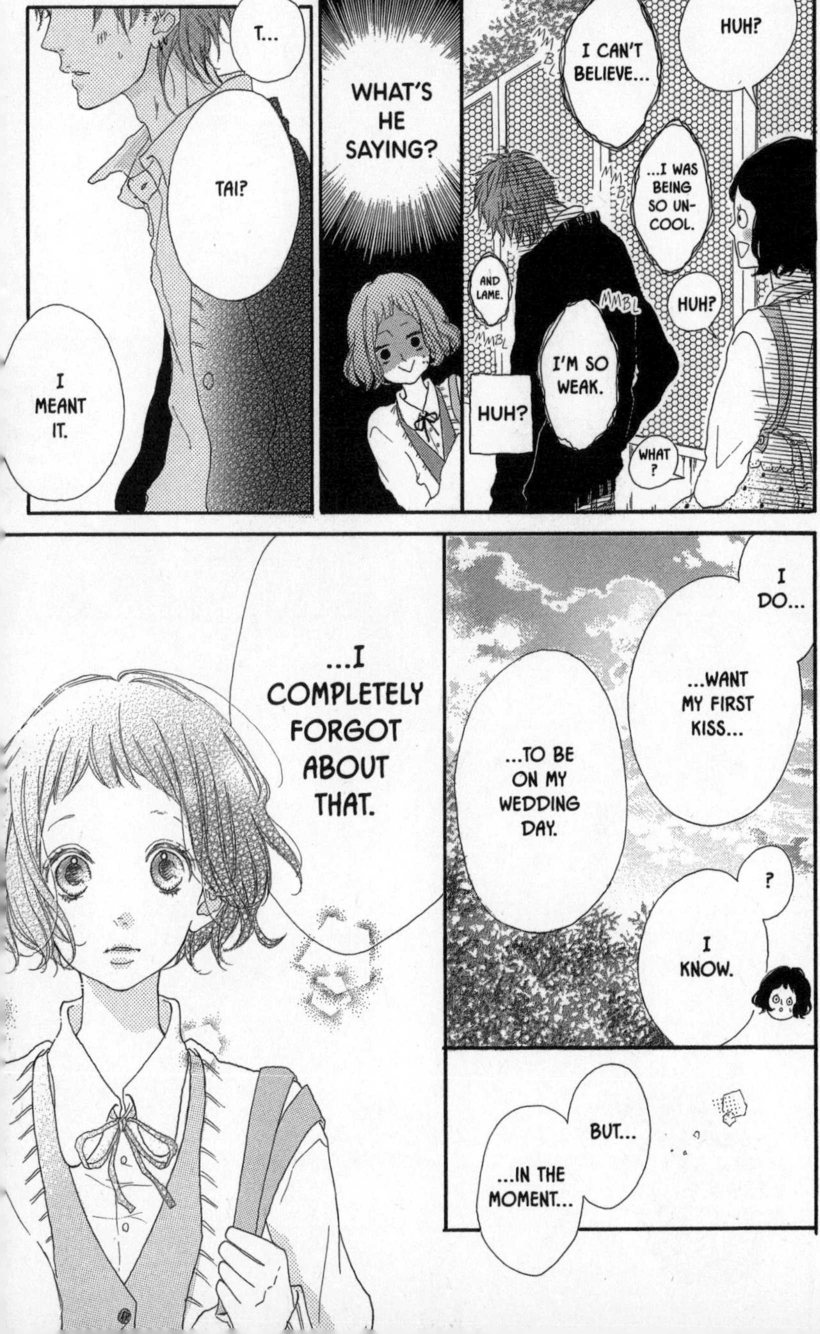
HUH?
I CAN'T BELIEVE...
MMBL
...I WAS BEING SO UN-COOL.
MMBL
HUH?
AND LAME.
MMBL
MMBL
I'M SO WEAK.
HUH?
WHAT?
WHAT'S HE SAYING?
T...
TAI?
I MEANT IT.
I DO...
...WANT MY FIRST KISS...
...TO BE ON MY WEDDING DAY.
?
I KNOW.
BUT...
...IN THE MOMENT...
...I COMPLETELY FORGOT ABOUT THAT.

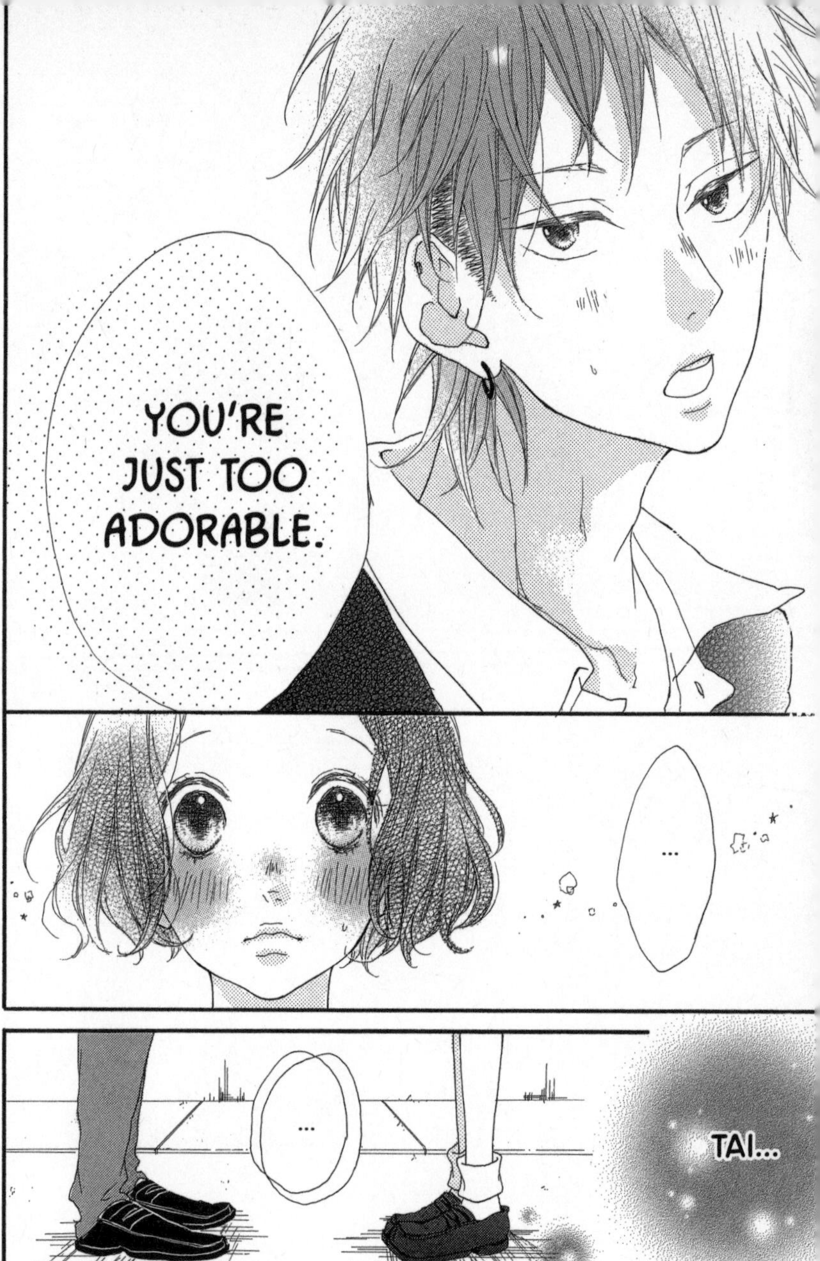
YOU'RE JUST TOO ADORABLE.
...
TAI...
...

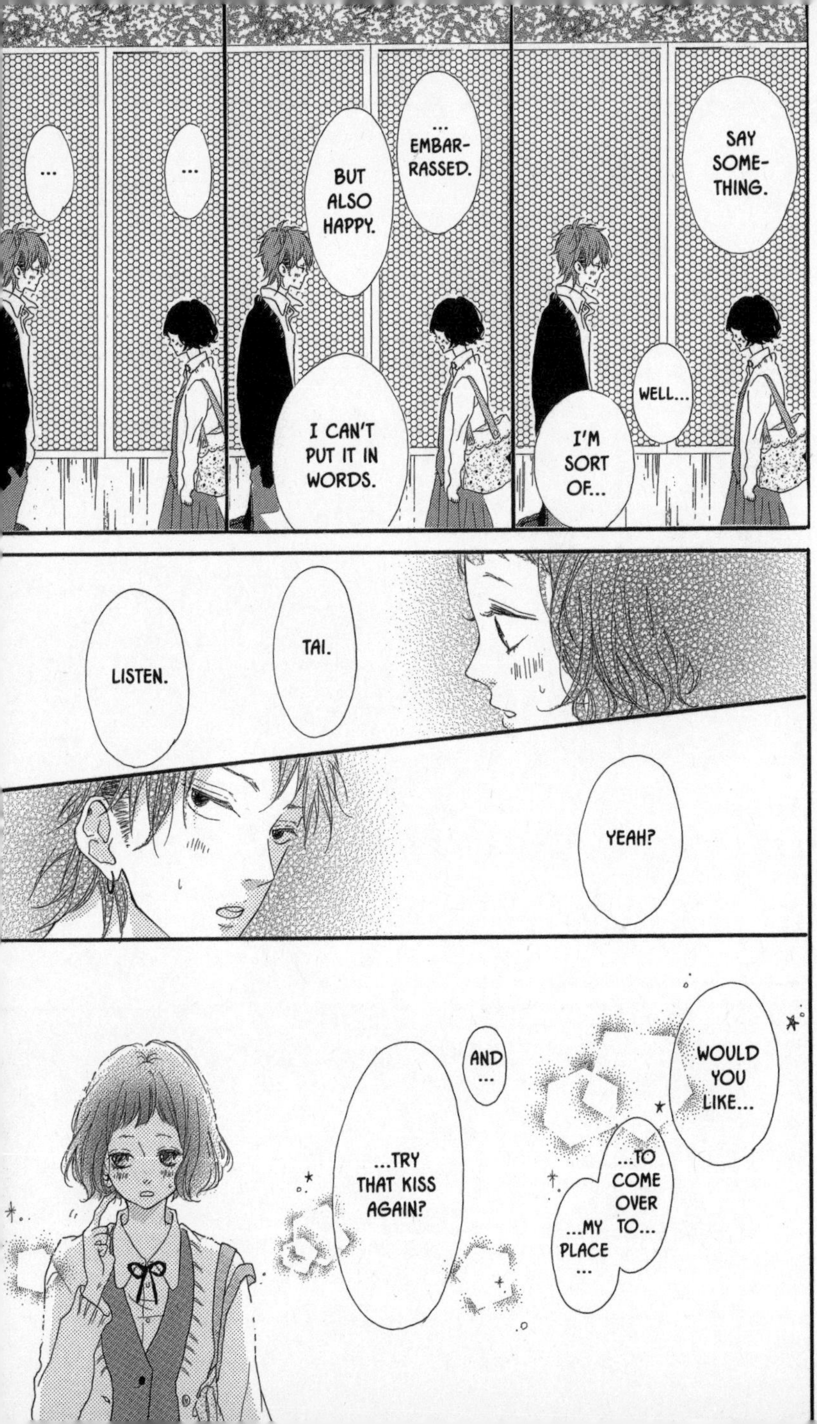
SAY SOME-THING.
WELL...
I'M SORT OF...
...EMBAR-RASSED.
BUT ALSO HAPPY.
I CAN'T PUT IT IN WORDS.
...
...
TAI.
LISTEN.
YEAH?
WOULD YOU LIKE...
...TO COME OVER TO...
...MY PLACE ...
AND ...
...TRY THAT KISS AGAIN?

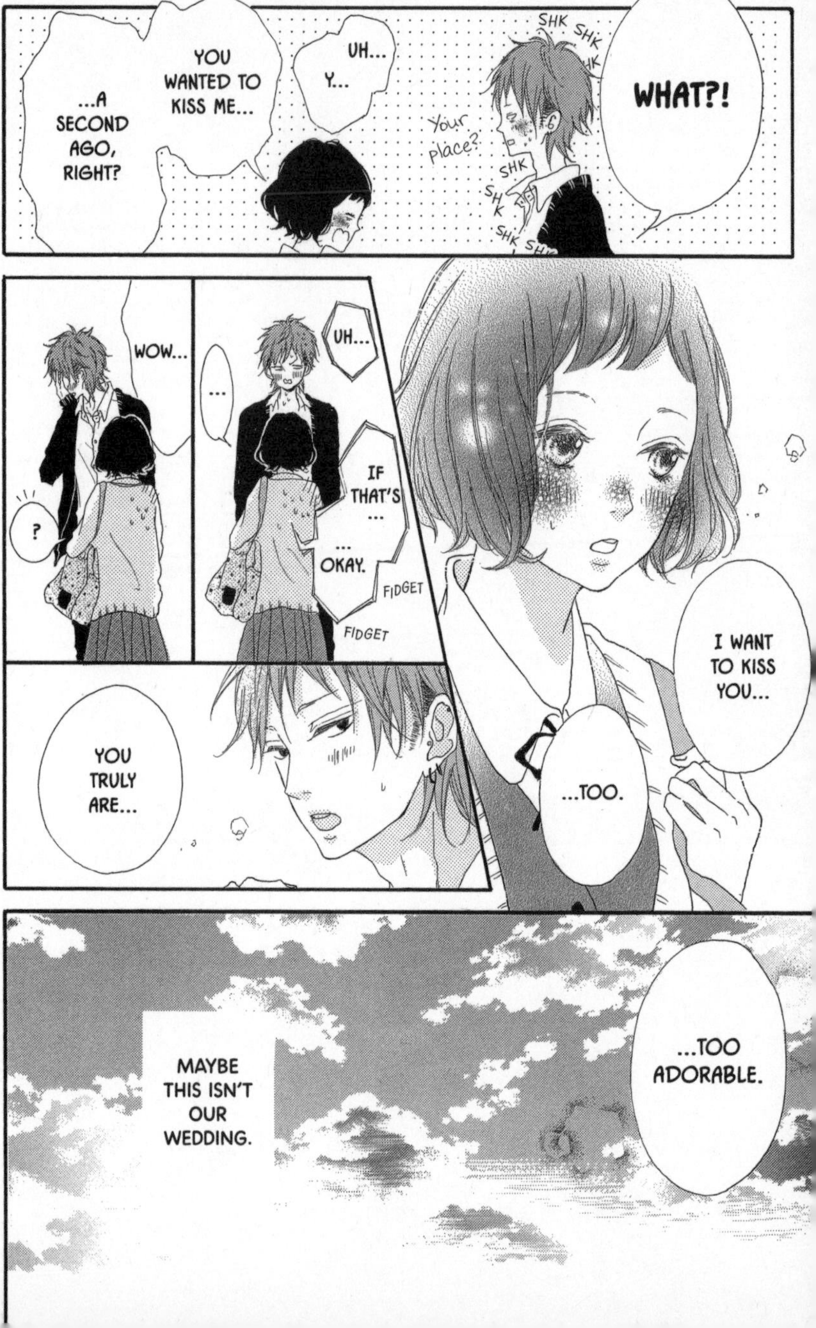
WHAT?!
SHK SHK SHK
Your place?
SHK SHK SHK SHK
UH... Y...
YOU WANTED TO KISS ME...
...A SECOND AGO, RIGHT?
I WANT TO KISS YOU...
...TOO.
UH...
...
IF THAT'S ... ... OKAY.
FIDGET FIDGET
WOW...
?
YOU TRULY ARE...
...TOO ADORABLE.
MAYBE THIS ISN'T OUR WEDDING.

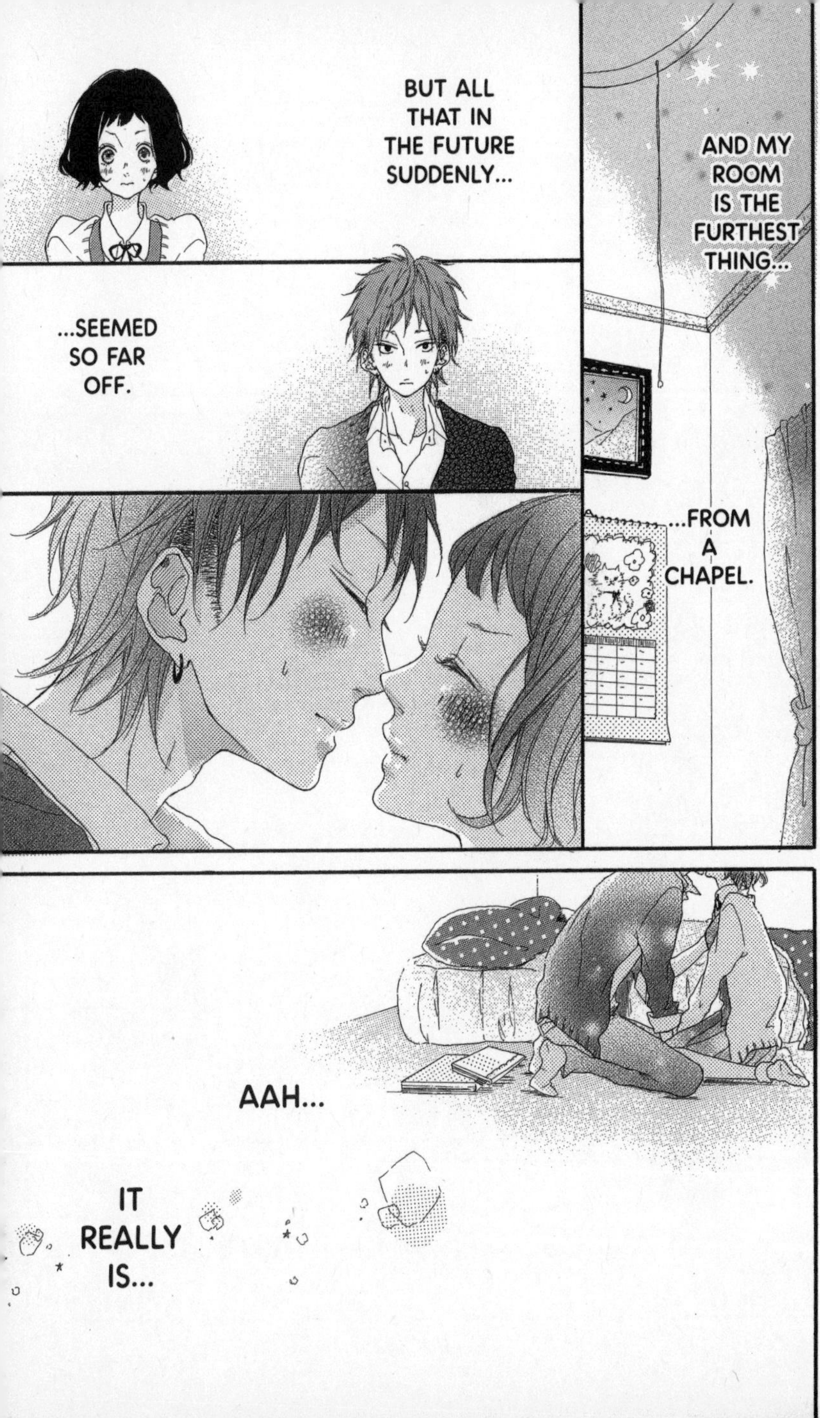
AND MY ROOM IS THE FURTHEST THING...
...FROM A CHAPEL.
BUT ALL THAT IN THE FUTURE SUDDENLY...
...SEEMED SO FAR OFF.
AAH...
IT REALLY IS...

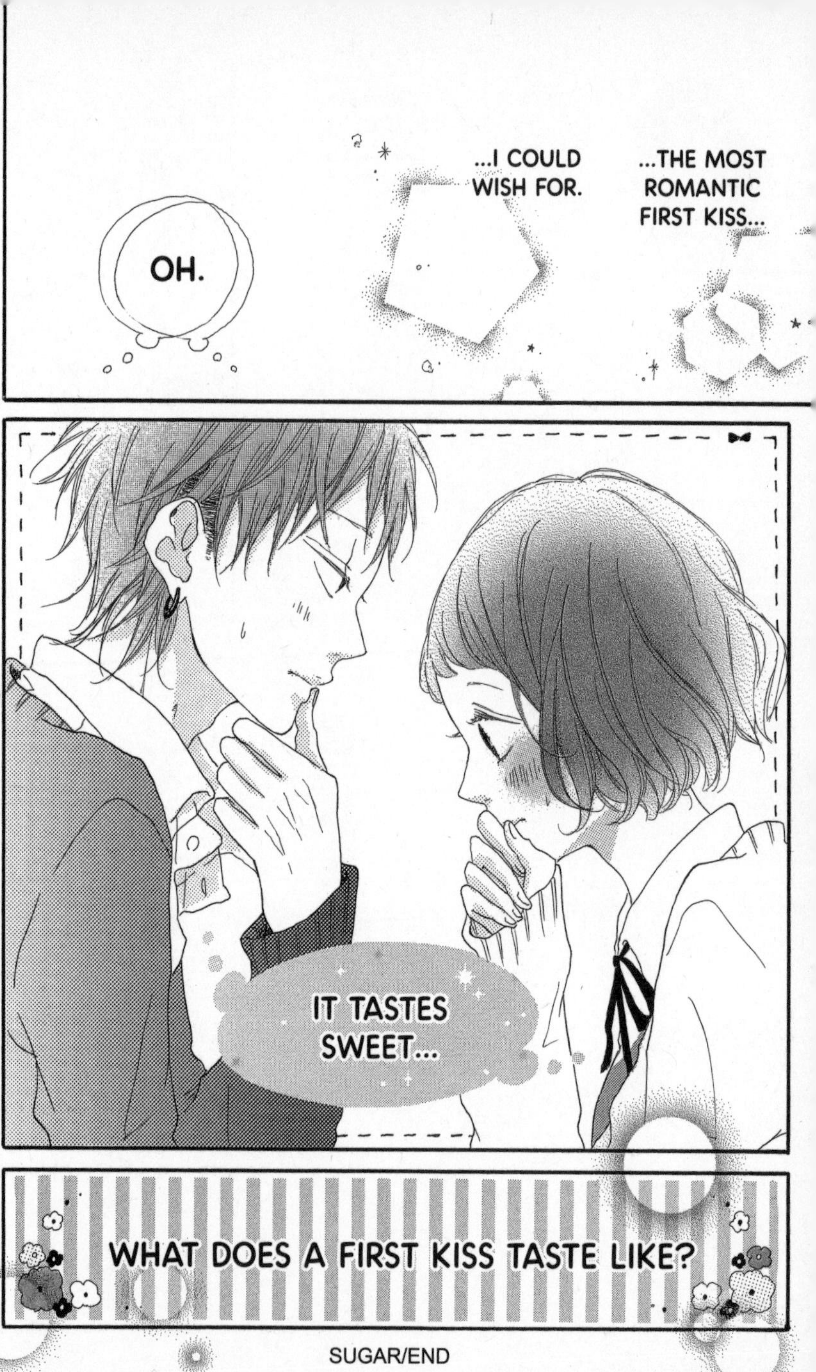
...THE MOST ROMANTIC FIRST KISS...
...I COULD WISH FOR.
OH.
IT TASTES SWEET...
WHAT DOES A FIRST KISS TASTE LIKE?

SUGAR/END

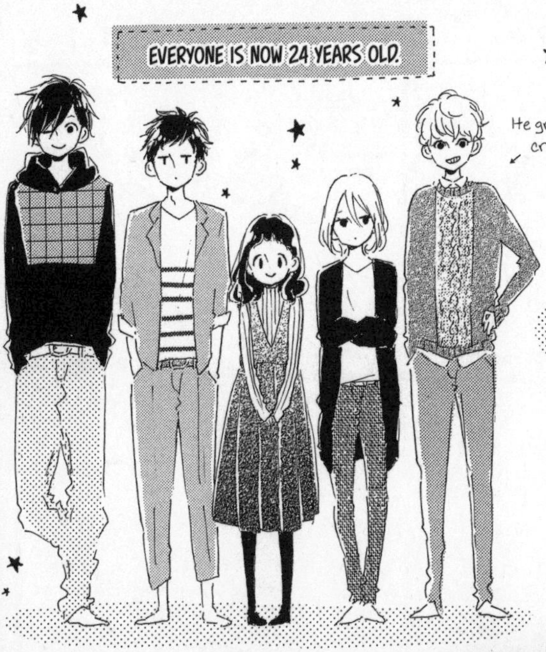
EVERYONE IS NOW 24 YEARS OLD.
He grew like crazy!

Bonus Comics

When We Go Out Drinking

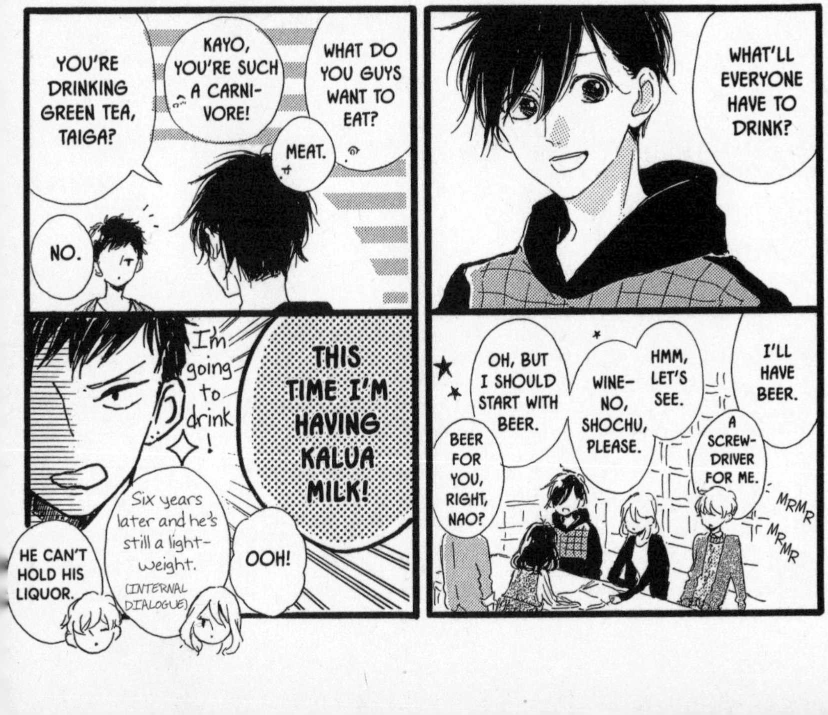
WHAT'LL EVERYONE HAVE TO DRINK?
WHAT DO YOU GUYS WANT TO EAT?
MEAT.
KAYO, YOU'RE SUCH A CARNIVORE!
YOU'RE DRINKING GREEN TEA, TAIGA?
NO.
I'LL HAVE BEER.
HMM, LET'S SEE.
A SCREWDRIVER FOR ME.
WINE—NO, SHOCHU, PLEASE.
OH, BUT I SHOULD START WITH BEER.
BEER FOR YOU, RIGHT, NAO?
MRMR
MRMR
THIS TIME I'M HAVING KALUA MILK!
I'm going to drink!
OOH!
Six years later and he's still a lightweight.
(INTERNAL DIALOGUE)
HE CAN'T HOLD HIS LIQUOR.

Onise + Alcohol

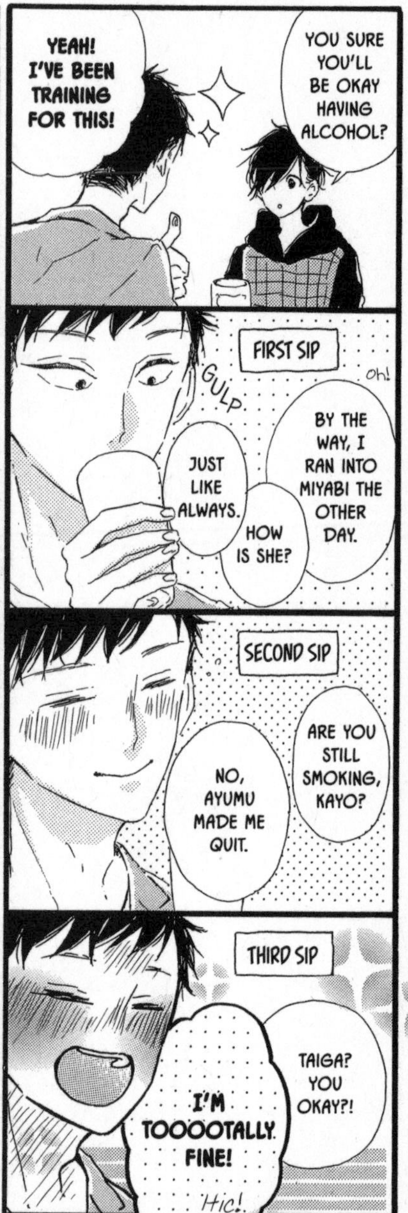
YOU SURE YOU'LL BE OKAY HAVING ALCOHOL?
YEAH! I'VE BEEN TRAINING FOR THIS!
FIRST SIP
Oh!
GULP
BY THE WAY, I RAN INTO MIYABI THE OTHER DAY.
HOW IS SHE?
JUST LIKE ALWAYS.
SECOND SIP
ARE YOU STILL SMOKING, KAYO?
NO, AYUMU MADE ME QUIT.
THIRD SIP
TAIGA? YOU OKAY?!
I'M TOOOOTALLY FINE!
Hic!

Yashiro + Alcohol

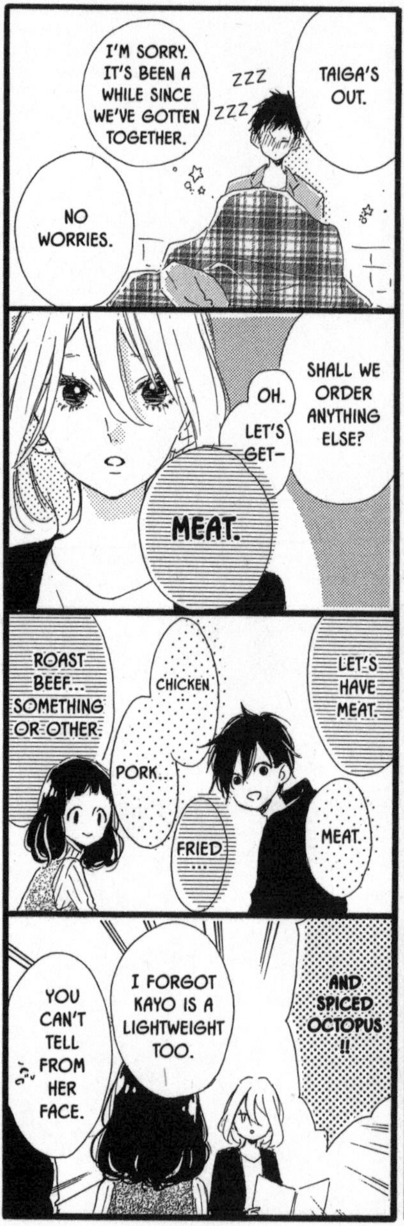
TAIGA'S OUT.
ZZZ
ZZZ
I'M SORRY. IT'S BEEN A WHILE SINCE WE'VE GOTTEN TOGETHER.
NO WORRIES.
SHALL WE ORDER ANYTHING ELSE?
OH.
LET'S GET—
MEAT.
LET'S HAVE MEAT.
MEAT.
CHICKEN...
ROAST BEEF... SOMETHING OR OTHER.
PORK...
FRIED...
AND SPICED OCTOPUS!!
I FORGOT KAYO IS A LIGHTWEIGHT TOO.
YOU CAN'T TELL FROM HER FACE.

Misaki + Alcohol

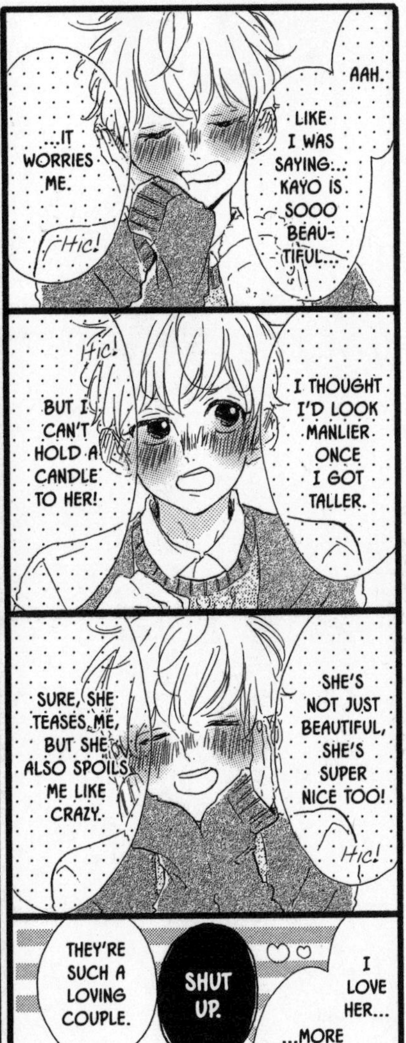
AAH. LIKE I WAS SAYING... KAYO IS SOOO BEAUTIFUL...
...IT WORRIES ME.
Hic!
I THOUGHT I'D LOOK MANLIER ONCE I GOT TALLER.
Hic!
BUT I CAN'T HOLD A CANDLE TO HER!
SHE'S NOT JUST BEAUTIFUL, SHE'S SUPER NICE TOO!
SURE, SHE TEASES ME, BUT SHE ALSO SPOILS ME LIKE CRAZY.
Hic!
I LOVE HER...
...MORE THAN ANYONE ELSE IN THE ENTIRE WORLD!
SHUT UP.
THEY'RE SUCH A LOVING COUPLE.
MISAKI WILL PROBABLY DIE OF EMBARRASSMENT IF HE REMEMBERS THIS.

Nao and Futami + Alchohol

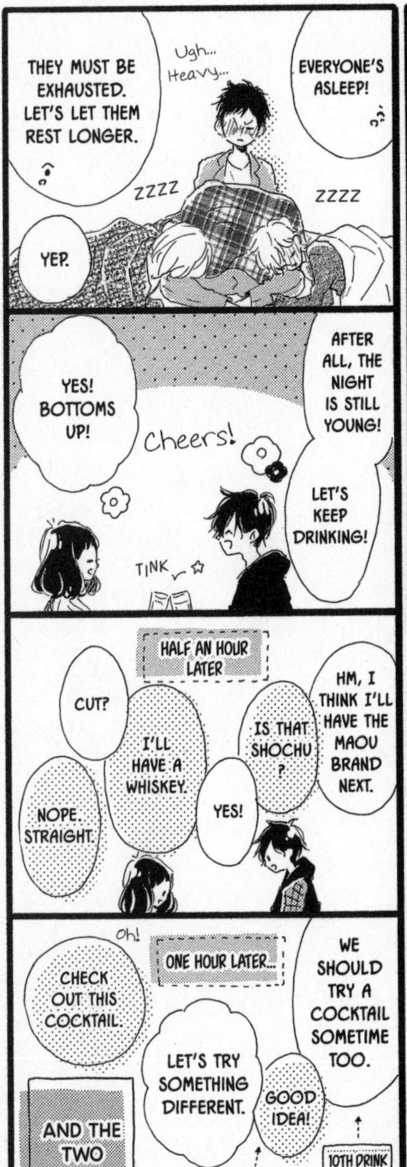
EVERYONE'S ASLEEP!
Ugh... Heavy...
THEY MUST BE EXHAUSTED. LET'S LET THEM REST LONGER.
ZZZZ
ZZZZ
YEP.
AFTER ALL, THE NIGHT IS STILL YOUNG!
LET'S KEEP DRINKING!
Cheers!
YES! BOTTOMS UP!
TINK
HALF AN HOUR LATER
HM, I THINK I'LL HAVE THE MAOU BRAND NEXT.
IS THAT SHOCHU?
YES!
I'LL HAVE A WHISKEY.
CUT?
NOPE. STRAIGHT.
WE SHOULD TRY A COCKTAIL SOMETIME TOO.
10TH DRINK
ONE HOUR LATER...
Oh!
CHECK OUT THIS COCKTAIL.
GOOD IDEA!
LET'S TRY SOMETHING DIFFERENT.
11TH DRINK
AND THE TWO KEPT ON GOING.

Bonus Comics

Our Family

(BASED OFF OF SOMETHING NAO SAID EARLIER)

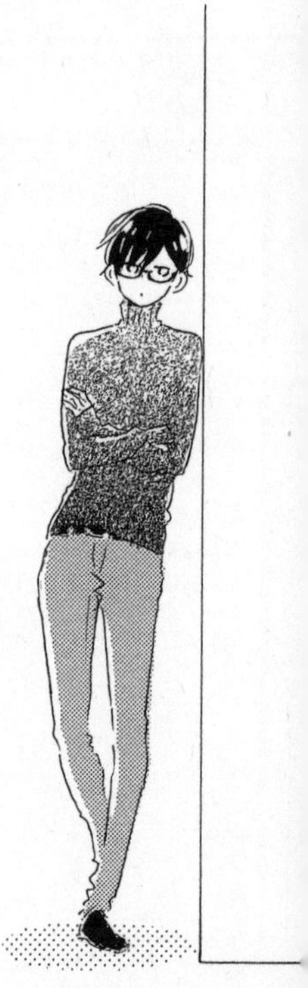

Sou

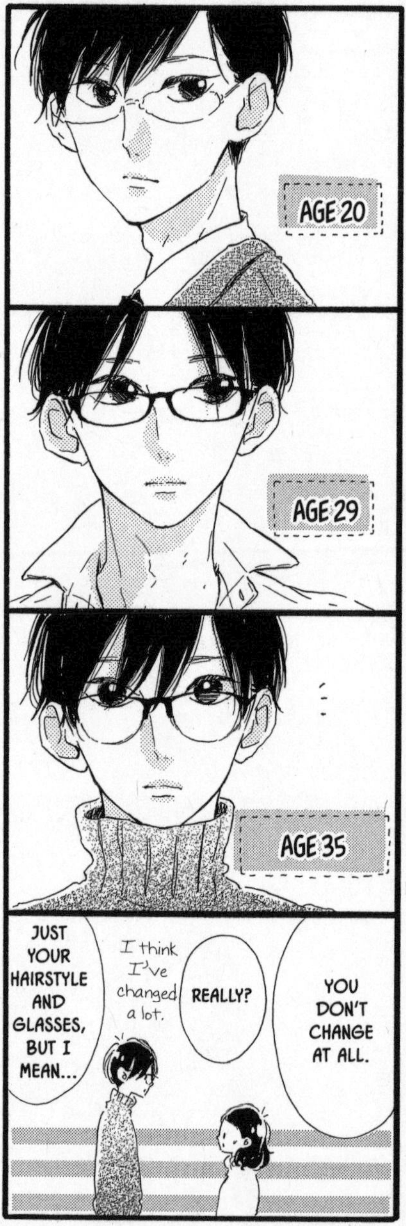

AGE 20
AGE 29
AGE 35
YOU DON'T CHANGE AT ALL.
REALLY?
I think I've changed a lot.
JUST YOUR HAIRSTYLE AND GLASSES, BUT I MEAN...

Onise's Big Brother

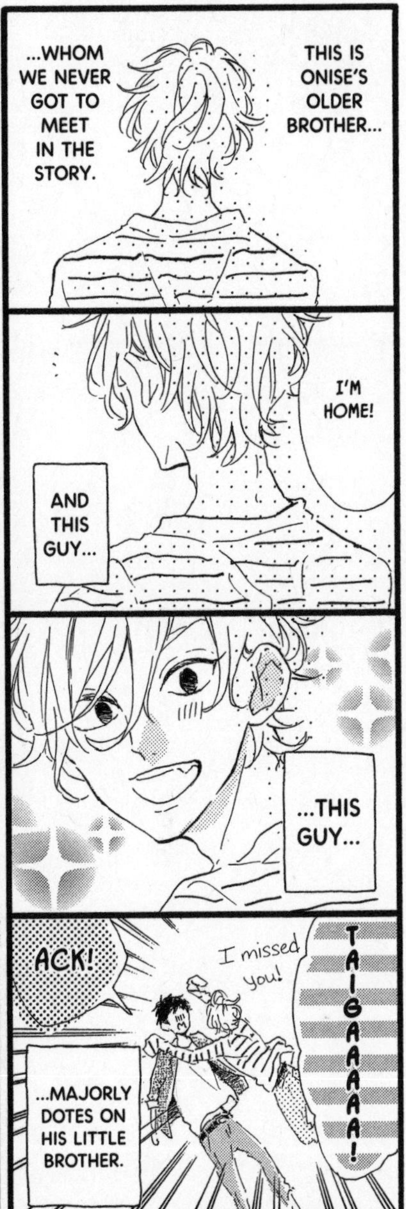

Onise's Big Brother 2

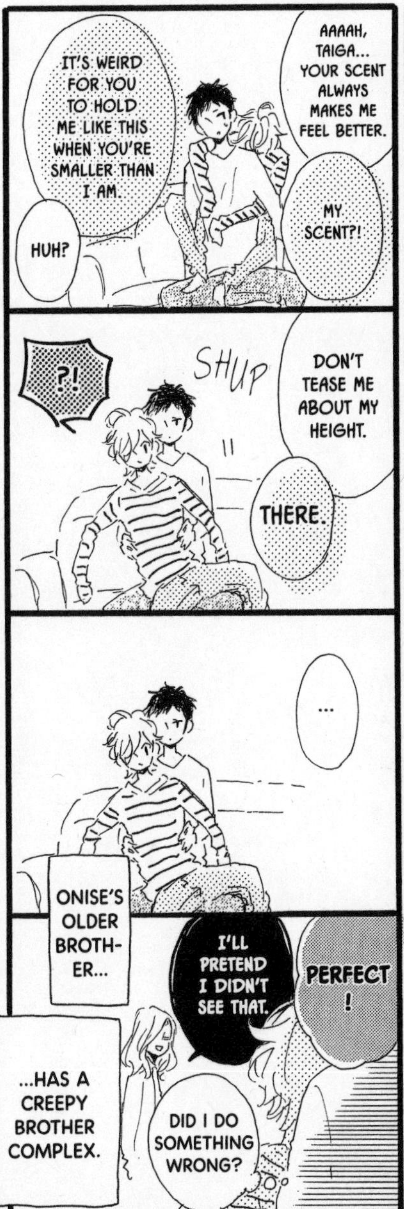

Thank you so much for picking up volume 8 of *Honey So Sweet*. This volume concludes the series. I want to thank everyone who stayed around to read it all.

Originally I'd intended to write Onise as more of a hero type, and Sou was going to have more complicated feelings for Nao that bordered on romantic instead of only familial, and I had planned a lot of other stuff too.

But I wasn't able to fit everything in like I'd wanted, so I'm ending this story with a healthy dose of humility.

I know I wouldn't have been able to continue this series the whole way through if it weren't for all my readers. Thank you so much for watching over me and for all the love you've given!

Until
we meet again!

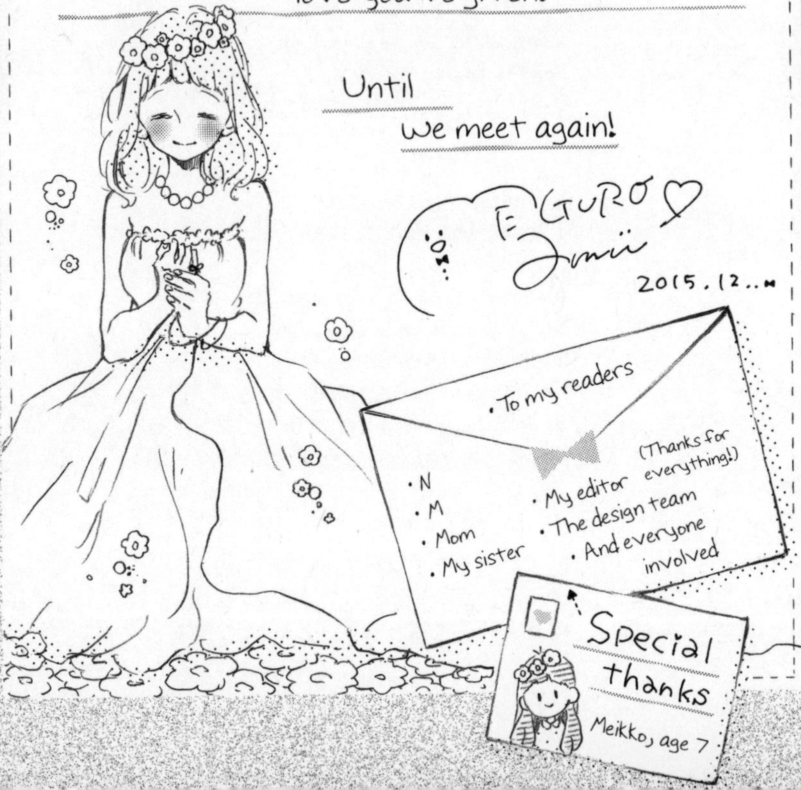

EGURO
Aimii
2015.12..
. To my readers
. N
. M
. Mom
. My sister
. My editor
. The design team
. And everyone involved
(Thanks for everything!)
Special thanks
Meikko, age 7

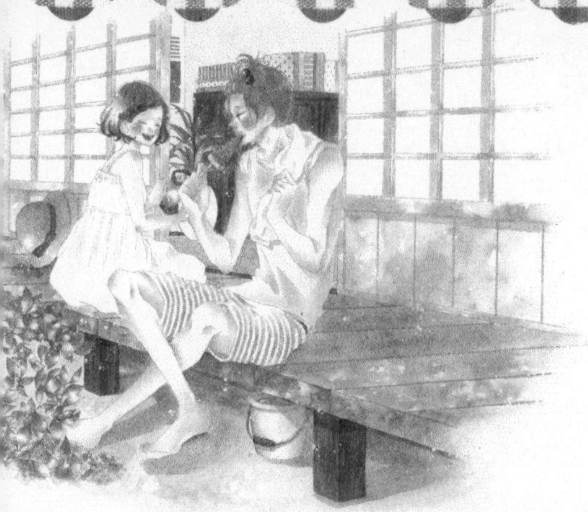

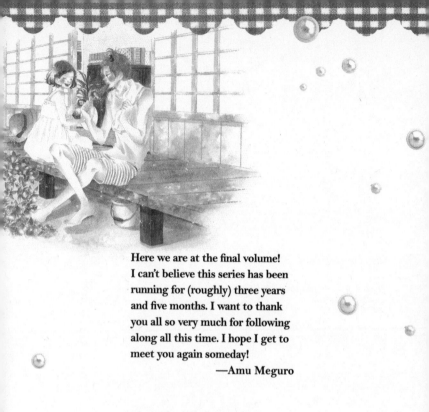

Here we are at the final volume! I can't believe this series has been running for (roughly) three years and five months. I want to thank you all so very much for following along all this time. I hope I get to meet you again someday!

—Amu Meguro

Newcomer Amu Meguro debuted with the one-shot manga *Makka na Ringo ni Kuchizuke O* (A Kiss for a Bright Red Apple). Born in Hokkaido, her hobbies are playing with her niece and eating. *Honey So Sweet* is her current series in *Bessatsu Margaret* magazine.

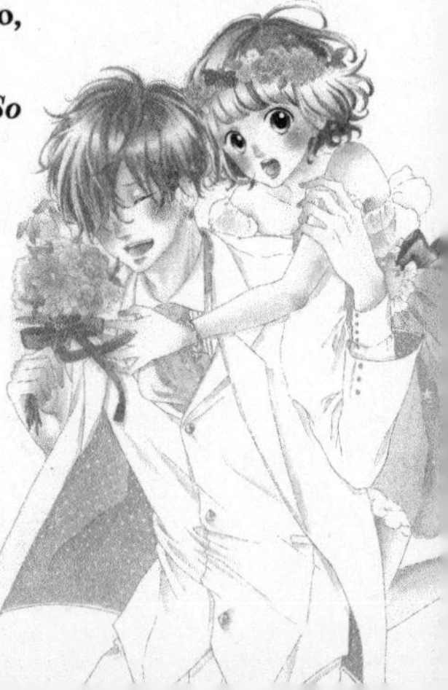

Honey
So Sweet

Shojo Beat Edition

Volume **8**

STORY AND ART BY
Amu Meguro

Translation/Katherine Schilling
Touch-Up Art & Lettering/Inori Fukuda Trant
Design/Izumi Evers
Editor/Nancy Thistlethwaite

HONEY © 2012 by Amu Meguro
All rights reserved.
First published in Japan in 2012 by SHUEISHA Inc., Tokyo.
English translation rights arranged by SHUEISHA Inc.

Printed in the U.S.A.

Published by VIZ Media, LLC
P.O. Box 77010
San Francisco, CA 94107

10 9 8 7 6 5 4 3 2 1
First printing, October 2017

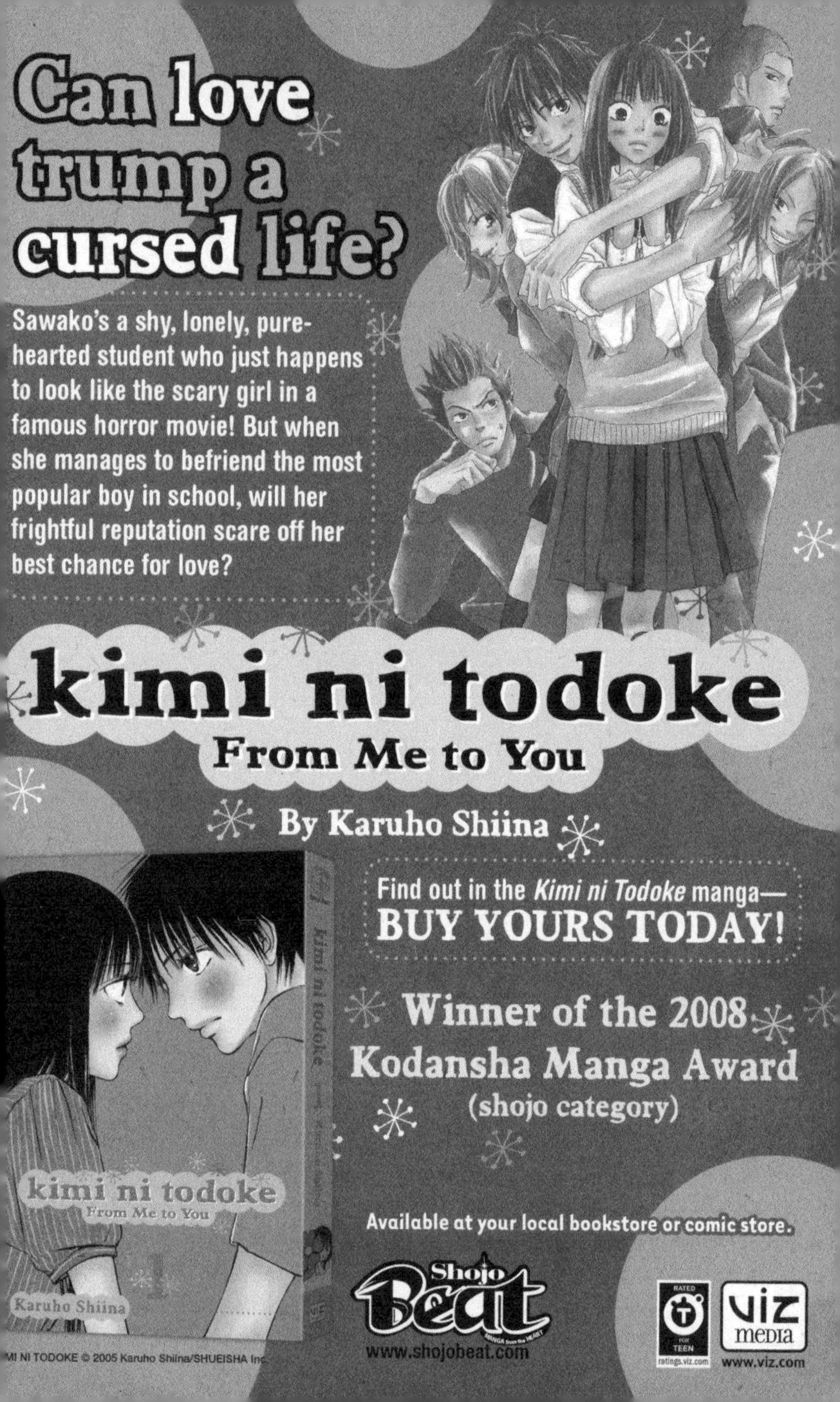

Can love trump a cursed life?
Sawako's a shy, lonely, pure-hearted student who just happens to look like the scary girl in a famous horror movie! But when she manages to befriend the most popular boy in school, will her frightful reputation scare off her best chance for love?
kimi ni todoke
From Me to You
By Karuho Shiina
kimi ni todoke
From Me to You
Karuho Shiina
Find out in the Kimi ni Todoke manga—
BUY YOURS TODAY!
Winner of the 2008 Kodansha Manga Award
(shojo category)
Available at your local bookstore or comic store.
Shojo Beat
www.shojobeat.com
RATED T FOR TEEN
ratings.viz.com
viz media
www.viz.com
MI NI TODOKE © 2005 Karuho Shiina/SHUEISHA Inc.

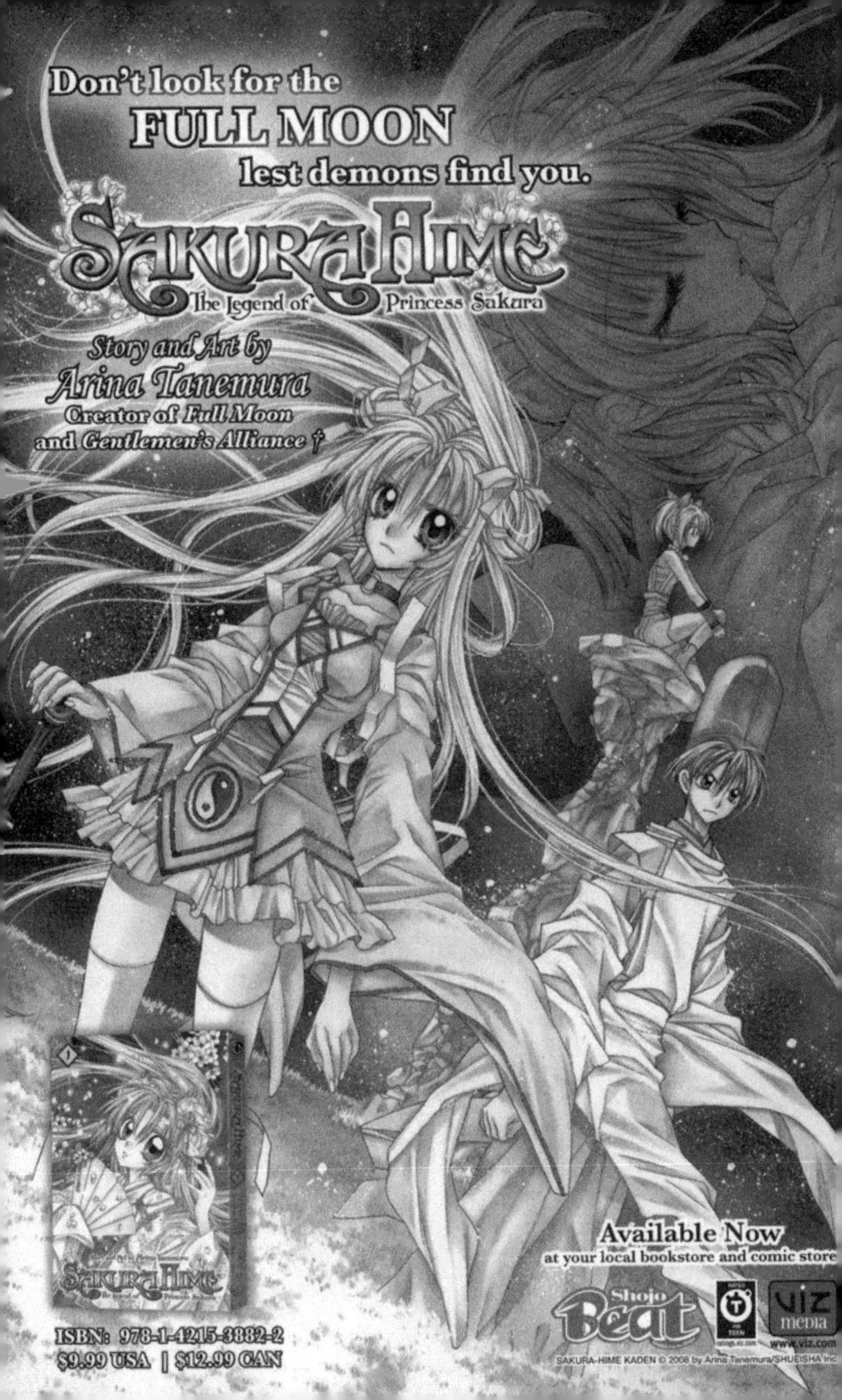

Don't look for the
FULL MOON
lest demons find you.
SAKURA HIME
The Legend of Princess Sakura
Story and Art by
Arina Tanemura
Creator of Full Moon
and Gentlemen's Alliance †
Available Now
at your local bookstore and comic store
Shojo Beat
VIZ media
www.viz.com
ISBN: 978-1-4215-3882-2
$9.99 USA | $12.99 CAN
SAKURA-HIME KADEN © 2008 by Arina Tanemura/SHUEISHA Inc.

You may be reading the wrong way!

This book reads right to left to maintain the original presentation and art of the Japanese edition, so action, sound effects and word balloons are reversed. This diagram shows how to follow the panels. Turn to the other side of the book to begin.

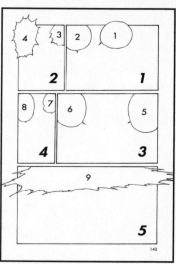